Down a Narrow Road

*Identity and Masculinity
in a Uyghur Community in
Xinjiang China*

Harvard East Asian Monographs 312

DOWN A NARROW ROAD

Identity and Masculinity in a Uyghur Community in Xinjiang China

Jay Dautcher

Published by the Harvard University Asia Center
Distributed by Harvard University Press
Cambridge (Massachusetts) and London 2009

© 2009 by the President and Fellows of Harvard College

Printed in the United States of America

The Harvard University Asia Center publishes a monograph series and, in coordination with the Fairbank Center for Chinese Studies, the Korea Institute, the Reischauer Institute of Japanese Studies, and other faculties and institutes, administers research projects designed to further scholarly understanding of China, Japan, Vietnam, Korea, and other Asian countries. The Center also sponsors projects addressing multidisciplinary and regional issues in Asia.

Library of Congress Cataloging-in-Publication Data

Dautcher, Jay, 1963-

Down a narrow road : identity and masculinity in a Uyghur community in Xinjiang China / Jay Dautcher.

   p. cm. -- (Harvard East Asian monographs ; 312)

Includes bibliographical references and index.

ISBN 978-0-674-03282-8 (cl : alk. paper)

   1. Uighur (Turkic people)--China--Xinjiang Uygur Zizhiqu--Social life and customs.

2. Family--China--Xinjiang Uygur Zizhiqu. 3. Men--China--Xinjiang Uygur Zizhiqu. I. Title.

DS731.U4D38 2009

306.0951'6--dc22

2008041015

Index by the author

☉   Printed on acid-free paper

Last figure below indicates year of this printing

18 17 16 15 14 13 12 11 10 09

Narrow Road

Yasin Muxpul

My eyes opened
   I came into the world
And saw your beautiful face
   Narrow road

Like to my dear mother's breast
   I clung to you
And you embraced me
   Narrow road

When I pass along
   the length of you
I could gaze upon you forever
   Narrow road

How can they call you narrow
   an entire world is within you
The fragrance of wild basil blooming
   Narrow road

Overflowing with the kindness of a
   thousand sweet-tempered mothers
Your love sets me aflame
   Narrow road

Whether I find myself in
   Paris or Istanbul
My soul is a bonfire of longing for you
   Narrow road

You are the dear mother who bore me
   Narrow road
You are the mother who raised me
   Narrow road
Protector of so many promising young
   girls and boys
You are a beautiful and beloved land
   Narrow road

---

köz échip
   alemge törelgende men
shu güzel hösningge baqtim
   tar kocha

jan anamning baghridek
   baghringgha men
qanmidim, baghrimni yaqtim
   tar kocha

boyliringdin ötkenimde
   herqachan
telmürüp toymay qaraymen
   tar kocha

kim seni tar deydu
   qoyning bir jahan
gül chichek reyhan puraysen
   tar kocha

sende xushxuy
   ming anining méhri jem
shunga men ishqingda yandim
   tar kocha

meyli parizh meyli
   istanbulda men
séghinish qelbimde gülxan
   tar kocha

méni tughqan jan anamsen
   tar kocha
méni östürgen anamsen
   tar kocha
shunche berna qiz-yigitke
   pasiban
bir güzel dilber makansen
   tar kocha

Acknowledgments

Support received from many individuals and organizations was critical in allowing me to complete this work, and I welcome this opportunity to acknowledge that help.

When I was a student at Beijing Normal University, Zhang Zichen and Zhong Jingwen introduced me to Chinese folklore. At the University of California, Berkeley, Alan Dundes, James Bosson, Stanley Brandes, Tom Gold, Aihwa Ong, Jack Potter, and Fred Wakeman helped train me as a social scientist and helped me secure the funding that allowed me to complete this research.

In Yining I am grateful to my host family for their generosity, and to the men, women, and children of Zawut and adjacent *mehelle* who made my year there so memorable. Local historian Is'haq Basiti explained to me much about Yining culture. The research and administrative staff of the Xinjiang Academy of Social Sciences (XASS) in Urumqi, my official hosts, and Abdüshükür Turdi, Liu Bin, Ismayil Tömür, and Guo Taishan in particular, kindly shared their insights and institutional resources.

Organizations that provided financial support for field research include the Anthropology Department, Graduate Fellowships Office, and Vice Chancellor's Office of the University of California, Berkeley, the Social Science Research Council, the Committee for Scholarly Communication with China, the Andrew W. Mellon Foundation, and the John D. and Catherine T. MacArthur Foundation.

Finally, the support and encouragement of many friends and mentors enabled and inspired me to complete the research and writing of this book. Folklorist Alan Dundes, historian Cheryl Barkey, and anthropologists Suzanne Gottschang, Lyn Jeffery, and Bahiyyih Watson read early drafts of my writing, and Stevan Harrell and Ralph Litzinger gave detailed reports on the manuscript; all provided valuable comments. Special thanks are due to Gardner Bovingdon, from whom I have learned much during our many conversations about Uyghur history and culture. Maria Stoilkova helped me read nineteenth-century Russian-language statistical records for Yining. Kurban Niyaz reviewed and advised me on translations of some of the Uyghur-language materials contained herein. John Emerson generously provided me with his original maps and other map data for Xinjiang, which appear here in a modified form.

J.D.

Contents

Foreword

Stevan Harrell

We can read Jay Dautcher's *Down a Narrow Road* in many ways. The most scholarly way to read it is as a book about identity discourses. We read that, for the Uyghur residents of the *mehelle*, or neighborhoods, of Yining city in the far northwest of Xinjiang, identity is a net of many strands: gender, locality, family, politics, language. In contrast to so many works about the Uyghurs that are all about ethnicity, about ethnonationalism, separatism, statism, and so many other abstract isms, *Narrow Road* portrays identity as emerging out of customs and practices of everyday life. As such, ethnic identity as Uyghurs is only one element of identity's complex, many-stranded net. In telling this story about identity, Dautcher not only gives us a fuller picture of identity than is possible if we concentrate on ethnicity, but, more important, shows us that ethnicity itself is something better understood through daily life than through abstract and imposed political categories.

The most delightful way to read *Down a Narrow Road* (and perhaps the least scholarly way) is simply as a series of good stories, vivid portraits, disturbing revelations, and sometimes obscure jokes about what it was like to live as a young man in a Uyghur neighborhood in the 1990s. Living with a family for over a year, speaking fluent Uyghur and

Chinese, taking part in family activities as well as the social gatherings of young men, Dautcher makes *mehelle* life real for us, and in doing so makes us appreciate that to be Uyghur is more than just to be Muslim, Turkic, Chinese citizen; it is to partake in a colorful, sometimes maddening, sometimes fun, series of social and spatial interactions that make the descriptive and narrative chapters in the book such a delight to read.

But the best way to read *Down a Narrow Road* is as a vindication of the value of ethnography for cross-cultural understanding. So much of the anthropology done in the People's Republic, particularly in minority communities, is rather thinner description than most of us authors would like to admit. Doing real ethnography in China is a challenge. Neither the state nor the academic establishment is very comfortable with the "intensive hanging out," the year-long or longer residence in a community observing and participating in everything one can, taking notes on home life, street life, work, play, and all else that crosses one's consciousness. Most research is much more directed, both by the requirements of visas and academic affiliations and by the dictates of doctoral committees and granting agencies. But Jay Dautcher somehow managed to combine the scholarly and the quotidian, to make the quotidian the basis of the scholarly, not to separate analysis from real life, but to make real life the basis of analysis. This is the first real ethnography of a Uyghur community, and we learn so much while entertaining ourselves with the account. The reader is, without doubt, "taken on a journey of discovery." *Bon Voyage!*

Characters

Personal names used in the book have in most cases been changed to ensure individuals' privacy. The following individuals are primary characters in the story of my year in Yining.

Abidem
Seventy-six years old, the head of an independent household in a courtyard shared with the household of her son Yakupjan and his family. Abidem's living descendants include seven children, thirty-seven grandchildren, and nineteen great-grandchildren, most of whom live within a few minutes' walk from her house.

Aysajan
An orphan, eight years old, born to a young woman in her twenties who had married Abidem's older brother when he was in his seventies. After Abidem's brother died, the mother fled, leaving Abidem to raise this child in her household, although without ever considering him to be a member of her family.

Rahine
Abidem's eldest living child, in her fifties, who lives in a rural village outside Yining with her husband and nine children. Rahine visits her mother's home regularly.

Aliye
Abidem's second oldest child, in her late forties, who is married to a hard-working man (a second marriage for both) with whom she shares responsibility for running a

successful vegetable stall near their home. Aliye and Anwarjan are raising two sons, Ablimit (age 15) and Ablikim (age 13), and a daughter, Mewlüdem (age 16).

Anwarjan   Husband of Abidem's second daughter, Aliye.

Yakupjan   Abidem's eldest living son, in his mid-forties, whose family lives in a household separate from Abidem's in a shared courtyard. Yakupjan is a merchant, a fruit wholesaler who has also been active in cross-border trade in Kazakhstan. Yakupjan and his wife, Gülzire, are raising four children, son Mehmud (age 18), daughters Xalidem (age 16) and Nuriye (age 9), and son Ilyar (age 7).

Gülzire   Wife of Abidem's son Yakupjan.

Anise   Fourth eldest child of Abidem, in her early forties, married to Ablimit Hajim.

Ablimit   Husband of Anise, Ablimit (also known as Haj'kam) is a
Hajim   shopkeeper equally devoted to accumulating wealth and presenting himself as a pious Muslim. Ablimit and Anise are raising four sons and one daughter. Their eldest child, Ablet (age 16), has recently begun a ten-year program of Qur'anic study.

Maynur   Abidem's fifth oldest child, in her mid-thirties, is the mother of girls Mahire (age 12) and Mukerrem (age 10). She divorced her husband after he hospitalized her with a severe beating, but ultimately returned to and remarried the man, a flashy reseller of used cars.

Memetjan   Sixth eldest child of Abidem, in his early thirties. At age thirteen Memetjan was selected to receive education and training in Uyghur music at the Central Institute of Nationalities in Beijing, where he grew up and now works as a teacher and performer of Uyghur music.

Senemgül   Abidem's youngest living child, in her late twenties, Senemgül married her sweetheart Téyipjan and has recently had two infant children, son Abdüshükür and daughter Tewsiye.

Téyipjan   Husband of Senemgül.

A Note on Language

This note provides a guide to the pronunciation of personal names and other Uyghur terms used in the book, drawing some examples from Hahn, *Spoken Uyghur*. Uyghur terms in the book are transliterated in Latin Script Uyghur, Chinese terms in *pinyin*.

The word Uyghur is usually pronounced in English as WEE-gur, although the Uyghur pronunciation is closer to OY-gore, as in "toy store."

The letter *a* is pronounced as the initial a in "aqua." The letter *e* is pronounced as in "get." A final syllable containing the letter *e* is usually stressed, giving Abidem (ah-bi-DEM), Anise (ah-ni-SEH), Aliye (ah-li-YEH), Ablet (ah-BLET), and so forth.

The letter *h* is unaspirated, as in "hour," and sounds close to a pause or stop, giving Mahire (ma-i-REH) and Rahine (ra-i-NEH). The term *mehelle* (neighborhood) is thus pronounced much like the three English words "met-et-let" minus their final consonants.

The letter *é* is pronounced like the e in "me," and the letter *i* is pronounced like the i in "pick," giving Téyipjan (tee-yip-JAN).

The sounds for *x*, *gh*, and *q* are challenging for English speakers. The letter *x* is pronounced like the *j* in the Spanish *joven* (youth). The sound of *gh* is similar to the *r* in the French *radio* (radio) or in the German

Rohre (tubes). The sound of *q* is similar to the *ch* in the German *acht* (eight). Less linguistically adventurous readers may wish to pronounce *x*, *gh*, and *q* as h, g, and k, respectively.

Place-names with established spellings have been retained, including Ili (EE-lee) and Urumqi (u-ROOM-chee).

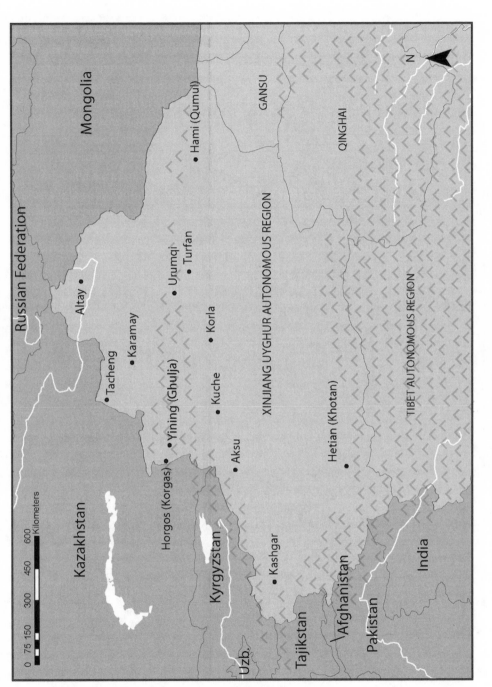

Map 1 The Xinjiang Uyghur Autonomous Region (courtesy of Human Rights Watch, © 2007).

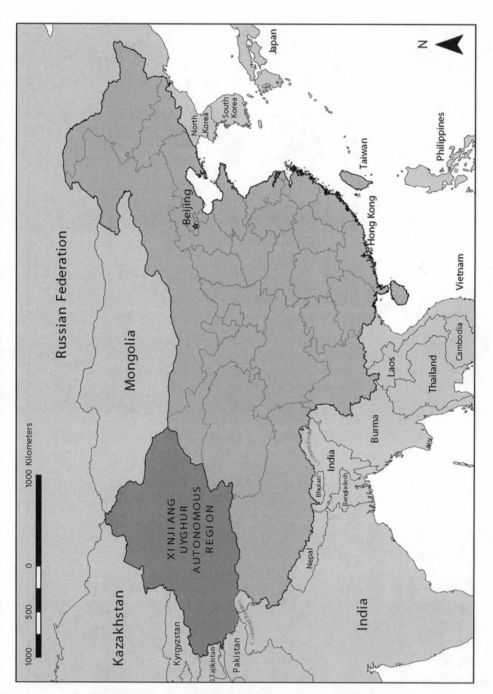

Map 2 The People's Republic of China, showing the location of the Xinjiang Uyghur Autonomous Region

Down a Narrow Road

---

*Identity and Masculinity
in a Uyghur Community in
Xinjiang China*

Introduction

Every story is a travel story.

—Michel de Certeau

If a man with no legs tells you he's going to swim across the river, don't believe him.

—Uyghur aphorism recorded circa 1875

I arrived in the city of Yining in northwest Xinjiang in the summer of 1995 with plans to conduct a year of ethnographic research into the marketing practices of Uyghur merchants. I had arranged to live in a suburban neighborhood on the outskirts of town with the family of a Uyghur friend I had made almost a decade earlier, when I lived in Beijing. As a field researcher, I dutifully spent my first days in Yining wandering through its bustling markets, chatting with merchants, and observing the flow of commercial and social activity. I had previously spent a year in Urumqi, Xinjiang's largest city, using that time to study Uyghur for six to eight hours each day and to socialize with Uyghur friends at night. By the time I arrived in Yining, my language skills were sufficient to allow me to interact, as did the men, women, and children around me, speaking entirely in Uyghur.

As the days passed, the conversations and personal dramas of my host family members and new friends from the marketplace quickly drew me into the rich life-world of an extended Uyghur family, a Uyghur suburban neighborhood, and the larger Uyghur community of Yining. Immersed in the language and lore of their daily lives, I realized how poorly existing scholarly works on Uyghurs, works that focused

almost exclusively on Uyghur ethnonationalism and Uyghur-Han relations, had prepared me to understand my subjects' daily lives. I expanded my research focus beyond the topic of Uyghurs' economic strategies
in the post-Mao era of economic reform and allowed myself to be
drawn into everything and anything of interest to my new Uyghur family and friends.

   This book presents the results of my attempt to make sense of everyday life in the predominately Uyghur suburbs of Yining[1] and to situate
that understanding into a broader account of Uyghur culture and social
life. My goal is to provide an ethnographic thick description of Uyghur
culture of the kind I wish had been available to me prior to my fieldwork.
In the four parts of this book, I explore topics ranging from child rearing
to wedding practices, from informal socializing to market activities to
forms of religious devotion. Uniting these topics and my analysis of them
is, first, an emphasis on the role folklore and personal narrative play in
helping individuals situate themselves in, as well as create, the communities and social groups in which they participate. A second connecting
thread is the critical impact of the male individual's concern to advance
his position in an agonistic world of interpersonal status competition on
the myriad external forms of social life in Uyghur communities.

   In one sense, the book does not deal with what is usually characterized in ethnographic literature as ethnicity per se. Instead, my narrative is framed around the terms *identity*, *community*, and *masculinity*. *Identity*,
because I seek to portray how Yining's Uyghurs experience and express
a set of individual and collective identities organized around concepts
of place, gender, family relations, friendships, occupation, and religious
practice. Unlike Uyghur intellectuals in Beijing and Urumqi, whose discussions of Uyghur identity drew on the same normative party-state
ethnicity discourse they sought to oppose, Yining Uyghurs showed few
traces of organizing their self-identities around explicit notions of "ethnic" or "minority" status. *Community*, because in virtually every aspect
of their daily lives the individuals and families I knew were drawn into
dense and overlapping networks of face-to-face social relationships that
bound them into a single social body, a community united by a shared
engagement with local differences as much as local commonalities of
daily life. *Masculinity*, because my account is weighted toward describing

Fig. 1   Ornate doorways allow passage through the high earthen walls that surround the court-yards of Uyghur homes. Here young children play in the small lane leading to Abidem's house in Zawut *mehelle* (photograph by the author, 1996).

the lives of men and the place of men's status competition within daily life in the community. This does not mean women's voices are absent; as a member of my host household, I interacted each day with the women of a large Uyghur family, listening to and participating in their private conversations about spouses and children, about their work inside and outside the home, and other aspects of their lives. During my year-long residence, I believe I collected as much information from women as I did from men; however, the lives of men and women's views about men and their relationships with them were typically at the center of these women's conversations. Although my account draws on women's voices, it does so to examine the lives of men.

In Part I, I introduce Uyghur community life by examining the importance of place and space as bases for individual and collective identities. In Part II, on gender and the life cycle, I examine the concerns expressed by Uyghur men and boys regarding the cultivation and performance of a masculine habitus. In the first three chapters in

Part II, I focus in turn on gender and child rearing, childhood play, and adult relationships, emphasizing in each the position of boys and men in these activities. In the next two chapters, my focus shifts exclusively to the lives of adult men, and in particular to two masculine institutions, nicknaming and a form of gathering known as *olturash*, in which men's abiding concern to build and maintain personal status by symbolically dominating other men figure centrally. In Part III, I consider the role of marketing and merchant culture as a domain in which men compete for status through their efforts to achieve wealth and position in the local community. Finally, in Part IV, I offer an account of vernacular Uyghur Islam and consider how men's competition for status shapes local religious sentiments and practices.

Most of the ethnographic materials I present here come from informal conversations conducted in Uyghur and are rendered here in English based on interview and field notes recorded within one or two days of the actual conversations. Longer passages quoting from those conversations were transcribed from video and audio recordings of interviews or events. To evoke for the reader some sense of my experiences in the field, I have incorporated excerpts from my field notes into the narrative, sometimes editing them slightly for the sake of clarity but without altering the meaning. Throughout the book personal names have been changed to protect individuals' privacy, with the exception of people whose accomplishments as scholars, authors, or entertainers have made them public figures in Xinjiang. A glossary listing Uyghur terms that appear in the text is provided in the back matter.

All translations from printed materials (these are mainly from Uyghur and Chinese) are my own unless otherwise noted. Given the lack of standardization of Uyghur orthography—each dictionary I purchased in Xinjiang seemed to offer new spellings for familiar words—I can only say that, in transcribing *mehelle* residents' speech, I attempted to match standard spellings as much as possible, but my interest in capturing local pronunciation patterns has in some cases produced variant spellings. Monetary amounts are given in Chinese *renminbi* in units of *yuan* (known colloquially as *kuai*) or in U.S. dollar equivalents at the exchange rate of eight *yuan* to the dollar.

This book is intended for readers interested in a general ethnographic account of life in a contemporary Uyghur community. Readers more deeply interested in Uyghur studies may find information of value in the doctoral dissertation on which this book is based; it includes annotations on historical, etymological, linguistic, and folkloristic details not included here and documents extensive connections between the folklore I encountered in Yining and folklore collected between the 1870s and the 1950s throughout Xinjiang and recorded in works by authors such as Gunnar Jarring, N. F. Katanov, Albert von Le Coq, Sergei Malov, Karl Menges, N. N. Pantusov, and W. Radloff. Taken together, those references illuminate the fact that many of the beliefs, practices, and oral folklore I found in Yining are not unique to that locality but are the vibrant contemporary expression of a shared cultural heritage that unites Uyghurs throughout Xinjiang. The extent to which geographical isolation, inter-oasis migration, and other factors have shaped patterns of difference within the shared culture of this region can only be considered when ethnographies from other oases become available for comparison.

Although this book tells a story about the lives of Uyghurs, that story is shaped through the lens of my experience as a first-time ethnographer engaged in field research. Because the book interweaves two stories, one about a Uyghur community, the other about my life in that community, perhaps a few words on this approach are in order. A good story, conventional wisdom suggests, is one in which the reader is taken on a journey of discovery. And a compelling ethnographic narrative might be compared to a journey from one side of a river to the other; a departure from the firm ground of the familiar, a traversing of the unfamiliar, and ultimately a return to the firm footing of a new understanding. Such a story would conjure up an idealized field research experience, in which the ethnographer plunges into a radically new environment, starts with no ground under his or her feet, and slowly gains confidence that he or she has arrived on a new shore and attained a secure epistemological footing in the host community's life-world. As a researcher in the field, however, I more often felt like the proverbial man with no legs attempting to swim across a river. In the beginning of my research, I was challenged to participate in a complex social world in a language in which I was far from perfectly conversant. As a writer, I struggled equally with a narrative form that presents as a linear, coherent whole fragments of understanding and insight accumulated through a nonlinear, disjointed, often quite disheartening process. The greater point, as I see it, is not whether I as an individual have proved myself capable of swimming across the river, but whether there ever is the possibility of finding firm ground on the other, the Others', shore. For me, a commitment to social science inquiry has grown to include a willingness to accept that one swims as best one can, and hopes for land-fall, as a sign of one's willingness to learn, to make mistakes, and to grow.

PART I

Local Identities of

Space and Place

Just as social groups reside in space, space itself inhabits a world of social categories and relationships. The three chapters of Part I describe the spatial relations of home and neighborhood, suburb and city, in Yining and show how these create a sense of belonging that lies at the foundation of Uyghur identity. Although the focus here is on identities based on space and place, other dimensions of personal identity examined more fully in subsequent chapters—gender, class, occupation, and religion—are foreshadowed here.

Zawut *mehelle*, the neighborhood I describe, is the pseudonymous focus of my field research. The house and courtyard I lived in, although tucked away on the corner of a narrow, dogleg dirt lane on Yining's periphery, stand at the center of my narrative. As the home I learned to know best, it was central to my experience of local life.[1] More important, as the home of Yining-born Abidem Nasréddin, who hosted me during my research, it was the social hub of a large extended kin network of native Yining residents. Abidem had borne fourteen children, and the experiences of her surviving descendants, a group that included seven children, thirty-seven grandchildren, and nineteen great-grandchildren, formed an important part of the social world I learned from during my research. Many of the families in her kin group lived just minutes away in adjacent neighborhoods, and it was a rare day when several of her children or grandchildren did not stop to visit and to share a meal or some recent gossip.

The following three chapters unfold by paralleling the expanding awareness of space I imagine a Zawut resident might develop as he or she travels through life. I begin with the home, the house and its courtyard, where infants take their first steps toward becoming persons. Then I describe a typical Uyghur *mehelle*, or residential neighborhood, along whose winding lanes young children laugh, play, and form informal age cohorts that often last lifetimes. Next, I describe the concentric ring such neighborhoods form around Yining's urbanizing center, a distinct suburban periphery that separates the city from the fertile fields and villages in the surrounding countryside. All these spaces are filled with the activities and social dramas examined in more detail in Parts II through IV. Indeed, the description of these spaces is intentionally filled with references to persons and events that are fully explained only in later chapters, a ploy intended to whet the reader's appetite. In this part, however, the main focus is on space and place.

Some comments are in order regarding the generality of the account offered here. Many Uyghur residents of Yining remember and sometimes speak of *mehelle* boundaries in places where Yining's urban center now stands, where Uyghur residents' adobe homes and walled courtyards have given way to concrete apartment buildings that house the increasing numbers of ethnic Han who work and live in the city. Although many Uyghurs still organize their perceptions of the city center through the remembered grid of its *mehelle*, ever fewer Uyghurs live there, and many of the sites that gave those *mehelle* their names and their distinctive characteristics have been torn down in the state-sponsored push to modernize. As a result, the notion of *mehelle* as a *kind* of space has emerged in Yining, a space associated with the many dozens of suburban neighborhoods that encircle Yining's urban center. To the casual observer, as well as in the eyes of the Uyghur families who live in them, this ring of neighborhoods remains a predominately Uyghur residential space encircling a Han city. When I write about Zawut, then, I am also writing generally about this suburban periphery and its dozens of neighborhoods. Although these *mehelle* exhibit subtle differences in form and feeling, the description of life in Zawut given here could apply equally well to most of them. When I use the phrase "*mehelle* residents," I refer to Uyghur residents of all Yining's *mehelle*, but not to residents of *mehelle* in other cities and towns in Xinjiang, about whom I make no claims.

For the Uyghurs who live in the *mehelle*—the children who spend their days playing in their narrow lanes, attending school, hawking apricots in the street from handcarts on the weekends; the men who trade in the markets, perhaps closing their stalls early in order to sneak off to drink with their friends by the riverside; the women who work in the local factories, who visit kinfolk bearing gifts and gossip—for all the residents of Yining's *mehelle*, the home remains a central place, the place from which all the day's activities begin and the place to which they all return. The home is where my story begins.

I

The Blessed Home

Residence and Identity in a
Uyghur Neighborhood

Saying "prosperity, come here," it's wanting to have a blessed (*beriketlik*) household, like this household.*

Look around, there's nothing here, but there is everything, too. Everything needed, Mom has somewhere.

— Senemgül, describing her mother Abidem's house

The physical arrangement of domestic and residential spaces in Zawut cannot be understood without situating those spaces in the wider social order that encompasses them. The spatial organization of domestic life is inseparable from many key categories of social identity in the lives of local residents. In Zawut, for example, an independent cooking stove is a key defining unit of the *öy* (household). One idiom for expressing marriage and the formation of a conjugal unit is to say that the couple has become "homed-and-stoved" (*öylük-ochaqliq*), or simply "homed" (*öylen-*), which suggests that they cook and reside apart from others. An *öy*, then, is a home, a social unit as well as an architectural one.

---

*The Uyghur term *beriket* (blessing) is cognate with the widely known Islamic concept of baraka.

Fig. 2 When weather permits, *mehelle* residents prepare and eat meals outdoors in walled-in court-yards. Here Abidem prepares dumplings for the evening meal. One of her daughters or grand-daughters will likely stop by to help before she is done. An evening meal usually consists of rice pilaf, dumplings, or homemade noodles served with meat and vegetables (photograph by the author, 1996).

Uyghur homes in Yining's suburbs are strikingly uniform in architec-tural style and method of construction. Floors are built on earthen foundations raised several feet off the ground. Walls are made either of fired brick or of rammed earth topped with locally made adobe brick. Flat roofs are simply made; poles are laid over the roof joists, then cov-ered with mats of reeds, a layer of straw, a layer of soil, and a topping of cinder or gravel. Although their rectilinear layouts vary, all homes are based on a single socio-spatial theme: a conjugal unit requires a two-room structure, an all-purpose *dalan* for living, dining, and sleeping, and a *saray* for entertaining guests. This division into one room for family use and one room for guests arises from the sharp distinction between the informal interactions of kin, friends, and neighbors that take place in the *dalan* and the more formal visits and gift exchanges of the *saray*, which are described using the terms "making guests" (*méhman qilish*) and "being guests" (*méhman bolush*).

Fitting this pattern is the home of Abidem Nasréddin, a woman who maintains an independent hearth and residence in a courtyard shared with the household of her eldest son, Yakupjan. The main spaces in Abidem's home—and the floor plan of her son's home is identical—are its two adjoining rectangular rooms, the *dalan* and the *saray*.

Abidem's *dalan* is perpetually full, not with material objects, but with the bustle of daily life. Few possessions are on display: a small wooden table, painted dark green, leans tilted on its side against a whitewashed wall; folded blankets lie neatly on a wooden chest; a bare forty-watt bulb hangs from one of three rough-hewn wooden beams. A few objects peek out from above the rafters, including a cloth bundle containing the shroud Abidem has been sewing in preparation for her eventual passing into the next world. This *dalan* is typical of such rooms in its further division into two adjacent sections, the *supa*, a twelve-by-fifteen-foot platform raised twenty inches above floor level, and the *tapsa*, a six-by-fifteen-foot floor made of brick. The *supa* here is built of solid earth, although in many homes *supa* have planked-over storage spaces inside. The *supa* is covered with mats of *kigiz*, a locally made thick wool felt, over which are laid carpets of soft wool or acrylic fiber with colorful geometric or floral designs. In well-to-do homes, carpets are often hung on walls as well, but the adobe walls in Abidem's modest *dalan* are bare except for a whitewash of lime. Even the single carpet on her *supa* is a bit too small, and the frayed *kigiz* underneath protrudes in a fifteen-inch swath running along the *supa*'s edge. *Kigiz* mats, although viewed as inferior to carpets, have their own allure, with paisley-like patterns dyed in purples and pinks on a dark cocoa field. Although *kigiz* are ubiquitous in Uyghur households, their designs are distinctive of the ethnic Kirgiz whose craftsmen have traditionally made the mats; as such, they are a reminder of links of exchange that have connected nomad and peasant in the region for centuries.

Despite its sparse decor, many of the household's daily activities take place here. For much of the year, meals are prepared here and eaten around the low table, with family and casual visitors seated on thin cotton pads placed directly on the *supa*. Sleeping takes place on the *supa* on bedding (more cotton pads, sheets, and blankets) that is stowed each day. In this room women mix dough in wooden troughs for the staple *nan* flatbread, mend and sew clothing, and rock infants strapped tightly into wooden cradles.

One trait of Uyghur spatial arrangements is their reproduction of the concern over personal status that emerges everywhere in local social life. Virtually all things in Uyghur life, from meals to musical instruments to merchant activities, are differentially valorized and associate those who bestow, use, or partake in them with varying degrees of status. Space is no exception, and the *tör*, or seat of honor, is the room's most important spot. Just as a person's lap is formed only when he or she sits, the seat of honor at a social gathering is not a permanent physical spot in a room but is created by the presence of those gathered. At social gatherings in Yining, participants typically sit in as circular an arrangement as possible; when men socialize, for example, they routinely monitor and comment on how well they are maintaining a physical symmetry. Despite this apparent egalitarianism, all such circles contain an inherent asymmetry. That spot on the *supa* seating platform taken as the *tör*—and taken is the right word, since men are keenly aware of the fierce if subtle status competitions waged to occupy it—is usually the point most distant from the edge of the *supa* adjacent to the floor. That edge, known as the *lep*, is the *supa*'s least prestigious part, and although it, too, is conceptually, not physically, demarcated, at Abidem's the protruding and well-worn *kigiz* appropriately marks that space.

On the fired-brick floor, a coal stove, handcrafted of steel by a local stovesmith, provides heat during the cold winters and serves as cookstove then as well. Near the stove a handmade galvanized tin water pail and a tin ladle made by the same stovesmith and purchased at his market stall are used to bring in clean water from a spigot in the courtyard. Against the end wall of the floor opposite the door hangs a thin cotton sheet, hiding a set of sturdy wooden shelves filled with bowls and jars of rock salt, homemade hot sauce, sweet clotted cream, refined sugar, sheep fat, vegetable oil, and *dimidi* holy water. Just inside the doorway that leads to the brick patio is the *pega*, the least prestigious part of the floor, where one leaves one's shoes before stepping up to the *supa*.

The *saray*, on the other hand, although brimming with objects, is most of the time quite empty. Where the living room is sparsely furnished but richly inhabited, the guest room is the opposite, richly decorated but on most days quite lifeless. All of the *saray* in Abidem's house is at floor level, although many *saray* in Yining, perhaps most, have raised *supa* seating platforms. Abidem's *saray* also does double duty as a space for storing various possessions. Here the walls are painted a bright sky blue, and the floor is carpeted. An iron bed frame holds a stack of cotton blankets— more than a dozen are on hand for overnight guests—each in a satin brocade cover hand-sewn by Abidem. Against one wall leans a low wooden table almost as long as the room is wide, on which Abidem spreads for guests a tablecloth and its offerings of hospitality. On a wooden desk, painted yellow and covered with oilcloth, sit two massive ceramic vases; one holds prepared sheep fat, the other a jumble of miscellaneous papers including various state-issued booklets and documents. Beside these sit more than fifty small serving bowls in different patterns, smaller bowls for tea, larger ones for noodles, on hand for large gatherings of kin and other guests. A framed glass panel painted in Arabic calligraphy with the phrase "In the name of God the most merciful" sits propped there as well. Two blanket chests covered in a lustrous golden metal sit in one corner, duplicate wedding gifts received by one of her daughters, and left here. The *saray*, like the *dalan*, has a large glass-paned window on the wall facing into the courtyard; its light allows Abidem to move several large potted plants inside during the cold winter months. In one corner stands a *chamadan*, a cylindrical tin vessel capable of holding the 40 to 50 kg of flour the household consumes each month.

Visitors exiting Abidem's house through its doorway step out onto a wide brick patio, which connects to her son's adjacent household, and down a set of steps leading into the courtyard. The patio is wide enough for a dozen family members to sit in the shade of the overhanging trellised grapevine and enjoy a meal, but only on a sunny day, for unlike most patios in Zawut, this one has no roof, one of many indications that this household is perhaps of more modest means than others in the neighborhood. Looking out over the courtyard (approx. 60 × 30 feet), a visitor's eye might fall first, at least in summer, on more broad-leaved grapevines laden with fruit or on Abidem's and her son's separate small garden plots, where bright marigolds surround pomegranate trees, tomato and pepper plants, and rows of corn. Apricot, apple, and peach trees, prized additions in many Zawut households, are absent here. Around the courtyard, however, are a number of other sites that figure centrally in household members' daily routines.

With the warm weather of late spring, Zawut residents shift their cooking arrangements to outdoor pavilions (*chayxana*), permitting them to keep the indoors cool while enjoying Yining's pleasant climate. A typical pavilion consists of a stove, molded from the courtyard's own clayey earth and painted with lime, and an adjacent raised sitting platform, roughly eight-by-eight feet, built of either earth or wood. Whereas coal is the main cooking fuel during winter, both wood and coal are used in outdoor stoves. Although many *chayxana* are elaborate, here a simple wooden platform, a worn-out *kigiz* mat, and a makeshift roof of poles and tar paper provide Abidem's household with all the comfort needed.

In the spring, residents mend any damage done to their outdoor stoves by the heavy snows of the previous winter, or may build the stove anew if the pavilion is to be shifted to a new site in the courtyard. These tasks are easily accomplished, although labor alone is not enough to complete them: both Abidem and Yakupjan's wife, Gülzire, mended or rebuilt their stoves in the spring of 1996, and in each case the women called all household members then present, plus visitors and neighborhood children, to gather around the new stove and laugh out loud for a few minutes as it was lit for the first time. The belief that this ensures the smooth passage of smoke through the stove and flue is an indication of how domestic spaces are imprinted with meaning through ritual action and daily practice. *Mehelle* residents describe foods prepared by women at the domestic hearth as "strength giving"; in contrast, foods made by men for sale in the marketplace, where this and other rituals are not performed, are said to be "hollow," "weak," and "false."

So that the women of the household may bake the staple *nan*, a leavened wheat flatbread, many courtyards contain a four-foot-high mound of earth built around a locally made clay liner to form a *tonur*, an opentopped beehive oven. Not all Zawut homes have ovens, however, and the joint use of *tonur* is common. Since each household bakes *nan*, a daylong operation, only once every fifteen to twenty-five days, a number of families might easily share a *tonur* without conflict. Families who borrow the use of a neighbor's or relative's *tonur* simply make sure it will be unused on a given day, bring their own firewood for fuel, and present the *tonur* owner with the gift of a whole *nan* when they are done. Baking *nan* is a laborious and difficult process often undertaken jointly by two or three women, and women without nearby kin often seek help from a willing neighbor, again in exchange for a portion of bread.

The outdoor latrine shared by both households stands in a far corner of the courtyard, a wide pit covered with a floor of thick planks into which a slot has been cut. The pit itself, I was told, was deep enough to last two years or more, at which point it would be emptied in winter, when it was frozen solid and could be chopped into blocks. A waist-high wall of unpainted adobe bricks provides some privacy, but the only protection from the elements comes from the overhead branches of a gnarled tree, which the women in the family are convinced is periodically haunted by ghosts (*jin*). No *mehelle* homes I visited had indoor plumbing, but most outdoor latrines were roofed over. An old book, perhaps a child's discarded elementary-school text, would be left there to be used as toilet paper. Here household members perform their daily toilet, washing face and hands, brushing teeth, and ablutions before prayer, squatting on the brick patio and leaning out over the earth below, pouring water from a small tin pitcher of water left there for that purpose.

Next to the latrine stands a long makeshift shed, consisting of a tar-paper roof tacked over an assortment of timbers and bricks. Yakupjan is stockpiling materials in expectation of building a new house in the courtyard in the coming year or two, as soon as he resolves a dispute with his trading partner that has tied up much of the profit he earned during a yearlong trading sojourn in Almaty, across the nearby border with Kazakhstan. Amid these building materials a space has been cleared to store coal, coarse chunks of bituminous cut by hand at a small local mine and delivered by donkey cart. At the opposite corner of the courtyard stands a detached one-room structure, built for Abidem's ailing elder brother to live in when he joined her household in 1990. Since his death in 1992, it has been rented out to a local kindergarten class, an arrangement that brings its own world of activity into the courtyard daily.

High walls of adobe brick and rammed earth surround the courtyard. Walls of seven feet or more are the norm in Yining, where every home is thus protected. Exterior house walls are often built along property lines and do double duty by forming a part of this perimeter enclosure. Each home has a strong gate of iron or thick wooden timbers that is locked at night. These entryways present formidable facades, although burglars easily circumvent them by sledge-hammering through adobe exterior walls straight into empty homes. On either side of the front gates of many homes small sitting ledges are built, for residents to use while they watch their children play, chatting with neighbors as they pass by.

Saining Boundaries

Architecture is nothing if not . . . a metaphor of the body, a modality that the body expresses to symbolize itself. A replica—and a double.

—Donatella Mazzoleni[1]

The prominent entryways of Zawut homes are a useful reminder that boundaries between spaces can also be critical elements of homes. Within Uyghur homes, boundaries such as thresholds and entranceways are marked with significance through a range of bodily practices, both mundane and extraordinary, that link these spatial boundaries with the transgressions of bodily boundaries that mark life-cycle passages, such as the parturition of a child from the mother's womb or the departure of breath from the body at the passage from this world to the next.

An errant child who unthinkingly sits or steps directly on the wooden threshold of the doorway leading into Abidem's house is quickly rebuked. Uyghur informants recorded by Katanov in 1892 attributed consequences such as foot ailments, a growth on the buttocks, the loss of friendship, and poor results from business activities to sitting or standing on the threshold; "Go stand on a threshold!" was also given as a generic insult.[2] The threshold also figures as a critical site in other bodily practices and protective rituals. Household members' toenails clippings, for example, were carefully buried under the threshold, based on the belief, in Abidem's words, that "on judgment day they will grow into a thick barrier of thorns and keep the infidels, the *xitay* [i.e., ethnic Han Chinese], out of the house." Ethnographic materials recorded in southern Xinjiang circa 1907 attest to this as a widespread element of Uyghur folk belief; by one such account, Satan will appear on Judgment Day riding his ass *marr-dadjal*, of which every hair is the string of a musical instrument. On that day, the nail clippings buried under the threshold will grow into thorny hedges, blocking doorways and preventing people from running out and joining in the music.[3]

Fig. 3   Households bake *nan* flatbread once every 3–4 weeks. Within days the *nan* become rock hard, and pieces must be soaked in salted milky tea to be eaten. Bread and tea with pickled vegetables are standard breakfast fare. Here daughter Maynur stands in Abidem's *dalan* preparing to mix dough on baking day (photograph by the author, 1996).

Another link between bodies and thresholds was highlighted when Abidem's ten-year-old granddaughter Mukerrem was sick with the mumps. After making the girl lie down with her head on the threshold, Abidem wiped her own booted foot several times against the child's neck while saining (reciting the short blessing *bismillahir rehmanir rehim*) in order to protect the child from evil influence. Abidem stressed that this curative ritual, performed on three consecutive days, was effective only if done by a woman who had given birth many times, in her own case, fourteen times. The more a woman's body has itself served as a passageway into this world, the more powerful is her ability to use a threshold to heal.

Abidem described for me another more elaborate threshold ritual, one her parents had told her many times had been performed on her soon after her birth. This paraphrase is based on her descriptions:

At the birth of a child, a passageway is dug out underneath the threshold of the parents' house, and the newborn is passed through it, passed by the mother from inside the house to the father outside. The father then "purchases" the child by handing back to the mother a small amount of wheat bran, which symbolizes something of insignificant value. Next, the child is taken up to the roof and lowered down through a skylight from the father back to the mother.

The ritual action here not only suggests a symbolic devaluation of the child done to evade the evil eye or other maleficent influences but also foreshadows the gendering of market exchange as a male sphere in contrast to the female domestic sphere.[4] Transforming the child into something purchased by the father can even be viewed as a particularly appropriate form of couvade* for a community of merchants; in the case of Abidem, she remembers her father as a prosperous dealer in livestock. From these examples, it should be clear that the domestic threshold is a site of rich symbolic meaning linked to many other aspects of social life, and that a comprehensive analysis of the grammar and vocabulary of Uyghur ritual action is needed.

Mazzoleni's insight, quoted as the epigraph to this section, that bodies and architectural spaces are in some sense homologous, should not be taken as a reductive positing of links between spatial openings in the home and bodily orifices. Rather, by recognizing a link between passages across architectural boundaries and the body's passage from one life-cycle stage to another, we can make sense of a number of ethnographic data. Just as the threshold plays a role in procuring longevity for a newborn and the recovery of health for an adolescent girl, the boundary between inside and outside the home articulates with conceptions of the transition from life to death. If this boundary can be undermined successfully, the normal transition of the individual to their

---

*Couvade refers to a range of cultural practices in which men ritually imitate aspects of childbirth in order to take symbolic credit for newborn children.

death can also be undermined, for instance, in order to secure their premature death. Malov, for example, recorded circa 1913 that among Uyghurs in the Yining area

Prayers, called *yada*, are recited over a live frog, and after each prayer, the frog is pricked with a needle. After a few pricks, the frog dies, and is buried under the gate of the person on whom the spell is cast. The person soon grows thin, pale, and dies. Relatives have been known to find the remains of the frog when they searched under the gate of the deceased person's house.[5]

By recognizing that this magic practice conjoins two passages, the first from inside to outside the home, the second from "this world" (*bu dunya*) to "that world" (*u dunya*), we can also shed some light on the question of why a frog is used. As Ádám Molnár points out in his discussion of Frazer's notion of sympathetic magic, frogs are associated worldwide with rain charms, given their symbolic connection to water; in Northwestern India, for example, live frogs are raised into the air to draw forth water from the skies.[6] The symbolic equivalence of "liquids with living and drying with dying" in connection with the evil eye belief complex found widely in Xinjiang suggests the link between water deprivation and death.[7] Elderly persons in some parts of Xinjiang, for example, are spoken of as *qurutqa*, "dried up, parched, withered."[8] For Uyghurs in this region, then, a dead frog buried under the ground represents an inversion of the rain-seeking ritual, an attempt to bring a kind of drought to an individual, the drying up of the liquid that symbolizes the life essence.

On a more quotidian level, household members regularly marked their passage out of the home and into the public space of neighborhood streets and the marketplace by saining themselves, reciting the protective blessing *bismillahir rehmanir rehim*, at the exact moment they exited through the courtyard gate. The special danger associated with transgressing the boundary between home, a space of reciprocal exchange among kin and guests, and the market, marked by agonistic haggling between strangers, is manifest in a number of ways. Until a newborn undergoes a protective ritual bathing ceremony on its fortieth day, for example, all visitors arriving from the marketplace must remain standing outside the home for several minutes. This practice was routinely followed by visitors to Abidem's home while her youngest daughter Senemgül rested there for forty days after giving birth to daughter Tewsiye. A second example is described in this field note passage.

Abidem and I walked to Fourstores today to buy flour. Each month she buys 30 kg of state-subsidized flour for around $6.00, and buys more as needed from private merchants at $8.00 for 25 kg.

The government people wouldn't issue next month's flour a day early—whether Abidem didn't know the date or the policy, I don't know—but she bought the privately sold 25 kg anyway. I told her I'd go on ahead, and carried the flour home quickly, sat it in the house, then went back out to make sure Abidem was walking home safely on the icy roads. Heading back I passed [Abidem's daughter] Maynur, who was walking on the main road past the turn-off to our house.

"Did you go to get flour?" she asked.

"Yes, but just private, the government's can't be picked up until tomorrow."

"Did you dump it in the *chamadan?*"

"Yeah," I responded, without really hearing her question, and then realizing that she had said *chamadan*, the tin flour bin. In fact I had just sat the sack on the floor. "Now why did she ask me that?" I thought. Abidem walked up.

"So, where are you heading off to?" She craned her head at Maynur and squinted a disapproving eye. The younger woman, caught with her face in powder and makeup, gave her explanations, and walked off arm-in-arm with a female friend. As soon as they were gone, Abidem turned to me and asked, "Did you pour the flour in the *chamadan?*" When I told her I had not, she looked visibly relieved. Then I remembered having seen her say *bismillahir rehmanir rehim* when dumping the flour. Both Maynur and Abidem had worried I would fill the *chamadan* without speaking this blessing, perhaps endangering a month's worth of food.

The home is a space always concerned with safeguarding its blessing. A child caught whistling inside a home, for example, is quickly scolded for "driving away the home's blessing (*beriket*)." For flour to be safely removed from the entangled domains of government and marketplace and transferred into the home, the moment of transition must be protected. Saining while cooking food is also a routine feature of domestic life for women, done, for example, each time noodles are dropped into boiling water. This is perhaps another reason why foods prepared at home by women, men and women alike agree, are "strength-giving," whereas market foods, prepared by men without saining, are "weak" and "empty."

Flexible Homes, Flexible Households

The cultural logic that shapes the spatial ordering of homes in Zawut incorporates dynamic as well as static elements. In Abidem's household, the frequent reorganization of domestic space was occasioned by seasonal requirements, such as the shift to the outdoor cookstove, as well as by the changing composition of the household and the changing relations among its members.

In the case of Abidem's household, spatial arrangements revealed the evolving boundaries of the social ties in the dual-family compound. In late autumn, for example, I discovered that Yakupjan had terminated his rental arrangement with the kindergarten when I found him building a wooden *supa* platform in the former schoolroom. He and his family then used the converted room as a wintertime cooking and eating space and as a sleeping space for him, his wife, and their two younger children. This smaller room was easier and less costly to heat and afforded an occasional private moment for Yakupjan and his wife, but the primary motivation behind the conversion was to permit Yakupjan to get away from his eldest son, Mehmud (age 18), who continued to sleep in the home's main *dalan*. An intense animosity between father and son grew throughout my stay—the two avoided eating meals together, for example—ending ultimately in a fist and knife fight between them. Trouble had been brewing "ever since Mehmud's nose had swollen up," Abidem explained, referring to the period after puberty when many parents find their children hard to handle.

Later that year, in the spring, I returned from a three-week absence to find Abidem's *chayxana* completely dismantled and her garden plot from the previous year bricked over. Abidem, too, had been surprised by these changes, which her son had made while she was in Urumqi, a fifteen-hour bus ride away, with her daughter Anise, who sought medical treatment. Her surprise gave way quickly to bitter, silent, angry resentment when she learned that Yakupjan, because he had decided to continue using his winter sleeping quarters throughout the summer and felt his mother's *chayxana* would be in his way, had simply destroyed it. When I asked him about bricking over his mother's garden, he shrugged and laughed. "She gets all her vegetables free from Aliye anyway," he said. Aliye did often bring over damaged and unsalable produce from her family's market stall, and Yakupjan perhaps resented not being given a share of this bounty, but he knew well that his mother valued the garden for its beauty and for the pleasure she derived from tending to it. As for the newly bricked-over space, Yakupjan used it all spring and summer as a convenient spot to wash his motorcycle, a weekly event, since men in the *mehelle* liked to keep their motorcycles clean. Reorganizations such as these highlight the difficulties households faced when sharing a courtyard. Such multihousehold courtyards were common, indeed the norm, in Zawut, and, judging from neighborhood gossip, most households had their share of ongoing antagonisms similar to those described here.

Just as spatial arrangements inside the home were flexible, so, too, was household composition. In the summer of 1995, Abidem, in her late seventies, still maintained a separate hearth and an independent household, home to a changing group of relatives. On my arrival in July, she was living with a boisterous ten-month-old grandson, Abdü-shükür, the first-born son of her youngest child, Senemgül. Abidem had been raising the boy for six months, ever since Senemgül had tipped a basin of boiling water onto herself and needed to recover from a bad scalding. Abidem provided this child care largely without compensation, a fact she occasionally grumbled about, although the child's parents would periodically give her small amounts of cash to help cover expenses. Senemgül, like most of Abidem's children, lived just a few minutes' walk away, and she stopped in daily for a meal or to see her son. Another resident was sad-faced Aysajan, eight years old, who was considered by all to be an orphan. When Abidem's elder brother was in his seventies, he had taken as his eighth wife—as one relative explained, "he needed someone to clean and cook for him"—a twenty-four-year-old woman from Aqsu, a town in southern Xinjiang. The young woman soon bore a child; when Abidem's brother took ill not long after, she ran away, abandoning her child to Abidem's care. Although Abidem did not view Aysajan as kin—no one in the family did—she had raised him on her own, feeding and clothing him using what little money she had. My arrival in July 1995 brought the household count to four. In January 1996 Senemgül gave birth to a daughter, Tewsiye, and for the six months after that Senemgül and both her children lived primarily in Abidem's home.

Senemgül was not the only child to return to Abidem's house for an extended stay. In the early 1990s, Abidem had also welcomed back into her home her daughter Maynur, then in her late twenties, who stayed for two years, in between divorcing her husband and then remarrying the same man. Maynur still quarreled frequently with her husband, and she returned regularly to stay at her mother's for days or weeks at a time, an addition of three people, since her daughters ages ten and twelve were sure to be around much of that time.

Members of the household of Abidem's son Yakupjan, like the members of Abidem's household, reappear throughout the following chapters; these include Yakupjan himself, age forty-three; his wife Gülzire, age forty; and their four children, boys Mehmud and Ilyar, ages eighteen and seven, and the two girls, Xalidem and Nuriye, ages sixteen and nine.

Changing Lifestyles: Moving Up and Moving Out

For some residents of Zawut and adjacent neighborhoods, a number of more permanent changes in the spatial configuration of domestic life were also under way, changes that involved both moving up and moving out. By moving up, I refer to the shift toward constructing new two- or three-story private residences in the *mehelle*, where single-story residences had long been the norm; by moving out, I mean the relocation of those few Uyghur families headed by an employee at a state work-unit out of suburban private dwellings and into concrete high-rise apartment buildings in the paved city center.

Moving Up

Nowadays these merchants are earning so much money that they are not only putting up fancy houses in this world, but they are thinking "In the next world, I want to do the same thing" and they have started building their graves to be just as fancy.

One merchant lays out fifty thousand *yuan* to have a fancy mausoleum built for himself. He gets this master bricklayer to come, the bricklayer was a master at speaking as well, and so he brings the guy over to the site, and gets all of the materials brought over. The bricklayer works for about a month, then the merchant drives up in his big [Volkswagen] Santana, and asks, "Master, is it all completed?"

"Nothing is missing, everything is all completed. The only thing missing is you."

—Muxtar Hésam, Yining jokester

Fig. 4   In the 1990s, prosperous *mehelle* families increasingly replaced their one-story adobe and rammed-earth homes with multistory buildings of masonry and concrete. Although home-building signaled rising affluence, residents understood it also resulted from the inability of married sons to acquire land for independent dwellings, a change they attributed to the pressure of incoming Han migrants (photograph by the author, 1996).

As more and more *mehelle* families prospered from trading in the private markets of Xinjiang and Central Asia in the 1990s, the building of new houses around Yining became common. And in building new houses, putting up highly ornamented homes of two or three stories became the norm. At times it seemed as if every lane in the *mehelle* had one or two households busy demolishing their single-story rammed-earth and adobe homes and building two-story brick houses. Indeed, the house Muxtar sat in as he told the above joke had recently been rebuilt into an elaborate two-story dwelling with an ornate, decoratively carved and painted wooden balcony. In the joke, the wise-cracking bricklayer takes the wealthy trader's own assumption, that the grave's completion is a desirable thing, and turns it against him, by sneaking in the suggestion that the rich man's death itself is desirable.

Where a casual visitor might have seen these bright facades as a clear sign of material prosperity, local residents understood that large houses signaled a more complex shift in residential patterns. Land was becoming increasingly scarce, a change residents attributed to the impact of Han immigrants to Xinjiang. Where once brothers would marry and establish independent residences away from their parents' home, usually in the same or adjacent *mehelle*, now three and even four brothers had begun to accept the need to live together in multistory houses.

Han labor crews were building most of these new Uyghur homes. Abidem's son-in-law Ablimit Hajim, for example, whom family members called Haj'kam, was having a large house constructed in the spring of 1996 in preparation for the eventual marriages of his four sons. Through a Han middleman, he had arranged for a crew of eighteen men and women from Sichuan to build his new home for around 50,000 *yuan* ($6,250). Uyghurs' reliance on Han homebuilders was not new—visitors to the region in the 1900s and 1930s commented on the presence of Han building crews and noted that Uyghurs appeared to derive an elevated sense of personal status from hiring Han as manual laborers—but specific building practices were changing due to market forces.[9] Haj'kam, for example, opted for a prefabricated cement slab roof in place of the traditional wood and mat construction when he learned the change would save him 300 *yuan*.

Given the suggestion in Muxtar's joke of popular resentment against wealthy merchants building extravagant homes, it is not surprising that Haj'kam disavowed any interest in building a "fancy" home. In fact, he went out of his way to express his intention to build a "plain" house, perhaps in part because he was a shopkeeper, selling everyday items to his neighbors from a small store attached to his house, and did not wish to appear to be earning too much from that business or to be trying to elevate himself over his customers. "He has to ask the neighbors about every little detail," his wife, Anise, griped to her mother one morning. "Even if we want to hang curtains in front of the windows, we have to ask every one of them what they think. He drives me crazy!"

This pious shopkeeper's posture of having wealth but not wishing to attract attention to the fact is the opposite of that found among many of Yining's marketplace traders, for whom fostering an appearance of wealth has become a key element in their strategy for success. Haj'kam was also rumored to have substantial wealth lent out at interest in support of the business ventures of other men. This is a common local practice, but the stigma it carries under Islamic custom made it a sensitive issue for this veteran of the pilgrimage to Mecca, who prays five times each day, which is more than most *mehelle* men. His frequent heavy-handed attempts to impress his poverty on friends and neighbors, Abidem suggested behind his back, were *set*, meaning both ugly and embarrassing.

Of ongoing concern to people building new houses was the state's increasing attempts to collect new construction-related taxes and permit fees. Haj'kam knew that building inspectors of some kind had come several times to his house to speak with him, but each time he slipped out a back entrance, having no better strategy at hand for avoiding making these payments.

Haj'kam often mentioned his plans to throw a *nezir* once the house was complete, describing it as a large party for friends, family, and neighbors who will present him with gifts. Haj'kam was looking forward to this, commenting in his gravelly, deadpan voice,

"When we have a *nezir* in October, it won't be chaotic (*qalaymiqan*). We won't be getting all sorts of presents we don't need, like carpets." His meaning is, he just wants cash. "I'm in debt for five thousand *yuan*," he complains.

Despite their considerable variation, all dwellings in the *mehelle*, whether new or old, plain or highly ornamented, for single or extended families, were based on the architectural elements described in this chapter, a feature they shared with Uyghur peasant homes in Yining's surrounding farming villages. As outlined above, these elements include high-walled courtyards containing fruit trees, grapevines, and garden plots, residences with rooms laid out in *dalan* and *saray* pairs, and outdoor clay ovens, earthen stoves, and shaded eating pavilions for summertime use. Newly built *mehelle* homes, despite their ornamental differences, provided the same facilities and permitted the same daily functions as before. Only when Uyghur families moved into apartment buildings in the city center did the spatial bases of domestic life change dramatically.

Moving Out

For the holidays, we were going to beat the carpets in our apartment clean, but there was no one at home except me and my dad. So my dad went to the Xenzu Bazar [a local market] and got four or five day-laborers to come. Well, they came, and we got the rugs outside, and they were beating away, *gup gup gup*. Tons of dirt was coming out, and one of them up and says to my dad, "Hey Hésam'ka, this one must be from the *dalan!*"

—Muxtar Hésam, Yining jokester

For a small number of Yining's Uyghurs, employment at state work-units brought the opportunity to reside in apartment buildings. For most, this came when success in the state educational system led to a government job assignment. In the case of the raconteur quoted above, the apartment came with the special status his father, Hésam, enjoyed as a nationally known performer in a state performance troupe. The floor plans of these apartments were based on layouts designed and made ubiquitous throughout China by Han and did not accord with the patterns of traditional Uyghur social life. For example, there was no *dalan* room with its raised *supa* platform. On occasions when I visited Uyghurs living in such apartments, the rooms were filled with manufactured furniture, couches and chairs, considered in China to be "western."

In the joke quoted above, the day-laborer teasingly suggests that although Hésam lives in a new apartment, supposedly a more "modern" living arrangement, his rug is still as dirty as it would be if he lived in a traditional house. The joke reveals local tensions not only about social stratification but also about changing patterns of social interaction, and it hints at the power of architecture to disrupt residents' abilities to participate in the reciprocal visitation practices central to Uyghur social life. Nor do apartment buildings provide facilities that allow residents to bake *nan*, a staple and symbolically important food item not available in local markets.*

---

*The *nan* sold in local markets (*bazar nan*) differs so greatly from homemade *nan* (*öy nan*) in taste and texture that *mehelle* residents view them as fundamentally incommensurate. Buyers of market *nan* include restaurants and food stalls, who serve it to customers, and people who serve it at large gatherings such as outdoor picnics or other social events.

Paved Streets and Other Changes in *Mehelle* Space

The impact of 1990s market success on the *mehelle* was not limited to the building of new private residences. Heavy rains and melting snow regularly turned *mehelle* lanes to mud, and on such days finely dressed residents setting off to market or on household visits could be seen stepping carefully around deep ruts and immense puddles. As I passed a particularly treacherous intersection one day walking with Abidem, she recalled a childhood memory of witnessing a horse so hopelessly mired in the mud at that same location that it broke its leg and was killed on the spot by its owner. Given the considerable inconvenience mud caused residents, it is not surprising that wealthier families were interested in paving *mehelle* lanes. At this time, Yining's paved city center was expanding outward incrementally, encroaching on the *mehelle* suburbs and bringing with it a tide of Han families, Han businesses, and Han architecture, all equally unwelcomed by Uyghur residents. But even deep inside the *mehelle*, new sections of paved road stood isolated, connecting to dirt lanes at either end. These paved sections, financed by the wealthy merchants whose homes fronted onto them, increasingly obscured the former sharp distinction between paved city thoroughfares and the dirt or gravel lanes of the *mehelle*. Although the benefits of such improvements were plain to local residents, these changes also signaled an increase in social stratification, an effect of the economic success enjoyed by Yining's more prosperous traders. This awareness was expressed in the following joke, recorded in Yining and sold widely in local markets on a manufactured cassette of songs and jokes.

There's a guy who's started going with a new girlfriend, and so he goes to her *mehelle*.

Now, her *mehelle*, it's full of dogs, so he goes there, and a dog runs right up and starts chasing him. It's chasing him, and he's so scared that he falls down to the ground and starts grabbing for rocks. But the girl's *mehelle*, it has paved streets. He's grabbing all around, but his hands are coming up empty. He keeps grabbing, and still nothing, finally he gets angry, and says, "I've never seen this kind of a girlfriend, one that ties up all the rocks and lets the dogs out!"   (Muxtar Hésam, Yining jokester)

This narrative nicely expresses the class tension I allude to, here embedded in a story of courtship. Note how, in his final line, Muxtar uses the word "girlfriend" as a metonym for the entire neighborhood; she *is* her neighborhood, a testament to the *mehelle*'s status as a critical unit of social identity. The young man visits her and sees that her neighborhood is fancier than his own. His humiliation is expressed in the attack of the dogs; he is afraid of the dogs but cannot fight them off, deprived of his weapons, his power to fight back, by the paving, which represents the affluence and social position of her family. The punch line presents a perfect symmetry in its reversal—instead of tying up the dogs and leaving the rocks strewn about, this neighborhood fixes the rocks in place and lets the dogs loose—and the joke "cracks" through its critique of the material and social changes associated with modernization and class differentiation.

———

In this chapter I have started to sketch some of the ways that the household provides the physical and cultural space at the core of the experience of being a *mehelle* resident. That picture is hardly complete, of course, and the chapters that follow return often to household spaces as they examine in more detail the daily dramas that shape much of social life in these communities. The next chapter crosses the threshold of the house and passes through the courtyard gate in order to look at the space of the *mehelle* beyond the home and to examine the profound affective importance the neighborhood holds as a basis for social identity in Yining. To do this, I turn now to the spatial and social organization of Yining's *mehelle* suburban ring as a whole.

2

Yining's *Mehelle* as Suburban Periphery

Nowadays, all of you know, the traffic cops are stopping donkey carts, they won't let them pass and enter the city.

One day, what do I see, but some guy coming down the road from Döng *mehelle* driving a donkey cart. Right when he is about to come to the city police [who stood each day at the junction of *mehelle* dirt lane and paved city street], he unhitches the donkey, loads it into the cart, and starts pulling it himself!

—Hésam Qurban, Yining jokester

Just as the organization of home and courtyard reflect and reproduce key features of Uyghur social life, so, too, do spatial and symbolic characteristics of suburban *mehelle* neighborhoods embody and express a number of revealing features about Yining society. The message of the above joke, in my reading, that the state is "making asses" out of Uyghurs, or more generally that onetime "natural" hierarchies of power are being inverted in the name of modernization, prompts us to consider more deeply Uyghurs' feelings for the rapidly changing *mehelle*.

Zawut *Mehelle*

To return home to Zawut *mehelle* from excursions into Yining's city center, Abidem and her neighbors would pass the point where the city's paved roads and bus service ended and walk several hundred meters farther down a series of winding, poplar-lined dirt roads. The manufacturing compound for which Zawut was named stood just across from where the narrow, dogleg lane leading to Abidem's courtyard veered away from the larger dirt road, which continued on toward the Ili River several kilometers away. In the mid-1990s, the defunct factory's only sites of daily activity were its small health clinic, open to the community at large, and the booth facing onto the street where guards kept watch over the compound's usually locked gate. In summer evenings men drifting out of the adjacent pool hall, or on their way home from a day spent sitting around a roadside pile of melons for sale, would slip quietly into the guardhouse to smoke hashish and tell jokes late into the night. Only on Sunday mornings were the gates thrown open, and the compound's large empty fields would be filled with rows of used television sets and immaculately washed motorcycles, secondhand goods brought by their owners to be sold through smooth-talking marketplace middlemen to other *mehelle* residents.

Most *mehelle* roads are dirt or gravel and are from eight to fifteen feet wide. All but the narrowest are lined with rows of poplars on either side, their trunks whitewashed from the ground up to a height of four to eight feet. Next to each row of trees runs a shallow channel of flowing water, then a raised dirt trail where residents walk when roads turn muddy. In addition to these broader dirt roads, networks of narrower, more twisted paths also weave their way through the *mehelle*. Entirely lining both sides of lanes and paths alike, high courtyard walls rise abruptly, adobe and brick walls washed in white lime or painted rich sky blue. Poorer neighborhoods look much the same, except that homes are smaller, the courtyards more densely packed together, and the walls facing the streets more likely to be left a dull, unpainted brown.

Like most of Yining's *mehelle*, Zawut had a number of new homes under construction, fewer perhaps than in the more prosperous *mehelle* adjacent to it, but as many or more than most. Like most *mehelle*, it had several small shops selling an assortment of everyday items and foodstuffs, convenient for residents who needed such items on short notice. Two health clinics operated in Zawut when I arrived, staffed by Uyghur or Uyghur-speaking Han nurses and doctors. In the spring of 1996, Zawut attracted a third clinic, set up by a Han doctor who rented a

Fig. 5   On the outskirts of Yining, this road leads from the city's urban center to the narrow winding dirt roads of Zawut. Covered horse-cart taxis wait here to carry passengers back into the *mehelle*. The sign at left reminds passersby in Uyghur and Chinese that *Mineral Resources Belong to the State!* (photograph by the author, 1996).

small room to ply his trade. This, too, was a trend throughout Yining; in the *mehelle* and in nearby villages Han doctors moonlighting from state hospitals set up private clinics and charged inflated prices for basic medicines.

In more prosperous *mehelle*, trash service was regular; ever-present piles of trash on the streets of poorer *mehelle* suggested services there were less comprehensive. As with other *mehelle*, the electricity went out frequently in Zawut, much more often than it did in the mostly Han city center, where street wiring and transformers were better maintained. *Mehelle* residents were responsible for maintaining the single wires that ran into their homes themselves, and short circuits due to rain or snow often seemed more the norm than the exception.

Although Zawut was in most ways typical of Yining's *mehelle*, certain differences did exist. Zawut had no mosques, for example. Men in Zawut invariably prayed at a large nearby mosque once each week, on Fridays, as did virtually all Uyghur men in Yining. In many *mehelle*, smaller daily-use mosques were also common. Wealthy merchants returning from the *haj* financed the construction of these small mosques, in part to promote the practice of performing five daily prayers. Large or small, neighborhood mosques functioned as centers for informal associational networks and reinforced a shared identity among their congregations. Although there was no strict relationship between *mehelle* boundaries and the spatial arrangement of mosques, the congregations of Yining's larger mosques usually lived in adjacent neighborhoods, and mosques anchored those neighborhoods spatially as centers of daily and weekly activity. For more senior men, they were a central focus of social activity; for younger men, billiard halls and gaming rooms with mahjong tables, of which Zawut had several, were often a more important place to congregate.

Zawut also lacked the steam baths that *mehelle* residents visited on a regular basis, usually once or twice a week. Several nearby bathhouses served their needs, however, providing users with private suites (a changing room, a washing room, and a steam-sauna room) for a fee of two to four *yuan* per hour. Although bathhouses were filled with men and women most days of the week, they were busiest on Friday mornings when men arrived to wash thoroughly before going to mosque. Men joked that Thursdays were the most frequent day for sexual activity between married couples, since the man would already be expecting to perform a full ablution (necessary after sexual contact) the next morning before praying at mosque.

One feature common to Zawut and surrounding *mehelle* was the gradual arrival of Han families into Uyghur neighborhoods, as Yining's Han population grew through in-migration. A large six-story brick dormitory to house the Han workers at a new pharmaceutical factory was under construction on the northern edge of Zawut. "Great One-Hundred-Year Plan" proclaimed the banner that hung from the site's construction crane tower, a none-too-subtle reminder to local residents that the Han in-migrants had come to stay.

Not every new project in the *mehelle* was built to house the growing Han population, however. In a Uyghur *mehelle* on the western edge of the city, Yining's municipal government had constructed what it hoped would be a tourist attraction, a gated park containing a statue of Lin Zexu, a famous Han statesman who resided in the area in the nineteenth century after being exiled there by the Qing emperor. Soon after

I first visited the site, I was invited to be a guest at several nearby homes, where residents recalled angrily how the government had taken land from Uyghur homeowners to build the monument. This in itself can be seen as an unintended but fitting tribute to Lin, considering that he was put in charge of Han colonization efforts in the area in 1844.[1] It is also ironic that a statue of Lin, a Han national hero remembered for standing up to the British during the Opium War, now looks out over communities of Uyghurs for whom heroin addiction is a major source of social problems, and who widely blame the Han for permitting the illicit trafficking of a drug they see as a genocidal poison.

One Mehelle *Is Still Five Fingers*

Like my neighbors, I was always proud to tell new acquaintances that I was from Zawut. Not because it was full of decent, reputable people, which it was, but because I felt I shared their sense of belonging to a specific place, to a specific group of people. Other *mehelle*, of course, were no less meaningful for the people who lived in them. When I saw Uyghur men from Yining making each other's acquaintance in Beijing or Urumqi, the first question they invariably asked each other was which *mehelle* they were from. According to one Uyghur phrase, one has a blood tie with one's *mehelle*; it is "the *mehelle* where one's umbilical cord blood has been spilt" (*kindik qéni tökülgen mehelle*). Another indication of the *mehelle*'s significance as a social unit is found in a local belief regarding the practice of performing male circumcision (*sünnet*). According to a version of that belief provided by Abidem, if the ceremony is performed when the child is six, the religious merit (*sawap*) goes to the child's mother. If the ceremony is done at age seven, the merit goes to the child's father. If at age eight, all merit goes to the *mehelle*. If we accept that here "mother" and "father" represent not so much individuals but entire kin lines, then *mehelle* is explicitly the next level of social identity beyond the kin group.

The importance of the *mehelle* as a basis for social identity among Uyghurs in other towns and cities in Xinjiang is likely to vary because of factors such as social structure and population size. One indication that *mehelle* identities are perhaps stronger in Yining than elsewhere is found in the liner notes of the more than four hundred cassette tapes of Uyghur popular and folk music produced throughout Xinjiang that I collected during my stay. In those notes, biographical information about artists from Yining uniformly includes their *mehelle* affiliation, whereas biographies of musicians from other oases do so only rarely. This is not to suggest that *mehelle* are unimportant in other oases; on the contrary, informal interviews with residents of other oases suggested they did exist and mattered greatly to Uyghurs throughout Xinjiang.

Despite the genuine solidarity created by shared *mehelle* identity, residents understood that feelings of solidarity coexisted with an awareness of the many distinctions and differences that shaped local society, as the following field note passage suggests.

After dinner Maynur finished washing the dishes, then went out up to the big street. Abidem was upset about it. Our neighbor on the corner stepped out of her doorway in the dark, and Abidem asked her, "Is Maynur at your place?"

"No," she replied.

Abidem turned to me, "I knew it, she's out in the street," she said, referring to Zawut's main thoroughfare. "If she sits out there, I get all worried inside."

"Why?"

"Well now, it's ugly, isn't it? There are all sorts of people walking by! My, but the women in this neighborhood just love to sit out on that street," she said scowling.

"Aren't they all one *mehelle* of people," I asked, just to press her. She raised her hand, clenched into a fist, then slowly uncurled her fingers.

"Five fingers, they're all different" (*besh qol oxshimaydu*). There are all kinds of people in a *mehelle*.

A Taxonomic Survey of Yining's *Mehelle*

During my research, I mapped out the rough boundaries of several dozen of Yining's *mehelle*. No maps or scholarly works in Uyghur or Chinese that I could locate acknowledged these boundaries or even listed the names of *mehelle*, despite the fact that for local Uyghurs they constituted perhaps the primary cultural categorization of both physical and social space. A review of some of these names highlights the inherent dynamism of local communities and community identities; *mehelle* emerge, grow, decline, are displaced, and disappear, all under the influence of myriad forces, including demographic change and socio-economic stratification. In the final analysis, *mehelle* boundaries are more social than physical, and a review of *mehelle* names reveals some of the social and economic bases for the organization of local communities, demonstrating that *mehelle* are shaped continually by local individuals, social groups, and events.

Many *mehelle* take their names from a craft or trade group. Names for such trades combine the name of a product, for example, *naghra* (kettle-drum), with the agentive suffix -*chi* (one who). The resulting compound is usually an ambiguous one; in this example, *naghrachi* might refer equally to one who makes drums, one who sells them, or one who performs with them—hence my temptation to translate *naghrachi* freely as "kettledrum-ist." When providing *mehelle* histories, residents were often unable (or reluctant) to distinguish communities of makers from communities of sellers. In the contemporary marketing of handicrafts, some local craftsmen produce for their own retail operations only, others sell to merchants who engage in either retailing or wholesaling, and many do both. The use of the ambiguous suffix -*chi* is fitting then, in that it captures nicely this blending of roles. *Mehelle* whose names derive from crafts include Naghrachi (kettledrum-ist); Namatmen (felt maker), where makers of a thick kind of felt lived; Könchi (leather-worker); Qazanchi (cauldron-ist); Töpchi, from a kind of hat made there; and Taqchiliq (horseshoeing).

Some *mehelle* are named after wealthy or prominent individuals. Ghapaway Kocha (*kocha* means "street") is named after Ghapar *bay*, or Ghapar "the rich man." Tajiway, whose residents were said to include a large proportion of ethnic Uzbeks, is named after a rich man who lived there, and derives from Taji (possibly *taiji*) + *bay*. Qaraway, residents suggested, derives either from *qara* (black) + *bay* (rich man), in which case *qara* is perhaps a nickname, given its derogatory implications, or more likely from *qariy* (the honorific "one who recites the Qur'an") + *bay*.

Other *mehelle* are named after specific sites, which in many cases have long since ceased to exist. Orda (palace) *mehelle* derives its name from the onetime residence of the *xakim beg*, a local official in the period of Qing rule in the area (ca. 1756–1911). Consul is an area in the city center named for the Russian consulate established there after a commercial treaty was signed in 1851. This wooded area with many buildings now operates as a state-run hotel. Moyka, according to residents, takes its name from the Russian word for "felt factory." Pen Zawut (plank factory) is a *mehelle* near the riverside. Töt Dukan (four stores) takes its name from a central crossroads with stores at each corner; the origin of Üch Dukan (three stores) is likewise evident. Térek Mazar (poplar shrine) takes its name from a saint shrine, or *mazar*, in the vicinity.

Other *mehelle* names relate to terrain and topographic features; indeed Uyghur place-names throughout Xinjiang are typically based on terrain features. Such terrain features, however, should not be considered irreducibly natural. Landscapes in Xinjiang have been transformed by human activity for millennia, and terrain features in the immediate Yining area are no exception. One subsection of Moyka *mehelle*, for example, was known widely as Azgal, meaning "hollow," in the sense of a slight depression or ravine. That hollow, noticeably lower than surrounding neighborhoods, was reportedly created by extensive brickmaking facilities that operated there long ago. The canal for which Ara Östeng (middle, or forked, canal) *mehelle* is named, like many canals in and around Yining, was dug under Qing rule by corvée labor provided by Uyghur peasants and townspeople. One *mehelle*, in which the bed of a canal spread out widely into a shallow creek, was known as Yéyiq Su (spreading water) or, in one variant, Yéyingqa Su.

Other neighborhoods, such as Jigdelik (oleaster orchard) and Top Térek (poplar grove), took their names from important local plants. Several prominent hillocks in the suburban fringe were named as *mehelle*, including Döng (hill), Qaradöng (black hill), and Topadöng, which may derive from *topa* (soil) or perhaps from *töpe* (upper part) + *döng*. Cultural categories can act as perceptual and cognitive filters for human awareness of the landscape. It is a striking coincidence, for example, that of all Yining's neighborhoods, Black Hill *mehelle* was viewed by residents of other *mehelle* as having the highest proportion of men engaged in the kinds of manual labor referred to derogatorily as "black work" (*qara ish*).

Numerous areas within Yining take their names from particular markets located there, but not all named areas constitute *mehelle*. Market areas that were considered *mehelle* include Alma Bazar (apple market) and Chilan Xangza (jujube street). Bide Bazar (clover market) and an area called Chinese market, on the other hand, were spoken of as locales rather than as actual neighborhoods. Residents referred to Chinese market either as Xitay Bazar or Xenzu Bazar (the ethnic label *xitay* has mild derogatory connotations, whereas the term *xenzu,* from the Chinese *hanzu,* or "ethnic Han," does not).

A number of *mehelle* names derive from translations or transliterations of non-Uyghur words, many of which have at this point worked their way into popular Uyghur consciousness. Xembeng, a name deriving from Chinese *hanbing* (Han soldiers), was formerly the site of a military encampment.* Qizil Bayraq (red flag) was formerly a part of Orda *mehelle,* but by the mid-1990s it was considered a distinct *mehelle,* taking its name from a standard Communist-era symbol. This is an interesting semiotic shift away from *orda,* the palace of a pre-Communist Uyghur official, to a symbol standing specifically for the Chinese Communist Party. Tereqiyiz *mehelle* is derived from Tereqi Yéza (Progress Village), a name presumably bestowed decades earlier under state-mandated collectivization. One *mehelle,* a broad flat area on the banks of the Ili River, is called Jirghilang, probably taking its name from the Mongolian *jirghalang* (enjoyment), since this area is a popular picnic site. Also near the river is Qongtaji *mehelle. Qun taiji* was the title of several Oyirat Mongol rulers in Ili. These two Mongol borrowings highlight the fact that the Ili River Valley was under Mongol influence for centuries prior to Qing rule.

These categories by no means exhaust the bases for *mehelle* naming. My inquiries into the origin of Alte Shu'ar (six slogans) *mehelle* led to arguments among several middle-aged men until one Abdurishit "the Matchmaker" settled the matter (at least for that day) with an account of how the "six slogans" faction, a Republican-era political movement, had started there. Some *mehelle* came into being when residents of some other locale migrated *en masse,* as is reputedly the case with Besh Kirem, whose initial residents I was told came from the southern Xinjiang town of Besh Kirem near Kashgar. The circumstances behind the name of Ayding (moonlight) *mehelle* were not known to the many Ayding residents I questioned, but this word's Mongolian origin suggests that the neighborhood may date to at least the 1700s, if not earlier.

---

*Han soldiers were garrisoned in Ili soon after the installation of the Manchu military governor there in 1762; as many as 10,700 of them by 1771 (Zeng Wenwu, *Zhongguo jingying xiyu shi,* 300).

Other *mehelle* names I inquired about but whose provenance I was not able to further identify, include Sherq (east); Paqa (frog); Teshlepki, eponymous with its large bazaar, possibly from Russian *deshevki* (low-price, cheap stuff); Törem, possibly from *teram* (a branching off of one stream into many); Pushman; Paytima Körük (foot-cloth bridge); Bay-köl (?); Bostan (oasis); Yéngi (new); and Ghalibiyet Kocha, which means "victory street," although which victory is not clear.

Most of the important questions one might ask about *mehelle* in Yining and elsewhere in Xinjiang remain to be answered. How fixed or fluid are the spatial boundaries of *mehelle* at any one point in time, or across time? What factors lead to the fission or fusion of neighborhoods? At this point I can only conjecture that critical junctures are likely to be marked by such things as the construction of a new building or the emergence of a charismatic merchant. In the mid-1990s, Ayding was one of Yining's most prosperous neighborhoods, with a great concentration of successful merchants, whose prominence and building activities created a number of named subdivisions within it, such as, Qexriman Kocha (hero street). Perhaps one day sub-*mehelle* such as this one will come to be viewed as separate *mehelle*.

The Pan-Neighborhood Identity of the *Ghuljiliq*

Although good-natured rivalries between residents of different *mehelle* were often invoked in Yining men's daily interactions, a strong sense of shared identity united the different *mehelle* vis-à-vis Uyghur residents of other cities. Local rivalries are expressed widely in Xinjiang, often taking the form of verbal teasing or folk rhymes by which residents of one locale insult residents of another, such as these two variant items I recorded from *Ghuljiliq* (Yining-native) Zawut residents regarding Kashgarians.

Kashgarian you dolt	*qeshqerliq qashang*
It has become springtime	*etiyaz boldi*
Throw away your ragged leather sandals	*choruqni tashlang*
Make yourself a drum	*dumbaqni yasang*
Kashgarian you dolt	*qeshqerliq qashang*
Scratch my back	*dümbemni qashlang*

It has become springtime   *etiyaz boldi*
Throw away your ragged sandals   *choruqni tashlang*

Before we can assume that the sentiments expressed in these verses strictly reflect rivalries between residents of different oases, however, we must first consider the extent to which waves of Uyghur migration into the Ili Valley from different areas of southern Xinjiang may have given rise to divisions and cleavages within Yining residence and identity patterns, such as, for example, between descendants of Yining's original Uyghur settlers, known as *taranchi*, who arrived from Turpan, Aqsu, and Uch-Turpan around 1755–60, and arrivals from Kashgar who came more than a century later. Whatever the case may be, these inter-oasis rivalries are reciprocated, as this verse recorded in 1935 from a Kashgar native about the *taranchi* residents of Yining attests.[2]

A *taranchi* is a fool   *taranchi digen axmaq*
In his girdle he has flint and steel   *bélide iken chaxmaq*
Whichever town he is in   *qaysi sheherde bar dur*
He is ready to sell his own town   *özining sheherini satmaq*

Note that the specific insult leveled at Yining-area Uyghurs is exactly that they lack a sufficiently developed sense of local-place loyalty!

Aural Community and Radio Yining

For the proud residents of Yining's many distinct *mehelle*, there was more than just physical proximity and a shared tradition of mutual teasing that united them into a single social body of *Ghuljiliq*. One local institution in particular was a key factor in producing a genuine sense of community among local residents.

Most mornings during my stay in Zawut, Abidem rose before dawn, performed her morning prayers, and began quietly attending to the first of the day's many chores. And always, at 6:30 A.M., she would turn on her radio to catch the beginning of the day's Uyghur-language broadcast. The year before, her grandson Mehmud, Yakupjan's oldest son, had slipped in and stolen her prized radio to sell for spending money. There wasn't much that could be done about Mehmud, even his father couldn't control him; as for the radio, she had gone out and bought a new one immediately, for a new programming format begun in 1993–94 had quickly become an indispensable part of her day. From morning to dusk a mixture of Uyghur folk and popular music, humorous sketches, poetry readings, and serialized passages from well-known Uyghur historical novels were presented in an all-Uyghur-language broadcast. As I walked through *mehelle* lanes and city streets, it often seemed to me that the entire Uyghur population of Yining was listening in; enough homes and market stalls played the station loudly that one was almost never out of earshot. This omnipresent soundscape not only created a unique sense of aural community in itself, the content of the broadcast also unified local knowledge about the city's happenings.

Talk radio was an important part of each day's programming. A main feature of such programs was that small children called in, often children as young as four or five. Always, although for no identifiable reason, they were asked to give (and gave) their full names and places of residence. Always the address began with a *mehelle* name; then the child would give directions to their home: ". . . then turn left at Abdurishit'akam's store, it's the fourth courtyard on the right."³ Few callers gave street numbers, since residents rarely used them. *Mehelle* doors often displayed three or four differently numbered state-issued plaques; residents added new plaques each time *mehelle* lanes were renumbered but few bothered to remove the old ones. The children were usually asked if they were calling from home and, if so, to give their home phone numbers. In face-to-face interactions men beamed with pride whenever a young child showed she or he had memorized their home phone number. I suspect that Yining's collective pride in its children was similar to that of individual parents, not just pride in the child's intelligence, but pride in their own status as privileged possessors of phones. Since it cost 3,200 *yuan* ($400) to install a home phone, a phone was a conspicuous marker of a trader's success in the marketplace.

Radio programs could also become sites of deeply felt emotional sharing between individuals, creating an intimacy that enhanced listeners' sense of community identity. One Sunday morning, a woman called an on-air request line. She gave her name and her age, fifty-three, to the program host, and tried unsuccessfully to choke back her tears. Sobbing, she said, "My dad died when I was five, tomorrow is my mother's birthday . . . she helped me to marry . . . (sobbing) . . . Could you play *Narrow Road* for her?"

The degree of her emotional openness, intense as it was, was not exceptional for adult callers; many shared intimate personal details about their lives. The song this caller requested immediately caught my ear, since it was one of my own favorite Uyghur songs, one I had heard sung live at informal gatherings of friends many times. To me its lyrics expressed beautifully the bond *mehelle* residents felt with the face-to-face social world and the physical space of the *mehelle*. In my reading, the song *Narrow Road* uses narrow *mehelle* lanes as a poetic figure for Uyghurs' materially modest but emotionally and culturally rich origins.[4] As the lyrics provided at the front of this book make clear, not even the marvels of Paris or Istanbul can diminish the deep longing a Uyghur traveler feels in his soul for the narrow streets of his hometown.

The station's cultural programming had a special value for its Yining audience as a background for routine activities even when the programs themselves were not a focus of attention. One summer afternoon, a passage from a novel set in the area around Yining, *Waves of the Ili River* (*Ili dolqunliri*), was being read aloud. Abidem broke off a conversation she was having on the *supa* with her next-door neighbor, commented to no one in particular that these were "important words" (*muhim gep*), and then returned to her chatting.

Mehelle residents identify strongly with Yining's long local musical tradition, and Uyghur-language music, much of it from contemporary Yining artists, made up a large part of the station's programming. Many songs played were about romantic love, a common theme in popular music. Songs popular during my stay included *Cute Girl* (*Omaq qiz*), *Souvenir* (*Yadikar*), *Pretty* (*Chirayliq*), and *Libra Flower* (*Mizan'gül*, a woman's name). Not all favorite songs were songs of love and romance, however. The following anti-heroin song was performed by the well-known child singer Abduqahar.

Heroin, don't smoke it, my dear older brothers
Your lives, don't throw them away, my dear older brothers
What has it given you, heroin, except for disaster?
Don't expect any good from it, my dear older brothers

Your beautiful youth, you only get one chance
In this world, people cannot blossom on poison
Heroin has brought mourning to so many homes
Open your eyes, blind dear older brothers

Because of you, mother and father wander like vagrants
Waiting for the time of bread and sweet pears
When you rejoin the ranks of the living, like everyone else
You, too, will enjoy the beauty of life, my dear brothers

Local music cassette merchants explained to me that many popular songs in the mid-1990s dealt with issues of heroin use and addiction. Most of these songs had been recorded by younger male performers between the ages of sixteen and twenty, the period when youths, both male and female, became increasingly at risk for drug addiction. This song, however, was popularized by a ten-year-old boy. Having a "younger brother" pleading with "older brothers" to respect themselves is powerfully ironic, since it is the ritual job of fictive older brothers, as we will see in Part II, to oblige younger brothers to respect them.

Occasionally songs were aired on the program that residents understood voiced thinly disguised pro-Uyghur or antigovernment sentiments. One example was the following song, which expressed a distinctly ethnonationalistic yearning for independence and Uyghur autonomy.

Coming into the world, you met only with hardship
Did you foresee that Destiny itself would betray you?
When nothing good appears, you make not a sound?
Won't you say something, you kindhearted, peaceful Uyghurs?

Some people, crying "Uyghur," raise a shout
Some people, being Uyghur, prepare to rout
Doesn't your conscience burn, doesn't it drive you at all?
Tell me, my kindhearted, peaceful Uyghurs

Some people would tell you that your fortune is tied to destiny
As they prepare to put the pincers to your gullible heart
If you don't pay such treatment back, will you ever attain the
    prosperity you hope for?
Tell me, my kindhearted, peaceful Uyghurs

Other songs played on the radio rekindled a sense of connection with local history. One gray winter morning, a distinctive nasal voice that Abidem knew well came through the radio, the voice of the blind singer Dawutjan, born and raised in Zawut, who had been a companion of her husband's throughout their lives. When Dawutjan began to sing *Canal Song* (*Östeng naxshisi*), a song she remembered first hearing more than sixty years earlier, she put down her sewing and looked off into the distance.

The bottom of the canal is hard, I chop but the spade can't cut through
The cruel, cold-hearted Begs* will not leave us alone
Chopping away at the canal, the spade it gets all bent
The poor, to do the rich man's tasks, from their villages get sent
The water in the rivers and canals, belongs to the *mirab*[†] alone
Nothing does he know of righteousness, his heart as black as stone
The *mirab*s ride on their ponies, and send water to the rich
If the poor but mention water, their heads are stuck in a ditch
Stop your digging, cruel masters, for the canal has filled with blood
Digging your waterway has starved us, and no one will give us food

Abidem shook her head and sighed deeply, "Oh, back when the tyrants were in power, back then, the people really suffered."

The radio station also served as a bulletin board for local happenings, one that was mostly but not entirely free of the formulaic phrases of state-scripted newscasts common in both Chinese and Uyghur media. Performances of a local children's dance troupe, the Blossoms (*ghunchaqlar*), were periodically announced. A traveling mummy exhibit was touted for weeks during its stay in town, falsely billing one of its mummies as the "Beauty of Loulan" (*Kirören güzéli*), a four-thousand-year-old archeological find that symbolized for many Uyghurs their ancient ties to Xinjiang's land. The actual mummy on display, the tour's museum-trained assistant confided to me, was "only from the thirteenth century." One series of radio spots advertised English language classes opening up in the evenings at an elementary school; other ads praised local small businesses for their quality merchandise and friendly service.

Not all news items were so cheery. One day in late November, I first heard the news of missing children: "Two boys, ages four and a half and five and a half, were taken the day before yesterday at 1:00 P.M.," an

---

*Begs were officials who ruled local Xinjiang society under Manchu supervision during Qing rule.
[†]The *mirab* was an official in charge of irrigation and water distribution.

announcer said in a somber voice. "We hope that if you have news, you will call." Abidem shook her head: "That makes five in one month. Three other kids have already disappeared in November alone." Like many news items, this became a topic for virtually everyone in town to gossip about, and two days later I sat with a group of men in the marketplace listening as they debated rumors that the children were stolen to be sold for their organs. Personal pleas from the missing children's parents broadcast on the radio in the days that followed put to rest any thought in my mind that the story of the kidnappings was itself possibly only a rumor.*

For many *mehelle* residents this diverse daily radio programming, from the intimate personal narratives of listener call-in programs to the poems, songs, and prose literature of Uyghur writers celebrating the delights of romantic love and the great history of the Uyghur people, provided a constant and immediate sense of participating in a local community of people with shared knowledge, shared beliefs, and a shared sense of belonging to the land of Xinjiang, a sense of belonging to place that, in their minds, none but other Uyghurs could share in in exactly the same way.

———

In this and the preceding chapter, I have discussed the place of home and neighborhood as bases for individual and collective identity among *mehelle* residents. In so doing, I have made only marginal references to the important contribution the state makes to shaping physical space in Xinjiang and to the ways that space is experienced by local residents. In the next chapter, I go beyond the home and the neighborhood to consider Uyghur ideas of belonging to the land of Xinjiang as a whole, and to examine more carefully the state's role in ordering local identities of place.

———

*One month earlier I had seen a dramatized television re-enactment of the recent capture in Urumqi of a gang of more than ten persons, all Han recently arrived from central China, who were arrested for stealing children to sell to unspecified buyers. Such dramatized real-crime programs are not widely viewed as fabricated, although such a possibility cannot be rule out.

3

Desettling the Land

The Destruction of Uyghur Chthonic Identity

Hey you! If you would be a man,
a real man, then be as heavy as the land

— Uyghur aphorism recorded circa 1875

In 1996 a published audiocassette tape circulated widely in Xinjiang under the title *It's Hard Being a Peasant*. Its contents included a series of poems narrating the suffering of Uyghur peasants in the 1990s. In the oil painting reproduced on its cover, the shoulders and bowed head of a Uyghur peasant rise out of the earth, an image in which the landscape and the soil of Xinjiang figure as the body of the Uyghur people. A tear rolls off the peasant's cheek onto checkerboard fields below, suggesting that Uyghurs' suffering has irrigated the region's populated desert oases for millennia. This image alone makes a striking case for the power and depth of Uyghurs' feelings of attachment to place. In this chapter, I examine Uyghur sentiments of belonging in Xinjiang, and I describe a largely hidden process of desettlement, a feature of Han rule in Xinjiang that threatens to dramatically reconfigure those sentiments.

To properly discern the ongoing desettlement of Uyghurs in Xinjiang, it helps to consider recent patterns of Han migration and settlement in the region and the impact of population transfer on Uyghur-

Han relations. Encompassing one-sixth of China's overall territory, Xinjiang offers a great promise of land for a country with a growing population. Much of Xinjiang is an uninhabitable desert, the Taklimakan, surrounded by the snow-capped Tianshan and Kunlun ranges. Most current population centers are long-settled oases nestled between mountain foothills and the desert's edge. When the Chinese Communist Party took control of most of the region in 1949, 80 percent of the local population was Uyghur, a Muslim ethnic group of peasants, craftsmen, and traders. At that time only 5 percent of Xinjiang's population was Han, China's national ethnic majority. As a result of intensive migration by Han into Xinjiang since 1949, much of it state sponsored under various party policies, by the late 1990s the Han and Uyghur populations had grown roughly even at around 8 million each.[1] Han population transfer into Xinjiang has been praised by state planners for making important contributions to agricultural production, urbanization, and border defense, as well as to eventual Uyghur assimilation.[2] Such comments, however, fail to consider the lived experiences of Uyghur communities in the face of that same migration.

In contemporary Yining, Uyghurs and Han live in worlds of face-to-face social interaction that are almost entirely separate. Residential settlement patterns remain largely segregated.[3] Uyghurs speak their own Turkic language, unrelated to Chinese, written in an Arabic script, whereas Xinjiang's Han populations speak either Mandarin or their home dialect, or both. Uyghurs and Han rarely learn much of the other's language. Han's consumption of pork and Uyghurs' strict observance of a pork taboo mean the groups cannot share food freely. Inter-group marriage is virtually nonexistent. Unable to exchange words, food, or people, the two groups have minimal mutual understanding, and interactions are strained. Growing numbers of Han outcompete Uyghurs for practically all material resources. Han dominate the local state apparatus and through it gain preferential access to economic opportunity, capital, jobs, and education.

Within Uyghur communities, anti-Han and antigovernment sentiments run high. Popular demonstrations are increasing and are increasingly violent. Islam has become a vehicle for political mobilization, despite a severe government crackdown on religious activities. The state is not unprepared for trouble; more than a million Han military personnel live in the region.[4] And the transfer of Han populations into Xinjiang continues, as state research teams "scientifically" project Xinjiang's total resettlement capacity to be in the tens of millions of persons. More than one million Han have been scheduled for ultimate relocation from the Three Gorges Dam project alone. What are the consequences of these demographic changes for Uyghurs in Xinjiang? One model available for use in answering this question is the concept of desettlement proposed below.

The Desettlement Concept

Feelings of personal identity and group membership are often grounded in metaphors of rootedness to land. The individual's attachment to place is reinforced through shared cognitive maps and embodied social practices that make place meaningful for a community. This aspect of identity, in which group members experience solidarity simultaneously with a social collective and with a physical place, may be called *chthonic identity*.* Personal and collective attachments to place are critical bases of identity in general, since claims to political entitlement are often understood and advanced through them. If a state can undermine the cognitive and material bases supporting this feeling of belonging, the ability of groups to advance claims to political entitlement is weakened.

To understand desettlement better, let us first consider the more familiar idea of resettlement. A state seeks access to land-based resources, finds its access impeded by the presence of some group of people, and responds by relocating that group elsewhere. In their new home, established cultural meanings of place and social uses of space no longer fit, and a sense of dislocation or crisis is produced as communities and individuals face unfamiliar difficulties. Several linked features of this process are worth noting. People know when they are being relocated. As a result, even relatively powerless groups can create strategies to cope with or to contest forced relocation, perhaps through hidden forms of resistance, perhaps through violence. States may silence protest through coercion or what anthropologist Laura Nader has

---

*From Greek *khthonios*, "of the earth."

called "administrative controlling processes," but the unfortunate consequences of resettlement—alcoholism, delinquency, and myriad forms of social suffering—are harder to conceal and are widely documented and investigated by scholars. Finally, third parties can engage with these visible processes in consequential ways, such as when the World Bank establishes mandatory guidelines for governments regarding the treatment of persons resettled as a result of bank-funded projects.[5] Resettlement, in sum, is a recognized concern widely addressed within both development activities and scholarly research.

Desettlement, as I use the term, emphasizes the conditions under which the social problems of resettlement occur without actual physical relocation. In Xinjiang the state seeks access to land-based resources in a region where sedentary Uyghurs are historically and culturally well situated. Even without moving them, it can displace them in other ways. If the cognitive maps, symbolic systems, and social practices of Uyghur chthonic identity can be systematically reordered by the state, Uyghurs' capacity to articulate claims to political entitlement based on their sense of belonging is weakened. My argument, then, is this: in twentieth-century Xinjiang, the Chinese state sought to undermine specific practices that bound Uyghur identity to place by literally disassembling the meanings of local identity and then reorganizing those meanings according to its own plan. As a result, I suggest, Uyghurs' capacity to define and defend their interests in the face of the state was diminished. To make my argument, I present three examples from among the symbolic systems, cognitive maps, and cultural practices through which Uyghurs' feelings of attachment to place are reproduced, and I consider how the state has attempted to reorganize these bases of Uyghur identity. The areas from which these examples are drawn can be summarized as monikers, maps, and *mazar*.

Monikers: Socionymic Analysis and Social Identity

A first step in understanding Uyghur collective identities is an investigation of the relevant *socionyms*. A socionym, in my usage, is any word used to name a social identity. In my usage, this neologism is more inclusive than existing terms; for a social label to be an "ethnonym," for example, the group named must arguably meet some set of characteristics necessary to be considered an "ethnic group." The more inclusive category of socionym, on the other hand, can be applied whenever an experience or perception of shared identity of any kind is salient enough in some local life-world to be recognized through a linguistic marker. Socionyms, words that name social groups, are rarely disinterested, objective labels and often contribute to the social, historical, and political processes of producing and ordering identities. In Xinjiang, socionyms link identity with the soil and with local place in self-evident ways.

Prior to the 1920s, the word "Uyghur" was virtually unused in Xinjiang. Back then, today's Uyghurs called themselves *yerlik*, literally "of the earth or land," or more colloquially, "locals." Ethnographic materials recorded as early as the 1870s show that the *yerlik* category referred only to today's Uyghurs and excluded all other ethnic groups, such as Han (*xitay*) and Hui (*donggan*).[6] At the same time, a second set of identity terms was also in widespread use.[7] Each term in that set was oasis-specific, such that inhabitants of Kashgar, Turpan, and other oases, for example, called themselves, and were called by others, Kashgarians (*Qeshqerliq*), Turpanians (*Turpanliq*), and so forth. Exceptions to this practice of building sub-*yerlik* socionyms out of toponyms include *taranchi*, a term that can be roughly glossed as "Turkestani agriculturalist of the Ili Valley," and *dolan*, a subethnic Uyghur group in southern Xinjiang.

The use of oasis-specific names does not in itself imply a lack of collective *yerlik* identity among these groups. That various observers have made such a leap shows what powerful instruments names can be for legitimizing claims to identity in the discourses of state administration and academic research, and supports my argument here about the importance of state manipulation of identity-culture categories in Xinjiang.[8] The terms of this Uyghur-language, mainly toponym-based socionymic system referred only to Uyghurs (*yerlik*), and contrasted with other terms of identity such as Chinese (*xitay*) or Manchu (*menju*). In this naming system, a *xitay*, or ethnic Han Chinese, could not be also a Turpanian, regardless of how long she or he had resided there. Uyghur vernacular language marked Uyghurs as "of the land/place," as the naturally embedded residents of the local landscape, and simultaneously marked ethnic others as being fundamentally and categorically incapable of being "locals."

In the 1920s this naming system was challenged when the Chinese state introduced ethnonyms and ethnic categories as instruments of nation-building. Adopting the term "Uyghur," a socionym otherwise abandoned around the tenth century, the state constructed Uyghurs as one group among others in a set of ascribed statuses (i.e., ethnic groups) under firm state control. Removed from categories related to Xinjiang's regional landscape and repositioned directly into the nationscape, Uyghurs become, in one favorite official phrase, "one of fourteen ethnic groups who reside in Xinjiang." In switching to an ascribed status system of ethnic identities, the state sought to make non-Han groups more interchangeable, more commensurate, even if their ostensible equality consisted primarily in their being marked as equal in a system of symbols adopted to serve the interests of a nation-state. Since the 1920s, of course, Uyghurs have come to widely embrace the term "Uyghur" as expressing a natural ethnic identity. Among themselves Uyghurs still use terms like *yerlik* and *Turpanliq*, but the state is not indifferent to these uses—the socionymic categories used by Uyghurs prior to the arrival of ethnicity discourse in Xinjiang are now erased by the state; for example, they generally do not appear in contemporary Uyghur dictionaries.

The significance of these changes was brought into sharp relief for me when I considered the local effects of a propaganda campaign that ran nationwide in 1990s China. In Xinjiang, huge billboards promoted slogans that reintroduced earlier identity categories based on place, using both the encompassing term "Xinjiang person" (*Xinjiang ren*) as well as various oasis-specific terms, for example "Turpanian" (*Tulupan ren*), but now these terms were deployed in Mandarin Chinese and inscribed around resettled Han populations. Over a period of seventy years, this administrative manipulation of identity categories has displaced a historical linguistic expression of Uyghur attachment to place, an effect achieved, ironically, each time the word "Uyghur" is invoked.

At a three-day conference in Urumqi in 1995 entitled "Cultural Anthropology and Xinjiang Culture," party-state policymakers presented the model of cultural identity that presumably lay behind that widespread propaganda campaign. In their prescriptive model, culture and identity were presented as a series of concentric circles. The innermost circle on their chart, positioned at the core of what they labeled "Xinjiang person identity," was an identity based on participation in the total "ethnic culture of Greater China" (*Zhonghua minzu wenhua*), a cultural identity shared by all (even diasporic) Chinese worldwide. The second concentric circle showed that the "Xinjiang person" next identifies as a "Chinese person" (*Zhongguo ren*) sharing in a unified "National Culture." As a resident of one of five northwestern provinces, the "Xinjiang person" then shares in "Northwest Culture" (*xibei wenhua*) and identifies as a "Northwesterner" (*xibei ren*). The next circle represented the specific identity of a "Xinjiang person" (*Xinjiang ren*), someone sharing in the common Xinjiang culture. Finally, the diagram showed, individuals share an identity with their co-residents, those from Urumqi are Urumqians (*Wulumuqi ren*), those from Kashgar are Kashgarians (*Kashi ren*), and so forth.

What about ethnic culture and ethnic identity? asked minority conference participants. The Han presenters explained to the dozens of ethnic minorities in the audience that "ethnic culture" still presented a conceptual challenge to them and admitted they were not sure where to fit it in, or if it fit at all. One thing, however, was made perfectly clear in a presentation to scholars one month later at the Xinjiang Academy of Social Sciences, at which attendance was obligatory. On that occasion, a Han party leader lecturing to a room full of minority researchers reported that despite Uyghurs' universal conversion to Islam more than 600 years earlier and despite the fact that today virtually all Uyghurs are practicing Muslims, the "international scholarly community" was nonetheless in agreement in concluding that Islam had never had any cultural influence in Xinjiang and that Islam was not relevant to any conceptualization of "Xinjiang culture" (*Xinjiang wenhua*), or of "ethnic culture" (*minzu wenhua*) in the region. China is a highly centralized state, and it is hardly surprising that a model of identity aligned with state interests consists of concentric circles centered around a centering center.

In sum, the state-sponsored administrative manipulation of socionyms plays a key role in supporting the managed demographic reorganization of the region by establishing a new set of place-based socionyms inscribed around, and thereby granting belonging to, new Han migrants.[9]

Mapping and Place-making

One challenge I regularly faced in my field research was simply following residents' directions for getting from place to place in the *mehelle*. "Go past the burned mosque," a friend would tell me, "wa—lk through Qazanchi *mehelle*, take a left, and go past the *noghay meschit*." Eventually I learned where to find the "burned mosque," which had been repaired thirty years earlier and showed no sign of damage. Because Uyghur speakers elongate words and heighten their pitch to vary the degree of emphasis, the utterances "you wa—lk and turn left" and "you wa——lk and turn left" are used to indicate distinctly different distances. Because no maps of Yining's neighborhoods existed, the exact beginning and end of Qazanchi *mehelle* were also always open to debate. And finally, the *noghay meschit* (Tatar mosque) had been torn down in the early 1970s, making it even harder to locate! A native resident might have been able to follow such directions easily, but to me they were often more mystifying than useful.

Although the directions given above are fictitious, the inclusion in them of two references to mosques is not arbitrary. Mosques not only anchored feelings of local community and shaped the social contours of *mehelle* boundaries, they also oriented residents spatially in the wider world. Mosques are built with a prayer niche (*qibla*) facing Mecca, physically situating local residents within the global community of Islam. *Mehelle* and mosques, then, were key elements both in Uyghurs' cognitive maps and in the place-making processes through which Uyghurs organized their local neighborhoods perceptually and physically.

The state's approach to mapping local place was quite different. Throughout China, the government regulates the production and circulation of printed maps. Xinjiang is a militarized border region where maps are especially sensitive. Yet even in Xinjiang many maps were available to me, tourist maps, roadmaps for truck drivers, maps sold in bus stations; even highly specialized maps containing information on such things as pollution sources and resource extraction sites could be purchased locally, although only in restricted-circulation publications. And like naming systems, I suggest, these printed maps can be read as encoding prescriptive models for the imagining of social and political landscapes.

Despite this plethora of maps, maps of locales within Xinjiang (and here I include city maps, county maps, and detailed provincial* maps) are printed only in Chinese, not Uyghur. This is especially striking given

---

*Xinjiang's exact status is provincial-level autonomous region.

that most other printed materials in Xinjiang, official and unofficial, are available in Uyghur-language versions. Uyghur writing and Chinese characters appear side by side on everything from street signs to candy wrappers, but maps with place-names in Uyghur are available only of the whole nation or else as overly simplified maps of the province. With printed maps, as with socionyms, Uyghurs are symbolically displaced from localities, shifted upward along an imagined hierarchy of place to be situated safely into the Han nation. Printed maps can show Uyghurs their position as Chinese nationals and as residents of Xinjiang but cannot be allowed to reflect to Uyghurs their embeddedness in *local* place.

Chinese-language maps of Yining and other locales within Xinjiang reveal significant lacunae. City maps of Yining, for example, ignore mosques and *mehelle. Mehelle* names and locations simply do not appear anywhere in the cultural products of the state. Mosques are also missing; only mosques that have been turned into official tourist sites are represented on maps, suggesting that this is part of the state's vision for Xinjiang's future. Outside urban areas, Uyghur place-names throughout Xinjiang typically draw on terrain features, such as villages named Forty Springs or Sand Hill. On Chinese-language maps, such names, if they appear at all, are transliterated into Chinese, and if something of their phonology remains, the meanings are entirely lost. For example, Black Lake in Uyghur is Qaraköl; in Chinese this becomes *ka-li-ku-li-hu*. In Mandarin such constructions sound like one of two things, baby talk or the conventional phrases that represent sounds made by animals (such as, in English, "cock-a-doodle-doo"). The effect is that Uyghur place-names become a basis for the exoticization, infantilization, and even bestialization of Uyghurs in the Han imagination. Not all Uyghur names suffer this fate, of course. Many ancient Uyghur names are simply replaced with completely new names in Chinese, names that de-emphasize the natural world, typically by conjoining a Han surname with some local man-made feature, such as the word for store or village.

The meanings of place for Uyghurs do not disappear with the printing of some maps or even with the presence of settlers using a new set of names. But maps do more than reveal an official utopian Uyghur Autonomous Region without Uyghurs. City maps and road maps in Chinese also facilitate Han mobility within and between Xinjiang's urban spaces. If Uyghurs wish to navigate their way through unfamiliar urban spaces, they must do so using instruments printed only in Chinese. Maps become one of a larger set of elements, together with things such as discriminatory zoning regulations and the coerced sale of Uyghur-owned land to Han in-migrants, that permanently affect Uyghurs' collective relationship with local place.

Mazar: The Tombs of Holy Men and Women

A third example of desettlement draws on the Uyghur practice of making pilgrimages to local shrines. In Xinjiang one aspect of Islamic practice involves making situational pilgrimages to *mazar*, or tombs of holy persons, often for purposes of healing sick bodies. This practice is widely described for other parts of the Muslim world as *ziyarat*, "visitation" (from Arabic *zaur*, "to visit"); in Uyghur vernacular the practice is called *tawab*.

One December day, Abidem announced to family members her intention to visit a nearby *mazar*. Her seven-year-old grandson Ilyar, Yakupjan's child, was ill, suffering an eye irritation brought on by excessive home video-game playing. As a result, Abidem and several other family members decided to visit Sultan Mazar, a trip I recorded in my field notes.

The main tomb, a man's tomb, consisted of a large well-made sepulchre (*tawut*) draped with a black embroidered canopy, housed in a forty-foot-high octagonal tower.

Abidem, Aliye, and I knelt down while Ablet [Abidem's sixteen-year-old grandson, who was studying to be an Islamic cleric] recited one verse from the Qur'an.

Abidem and her group then left the main tomb, neither leaving nor taking anything, and went out to a much smaller tomb standing a few dozen yards away. This tomb, only half as large as the last one, was the tomb of a woman. Onto the branches of the trees that surrounded it visitors had tied dozens of small tufts of cloth. Abidem stooped down and gathered up a handful of earth lying a few inches from the tomb.

At home that evening Abidem rubbed some of the soil over Ilyar's eyes. Months later she would dissolve the same soil into water used to wash her newborn granddaughter Tewsiye in a ritual bathing ceremony. Ingesting *mazar* soil is a widely documented part of *mazar* visitation

throughout Xinjiang and the surrounding area.[10] Archeological research
suggests that *mazar* sites in Xinjiang have existed for millennia as sites
of healing power emanating from the earth.[11] When Buddhism flourished in Xinjiang between the second and seventh centuries C.E., local
inhabitants cast these sites as Buddhist shrines. With the arrival of Islam beginning in the ninth century, they were recast as Islamic shrines
and linked with Islamic saints' legends. Beneath these surface changes,
the power of these sites continues to come from, and to bind Uyghur
identity into, the earth. Shrines are seen as places where legendary
"great" (*ulugh*) Uyghur persons have been interred and absorbed into
the earth, earth that can be gathered and absorbed into living Uyghur
bodies. The recovery of many dozens of well-preserved corpses from
sites of ancient settlements on the periphery of the Taklimakan desert
has provoked a strong response from Uyghur communities in Xinjiang.
Desiccated mummies taken directly from the earth provide Uyghurs
with potent ready-made symbols of their autochthonous identity. Uyghurs I spoke with unquestioningly understood these mummies to be
their direct "Uyghur" ancestors.

What role does the state play in shaping *mazar* practices? In the new
landscape of Han modernity, the role for *mazar*, like mosques, is as
tourist sites. When Abidem arrived at the *mazar*, she commented that
the eight-foot-high iron barrier that surrounded the site had been added
since her last visit several years earlier. A new plaque confirmed that the
state tourism administration bureau had been given jurisdiction over
the site. Tickets had been printed up to regulate entrance, the Uyghur
gatekeeper told us, but had not yet been delivered, and he let our group
in for free. As Abidem had done on previous visits, she presented the
gatekeeper with a piece of cloth as a special gift. No longer were visitors permitted to prepare a meal in the *mazar*'s communal cooking pot,
however, something Abidem described as one of the most critical elements in a successful *mazar* visit.

In the Chinese state's exercise of administrative control over naming
systems, map production, and the folk religious practices of *mazar* visitation in Xinjiang, a common outcome is discernible. That outcome is
one in which Uyghurs are desettled from the land, symbolically dislo-
cated from fully inhabiting local place. The processes described here
are, of course, not unique to Xinjiang; on the contrary, the desettlement

concept may be useful generally in emphasizing the perspective that chthonic identity, the inseparable feeling of belonging simultaneously to a group and a place, is always shaped within fields of power. Groups everywhere experience social dislocation as the spatial organization of daily life is transformed around them, often by forces outside their control or perception. The intentional reorganization of identities by powerful actors like states is a widespread feature of the modern world. In the case of Xinjiang, it can be argued that desettlement points to a coherent pattern of state intervention in local identities, one that, in my opinion, does not bode well for the region's future. In Xinjiang, state efforts to reorganize local identity undermine Uyghur attachment to place, and although their final impact is unclear, it is apparent that they are intended to serve as an ideological prop for the managed demographic reorganization of the region. Only further ethnographic examination of the links between symbolic and material processes in the interplay of culture, power, and identity can help us to better understand these processes and their outcomes.

This concludes Part I, and with it the close focus on the meanings of space and place for *mehelle* residents. In subsequent chapters, the familiar spaces of home and courtyard, shady *mehelle* street corner and bustling city bazaar, do not disappear; rather, they provide a backdrop for the diverse social dramas and personal narratives we will encounter as we examine other aspects of daily life for *mehelle* residents.

PART II

Gender and the Life Cycle

Five years ago, I asked my dad, "Dad, how old are you?"

"I'm sixty," he said.

Then this year I asked him again, "Dad, how old are you?" and he says he's sixty years old.

"Huh? But, five years ago when I asked, you said you were sixty. This year how can you still say you are sixty?"

"My child, a lad (*yigit*) never goes back on his word."

—Muxtar Hésam, Yining jokester

In the five chapters of Part II, I present ethnographic materials that bear on *mehelle* residents' passage through the life cycle, specifically on the formation and expression of masculine identity. In the first three chapters, I examine three periods in the lives of *mehelle* residents: the postpartum period and early infancy; late infancy and early adolescence; and courtship, adult gender relations, and concepts of sexuality. In these chapters I rely on folklore and personal narratives provided by *mehelle* residents to explore Uyghur ideas about the events and experiences typical of these periods of life. Although these first three chapters address the experiences of both boys and girls, women and men, my presentation is shaped by a concern to provide background for the focus on masculinity that emerges in the remainder of the book. In the final two chapters of this part, I begin that focus by examining two institutions that stand at the center of men's everyday social interactions, the festive gathering known as the *olturash* and the nicknaming practices that, together, bind male *mehelle* residents into a single community of men. Here, as in Part III on economic life and Part IV on religious life, my emphasis shifts almost entirely to a concern with the lives of men.

The value of a life-cycle approach for understanding the gendering of Uyghur social life, and for understanding Uyghur masculinity in particular, is indicated for two reasons. First, experiences in infancy, childhood, and adolescence are widely theorized as being causally related to adult personality and social identity. Second, *mehelle* conceptualizations of adult masculinity are frequently and explicitly linked to ideas about adolescence. This is suggested in the joke quoted above, in which Hésam invokes his status as a *yigit*, a "youthful lad," even at the age of sixty-five. To fully understand the connection between adolescence and adult masculinity that men listening to this joke would take for granted, a review of some basic categories of age, gender, and kinship in Uyghur may be useful.

Age, Gender, and Kinship in the Uyghur Life Cycle

Neonates are often addressed as *elley* before they are named, which usually takes place in a ceremony held on the third or seventh day after birth. Uyghur dictionaries translate *elley* as "cradlesong" or "lullaby," and *elengle-* as "to cause to sway or rock gently." Uyghur women have long used cradles and hammocks to swing babies back and forth gently. Infants are called *bowaq*, a word whose phonetic relationship with *bowa* (grandfather) suggests that a special link exists between infant and grandparent.[1] Although published sources imply that *bowaq* is gender neutral, in Yining I observed the use of *bowaq* only for male infants; female infants were referred to as *böpe*, a term phonetically similar to *büwi*, an honorific used for older women. Given their phonological parallelism, it is likely that *bowaq/bowa* and *böpe/büwi* are paired terms used separately for males and females. Another gender-neutral term for infant is *engge*.

In Zawut, the most commonly used word for "child" in general was *bala*. This word was used in such phrases as "my child" (*balam*), or "the child of A" (*A-ning balisi*). To emphasize the meaning of "small child," Zawut residents used the singular *ushshaq bala* (small/slender child) or *kichik bala* (small child). The plural *ushshaqlar* (small/slender ones) was often used alone as a term of collective reference. As a term for young boys and girls, *bala* by itself is gender neutral and can be modified by the gender terms "boy" (*oghul*) and "girl" (*qiz*) to produce *qiz-bala* and *oghul-bala*.

In addition to these meanings, the word *bala* is also commonly used without modifiers to refer in earnest to any man middle-aged or younger, up to roughly the ages of fifty to fifty-five. Although *bala* is gender-neutral when applied to children, as a reference to adults it is used only for men. Furthermore, whereas *qiz-bala* is used only for a female child, *oghul-bala* is a term routinely applied to a grown man, specifically in order to emphasize his masculine character beyond his generic status as a male. One Uyghur man, for example, in pressing me to give him my sunglasses as a gift, said, "Come on, be an *oghul-bala*." In this phrase an idealized adult-male personality type is expressed through the metaphorical extension of a childhood status.

In the Mandarin Chinese vernacular of Xinjiang, Han have borrowed the Uyghur *bala* and given it a slightly different meaning. In Chinese, *balangzi* refers only to Uyghur adolescents. This Chinese form corresponds closely with the Uyghur *bala* + -*ng* = *balang*, the familiar form of "your child." For a Chinese speaker, however, this word resonates distinctly with the word *langzi*, "wolf," so that *balangzi* becomes "*ba*-wolf," a phrase that conjures up images of a dangerous animal, cruel and clever, that preys on unsuspecting innocents. And indeed, a Han woman born and raised in Xinjiang explained the word's two main meanings to me as follows. First, it is a derogatory term for Uyghur youths whom Han perceive to be dangerous, those who, in their eyes, loiter in public places, break the law, and threaten the social order. Second, the term is used by Han parents much like the fictive American "bogey-man" is used, to scare children into a desired behavior. A Han parent might say "If you are not good, the *balangzi* will take you." No amount of state propagandizing for ethnic unity is likely to undo the deep imprint of this child-against-child anti-Uyghur stereotyping. Interestingly, some Uyghurs have reincorporated the word *balangzi* into their own Mandarin speech patterns, making the word a term of ethnic pride with no negative connotations.

The life-cycle phase of being a *bala* (child) ends at puberty (*balaghet*), although males continue to be called *bala* for decades, with a meaning roughly equivalent to the American colloquial term "guy." In the joke given at the start of this chapter, the sixty-five-year-old Hésam claimed to be a *yigit*, a term whose core meaning is "a young man, a youth, a lad." To be a *yigit* is to be virile and assertive. Its use in reference to older adult men finds perhaps its closest parallel in American English in the phrase "one of the boys." It is particularly ironic that Hésam asserts both his status as a "youthful lad" and his respect for the code of honor that that status imposes on him in order to deny his aging, since it is aging that marks his inevitable passage out of the community of adult men beholden to each other through those moral codes. When adult men call themselves *oghul-bala* or *yigit*, then, their claim to a well-defined gender identity is inseparable from a simultaneous symbolic assertion of their adolescent status.

The most common term for "person" is *adem*, which is used for both males and females. However, *adem*, which is cognate with the biblical Adam, conflates the meanings of "person" and "male person" much as do the terms "man" and "mankind" in English. A gender bias is evident here, then, in that the category of person becomes associated with men in a special way. A second term, *kishi*, is a slightly more vernacular and gender-neutral term for "person." Standard terms for "man/men" and "woman/women" are *er/erler* and *ayal/ayallar*. These terms designate a gendered status and also suggest the life-cycle status of a married individual: to call a man *er* is to imply his status as a husband; to emphasize simply that a person is an adult male, the compound *er kishi* (man-person) is typically used. *Ayal* carries a trace of the meaning of "wife," but is used in Yining vernacular as a general term for "adult woman"; *xotun* is more commonly used for "wife." The term *yoldash* (fellow-traveler) used by some educated Uyghurs for their spouses, a term that suggests the socialist-era Chinese *tongzhi* (comrade), is not heard in the *mehelle*. Married couples in the *mehelle* freely use each other's given names as terms of address, although some women with children both address and refer to their husbands as *dadisi*, meaning "[his/her/their] father."

Zawut residents classify kin according to two main categories, *tughqan* (consanguines) and *quda* (affines). The term *tughqan*, the past participle of the verb *tughmaq* (to give birth), literally means "birthed." To say, "I am kin with that person," then, is akin to saying "I am 'born' with that person." On several occasions Abidem's family members expressed the shared identity felt between kin using the proverb

Meat and fat are one kin	*gösh yagh bilen bir tughqan*
The onion's browning is browned	*piyaz köygénini köygen*

The meaning of this second line becomes more sensible in light of a variant collected in the 1930s.[2]

Meat and fat are one kin	*gösh bilen yagh bir tuqqan*
It does no good to brown the onion	*piyazning köygéni bikar*

These items suggest that kin always remain kin, no matter how poorly they may treat each other, whereas a nonrelative will never be viewed as a relation regardless of how much he may try to behave like one. Yakupjan one day quoted the above proverb while pointing to Aysajan, the orphan raised by Abidem, adding by way of explanation, "He is an onion." Aysajan, who had lived with Abidem for all of his eight years, was indeed not treated like a family member. He was verbally abused many times each day—a typical day's comments might include "you stupid cow, what are we doing raising you, too dumb to even stay alive"; "you corpse"; "so stupid he can't even stick his fingers in his mouth"—mostly by Abidem, for whom he was a convenient scapegoat for her frustrations and physical suffering.[3]

In addition to *tughqan* and *quda* relations, the category of *baja* was also widely known to *mehelle* residents; men are *baja* with each other if they are married to sisters. All the men I asked agreed that *baja* relationships were typically marked with latent animosity, but none was able to satisfy my request for an explanation. One man struggled for a moment, then smiled in triumph, and said

When one *baja* sees another *baja*	*baja baja körse*
His asshole itches	*qong qichishidu*
He acts like he has scabies	*qitirghuliq qilidu*

"Don't you get it?" he asked, looking at me expectantly. "His asshole itches!" At the time his use of this particular metaphor to describe the behavior of a man uneasy in his relations with another man raised more questions for me than it resolved. In the chapters that follow, however, the opportunity to explore in depth the vernacular metaphors *mehelle* men use to characterize both the normative and the deviant masculine habitus will allow us to find an answer of sorts.

4

Gleaming Eyes, Evil Eyes

Cradle and Cure in Uyghur

Child Rearing

The crow says "My baby is white"   *kagha balam apaq*
The hedgehog says "My baby is soft"   *kirpe balam yumshaq*

— Abidem, citing a Uyghur proverb

A Uyghur woman preparing to give birth is said to have "gleaming eyes" (*köz yorush*). Once her child is born, her eyes may no longer gleam, but as the proverb quoted above suggests, they will continue to look on her newborn child in a special way. Just as the crow sees her baby as the whitest of all, a mother sees her child as a superlative and unique individual.

Much of the information presented in this chapter derives from observing at close quarters the rearing of two infants and the raising of a number of older children, primarily the dozen or more grandchildren of Abidem I saw on a daily basis, over the course of one year. I observed interactions among children and between children and various adults, including their parents, and I was also privy to many conversations between parents regarding specific issues of child rearing. Based on my informal observations of other children and on the overall typicality of Abidem's kin group, I am confident that these materials demonstrate general features of *mehelle* residents' experiences in the early stages of

life. To put it another way, I am confident, Uyghur folk wisdom to the
contrary, that the infants I observed were neither whiter nor softer than
other *mehelle* children.

Birth

Before a child can be born, the woman must conceive and successfully
complete her pregnancy. A Uyghur woman who has difficulty conceiv-
ing might visit a local shrine (*mazar*) to perform prayers and to tie small
scraps of cloth (*tugh* or *tugh-alem*) onto tree branches. *Mehelle* women
spoke of such practices as still common, and the cloths I observed during the *mazar* visit described in Chapter 3 bear witness to this practice.
In Zawut, however, the only couple I knew experiencing infertility had
preferred to seek help from state biomedical practitioners, before ultimately adopting a young son.

A range of traditional avoidance practices are known and followed
by pregnant Uyghur women, according to Uyghur scholars who document such beliefs. Eating camel meat, for example, is said to prolong
pregnancy. And a pregnant woman must not see rabbits or eat their
meat, or her child will have a harelip.[1] In Zawut, however, I saw little of
such things. Abidem's daughter Senemgül (age 27) was a daily visitor to
her mother's house during the six months prior to her delivery of a
child in January 1996. Although I saw Senemgül frequently, I never observed her following any specific avoidance practices, nor were such
practices a topic in conversations when I was present. Instead, traditional avoidance concerns had given way to more practical ones—
avoiding the agents who enforced the birth-control policies of China's
party-state. Senemgül, whose son Abdüshükür was only sixteen months
old when her second child was born, was particularly anxious about
keeping the spinning factory, where she had worked since the age of sixteen, from learning about these too closely spaced children.* "The fine,"
she said dramatically, "would be 20,000 *yuan* [$2,500]." Although no
one was certain what the consequences would be—each of her family

---

*Senemgül had begun an extended sick leave many months earlier while recovering
from a bad burn and had not been seen by officials at her work-unit for quite some
time. She was thus able to evade detection.

members cited a different amount of money as the fine—they were in agreement that the birth would have repercussions. Senemgül's husband, Téyipjan, in his usual confident tone, proposed one solution: "The simplest way will be the best, a carton of Marlboros and 25 *som* [$3.15] for a paper [i.e., as a bribe to obtain fake documentation]." Although his guess was low, he was not far off.

Senemgül ultimately paid 300 *yuan* ($37.50) to obtain a new household registration booklet with her own photo but issued in her older sister's name, a booklet in which no children had yet been registered. She also selected the hospital for her delivery based mainly on her desire to avoid state scrutiny. The small facility in Qaradöng *mehelle* where she chose to deliver was reputedly lax in monitoring births, and Uyghur women from nearby villages were known to go there to avoid the more efficient state bureaucracies that monitored their village-level facilities. In the weeks after the birth, Senemgül returned to that hospital, presenting the new booklet bearing her sister's name while claiming this was her first, not second, birth. "The hospital won't care," Senemgül's sisters nodded in agreement, "as long as there is paperwork."

Senemgül's water broke before dawn one morning, and she traveled at first light with her husband by taxi from their home—they lived in two rented rooms in another Uyghur family's courtyard—to the small hospital roughly two kilometers away. Her mother, a sister, a niece, and I joined her and her husband there by 7:00 A.M., and we waited with her all morning, sitting on a wooden bed frame in an otherwise bare room. At 2:30 P.M. Senemgül went next door to the equally bare delivery room and lay down on another wooden table, covered with her own bedding. On the advice of her older sister she asked for an injection to induce birth, and minutes later, after screaming "O soul, o soul" (*wayjan, wayjan*) a few times, she gave birth to a healthy 2.9-kg girl, assisted by a female Uyghur obstetrician and a younger Uyghur midwife.

That evening Senemgül's mother and sister, who had left the hospital to take care of household chores, returned for a visit. After a brief chat, Abidem opened a cloth folded around several handfuls of walnuts, a food usually served to guests, and gave some to all present. Each person ate without ritual, as if the walnuts were simply a snack. Then Abidem used her finger to smear a paste of chewed walnut over the baby's mouth, saying to me:

"It is so that she may speak like 'cracking/lightning' (*chaqmaqdek gep qilsun*)."

I asked her to explain, and she went on. "We give babies walnuts, which you have to crack, right? They go 'crack-crack' (*chaq-chaq*), so that the child will speak well."

"You mean," I asked her, "like saying a joke (*chaqchaq*), so they learn to tell jokes well?"

"No, we say 'may (s)he speak like walnuts cracking open' (*yangaq chaqqandek gep qilsun*)."

Abidem later described for me how the cracking of a walnut was a metaphor for effortless and instantaneous speaking, the opposite, she said, of stuttering. Another metaphor is suggested by a second meaning of *chaqmaqdek*, "like a flash of lightning." This is one of many indications we will see of Uyghurs' lifelong concern with speaking ability and quick-wittedness, skills that allow individuals to avoid being bested in everyday forms of verbal jousting. Several weeks after the birth, after Senemgül had moved back to her mother's house, I was swiftly corrected when Abidem saw my first attempt to burp the baby by patting her on her back. She explained that such patting was to be avoided since it would make her tongue "not cracking." Several of the women who visited the infant after her birth also mentioned the practice of smearing honey on a neonate's mouth, a custom thought to ensure the infant's ability to speak "sweet words" (*tatliq söz*). Although my research focused on the role of verbal skill in men's interactions, the speaking ability of girls and women was also valued in *mehelle* society.

The sympathetic magical transference of properties from other substances onto Senemgül's child extended to the spreading of placental blood on her cheeks and lips, also a widespread Uyghur practice. On the day of the birth, Senemgül's sister Maynur denied that this had been done, but later acknowledged that she had been embarrassed to admit to the practice to me in the presence of the obstetrician. Soon after the delivery, though, Maynur had indeed requested that the midwife do so. Another of Abidem's daughters put it this way. "Blood is spread on the cheeks and lips so that they will be red when she grows up. Then on the third day or so, some black shit-like stuff (*poqdek néme*) [i.e., meconium] comes out and is spread on her brows to make them black."

In daily speech and in various genres of folk narrative, the "black brows" of a man or woman, especially a lover, is a common trope denoting both physical attractiveness and positive character. In the weeks that followed, visiting friends and relatives often commented on the blackness of the child's brows relative to those of other infants they had known.

The forms of Uyghur parturition customs and their local meanings are likely to vary widely throughout Xinjiang. Abdukérim Raxman lists a number of such practices, including hanging a red cloth from the ceiling of the room where a woman is delivering.[2] "Of course, this is a remnant from shamanism," he notes, ignoring possible symbolic meanings of the red cloth. At a number of Uyghur weddings I attended, the bride was at one point made to step onto a large piece of red cloth, whereupon the groom's male friends crowded toward her, vigorously grabbing the cloth and pulling it to pieces. On her wedding day, I was told, a bride's new mother-in-law may give her (through an intermediary) a stack of white cloths, which the bride must return the following morning covered with blood. The blood symbolism of a red cloth displayed at a wedding, after a couple's first sexual encounter, and finally on the birth of a child, seems likely.

Senemgül considered the hospital where she delivered to be well suited for her purposes, even if it was located just at the boundary between city and *mehelle* in a part of town Zawut residents considered less prosperous than their own. The area's slightly ramshackle courtyards, a few piles of trash dumped on the roadside, and a permanent cluster of tough-looking adolescents gathered at the nearest street corner—"They're selling heroin," Téyipjan said knowingly—distinguished the scene from the better-equipped hospitals and nicer neighborhoods closer to Zawut. Even though Senemgül had wanted to avoid the more efficient bureaucracies of those hospitals, for several days she expressed regret that she had not gone to a larger hospital if only because those hospitals, she had been told, gave each child a plastic medallion bearing his or her Chinese zodiac sign. As a favor, I went to a large hospital to request a medal for her child: "She was born in the Year of the Rat," Senemgül had assured me. Nurses at the hospital, however, were still issuing medallions for the Year of the Pig, explaining that the Chinese New Year was still several weeks away. Given Uyghurs' aversion to all things pig-related, I left empty-handed and told Senemgül the hospital had run out.

The evening of the day Senemgül delivered, her husband, Téyipjan, walked into his parents' *dalan* at dinnertime, a smile on his face.

"Well?" they asked, sensing his special mood.

"Well what?" he replied. "Oh . . . news? Yeah, there's news. But I'm kind of empty-handed." He smiled mischievously. His mother stepped into the adjoining *saray*, opened a small cabinet, and removed the first two women's gifting objects within reach, a brightly colored headscarf and a package of nylons. She passed them to him.

"That's better," he smiled. "It's a girl."

This field note passage describes the giving of the *söyünche,* a present bestowed on a bearer of good news.[3] The objects given here were chosen from a stack of gifting objects (*edimechilik*) that Téyipjan's mother, like virtually all women in the *mehelle*, kept on hand for use in women's frequent gift exchanges. The scarf and nylons had little significance to anyone once the exchange was over, and when Téyipjan brought them the next day to show his wife, who was reclining on the *supa* at her mother's house, he surrendered them to the first woman there who claimed them. On a number of occasions I saw adults and children demand a *söyünche* in order to tease someone who wished to know a particular piece of news, although this was the only time I actually witnessed the presenting of a *söyünche*.

A Uyghur Naming Ceremony

A new father, while anxiously looking for a cleric to officiate at the naming of his newborn, bumps into a local jokester. The jokester says, "Lucky you bumped into me. Around here I name all the babies, I'm your guy. So, uh, how much are you planning on paying?"

"Five *som* [$0.60]."

"Five *som*! What kind of name are you going to get for that? For five *som*, you get Sauntaxun, Mauntaxun. So what's the baby's name going to be, anyway?"

"Mutellip."

"You know as well as I do, that's a twenty-five-*som* name!"

—Hésam Qurban, Yining jokester

After her birth, the infant was referred to only as *elley,* for she was not to be named until her third day. The first few days after the infant's birth were busy days at Abidem's house. The infant, who had been swaddled in blankets at the hospital, was dressed in her first piece of clothing, a sleeved gown of fine muslin with no hemmed edges. Abidem explained that hems would negatively affect her ability to learn to walk. During those first few days, family members discussed with interest the question of what the infant would be named. Abidem suggested Rozgül or Ramizanxan, each of which compounded a reference to the occurrence of her birth during the month of Ramadan with a suffix common to women's names, *-gül* (flower) or *-xan* (short for *xanqiz*, "princess"). One of Senemgül's adolescent nieces suggested her new cousin be named Kiroren-güzéli (Beauty of Loulan), the name of a four-thousand-year-old mummified woman's body that had inspired a recent mummy craze in Uyghur popular culture due to its significance as a symbol of Uyghur indigeneity and cultural identity. Senemgül herself, her husband told me, secretly preferred Arzugül (Hope-flower), since it was alliterative with the name of her first child, Abdüshükür.

The joke quoted above about a newborn's naming ceremony reveals *mehelle* residents' association of certain proper names, in this case Sauntaxun (Semet-axun) and Mauntaxun (Memet-axun), with peasant backwardness and the relative poverty of rural areas. In the joke, peasants' given names are literally worth less than names popular among suburbanites. These ideas about names, which reveal a suburbanite distinction between the low value of a rural identity and the high value of a suburban *mehelle* identity, suggest that individuals are likely to appraise given names through a complex filter of place-based and other status hierarchies.

On the day the infant was to be named, Téyipjan's mother, Meryam, arrived by herself precisely at noon and sat for an hour, waiting for her husband, Iminjan, to arrive. As the baby's paternal grandfather, Iminjan was her *ustixan igisi*, literally the "owner/master of [her] bones," and he alone could choose the name. "If I were to pick the name, now wouldn't that be ugly (*set*)?" Abidem said, using the term she most often applied to inappropriate or dishonorable behavior. Although some accounts mention the practice of calling a religious specialist to the home to "put" the name in exchange for a fee, on this day the infant's paternal grandfather would "put" her name himself and receive payment in the form of a gift.

While waiting for Iminjan to arrive, Senemgül's family members discussed with Meryam the names they had come up with. Anise asked for opinions on the name Zulfiye, which she said she liked. Then Senemgül spoke up. "I thought of Perhize," she said cheerily, giving a name I knew was actually preferred by her sister, perhaps because she had anticipated her mother-in-law's response, which was stony silence. Senemgül was quite forward even to profess an opinion in front of her mother-in-law.

After waiting an hour, Meryam had to return home, she said, to prepare for overnight guests who would be arriving at her home that afternoon. A few minutes after she had gone, her husband finally arrived and joined the conversation about names.

"I've got one in my heart too," Iminjan said, "Tewsiye. It was my elder sister's name, it's a great name (*ulugh at*)."

Abidem, though she had no actual say in the matter, defended her own suggestion and her pride, "Well Ramizanxan is a great name too," I heard her say, as I carried the coal bucket outside to make more space for visitors in the crowded room. As I stepped back inside, Abidem said, "Well, I'll get a prayer-sheet (*jeynamaz*)."[4]

Iminjan climbed up onto the *supa* and stood holding the baby in his hands. The child was bundled in her regular swaddling clothes, but had a new blue and white striped cloth laid over her, a gift from her Aunt Anise. Standing erect, Iminjan recited a short prayer, then bent at the waist and rolled the baby 360° away from him along the *jeynamaz*, as if he were rolling a log, saying aloud as he did so, "From this day on, your name is Tewsiye."[*] As she lay there, her uncle Yakupjan stepped up onto the *supa* and placed a 10 *yuan* note at her left ear, then Iminjan placed a 10 *yuan* note at her right ear. Several people present later agreed that the amount could vary "depending on one's heart." Then Iminjan picked her up and sat down with her on the edge of the *supa*.

Abidem presented Iminjan with the cloth that had been used to cover the baby, along with one kg of rock sugar (*nawat*). Then she took out four more gifts, hand towels, which she gave to Yakupjan, Téyipjan, Senemgül, and me.

As the child is rolled, she is turned face down, away from all present, a ritual removal from the group; when she returns, or is literally re-turned face up, she returns as a person with a name.

---

[*]By some accounts it is typical at this point for the man to whisper the call to prayer in the child's ear, but my field notes make no mention of this.

This incident incorporates two elements common in personal naming in the *mehelle*. First, before the ceremony, the infant's paternal grandfather stated his interest in passing on a name from a previous generation; this is a commonly voiced cultural ideal. Second, Senemgül had stated a preference for alliteration in her children's names. In Yining it was quite common for siblings' names to begin with the same letter, to share one or more syllables, or to display some other external similarities. Both these features enhance the capacity of the personal name to mark the individual as a member of their kin group, the first across generations, the second within them. Personal names, then, reinforce the individual's sense of belonging within the kin group.

The day after the naming ceremony I witnessed an exchange between Senemgül and her mother-in-law, Meryam, who had left before the ceremony began.

"So he ended up calling her Tewsiye, did he?" Meryam asked rhetorically, surely knowing that he had.

"Yes," Senemgül said, nodding her head. "Tewsiye as a name, I've never heard it before."

"Oh, we saw it in a Pakistani movie," her mother-in-law volunteered. "Nonbelievers say it of Muslims when they [i.e., Muslims] give guidance (*tewsiye qilish*) or give advice (*dalalet qilish*) to them."

After witnessing this interaction I had to wonder if Iminjan's claim that the name had belonged to his elder sister was true or was only an attempt to justify bestowing a name he had heard in a film.

Protective Names and *Irim* Practices

On a well-trafficked dirt road connecting Zawut to an adjacent *mehelle*, a faded wooden sign identifies one small building as the Purchased (*setiwaldi*) Health Clinic. The reader who recalls the protective ritual described in Chapter 1 might guess that the word "Purchased" here is the physician's name. Symbolically "sold" soon after her birth by her mother to her father for a quantity of wheat bran, Abidem, too, had been informally called Setiwaldixan, *setiwaldi* plus the feminine suffix *-xan*. Because she had, during the same ritual event, been pulled back into the house through a skylight, she was also called Tartiwaldixan,

literally "pulled" + *-xan*. During my fieldwork in Yining, I also encountered the word *soghriwaldi* used as an adult personal name—one Uyghur
dictionary gives *sughur-* as "to pull out of"—which I take to be a syno-
nym of *tartiwaldi* and most likely a marker of a similar protective ritual.
These names, then, memorialize a kind of ritual event referred to by
mehelle residents as *irim*, or *irimliq*, and invoke memories of those rituals
each time they are uttered.

In Yining I was not able to determine if such names were ever given
as proper names, that is, bestowed by the *ustixan igisi* or a religious specialist during the initial naming ritual. My understanding is that they
rarely or never were. Instead, such names were secondary names, used
in place of true given names during childhood and abandoned in most
but not all cases before puberty. Other protective names were bestowed on young children without an associated ritual. Such names
given to small children include Toxti (Stopped) for boys and Toxtagül
(Stopped + flower) for girls. In the face of high infant mortality rates—
Abidem, for example, lost six of her fourteen children at birth or soon
after—such names express parents' hopes that the child will remain in
this world. Abidem's granddaughter Mukerrem was given the name
Toxtagül, which she used happily until around the age of nine, at which
point she became adamant that others, adults and children alike, use her
given name. Other fixing names, all bestowed without ritual, include
Turdi (Stayed) and Tursun (May-he-stay) for boys, and Tursungül
(May-she-stay + flower) and Tursunay (May-she-stay + moon) for girls.

The potent magic attributed to protective names can have unfortunate consequences for the name bearers. Abidem once recalled for me
from her childhood a song about local tyrants who forced peasants to
build earthen barriers against the flooding Ili River in the 1920s. Although this detail was not in the lyrics themselves, she described how
those tyrants gathered up individuals named Toxti or Tursun and threw
them in the river to stop the waters from rising any higher. The Swedish missionary Ahlbert, writing in 1920, reported as fact that two similarly named men had been killed for this same reason, drowned in a
river in southern Xinjiang that had broken its levee.[5]

A number of other diverse activities were also categorized as *irim* by
Zawut residents. One *irim* practice was referred to as "causing breath to

be put" (*dem saldurush*). Abidem recalled hearing stories of how she fell sick soon after her birth, and how her father insisted that a blemish (*dagh*) be put on her forehead for her protection. Her explanation is paraphrased here.

When a child is born and takes sick, if he cries a lot, a person takes a copper cash [i.e., a round coin with a square hole in it] and places it on the forehead of the child, when the child is lying down. A bead is heated and placed in the hole, leaving a mark. That makes the child healthier and better behaved.[6]

It is likely, I suggest, that a key element of the "breath-putting" ritual is missing in Abidem's account, one involving the ritual breathing or pseudo-spitting gesture performed, as we will see below, to drive away spirits and in the making of *dimidi* (holy water). Another possibility is that this *irim* practice is called *dem saldurush* due to the expectation that it will fix the child's breath in the body, so that he or she will live.[7] Another form of *irim* was described by Abidem in this way:

If a child is born in the lunar month of *seper*, it is dangerous. The child or mother may go on a journey [i.e., die and pass on to the next world], and so the father throws a bag over his shoulder, and says, "I'm going on a journey." Then he goes out and walks around for a few hours.

According to her belief, without the father's prophylactic perambulation, the mother or child will likely meet with an unexpected journey of her or his own to the next world.

Cradling Culture

On their seventh day, Uyghur newborns are strapped to a wooden cradle (*böshük*), where they will spend a good deal of the coming year. Before the child is cradled for the first time, a ceremony is held involving the *tash bala* (stone child). On the seventh day of infant Tewsiye's life, a large group of women (fourteen adults), including members of the child's maternal and paternal kin, came to Abidem's house to witness this cradling ceremony. When the ceremony described below took place, most of the visitors were sitting haphazardly around the *supa* in the *dalan*, where Senemgül would remain, her infant at her side, until the end of a forty-day rest period.

Fig. 6   Senemgül leans over a handmade wooden cradle. Her daughter, Tewsiye, like most *mehelle* infants, was swaddled securely for many hours each day. Here the cradle sits on a carpeted platform (*supa*) that occupies most of the room, a common feature in neighborhood homes (photograph by the author, 1996).

The infant's two grandmothers sat on opposite sides of the cradle. Abidem held Tewsiye, while the paternal grandmother Meryam held an object roughly the size of a building brick, which had been wrapped completely in a white cloth. Later I learned it was a large black stone from the river, one Abidem had reused for several grandchildren.

Before they began, one of the other women stepped out in the street to call into the room more than ten neighborhood children who had been out playing in the deep snow. After the children entered, the two grandmothers abruptly began to speak.

"My real child I'll put in!" said Abidem.

"My stone child I'll put in!" countered Meryam.

"My real child I'll put in!" repeated Abidem.

"My stone child I'll put in!" said Meryam again. During these and several more repetitions of the same lines, the child and stone were alternately swung over the cradle, as if the women were competing to put them inside. On her sixth try, Abidem "won" the contest and gently placed Tewsiye into the cradle.[8] The stone baby was briefly tucked under the blanket by her side; then, since this particular stone was judged too large to remain there, it was put on the *supa* directly under the cradle. An hour later, after Tewsiye had been strapped into the cradle properly, Abidem smiled.

"May she be heavier" (*éghiraq bolsun*).

The kinesthetic element of the competition between stone and child, each in turn physically occupying the cradle, suggests the idea that the stone is used to mislead either maleficent spirits or a jealous eye or tongue, or to somehow draw them away from the real child. Abidem's final comment suggests a complementary interpretation, namely, that the stone symbolizes a wish for the child's fixedness and attachment to this world, the stone's weight serving as a metaphor for the child's longevity. Meryam, in response to my queries about why the stone was left in proximity to the child, explained more pragmatically, "It stays there so the baby sleeps just like a stone."

After Abidem placed Tewsiye into the cradle, one step still remained in the *tash bala* ceremony. As Tewsiye lay quietly on the cradle's main platform, Abidem took a bag of hard sugar candies and passed it through the cradle, above Tewsiye's body but below the handle that ran from head to foot down the cradle's centerline, and into the hands of Meryam, who was still seated across from her. Meryam handed the bag back, this time passing it under the cradle, which stood several inches off the carpet on high rockers. Once the candy, which the women referred to as *chachqu* or *chachqa* (sprinklings), had completed a full circuit around the cradle, it was thrown in handfuls into the crowd of children standing by the doorway. Several women also handed to the children walnuts and small breads baked for the occasion.

"It's to trick the little kids," one woman said bluntly. "There are no little kids here," she continued, a phrase whose meaning was ambiguous, given that there were more than a dozen children in the room at the time. "But if there were," she went on, "it's to fool them."

This comment might have been meant to suggest that the newly cradled infant had no potentially jealous young siblings, implying presumably that sixteen-month-old Abdüshükür, who was present, was too young to even understand. Another possible reading of her comment was that the cradled infant had no siblings who were still breastfeeding; Abdüshükür had switched to eating solid foods in his fourth month, after his mother sustained a serious burn from scalding water.

In either case, the comment supports the interpretation that *chachqu* were offered to keep older children, possibly siblings, from being jealous. In this interpretation "sprinklings" are what Stanley Brandes, following George Foster, has called a "sop," an object offered to keep other children from being jealous.[9] Another possibility, given that the children leave with the candy, is that the candy, once passed around the cradle, draws into itself any maleficent entities, which are then sent off with the neighborhood children.

Although different in minor details, another firsthand account of a Uyghur cradling ceremony, this one recorded in 1891, shows a near identical use of *chachqu*.

On the day the baby will be put in the cradle, seven elder women are called. They take seats, three on each side of the cradle, one by the child's head. A platter of fried dough cakes is set under the child, and the women each take a handful and sprinkle them over and under the cradle. Afterward they are given to young children.[10]

Note that, just as with the *irim* practice of passing the newborn in a circuit around the house, first under the threshold and then over the roof, in both accounts of this ceremony the "sprinklings" were passed in a circuit around the cradle. But why is the candy thrown and not handed to people or placed somewhere that those present can reach out and take it themselves? One interpretation is hinted at by a phrase Abidem recited several days later in reply to my questions about the event.

Sprinkle the sprinklings!   *chachqu chach*
See your fortune!   *bextingni kör*

This was not spoken while throwing candy, she explained, it was simply a saying that "everyone knows." According to these lines, if one is able to grab a lot of candy, one has lots of fortune; otherwise one does not. This can be understood more clearly by considering the fact that sprinklings were also thrown to children at Abidem's house on the day Senemgül delivered Tewsiye, when mother and child were still at the hospital. "This ensures Senemgül has babies," her mother explained. If we view sprinkling as a form of exchange, it is one in which the direct relationship between giver and receiver is occluded, much like the way hiding eggs in an Easter egg hunt (to take an American example) mystifies the fact that they emanate from parents. Why do Uyghur adults create a fictional giver, here the hand of destiny, through the use of a seemingly randomized means of giving (scattering the candy)? Perhaps to suggest that the arrival of the baby and the baby's personal qualities are given by chance and that the baby has a destiny not determined directly by parents. They give it life but cannot be held responsible for giving it happiness, wealth, health, and so forth, just as a person who sprinkles *chachqu* provides the candy but chooses to emphasize the randomness of its distribution.

The Cradle

Once the *chachqu* had been tossed to the children, the women turned their attention to preparing the cradle. The infant, who had been merely laid into the cradle, was lifted out, and a proper cradling was begun. According to one account, a special role in the first cradling is played by an older woman who serves as the "cradle-mother" (*böshük anisi*) or "*irim*-ist" (*irimchi*), and whose secret family tradition (*udum*) is followed in preparing the cradle.[11] Nothing had been said aloud to indicate if one of the grandmothers held this status or not, but Meryam had brought several special objects to put in the cradle with the child. Under the cotton mattress pad she placed two mimeographed prayer pamphlets (*risale*) and a small glass bottle of medicine (*dora*). For boys, a knife is typically placed under the mattress beneath the head; for girls, a small mirror. The mirror's purpose is to ensure that "black does not press down" (*qara bésip qalmasliq*), in other words, that the child will not *jöylep* (see hallucinations; experience delirium; have evil dreams). Abidem had sewn two evil eye amulets (*tumar*), one of which was hung from the cradle, the other around the infant's neck.

A Uyghur cradle is built of wood and painted in bright colors. It has no sidewalls, a design feature that permits the mother to nurse by leaning over the cradle from either side. End-walls at the child's head and feet are made from turned stiles set into a curved hoop. These end-walls are connected by a handle, a turned rod 2–3 inches in diameter, which sits approximately 15 inches over the main platform. When the baby is placed on its back in position in the cradle, this rod runs the entire length of the cradle directly over the child. The cradle platform itself is flat; in Tewsiye's cradle it measured 16 × 27 inches and sat raised on rockers 9 inches off the floor. This platform has a round hole (*oyuqche*) 4 inches in diameter cut through at its center. A padded cloth torus—the *jak tumaq* (or simply *kallek*, meaning "hoop")—1 inch high and 5 inches across sits over this hole. A special 6-inch-high clay vessel, the *kültük* (also called the *jak*, or *garshuq*), drops down through the torus and the *oyuqche* both, extending down 4–5 inches below the cradle, the lip of the *kültük* fitting exactly over the torus. Pads are placed on the platform around the protruding *kallek* and *kültük* making a smooth surface for the baby to lie on. The child is usually wrapped in a two- or three-piece swaddling cloth, called the *zaka* or *yögek*. Before being secured in place, a special wooden tube called a *shümek* connects the child's urethra to the *kültük*, to drain urine while the child is cradled. A boy's *shümek* resembles a wooden tobacco-pipe; the penis fits into the bowl, the stem extends down into the *kültük*.* A girl's first *shümek* is often homemade; a smooth reed tube has a hole burned into its side near one end (cutting the hole would leave splinters) and this hole is then pressed against the urethra. The child is secured to the cradle using *qolwas*, quilted cloth pads placed over the infant's hands, which are then tied with *qoltartqan*, pieces of fabric with cords on them which pull the hands of the infant tightly against the body. The child is then covered with a special blanket (*u'da*); a pillow (*yastuq*) is also used. Other swaddling implements include pads that restrain elbows and knees, called *jeyneklik* and *tizliq*, respectively.

The "Forty Water"

During infant Tewsiye's first few weeks, caregivers constantly encouraged her to take a pacifier and were happy when, after about a month, she finally began to accept it. Tewsiye nursed while strapped in the crib and was removed mainly to have a dirty diaper-cloth changed or to be oiled. Babies were oiled regularly with rendered sheep fat, since this was

---

*It was a running joke in the *mehelle* that Han shoppers would see boys' *shümek* for sale in local markets and place them in their mouths, thinking they were tobacco pipes.

thought to keep them from being "hit" by cold or by wind. The stone child remained under the cradle until the fortieth day, when another ceremony was held for the child.

On the morning of Tewsiye's fortieth day, Abidem scrubbed clean a red and white enamel basin and sat it on the *supa*. "Put some water in there," she said to her oldest daughter, Rahine, who was already lifting a ladle of cold water out of the pail in the corner. Abidem sat the basin on the stove, then dropped a large handful of dried twigs of *adrasman* (*Peganum harmala*) into the water. Reaching into a pocket hidden under her dress, she took out a knotted blue handkerchief. Inside were two or three tablespoons of fine soil she had scooped up from beside a grave at Sultan Mazar, a local saint shrine. She sprinkled some into the basin, then knotted the blue cloth back up carefully, muttering a promise to give the remainder to Rahine, who herself had borne nine children, and would surely be able to use it for her own grandchildren. But the knotted blue rag disappeared under Abidem's dress before Rahine had time to comment.

Rahine stepped into the *saray*, where foods served to guests were stored—candies and cookies and other treats, left in their stacked serving dishes—and returned with two large cubes of sugar. She held them up to her mother, who nodded, and she tossed them in. Next they added a large handful of rock salt. Abidem had put a skewer of lamb meat into the fire, and she pulled the cooked meat off and dropped it into the basin. The women took a gold ring from Senemgül and dropped that in as well. During their preparations I had been chatting with them, and when Yakupjan wandered in from next door, he overheard me asking the women what wish I should offer Tewsiye during the ceremony that was to begin shortly.

"Hey Ismayil,* you should say 'May she be a naughty girl! May she not come in from outside!'"

---

*In 1988 Uyghur friends in Beijing had adopted the habit of called me Ismayil. In Yining, *mehelle* men who tried to call me Jay invariably pronounced my name as *jeyk*, a word best known as the sound a fighting cock makes when he turns tail and flees from a cockfight. "Fleeing chicken" didn't strike me as an auspicious name, and so I continued to use Ismayil throughout my field research.

"No matter what we say," Abidem interrupted, "she'll turn out just like her mom and dad. If they are good, she'll turn out good. It doesn't matter what we say." This was a none-too-subtle dig at Yakupjan, I thought, whose son Mehmud gave both his father and his grandmother more than their fair share of aggravation.

The water in the basin had been warmed on the coal stove by the time the twenty or so close relatives who were expected had arrived. Adults stood or sat and children scampered noisily around Abidem's two small rooms as Yakupjan carried the basin of water into the *saray*. He walked over to the oldest person present, the mother-in-law of Abidem's daughter Aliye, who sat on the floor beside the long low table. Slowly, but with a steady hand, the old woman spooned water from the red and white enamel basin held by Yakupjan into an empty green basin on the table. With each sentence she spoke she transferred another spoonful of water.

In the name of God the merciful. May she be a Muslim! May she be considerate of others! May she be a good master of God's heaven! May she be gentle! May she be long-lived!

Next came the baby's paternal grandmother Meryam, with four wishes.

In the name of God the merciful. May she live long! May she have a white [i.e., kind] heart! May she be considerate of others! May she be devout!

While Meryam was spooning water, her sister asked Abidem, "Did you add rock sugar?" Abidem nodded in the affirmative. "Of course. Sure we put it in." In fact she had used sugar cubes and, at the time, had voiced her own regret that there was no rock sugar in the house, but she kept this detail to herself; this was no time for problems with the in-laws. Taking the next turn at the spoon was Abidem herself, with three wishes. Then, in approximately declining order of age, first all the adult women present spooned water, then the adult men, and lastly all the children present. Through these actions, the spoken words and the breaths that transmitted them were imparted into the fluid, which was later used to ritually bathe the infant for protection.

Most of the adults offered two wishes, some one or three, and most of the children offered a single wish. There was much repetition of wishes that had already been given. Wishes included "May she have a conscience!," "May she be prosperous!," "May she be a good girl!," and "May she be intelligent!" Differences in wishes for male and female infants are likely to reveal significantly different expectations for boys and girls, and I regretted not having occasion to attend another forty water ceremony during my research. By far the most frequently offered wish for Tewsiye was one I suspect would never be uttered for a male child: "May she be docile!"

During the spooning, a dozen neighborhood children had been invited in. When the spooning was completed, the children happily took candy and walnuts handed to them by Senemgül and Gülzire, Yakupjan's wife, and then quickly left.

"We should be giving candy, walnuts, and small *toqash* breads," Abidem said to me, "but we are giving store-bought cookies, since we didn't have time to bake *toqash* in advance."

Aliye chimed in with her own explanation, "If forty-one *toqash* and walnuts are not given to the neighborhood children, the baby grows up to have a bad temper and a mean character."

I asked Abidem if these candies and nuts were *chachqu*.

"No," she replied, "it's just an offering (*nezir sediqe*), it's just to let the kids play and be happy."

In Aliye's explanation I take the number forty-one to mean roughly "a good amount, and then some," much as the number 101 is used in English. Despite Abidem's categorizing these offerings as a generic social prestation, the interpretation suggested above for *chachqu*, of giving the children something that they take away and consume, perhaps taking a threatening tongue or an evil eye with them, is still relevant here.

Throughout the ladling of water, Tewsiye had remained in her cradle virtually ignored. In warmer months, the ladling is often done directly onto the child. Since it was winter, however, and there was concern that the room would be cold due to the single door being repeatedly opened and shut, the actual bathing of the child took place later that evening without ceremony.

The women present offered a range of explanations for why various objects had been placed in the basin. Gold was put there "so that she may be precious as gold." The dried *adrasman* was so that "she is not touched by eyes or tongues." This herb was frequently burned in *mehelle* homes as a purificatory measure against the evil eye. The soil from the *mazar* was put there "so that she becomes great (*ulugh*), like the person in the grave." The sugar, they explained, was "so that her words will be sweet." The meat ensured that if the child was ever "wounded or cut with a knife, she will heal well." I asked next about the salt. When the women answered quickly "same as for meat," I took it as a sign they were tired of my questions, especially given the important role salt played in other rituals for expelling evil spirits or an evil eye.[12]

Eating and Excreting:
Children's Body Control

The two children say "bread"	*ikki bala nan deydu*
The angel of death says "soul"	*izréyil jan deydu*
	—Abidem, citing a Uyghur proverb

Once weaned from the breast, a child is fed by caregivers who chew plain noodles or bread dipped in tea and spit the chewed food into his or her mouth. Abdüshükür took food in this manner until his fourteenth month, when he began to demand first that the food be spit into his hand, then later into a spoon, so that he could put it in his own mouth. Like other young children in Zawut, the split-crotch pants he wore once he began to crawl, and then later walk, allowed him to defecate and urinate without fuss. Whichever woman or young girl was watching him would hold him over a pan when needed. To get him to go, they would often rub his inner thighs with their fingers as they held him. For several months Abdüshükür was constantly eating lime from off the walls around the *supa*, despite efforts to cover all parts of the walls in his reach with a makeshift fabric wainscot. This habit, Abidem believed, caused his frequent constipation, and she often gave him a soap-water enema from a basin using a turkey baster.

Like other Uyghur children, Abdüshükür was frequently referred to using terms that addressed his lack of bodily control. He was often called "pisser" (*süygek*, literally "prone to urinate"), since he in fact urinated on the *supa* carpet frequently. He also shat quite often on the same carpet, and so was also called "shitter" (*chichqaq*, "prone to shitting"). Although older children are often teased good-naturedly about farting, parents recognized infants' farting as a sign of discomfort.

Yesterday I was sitting next to Tewsiye, who was asleep on the *supa*, not cradled. Abidem asked me from across the room to cover the baby's feet with the blanket, and the moment I did so, she emitted a loud fart. I chuckled in surprise, and Abidem immediately commented,

"Stomach pains."

"Since when?" I asked. I hadn't known Tewsiye wasn't feeling well. Abidem cocked her head at me, realizing I had not gotten her point.

"If you laugh, her stomach will hurt. When babies fart or shit, you're not supposed to laugh." She said she had learned this as a child.

Soon after Tewsiye was born, Senemgül also began eating seeds purchased from a local folk herbalist, in an attempt to change the quality of her breast milk and thereby reduce the baby's gas.

The Evil Eye and Curative Practices

The evil eye belief complex is found widely in Xinjiang, and infants in the *mehelle* thought to be afflicted might be treated with a number of remedies. A child who is sick, crying, and whining is often thought to have become afflicted by the evil eye. People say that the child has become "prone to crying" (*éngiz bolup qaptu*). To cure the child, a gauze cloth soaked in a paste of ground nutmeg and whipped egg yolk is applied to the child's head. As the gauze is wrapped around the child's head, the fluid drips onto his or her face; this is always left in place. An infant treated with such a poultice quickly gets a dirty face, since the sticky fluid attracts dirt. This, too, is left to wear off on its own and is expressly not washed off. This may serve the useful function of keeping the baby looking dirty and unattractive and thereby reduce the envy and jealousy believed to attract the evil eye. "When Yakupjan was cradled," Abidem recalled of her adult son, "he was so cute my older brother smeared coal dust on his face every day."

Despite the threat of the evil eye, adults are not unwilling to praise infants. Abidem was pleased to remark on Abdüshükür's health and attractiveness, calling him a "ram-like child." Many relatives praised Tewsiye and commented on how attractive and black her eyebrows were. But certainly some forms of praise were dangerous. Several months after Tewsiye was born, Senemgül cut her finger while dicing vegetables at home. Abidem shook her head when she heard, saying:

She attracted a malediction (*chetnep ketti*). Someone said she was lucky, with her two nice kids. She's un-self-consciously pretty, so she cut her finger. She should incense all of the utensils of the house with some burning *adrasman*. That neighbor of ours has a bad eye. It's dangerous for Senemgül.

When a child is threatened by unwanted praise or other maleficence, means are available to expel this bad influence. One such method is used to combat a condition referred to as "having hunger enter" (*ach kirmek*), meaning that the hunger of the person with the evil eye enters into the victim. "It means you are hit with evil because you are stared at while eating," Abidem explained. A Uyghur dictionary definition confirmed Abidem's explanation.

To have hunger enter: According to a superstitious belief, the occurrence of a condition of vomiting, stomach aches, yawning, and so forth, caused in a person due to their being looked upon with hungry eyes by another person when eating.[13]

During my research, I observed Abidem attempt to remove this condition several times for each of Senemgül's two children. Although I can offer only a partial account here, it is to my knowledge the only published description of this practice. She called her act *ashlash*, meaning "to pacify, soothe, calm." First, she put a handful of salt or ashes into small bowl. On one occasion, Abidem explained to a woman visiting from the countryside that she used ashes because there was no wheat bran, suggesting that bran is an acceptable or even preferable alternative. She then took an amount of either ash or salt into her hand, or in some cases held the bowl in both hands, and with the hand or bowl patted the child all over the body, as she recited the verses given below. After the recitation, she threw the material from her hand or the bowl into the fire, simultaneous with the utterance of the final line of the verse.

From that grave	*ashu gördi*
From that grave	*ashu gördi*
From that grave	*ashu gördi*
[This line is repeated five to fifteen times total]	
Come out of the grave	*chiq gördi*
Come out of the grave	*chiq gördi*
[This line is repeated two to five times total]	

Fig. 7 A small child experiencing bodily discomfort may be seen as having fallen victim to an evil eye or tongue. Here Abdüshükür, held by his father, wears the remains of a protective poultice that had been applied to his head and face by his grandmother several days earlier, an intervention intended to drive or keep away such maleficent influences (photograph by the author, 1996).

If you're coming out, then you're out	*chiqsang chiqting*
If you're not coming out	*chiqmisang*
Up your asshole, a reed I'll ignite	*qonggha borini qalap*
And set you on fire!	*ot qoyiwétimen*

I was initially tempted to view *ashu gördi* as a modified pronunciation of *ach kirdi* (in part because *ch* is often pronounced *sh* in Yining dialect), giving the first lines the meaning "hunger has entered." Uyghur scholar Kurban Niyaz (personal communication) has suggested the more likely interpretation that *gördi* should be read as *gör* + *din* (from the grave), based on his view that "it is commonly believed that devils come from graves." The underlying idea, presumably, is that a maleficent entity, from the safety of its grave, is afflicting the child; to cure the child, the entity must be dislodged from its grave to a place where it can do no harm. A variant of the final verse Abidem used on another occasion, given here, shows that the wording can be altered.

If you're coming out, then you're out!	*chiqsang chiqting*
If you're not coming out,	*chiqmisang*
In your asshole I'll start a fire	*qonggha ot yéqip*
And burn you with reeds	*bora bilen köydüriwétimen*

A longer version of an *ashlash* verse that I recorded on one occasion included the motif of removing the maleficent agent and banishing it into
"a nearby crumbling wall."[14] One possible reason for the use of fire
in this rite of expulsion is suggested in the phrase "grabbed by fire" (*ot
tutti*), naming a condition Abidem described as "the same as being entered by hunger." If fire has taken hold of the infant, it makes sense
that like can be used to drive away like.

On occasion Abidem also performed another curative practice, one
she called *uchughdash*. One Uyghur dictionary gives the meaning of this
term as "to expel something bad" and provides the example "the witch
expelled the disease." In its passive form this verb is also given as "to
be bashed, pounded, assaulted." The link between "expelling something
bad" and "being bashed and pounded" was apparent in a scene I witnessed in 1992, when Abidem undertook to *uchughdash* her son Memetjan, then age thirty, after he broke two toes crossing a stream barefoot.
With her son lying face up on the carpet of the *saray*, Abidem took (in
her words) "forty-one branches from a tree" and hit him forcefully
more than a dozen times over his entire body. She then threw a handful
of *dimidi* water into each of his eyes.

Dimidi water, used in many protective rituals, can be made in a number of ways. The best water for making *dimidi*, according to a number
of accounts, is water collected from *leyzeng*, the first rainfall of spring,
using any clean vessel. The second rain of spring, known as *abdurexmet*,
is also acceptable, although not as good. During *qurban heyt* (The Festival of Sacrifice), Abidem handed young Aysajan a glass jar of *leyzeng* water she had been preserving and sent him to stand outside a large
mosque as worshippers exited after prayers. As the men left, they "put
their breath" (*dem salmaq*) onto it, Abidem explained, which she demonstrated by breathing out while making a whispering sound akin to sip-
ping a hot beverage.[15]

Dimidi can also be made by having one individual recite verses from
the Qur'an over the open vessel of water. Anwarjan, Abidem's son-in-
law, explained the practice this way.

"They read thirty-two Qur'anic verses. At the end of each verse, they say *su* once. It takes ten or fifteen minutes to read each verse, and when they're done, the *dimidi* is made. [The power of *dimidi* is such that] it keeps a curse from having any effect."

"How would someone put a curse?" I asked him.

"Like if while speaking a curse, they stepped on bread, or held a Qur'an," he said, mentioning actions that turn an otherwise routine expression of ill will into a curse.

"Or if they say 'May bread strike me' or 'May I go blind,'" Yakupjan interjected. Abidem heard all this talk of oaths, which she disapproved of greatly, and spoke up.

"Bread is great (*ulugh*)," she said. "The Qur'an is great (*ulugh*). They don't really hit you."

To clarify, in making his explanation Anwarjan did not actually pronounce the word *su*, which in Uyghur means (surely not coincidentally) "water." Rather, he made a spitting gesture with his lips while making a short hissing sound (best approximated phonetically as "su"), as if spitting dry air. Months later, toward the end of Ramadan, Abidem invited to her home her grandson Ablet, who was learning to recite the Qur'an. The sixteen-year-old read a passage from the Qur'an, the *süre yasin*, over a bowl of water one evening, making it into *dimidi*, which Abidem drank along with other family members the next evening at *iptar*, the fast-breaking meal.

———

Once the child has safely passed through early infancy and begins to walk, she or he is soon ready to leave the cradle and the domestic confines of the *dalan* and to enter the world of play, a subject examined in detail in the following chapter on the language and lore of Uyghur childhood.

5

At Play in the *Mehelle*

The Language and Lore of
Uyghur Childhood

Play [is] a world in which you are what you become through your ability to control your body while mastering the rules of the game—and the rules for changing the rules.

— Roger D. Abrahams

The unpaved lanes of Yining's *mehelle* were often filled with the noisy play of neighborhood children. As soon as young infants learned to walk, they would be in the streets with older children throughout the day, shepherded about by siblings, cousins, or neighbors, and led to participate in a range of play activities. The lives of children were not all play, of course. It was common to see children as young as six or seven roaming local markets selling plastic bags, matchboxes, or glasses of tea. During such activities children often traveled in groups and most times seemed to be having fun while also earnestly pursuing profit. Older female children also contributed significant amounts of labor in the home, washing dishes, scrubbing and sweeping floors, and completing other chores. It was in the activities of informal play, however, which took place in courtyards and *mehelle* lanes, that children developed much of their sociality, away from the direct intervention of adults, in the semiautonomous world of play. Semiautonomous, I say, since adults did participate in many ways in the play of children.

In this chapter I consider folklore and play activities in children's lives, to look there for insight into the development of adult social identities, particularly the identities of men. The chapter also examines the social meanings behind certain exchanges between children and their adult caregivers. In considering features of adult-child verbal and play interactions, I focus on patterns in which adults tease and provoke young children, boys in particular, given the centrality of mutual provocation in adult interactions. Girls' experiences of the transition into adult gender identity differ from those of boys, it might be argued, in part because female role models surround them from a young age. In the *mehelle*, where children's caregivers are virtually all female, girls play with cradles and dolls alongside young women caring for real infants, and play at household chores before they are asked to perform them in earnest. Uyghur boys have a harder time observing their fathers' activities, since men remain away from the home for the greater part of most days. Consequently, according to this line of reasoning, boys' heightened efforts to present a masculine identity during adolescence serve in part to help them overcome the influence of the female role models provided by women who raised them.[1] Many of the materials presented below, I suggest, support such an argument.

Interaction Between Adult and Infant

Given the concerns adults express about an infant's future speaking ability, it is worth considering in more detail how men and women in the *mehelle* speak to their young children. First, infants are often addressed using "spoiling names" (*erkiletme nam*), names of endearment given to infants by adults soon after birth. In Zawut adults used these names in an informal and spontaneous way; a particular child is addressed by many such names, no consensus is sought, and such names are used only for the first few years and then forgotten. Senemgül's daughter, Tewsiye, was frequently addressed as Tewsiye *ay* (moon), a phrase in which the *ay* is a spoiling name. Other spoiling names include, for boys, "my master" (*ghojam*), "my Beg" (*bégim*), "my lamb" (*paqlinim* or *qozam*), "my sparrow-hawk" (*qurghuyum*), "my rabbit-hawk" (*qaricho-gham*), "my baby camel" (*botam*), and "my mosquito" (*pashayim*); and for girls, "my dear moon" (*jan ayim*), "my bead" (*munchiqim*), "my flower" (*gülüm*), "my gold" (*altunum*), "my rosefinch" (*tumuchuqum*), "my Venus" (*cholpanim*), and "fairy princess" (*peri xan*).[2] As is evident here, a significant gender division is communicated early in children's lives through the strictly different sets of words used for boys and girls.

Infants are often addressed in a special manner that expresses the emotional relationship expected between parent and young child, a type of speaking called *erkiletmek*, literally "to cause to be spoiled." "Spoiling talk" (*erkiliten gep*) is roughly equivalent to the American vernacular term "baby talk." The root these words share, *erke*, has the core meaning of "spoiled" or "acting spoiled"; *erkiliten gep* is literally "causing-them-to-be-spoiled language." Children are no longer spoken to this way once they reach the age of four or five, suggesting that the end of "spoiling name" use coincides with the passage of the child into a new phase of social identity, when a new set of expectations about emotional and behavioral control are presented by the child's adult kin.

Although an exact etymology of the word *erke* is unavailable, it is striking that *er* is "man" and *erkek* is "masculine," yet *erke*, when used to describe an older child or a man, shifts from meaning "spoiled" to meaning more specifically "effeminate." This cluster of meanings suggests a range of cultural and semantic relationships. In later adolescence, the term *erke-naynaq* is used to describe a boy who is spoiled and behaving naughtily. *Naynaqlash* alone, as a verb, means: (1) to walk swinging one's hips; and (2) to be flighty or frivolous. Each of these meanings, one a behavior, the other an emotional attribute, is associated by *mehelle* men with an exaggerated femininity. Taken together, this suggests that adults consciously spoil children when young, but that boys who fail to make a radical shift away from the identity such behavior promotes are explicitly considered effeminate. Below we will see signs that suggest a boy's transition from spoiled child doted on by women to properly gendered adolescent is marked with anxiety.

Although children are cuddled and spoken to sweetly, they can also easily become the recipients of harsh invective. Adult caregivers swear at infants often: Abidem might bark at fourteen-month-old Abdüshükür "You bastard whoreson!"[3] In turn, young boys are not unwilling to use similarly harsh language with their elders, who often welcome this as a sign of the child's inherent willfulness and willingness to assert himself without regard for others. Both of these, we will see, are prized personality traits in adult men.

Adult women enjoyed teasing young children during play. Below are two examples of rhymes spoken to the pre-verbal Abdüshükür when he was between thirteen and fifteen months old. When singing, women would often move their arms or sway their entire bodies along with the rhythm of the words.

Baroom, baroom	*dombur dombur maqqa*
The donkey is in the leaves	*ishek yopurmaqqa*
A letter came from Almaty	*amatudin xet keptu*
Saying Abdüshükür is a farter	*Abdüshükür osurghaqqa*

The singer explained that *dombur maqqa* is a playful manipulation of the word *dombaq* (drum), and represents a loud, booming, farting sound. The second rhyme draws on the same theme of passing gas.

Snow was falling, smitter smatter	*qarla yaghdi lep lep*
Rabbit came hopping, pitter patter	*toshqan keldi sekrep*
I grabbed him, 'twas an easy matter	*tutiwaldim eplep*
I stuffed him in the pot, all-a-clatter	*qazan saldim keplep*
I put the lid on, without a splatter	*tuwaqni yapdim pemlep*
I swallowed him down, "gulp gulp"	*yutiwettim ghort-ghort*
And farted him out, "blulp blulp"	*osiriwettim bort-bort*

Babies in Zawut were frequently teased, at least in Abidem's household, for being "prone-to-fart" (*osurghaq*), "prone-to-pee" (*süygek*), or "prone-to-shit" (*chichqaq*). From a young age, Abdüshükür was teased about an inability to control his bodily functions, despite the prohibition against laughing at an infant's farting, which was believed to further distress the infant.

Lullabies

Young girls and adult women often sang to children in their care, to younger infants strapped into cradles and to older infants swinging in cloth hammocks above the *supa*. Although men sang frequently to one another at their own all-male gatherings, I never saw a man or boy sing to a child. Several women insisted that to learn about lullabies I should talk to local Uzbek women—Yining has several thousand Uzbek residents, many of whom live in a *mehelle* adjacent to Zawut—whose singing of lullabies they believed to be superior to their own. Despite these disavowals, I was able to collect a number of verses sung by different women to Tewsiye.

Short, one-line verses were regularly spoken or sung while the infant was being bathed or held. Senemgül would often sing "Tewsiye moon, the tea in my tea bowl" (*Tewsiye ay, chinemdiki chay*) as she bathed her baby. The moon is a frequent metaphor in Uyghur folk narrative representing the beautiful face of a loved one. Other verses sung to Tewsiye sounded much like children's own folklore, with short, staccato, rhyming lines. The following verse was sung to her often by Abidem.

White girl, whitest girl	*aq qiz apaq qiz*
Black girl, road-rut girl	*qara qiz katang qiz*
Lie down in the leaves, girl	*yopurmaqqa yatang qiz*
You are fit for a king, girl	*xanlargha layiq qiz*
You would be wasted on a Beg, girl	*beglerge zaye qiz*

The next verse was often sung in response to the child's cries.

Rock, rock, my white child	*elle elle aq böpem*
Lie in your white cradle, my child	*aq böshükte yat böpem*
Here comes your mother now	*hazir apingiz kélidu*
She'll give you her nipple	*sizge memem béridu*

Not all verses were so comforting, however, as I discovered listening to a verse sung by Abidem to a decidedly more mournful melody.

For three hundred sixty days	*üch yüz atmish künlerde*
You don't get sleepy at night	*uyqung kelmes tünlerde*
There are so many little babes	*ushshaq baliliri tola*
Crying out on the desert's edge	*yighlighanda chöl yerde*
Rock my child, rock my child, rock	*elle balam elle balam elle*

Initially I heard in these lines a veiled threat, if only a joking one, to abandon the child "out on the desert's edge." This interpretation drew on my knowing that Abidem was often deeply exhausted by tending two babies all night long, a situation that frustrated her and caused her to make resentful comments about the demands placed on her by the task.

A different interpretation can be offered in light of a text I subsequently uncovered, the likely source of these lines. That text is of a Uyghur folk song recorded in Yining in the 1870s and published in Uyghur in 1881. Many parallels exist between the situation of the woman whose plight is described in the song and that of Abidem. Both have lost their husbands, and both are confronting their own mortality. The singer tells of suffering untold pain and of seeing young people passing through life like water bubbling in a stream, while she is like a dried-up blossom fallen from a tree, growing more yellow with each passing day. Abidem, too, was outspoken about her own physical pains and referred almost daily to her future journey to the next world. I quote the 1881 variant at length, given the interesting parallels the verses have with Abidem's life.[4]

For three hundred sixty days	*üch yüz atmish künlerde*
I couldn't sleep at night	*uxlamidim tünlerde*
There are so many little babes	*ushaq balilar tola*
Crying out in the barren lands	*yighlighan dur jöllerde*
Should I speak of my father's situation?	*atamning xalini deymu*
Should I speak of my own hardships?	*özümning derdini deymu*
Should I speak of the Chinese tyrants?	*xitayning zalimni deymu*
Should I die without telling my sufferings?	*derdim eytmay öleymu*
Inside me, my sorrows are many	*ichimde derdim tola*
To whom will I speak of my hardships?	*derdimni kimge eytay*
My father and mother are no more	*atam bilen anam yoq*
I leave with naught but my head	*béshimni élip kétey*
All that was left of your home was a hatchet	*öyüng qélip dur bir palta*
I picked it up and put it in a chest	*élip sanduqqa men saldim*
To my mother-in-law and father-in-law	*qiyin atam bilen anam*
Only I am left to say "I am your son"*	*men oghlungni dep qaldim*
The people going to Tashkent	*tashkentke ketken xelqlerning*
Have silver tucked at their bosoms	*qoyunida kümüshi bar*
Run, my older and younger brothers	*yurunglar agha inilar*
It's an accursed state of affairs in Ili	*ilining le'in ishi bar*
My own name is Meyumxan	*özüm éti Meyumxan*
My sister's name is Minexan	*singlim éti Minexan*

———

*Meaning that her husband, their son, has died.

I heard in advance of the coming	*awal anglaghan bolsam*
unrest	*bilen*
And we left together right away	*turup ketkeshken*
On these roads there are	*bu yollarda bar iken*
Stones that stick up through the sands	*qum sekligen tashlar*
Like water flowing in a stream	*ériqdiki sugha oxshash*
The young folk are going on their way	*kétip baridur yashlar*
As I pass through my life	*kétip barghan ömrümgha*
I hurt so much, so much	*toladin tola aghraymen*
Like a dried leaf fallen to the ground	*yerge chüshken xazan dek*
Day by day I turn more yellow	*kündin kün'ge saghraymen*

As I collected women's verses, I was surprised to find that several songs women identified as lullabies dealt with romantic and even erotic love between adult men and women. Tewsiye's maternal aunt Rahine had married into a peasant family in the nearby village of Turpanyüz in the 1960s, when her family had been sent to live there during China's Cultural Revolution. During one of Rahine's extended visits to her mother's house, I asked her if she might sing slowly, so that I could write down, one of the lullabies she sang to Tewsiye. Embarrassed, she sang awkwardly and in a slow rhythm the line "Sleep, my child, sleep, my child, sleep, don't cry." Then, turning her face away from me, she sang this verse in a whisper.[5]

From mountains high	*igiz igiz taghlardin*
I slid down to you	*sirildim sizge*
Like a rosebud	*qizil gülning ghunchisidek*
I bent down to you	*égildim sizge*
Do you know or don't you	*bilemsiz bilmemsiz*
How you fill me with desire	*xushtarmen sizge*
If I die in love	*xushtarliqta ölüp ketsem*
It will be unrequited	*ugalim sizge*

For a few minutes, she discussed with her mother the words to a lullaby she remembered from years earlier and then slowly began to sing.[6]

At the top of the wall he sits	*tam töpiside olturidu*
That happy-go-lucky, well-built lad	*shox shi boyliq shol yigit*

If I offer him an apple, he's unwilling	*alma bersem unimaydu*
That *barbira* golden boy	*barbira altun yigit*
White thorn, whitest thorn	*aq tiken apaq tiken*
With flowers all around it	*chöriside gül bar iken*
Goldenboy's appearance	*altun yigitning sürtte*
Has a *sultanchi*	*sultanchi bar*
I picked a flower, and put it in the jug	*gülni üzüp küpke saldim*
There is wine in the jug	*küpde haraq bar iken*

The following lullaby again presents a story about romantic love, this time in a verse sung to Tewsiye by her Aunt Maynur.

Rock, my child, rock	*elle balam elle*
Rock, my child, rock	*elle balam elle*
The sheep's head is under the trellis	*kalla barangliqta*
Your key is hidden in the mortar and pestle	*kilting soqatashta*
Come in, come in, and eat up	*chiqip chiqip yengla*
Rock, my child, rock	*elle balam elle*
There are walnuts in the walnut trees	*tolimu yangaqliqta*
The candies are under the grape-trellis	*chelge barangliqta*
Oleaster-dates are between the cornrows	*jigde qonaqliqta*
Rock, my child, rock	*elle balam elle*
Raisins and seeds are under the trellis	*kishmish barangliqta*
Apricots are in the flowerbeds	*ürük zarliqta*
Rock, my child, rock	*elle balam elle*

The words, Maynur explained, express the point of view of a woman rocking her child inside a house. She is expecting a visit from her lover and has prepared a number of snacks for him, which she has hidden around the courtyard, when her husband arrives home unexpectedly. As noted above, *mehelle* men would typically remain away from home throughout the morning and afternoon. To signal to her lover that he should not knock while her husband is home, she sings this song, informing him about the foods that await him outside, so that he will stay hidden in the courtyard and consume them while he waits for her husband to depart.

Play Activities and Gender Relations

Abidem's household conveniently provided the opportunity to com-
pare procedures for rearing very young male and female children. At
Abidem's, female kin were responsible for virtually all child care, including watching Abdüshükür and Tewsiye throughout the day.

One striking feature of the play I observed between adults and
young children was the constant attention paid by female adult kin to
the penis and scrotum of Abdüshükür between the ages of ten and
twenty-one months. His genitals were regularly, although always fairly
briefly, made a focal point of interaction by adult women who kissed,
rubbed, or blew air on them. Most common, however, was for adult
female kin to pretend to eat the penis, either by holding it to their
mouths or by attempting to pinch it between their fingers, which they
then put to their mouths. The penis was often spoken of as a piece of
candy. Three typical incidents are presented in these field note excerpts.

Abidem squeezed his penis, and said "I'll eat your little candy right up, I will."

Abidem squeezed his penis, and said "I'll feed this little candy to someone."

Maynur makes a pinching motion at his penis, then puts her hand to her
mouth and squeals in delight, as if it were incredibly tasty and sweet.

I witnessed Abdüshükür's adult female kin kissing his penis up to
when he was twenty-one months old. No men participated in such behavior toward infants, and I never saw any playful attention paid to a
female infant's genitals by anyone. Several dimensions of the genital
manipulation of male infants relate to themes visible in the experiences
of older males discussed in subsequent chapters. First, women present
themselves as deeply interested in the male penis. Second, women are
seen as potential threatening devourers of male genitalia. Third, the
possibility is raised that the penis can be removed from the body or
otherwise made to disappear. This in turn raises the concern that the
penis, and by extension the masculine identity itself, is neither stable
nor permanently fixed.

At thirteen months, Abdüshükür was able to walk several steps
without falling. His mother and other female adult kin then enjoyed
playing a game with him, throwing a wadded-up piece of cotton (which
they called a "mouse") between his legs as he took a few hesitant steps

from one seated woman to the next. The women playing this game knew, even if the toddler did not, that "playing cat and mouse" was a common folk metaphor for marital sexual relations, a metaphor that casts the penis as the mouse and the vagina as the devouring cat. In this game adult women toss the mouse back and forth between the legs of a male infant, who never succeeds at taking possession of his mouse, thwarted endlessly by the women, who laugh uproariously at his futile efforts. If we recognize in this the male child's inability to securely claim his own symbolic penis, we can better understand some features of adult men's concerns with the performance of their masculine identities.

Another common form of play involved encouraging or compelling the young child to perform for others. Abdüshükür, who at seventeen months was not yet speaking, was frequently made to "sing" or "dance" for a group of adults seated around the *supa*. Holding in his hand some object as a pretend microphone, or with his hands held over his head and making motions as if snapping his fingers, he would walk around the *supa* beaming with happiness. Infants, especially girls but also boys, are encouraged to dance long before they can stand, by adults who do so by snapping their fingers, repeating the phrase *nay-nay* and twisting their hands in a manner reminiscent of the motions of Uyghur *usul* dance. Adults prompting infants to dance is widespread in Xinjiang, and the activity is referred to as "to nay-nay" (*nay-nay qilish*).

Women interacted with infant children far more often than did men, but as young boys become capable of taking part in more challenging play activities, men gradually began to spend more time playing with them. Play activities shared by men and older boys are discussed shortly, in this chapter. One striking example of play between men and very young boys did occur frequently, however. On more than a dozen occasions, I witnessed an adult man pull down, or attempt to pull down, the pants of a boy aged roughly four to six. On each occasion the man verbally teased the child by asking "Are you a boy?" or "Are you a boy or a girl?" On many more occasions, men asked the same question in a teasing manner without attempting to pull down the child's pants. In all instances, the intent was clearly to challenge the boy to display his penis and thereby prove his gender. This was not done between male kin; usually it was done by men who were friends with the child's male kin. Such behavior suggests a number of possible interpretations. In my view, this taunting creates anxiety for young boys, insofar as they begin to see their gender as something that might change; thus, it teaches them to vigilantly maintain and assertively proclaim their gender identity. This behavior also reinforces for boys their confidence that whenever their gender identity is in doubt, they can always demonstrate their penis in order to clear up all ambiguity.

Body Language: Finger and Hand Rhymes

Of the many adults who played with Abdüshükür, only his mother regularly played with him in what seemed to me a pedagogic fashion, for example, by simultaneously touching and naming his various body parts. Other adults were more likely to play by teasing or provoking him, something his mother did as well. One frequent play activity consisted of gently pinching his fingers one at a time while reciting a five-line verse such as the following.

Thumb   *besh maltak*
   "*besh maltak* is the name of the thumb . . ."
Index finger   *besh rayaytak*
   " . . . his neighbor is *béshi rayaytak*. *Aytak* means the same as *yaylaq* (pasture, grazing area) . . ."
The middle one is a pasture   *otturanchi yaylaq*
   " . . . this means the middle one is fat and does no work. It's big around, like someone who never works, just eats a lot and plays all the time, of someone like that we say he plays like a pasture (*yaylaqdek oynap yürgen*) . . ."
The little master *mimi*   *ghojiya mimi*
   " . . . what's *mimi*? It's like, if you were talking baby-talk to kids, if they were being bad, and you'd say, 'you're a little *mimi*,' to tease them that they were behaving like little kids."
A tiny little *chichi*   *kichige chichi*

Here is another such rhyme.

Thumb   *bash barmaq*
Joint finger   *bamal barmaq*
Oltan poplar   *oltan térek*
Master-older-brother is a Muslim   *ghojakam mömin*
The littlest one is Tai-the-tassel   *kichikinem Tai pöpük*

The following five-line rhyme was spoken while squeezing one finger in turn, from thumb to littlest finger.

Let's go	*yürunglar*
To where?	*nege*
To the melon field [to steal melons]	*qoghunluqqa*
Aren't you afraid of God?	*xudayimdin qorqmamsiler*
We'll take some . . . and flee!	*alimiz . . . qachamiz*

Stealing melons often arose as a trope of rural life in the narratives of *mehelle* men, who nostalgically recalled their adventures stealing melons as boys. By telling stories about stealing melons, men portray themselves as having been both bold and mischievous, traits that men widely admire.

Uyghur children also learned to play various games involving hand rhymes. Abdüshükür's female cousin Nuriye (age 9) was playing a hand-patting game with him when he was just eleven months old. As they clapped their hands together, seated in the shade of the courtyard's outdoor summer eating pavilion, the girl repeated the following words.

One fish	*bir béliq*
Two bears	*ikki éyiq*
Three grapes	*üch üzüm*
Four holes	*töt töshük*
Five "fivestones"	*besh beshtash*
Six skinnies	*alte awaq*
Seven singles	*yette yekke*
Eight baskets	*sekkiz siwet*
Nine clubs	*toqquz toqmaq*
Ten battles	*on urush*
Yeast leavening	*xémirturush*

Note the alliteration in Uyghur (absent in the translation) between the word for the item associated with each number and the number itself. "Fivestones," the item named in number five, is itself a common game in the *mehelle*, most often played by young girls.[7]

Older Children's Games and Sexuality

As soon as children learn to walk and are freed from the regimen of being tightly swaddled in their cradles, they begin to participate, often led
by older siblings or cousins, in the gaming and play of neighborhood
children. Within the rich world of Uyghur children's play, I limit myself
here to a consideration of those activities of visibly greatest interest to
mehelle boys. Wintertime play activities, which usually took place in the
lanes and courtyards of Zawut, were readily observable during my field
research. During the summer, however, boys were more likely to venture away from the home and *mehelle* to play in the orchards, parks, and
urban spaces of Yining and its environs. Hence, the main forms of
boys' play I witnessed were concentrated over the winter months.
Nonetheless, in the activities I observed a clear pattern emerges.

During the days of Yining's long winter, icy snow-packed *mehelle*
lanes were dotted everywhere with clusters of boys playing for hours on
end with tops (*pirqirghuch*), which they or their fathers built out of metal
and wood. Tops are set in motion, always on icy surfaces to reduce fric-
tion, using a whip made of a stick eighteen to thirty-six inches long, to
one end of which is fastened an equally long segment of rope made of
thick string or twisted fabric. The rope is wrapped around the top, and
with a skilled flick of the whip's handle the top is set spinning, then
immediately whipped to increase its momentum. The first challenge in
the highly competitive domain of top spinning is to get one's top into a
stable upright position by whipping it. Once a boy can keep his top up,
he is able to compete with other boys to see whose top can stay up
longest. Usually four to six boys stood together, taking turns competing
in pairs in front of the others, who watched the contest with interest.
When tops collided, one was usually sent flying, giving a clear victory to
the boy whose top remained. There was no additional procedure associated with winning or losing, no keeping score, just briefly recognized
honor for the victor and embarrassment for the loser. These sessions
were an early arena in which boys competed for status in front of an
audience of peers. The seven-year-old boy living in Abidem's courtyard,
Yakupjan's youngest child Ilyar, was deeply invested in his top-spinning
ability. In this he received great encouragement from his father, who

Fig. 8   Once a child learns to walk, older siblings and cousins are encouraged to lead him or her away from the direct supervision of adults into the world of play. Here Ilyar teaches his young cousin Abdüshükür to play with marbles (photograph by the author, 1996).

made him a strong steel top of used machine parts and flooded a section of the family's courtyard with water to use as a practice rink. At the
beginning of top season, Ilyar remained outdoors in the freezing tem-
peratures, whipping his top until his hand became badly blistered from
the repetitive gesture. Yakupjan took great pride in his son's accomplishments. The toddler Abdüshükür, at sixteen months, often demanded a turn at the whip and would happily beat the motionless top
for minutes on end.

The flying of kites (*leglek*) was perhaps the second most popular winter
pastime for boys. On clear and windy days, the skies over Zawut would
often reveal six to ten kites flown by neighborhood children, and the
skies of adjacent *mehelle* were no less crowded. Kites were small and light,
often homemade, about twelve or fourteen inches square. Older boys
made and sold kites, and Abidem's grandsons Ablikim and Ablimit sold
their own homemade kites to neighborhood children for 3 *mao* ($0.04)
apiece. Aysajan the orphan, without even this amount to purchase a kite,
and without a father to help him make one, amused himself with a

homemade kite, a single sheet of paper attached to a length of magnetic tape taken from a discarded music cassette.

A third play activity of young boys seen in the lanes of the *mehelle* was the rolling of an iron hoop with an iron rod (*jirildaq*). Here, too, as with tops and kites, the point was to demonstrate one's ability to master the techniques needed to keep the play object in an upright position for as long as possible.[8]

These three forms of play, the most common toy-based play activities I observed among boys in the *mehelle*, share an obvious theme. In each, the main concern is to get the play object up and then to keep it up. As is particularly evident in the game of tops, the object for each boy is explicitly to demonstrate that his top can stay up longer than, and thereby defeat, the tops of other boys. These examples suggest boys' early exposure to a set of gestural and verbal metaphors in which dominance is uprightness, metaphors that reappear in the verbal jousting of adult men discussed in subsequent chapters.

Counting-out Rhymes

Counting-out rhymes are narrative devices that provide a specific frame for the play that follows. Through these usually complex verbal performances, the normal frame of everyday life is ruptured, and participants are transported into the collective and liminal world of play.[9] In *mehelle* play, a first counting-out rhyme is used to eliminate one person from the play group, the same or a different rhyme is used to eliminate a second person, and so on, until a single person remains. That person then assumes the "it" role.

A range of male and female adults recalled and recited for me the verses presented here. This first verse, according to the man who recited it, consists largely of nonsense syllables.

enni wenni arken body	*enni wenni arken tenni*
Barn tobacco tomato	*axor maxor pemidor*
es wes ki ku lu ku was	*es wes ki ku lu ku was*

Nonsense syllables, which are common in counting-out rhymes and other forms of children's speech, only enhance such rhymes' usefulness for demonstrating verbal agility.[10] The semantic indeterminacy of the item above was somewhat reduced in a second variant, according to the explanation of the forty-seven-year-old *mehelle* woman who provided it.

enni wenni brawny body
Barn tobacco tomato
Doll, you!

enni wenni türken tenni
axor maxor pemidor
kik liku was

The woman, who had learned to speak Russian at a privately run Russian elementary school in Yining, recalled believing as a child that the last line derived from Russian *kukla* (doll) and *vas* (you). The following verse was also widely known in the *mehelle*.

To the mountain, to the shmountain
Chain and bracelet
Where's your bracelet?
At the mountain
Mountain's mine, grave is mine
Chinese girl named "Egg-flower"
My dad's name is *poza*
In his pocket is a jug
Take it, my girl, the lizard
My right hand, my left hand
My pinky finger, *chim*, out!

taqqa tuqqa
zenjir halqa
halqang nede
taghda
tagh méning gör méning
qitay qizi Toxumgül
dadam éti poza
yanchuqida koza
éling qizim keslenchük
ong qolum song qolum
chimeltikim chim chiq

The following two counting-out rhymes were elicited from Abidem's daughter Maynur. In the first, the phrase "the time of beaded bonnets" is a reference to infanthood.

I took it, I gave it
  gössüm, I sold it
With my cap,
  I lowered my chin
Tightly pull on the beaded bonnet
In the time of beaded bonnets
Moon and sun
"Thunder-thunder," "drizzle"

*edim bedim [aldim berdim]**
  gössüm sedim [sattim]
shepkem bilen
  éngedim [engishidim]
him-him majan [marjan] bök
majan bökning zamanida
ay bilen kün
tarax-turux sim

---

*Here and below, square brackets enclose more standard spellings of words with altered pronunciation.

In the final line above, *tarax-turux* and *sim* are onomatopoeias for the sounds of thunder and drizzling rain.

Tea, tea, red tea	*chay chay pemil chay*
Tea that's come from the Six Cities*	*alte sheherdin kelgen chay*
In the heart it plays	*yürekde oynaydu*
At the fingernail it stays	*tirnaqda toxtaydu*
Bring me the prayer cap!	*helepbe shelepbe [elipber shilepe]*
Polish my boots for me!	*ötükümni maylap ber*
I won't take an old woman for a wife	*jugan xotun almaymen*
Bring me a fifteen-year-old maiden!	*on besh yashliq qiz ep ber*

Teasing Through Names

Name-teasing rhymes were common among *mehelle* children. That such rhymes may provide insight into the gendering of social identity during childhood is attested to by the fact that such rhymes target only males. *Mehelle* residents did not categorically deny the existence of such rhymes for girls, but none of the adult men, adult women, boys, or girls from whom I elicited name rhymes could recall any examples of rhymes for girls' names. In name-teasing rhymes, each rhyme has a fixed association with one and only one given name, so that the name used in a particular teasing rhyme does not vary even when external linguistic factors such as rhyme or alliteration do not make one name more obviously suitable than another. As such, these rhymes suggest that each generation reproduces certain taunts about the failure to comply with social norms, regardless of whether the persons so stigmatized are deserving or not. Consider, for example, the following.

Musa, go up the hill and fart!	*Musa döngge chiqip osa*

Another taunt is the following.

Abduraxman, like a haw-fruit	*Abduraxman jigidek*
[i.e., of small stature]	*[jigdedek]*
Eats five flatbreads	*besh nan yigidek*

---

*"Six Cities" is a traditional name for the oases situated along the periphery of the Taklimakan Desert in southern Xinjiang.

| Can't get up in the morning | *etigende qopalmay* |
| Just drinks noodle soup | *mentang ichigidek* |

Here the butt of the joke is teased, as one man explained, "because his belly is bad" (*qerini yaman*), meaning that he is a glutton. Another verse gives

| Kérim throat | *Kérim kikitek* [*kekirdek*] |
| Eats five flatbreads | *besh nan yigidek* |

The Kérims and Abduraxmans of the world are forever condemned, at least in the world of children's play, for being gluttons. The Tursuns, however, have it even worse.

| Tursun, may God beat you | *Tursun xuda ursun* |
| May you eat noodles and get diarrhea | *lengmen yep iching sursun* |

As in the first example given above, the victim here is teased for not being able to keep his anus shut. *Shatraq* (diarrhea, diarrheic), because it evokes images of an out-of-control anus, is an adjective frequently ascribed to adult men who lack self-control. Note also that the phrase "May God beat me" is frequently used in swearing oaths.

In only one case did I encounter a name-teasing rhyme dealing with the issue of adult sexuality. The item below, collected from a fifty-two-year-old *mehelle* man, replaces several lines in one of the verses given above to produce the following.

Abduraxman, like a haw-fruit	*Abduraxman jigidek*
Eats five flatbreads	*besh nan yigidek*
Has a house in Plank Factory *mehelle*	*pen zawutta öyi bar*
Has a girl with a cat-cunt	*müshük totaq qizi bar*
Meow	*miyaw*

This verse references the analogy vagina is to penis as cat is to mouse, which recurs in *mehelle* folklore. Despite the uncertain relationship between Abduraxman and his girl, the phrase "playing cat and mouse" was typically used to refer strictly to marital sexual relations, perhaps because there male apprehension about the power of female sexuality was heightened. In this analogy, the vagina/cat preys on, has claws and teeth to devour, the penis/mouse. Vernacular expressions for extramarital sexual intercourse, on the other hand, typically employed metaphors of food consumption, evoking the control men enjoyed believing they exercised over their mistresses. Additional metaphors for adult sexuality are considered in the next chapter.

Body Products: The Disposal of Teeth

A method used by adults and children to dispose of toenails, burying them under the domestic threshold in preparation for Judgment Day, was presented in Chapter 1. Here I describe an additional item of Uyghur body product folklore, one related to the disposal of teeth. When Mukerrem (age 10) lost a tooth at Abidem's house one January afternoon, she shoved the tooth inside a piece of home-baked *nan* bread, ran out of the house, and fed the bread and tooth together to her uncle's dog, while saying

Pearly tooth, give to me!	*ünche chishni manga ber*
Hatchet tooth, take for yourself!	*palta chishni özeng al*

A variant of this verse I elicited at a later date is

Your pearly tooth, give to me!	*ünche chishingni manga ber*
Your thick tooth, you take!	*yoghan chishingni sen al*

Although numerous *mehelle* residents explained this transaction in terms of the desire to have teeth as strong and as well formed as canine teeth, I mention here one other practice involving feeding bread to dogs, to encourage future exploration of possible links between these practices.

Mehelle residents often demonstrated a deep reverence for bread. Like holy saints and the Qur'an, bread was considered "great" (*ulugh*), and men swearing oaths often said "swear to bread" in place of "swear to God." When *nan* flatbread was given as a gift or loaned (to be repaid later) to friends, kin, or neighbors, it was always given in whole loaves. Bread broken into pieces was given only as alms to beggars, including both those who begged for sustenance and those who performed the ritual Ramadan begging described in Chapter 12. Most important, scraps of bread were never discarded but were always collected and saved to be eaten in some form later. Given this reverence for bread, it was striking to me that the two instances in which I saw bread disposed of in another way involved feeding bread to dogs. The second instance was in a practice Abidem described as follows.

A person with a foot ailment feeds a piece of bread to a dog and says, "That's for Master Qitmir (*Qitmir ghojam*)." The dog eats the bread, and when he leaves he takes the pain with him.

Qitmir (or Kitmer) is the name usually given to the dog in the legend of the Seven Sleepers of Ephesus, which circulates widely in Xinjiang and Central Asia generally.[11] In Uyghur variants of this legend, the dog Qitmir's legs are either broken or cut off by a group of men who do not wish him to follow along on their quest to find God; later his feet are miraculously restored.[12] Qitmir's recovery of his feet is perhaps the reason why the power to cure foot ailments is attributed to him.

Compelled Food Sharing

Unlike the institutions of adult gift exchange discussed in the next chapter, which disguise dynamics of competition within the reciprocal practices of hosting parties, making guests of friends and kin, and the occasional lending of goods or money, food exchange among children reveals more direct elements of competition. Through the practice described here, the child learns that skill and speed in reciting verbal formulas can force other children to submit and surrender their food. The practice, as I observed it in Zawut, works as follows. If A sees B eating food of some kind, A can initiate a game to compel B to hand over the food by saying *sori*.* If B is fast enough to begin to say *ésim* (in one variant, *ésimda*) before A has completed uttering *sori*, B can keep the food; otherwise she or he must hand the food to A. I first saw the game played by two girls, ages eight and ten. Later I tried to elicit an explanation of the game from the mother of one of the girls, who had been watching as well. The woman cryptically offered only the following verse by way of explanation.

Friends, friends, flower-meadow friends	*dos dos chimen dos*
Whatever we find, we eat equally	*néme tapsaq teng yeymiz*
Cock-a-doodle-doo	*qi-qi-qi*

---

*The root *sor-* means "to ask," and although the *-ri* is not a recognizable tense ending, the meaning of *sori* may lie close to "I ask for it."

The metaphorical use of "flower" to describe the period of childhood is also found in a number of adult verses describing attitudes about youth, to which I now turn.

Adult Attitudes About Youth

Young people say "I'm leaving"   *yashlar kétey deydu*
Old people say "I'm dying"   *qérilar öley deydu*
                                    —Abidem, citing a Uyghur proverb

One evening over dinner at Abidem's house, her son Yakupjan and son-in-law Téyipjan exchanged complaints about Yining's traffic police, who stood throughout the day at many of the city's major intersections, denying passage to donkey carts and horse-cart taxis, and inspecting motorists' papers in hopes of finding violations. The policemen regularly extracted fines for motorcycle violations, virtually always for missing documents, yet appeared indifferent to the countless moving violations that occurred around them. In describing the behavior of these police, Yakupjan cited the Uyghur proverb

When you have teeth, eat meat!   *chishning barida gösh ye*

I took his comment to mean that since the police could get away with it, it was to be expected that they would take advantage of their position, consuming what bribes or fines they could. When I asked him to explain the proverb, however, hoping to confirm my interpretation, his only response was to recite the following verse.

When I was a child, I reigned as a King   *yashliqim padishahliqim*
From every direction flowers came   *her tereptin gül kélur*
Who knew that just five days later   *tangla besh kündin kéyin*
No one would come to your side   *séning qéshinggha kim kélur*

I was delighted Yakupjan had provided me with yet another verse to record, but I told him I still wanted to hear him explain the meaning of the original proverb, and now the meaning of this second verse as well. He looked at me in surprise. Then, with a grin that suggested he sensed full well my frustration, he said, "You still don't get it? How about this one."

When you have a horse   *sen étingning barida*
Don't gallop downhill   *oyman'gha chapmay*
Gallop uphill   *döngge chap*

Ultimately Yakupjan did give in and share with me what each of these verses meant to him, confirming the interpretation that youth is a time when one is able to take advantage of the world around one, when one gets what one wants, when one has teeth to bite and a horse that can gallop uphill. Later I recalled having seen another reference to youth as a time of flowers, this in a 1930s-era collection of Uyghur proverbs I had among my books, and I was able to locate and discuss with Yakupjan and others that item as well, which is as follows.[13]

In the time of flowers [i.e., youth],   *gül waqtida*
    squeeze your flower shut   *gülüngni qis*
When the flowers are finished,   *gul tügiside*
    squeeze your anus shut   *qongangni qis*

This verse, I learned, was known to many *mehelle* adults, all of whom agreed that it described adult nostalgia for childhood as a time when everything comes easily. The final admonition to "squeeze your anus shut" refers to the norm that an adult must know how to maintain self-control. The use of a clenched anus as a metaphor for self-control is examined in more detail in the discussion of nicknaming in Chapter 8.

———

If childhood is a time of flowers, the transition into adulthood is a period of increasing social obligations, a time when young men face new demands to establish a more autonomous sense of self-identity and to take their place in the local community by participating in adult social activities. In the following chapter, I explore the experiences of older boys and girls in the *mehelle* as they court and wed, and as they find expression in their adult lives of the gendered sociality that has been inculcated in them during their youth.

6

Marriage, Mistresses, and Masculinity

Gender and Adult Social Life

When the turtledove sings, it cries
"He fears his wife, he fears his wife."

— Gheni, male *mehelle* resident (age 33)

For men in the *mehelle*, a concern with managing relationships with women, not surprisingly, was a recurring feature in their performance of masculine identities. In this chapter, I present a range of materials, mainly folklore and personal narratives, regarding male-female relations in the *mehelle*. I first discuss courtship activities and the wedding ceremony and then examine adult relationships between men and women, comparing marital relations with the social activities that accompany men's extramarital relationships. After this, I examine the gendering of guesting and gifting practices in the lives of men and women. A recurring theme in the materials presented here is suggested by the epigraph to this chapter, in which even the birds in the sky wait ready to taunt a man if he fails to demonstrate that his masculinity consists in dominating, and not being dominated by, women.

Courtship

In contemporary Xinjiang, state marriage laws passed in the 1950s prohibit the polygamy formerly sanctioned by Islamic law. Travelers' accounts dating back a century prior to the passage of those laws, however, suggest that polygamy was never a deeply ingrained feature of local society.

A historical perspective on local courting practices is found in materials collected by N. N. Pantusov in Yining in the 1870s, which document ribald courting parties (*mejlis*) that took place between groups of boys and girls. According to one account, boys initiated a musical exchange by singing verses such as the following.[1]

The moon is your face,	*ay yüzliri*
and a flower the bud of your lips	*gül libliri ghunche*
And a bud is not yet a flower,	*ghunche gül emes*
do not open, bud	*échilma ghunche*
Don't be someone's dream come true	*bolmaydur kishining murat hasil*
Don't be the sweetheart of their heart,	*könglidiki yari bolma*
young blossom	*ghunche*
Each day one thousand times,	*séni her künde ming*
I long to see you	*körgüm kélédur*
I long to hold you to my breast,	*quchaqimgha élip*
and kiss you	*süygüm kélédur*
I long to run *mudam* with	*séning bilen mudam yürgüm*
you	*kélédur*
If you don't look at me,	*manga bir baqmasang*
I long to die	*ölgüm kélédur*

Girls replied with verses of their own, such as the following.

Kiss me, my dear, I will be	*süy méni janim men séningki*
your own	*bolay*
Don't let your heart break, my sweet	*buzma könglüngni nigarim*
Until death, I'll be your slave	*ölgüche qulung bolay*
In the garden you watered with your pitcher	*baghda chögen sarghérip-tur*
You watered me into the ground	*yer sarghatti méni*
You were on fire, your eyes like embers	*özi otluq közi choghluq*
You made me weep and moan	*zar yighlatti méni*

| I could not stand the fire of your passion | *otungizgha chidiyalmaymen* |
| And my tears of blood flowed | *qan yighlap-yürdüm* |

In the dozens of verses Pantusov provides, images of boys watering plants with their watering pots and of girls as unopened flowers, unable to withstand boys' actions, are common. These can be readily understood as metaphors for adolescent sexuality, particularly for female virginity and male desire. Although the image of "crying blood" is widely used in vernacular Uyghur to mean "crying intensely," it seems relevant in the face of the numerous metaphors for virginity around it to consider the possibility that "tears of blood" might refer also, at least in this context, to the breaking of the hymen.

Younger boys, Pantusov notes, in addition to expressing desire for girls younger than or the same age as themselves, might also address older, more experienced girls (who delighted in teasing younger boys), by singing verses such as the following.

My melon may be small, but if I were	*kichikkine chilgemni*
to offer it to you, you'd eat it	*ichip bersem yersiz*
You say that the one on the seat of honor	*tördikini chong dep*
is big, and that I am small	*méni kichik der siz*
But when we are playing, the two of us,	*oynashqanda ikkimiz*
I'll make you cry	*yighlaturmen sizni*
And when you are pressed down beneath	*astinimgha basqanda*
me, then you'll call me older brother	*akam dersiz bizni*

In this last verse we see that boys are aware older females might taunt and tease them for having a "small melon," and that the full demonstration of their masculinity includes proving their ability to literally make women cry by sexually or physically dominating them.

In the 1990s I encountered no evidence that courting parties still took place; nonetheless, most matches in the *mehelle* resulted from courting between adolescents or young adults unsupervised by their parents or other older kin. One of Abidem's grandsons, at the age of sixteen, was considered by all adults in the family to be "good at earning money," and he himself said that he expected soon to be able to court a girl with the intention of marriage. He was caught several times at his family's produce stand giving away vegetables to two girls his age who often came to talk with him, drawing the ire of his more profit-minded thirteen-year-old brother. Another of Abidem's grandsons, eighteen-year-old Mehmud, on the other hand, rarely had any money, and his parents and older kin often spoke of their concern for his future, and of his need to establish an occupation.

When boys do begin to court girls, it is likely that anxieties about encountering a female sexuality more powerful and more experienced than their own, such as were hinted at in the verses above, may be part of that courtship experience. Consider, for example, the tensions revealed in the following joke, which circulated in Yining in the 1990s.

One day a guy is sitting with his girlfriend in an orchard, and he asks her, "Ayshibü, before going with me, how many other guys did you go with?"

She gets all shy and turns around and sits facing the other way. After she's been sitting there for a while, the kid is thinking, "I shouldn't have asked, now she must be angry at me," and he gives her a big slap on the back.

"Don't be angry, Ayshibü," he says, and she snaps back, "Sit still, or I'll lose count!"

This joke evokes the tensions that exist for men when comparing their own levels of experience and desire with those of their partners, and gives voice to men's anxieties that women will prove more experienced than they.

The Wedding Ceremony

Most adults in the *mehelle* first married in their late teens or early twenties to partners they themselves had chosen. When a courting couple is ready to be married, the services of a matchmaker (*elchi*), typically an older man, are secured. For the wedding of Nurnisa, the daughter of one of Abidem's neighbors, the matchmaker described his role in the wedding to me in this way.[2]

The matchmaker goes to the girl's house and writes down, in conversation with her family, the wedding present list (*toyluq*). The boy's side shortens the list. The girl's side agrees to the changes. Three or four of the bride's female kin bring fabric (*rexmet-tazim*) for new outfits for the groom's immediate kin. The boy's side then writes a guest list for the "whiteness tea" (*aqliq chay*).

The "whiteness tea" is held by the bride's family for the groom's family, based on a guest list set by the latter in an attempt to receive a benefit equal to what they themselves will give the bride's family in the form of wedding presents. Several days before the wedding, an additional "consulting tea" (*meslihet chay*) is held by the groom for his male friends, as a sort of bachelor party. These gatherings are conducted much as other men's gatherings are, with drinking, music, and laughter. One added feature is that the men decide, working all together or in small groups, who to invite to the wedding, and they fill out invitation cards that will be delivered to the invitees over the next few days.

On the day before Nurnisa's wedding, while preparations were under way throughout the house, the matchmaker made a visit to the bride's home and made a brief speech to her friends and family.

In our hearts, we hope that this wedding will be pretty (*chirayliq*), will be good, that it will be very uniting. Making a name for ourselves, gaining status, for us such things are not possible here, instead, we hope just that it can be nice and simple. . . . This is a widow's family, a poor family. She has spent 2,000 *yuan*, the widow, spent so much money, weddings cost so much. But we say, "So what if money is scarce, we ourselves can still be elegant" (*pul az bolsun, ozi saz bolsun*).

After he was done, the bride's mother praised his speech, saying, "What you have said is right, words are not to eat or drink (*gep ichmek yémek emes*)." This ambiguous phrase permits at least two readings. In one sense, the phrase can be taken to mean "words spoken are not like food or drink," that is to say, words spoken are an enduring good, unlike food, which is "pissed and shit away." "Eaten-and-pissed" (*yégen-süygen*) and "pissed-and-shit" (*süygen-chichqan*) are common phrases for describing something without enduring value. An equally plausible parsing of the phrase would render it as "drinking and eating are not worth speaking about." In this sense the sentence is an attempt to deny what the speaker knows all too well—that a main focus of neighborhood gossip after a wedding is the quality and quantity of food served to guests.

During the wedding ceremony itself, as a part of the rite that transforms the two individuals into a single conjugal unit, the importance of bread as a source of strength for the new household is indicated by its use in bracketing the actual taking of vows. Immediately before vows are exchanged, the woman covers her head with a scarf and places two pieces of *nan* bread into a bowl of salt water. The man is asked three times if he takes the woman, twice remaining silent "out of shame (*xijil-liq*) in front of his elders," and the third time saying, "I take her."[3] She, too, is asked twice if she accepts, and then again a third time, when she finally whispers her assent to the age-mates and relatives who stand at her side. Then all rise and congratulate the pair. The bride and groom now see who can be quickest to remove the bread from the bowl of salt water and feed it to their friends.

Throughout the day of Nurnisa's wedding, traditional congratulatory verses were spoken to the groom, including "May there be a child at your head and riches at your feet" and "May you have a child in front of you and riches behind you." Verses spoken to the bride were all variants of the phrase "May your head be a head and may your feet be a stone." One married woman explained the reference to the stone as a figurative way of saying "May the new bride stay in her new house."

Some *mehelle* residents recalled a past tradition of the bride's male kin rolling her up inside a carpet before handing her over to the groom and his kin, at which point a representative of the bride's patriline would speak the phrase "The bones are ours, the flesh is yours" (*ustixani bizning, göshi silerning*). No one could recall the last time a rug had been used in a *mehelle* wedding—as with many practices they viewed as "traditional," several suburban residents commented that in the countryside such things still flourished—but the verse was still routinely spoken when the bride passed to the groom's kin. Just as the patriline is referred to as the "owner/master of the bones" during a child's naming ceremony, here the phrase invokes the idea that the bones of the bride remain the property of her patriline, and only her flesh is symbolically given over to the patriline of the groom. *Mehelle* residents explained that this verse was also used in the past whenever a child was taken to religious specialists to undergo training in Islamic prayer and practice. In both cases, to paraphrase residents' explanations, the implication was "You may physically discipline the flesh of this person, but do not go too far, for if the punishment goes too deep, it will be considered an affront to the bones, which we will still defend as a matter of honor."

Wedding celebrations are spread over three days. On the wedding day itself, a banquet (*toy*) is held; on the second day, a "groom's invitational" (*oghul terepning chirliqi*) is held; on the third day, a "bride's invitational" (*qizning chirliqi*) is held. In several ways, these wedding gatherings exemplify a general pattern in the spatial and temporal organization of mixed-gender social events. First, women and men are typically invited to arrive at different times, women arriving around noon and men joining them only later in the evening. Second, women sit and socialize together for many hours, whereas men stay only for a banquet meal. Finally, when men and women are present together at social events, they do not sit with each other; in the case of large wedding banquets, for example, they sit at tables on separate sides of the room.

Throughout the four days of the wedding (the preparation day and days for the wedding ceremony and the groom's and bride's invitationals), the groom's male kin will, at various times, be present as guests or casual visitors in the bride's home. During one of these visits, it is expected that they will steal a number of items. The first is a pair of bowls. The men take these two bowls to the home of the groom's parents, where they are placed at the bottom of a wooden blanket chest upside down, to be left there until the bride bears a child. The similarity between two upturned bowls and the breasts that will nourish the patriline's future member suggests this is a magical means for ensuring a strong supply of milk for the child, a supply as plentiful as milk pouring from an overturned bowl. The other stolen item is one of the nails on which cloths and utensils are hung near the cookstove of the bride's home. This nail is removed and nailed up over the hearth in the bride's new home. This, residents explained, ensures that the bride will "stay" with her new family. Given the high frequency of divorce in Xinjiang, remarked on by observers of the region for more than century, it is likely that "stay" here refers more to the stability of the marriage than to the bride's health.

Women Who Flee

Not all *mehelle* couples were joined together through weddings negotiated in advance by kin groups, however, as I first learned in a somewhat dramatic manner. One mid-morning in May, as I left Abidem's house and walked out onto the main lane, I saw a large crowd gathered around Abidem's neighbor Dilshat (age 22). Rivulets of blood streamed down his face, mixed with what I soon realized was beer. A hefty woman stood yelling fiercely at Dilshat; he seemed quite terrified. The onlooker next to me pointed to the woman and explained cryptically: "He said 'I'm taking a fleeing girl,' so she broke a beer bottle over his head." Dilshat was having a tough time of it—the woman had six or seven years and forty pounds on him, and was using both to her advantage. As soon as the woman's tirade lost some of its momentum, Dilshat turned his back and scurried down the lane into his courtyard, directly across from Abidem's. I followed him down but stepped instead into Abidem's courtyard, where a girl of seventeen was squatting behind the gate. Dilshat soon came over to join her, and together they explained their situation to Abidem. The woman who had attacked him was his elder sister. He had taken this girl, he said, introducing her as his bride, but since he had no money for a wedding, the girl chose to "flee" her own family to join him. Such a union is seen as shameful for both kin groups. Men who take "fleeing" brides are criticized for "stealing" their brides, although the same people who called this "stealing" acknowledged in this and several similar cases I learned of afterward that the woman herself has always chosen to flee. Nonetheless, this was viewed as stealing in a social sense, since the alliance was not formalized through reciprocal exchanges between kin groups.

In some cases of "fleeing," kin groups are able to negotiate an alliance through an exchange of gifts after the fact. Abidem herself had visited a town some 40 km from Yining to work out the exchanges to be made in such a situation. As the oldest living member of her patriline, Abidem had been recruited by the groom's parents to supervise the negotiations. She and I traveled to the town by bus and waited in vain for the groom and his friends to arrive on their motorcycles, which we later learned had broken down on their way to meet us. As we waited, Abidem asked the driver of a passing horse-cart taxi if he "knew of a girl nearby who 'fled' away to a boy at Bayköl *mehelle*." The man shrugged his shoulders and called over a girl of nineteen or so. He asked her the same question, but she, too, was stumped. "There are lots of girls around here who flee," she said. "It's hard to tell." After waiting several hours, Abidem and I returned home, and I never did learn how the matter was resolved.

Married Life

Even within the marriages of Abidem's five daughters, about which I learned and observed a good deal, the considerable differences between married partners' affective bonds belie any simple generalizations about Uyghur marriages. The following vignettes from my field notes, however, do demonstrate something of the range of marital attitudes present in Yining's *mehelle*.

This evening I found Senemgül at home in a bad mood. Téyipjan [her husband] told her yesterday he was going to go visit kin in Turpanyüz, but he had actually gone to party with friends—Maynur told me this earlier that day—and he stayed in the countryside overnight.

"Has Téyipjan appeared yet?" I asked her, assuming that by this time he was back.

"No!" she said, eyes flashing in anger. "He called last night, he and his friends, 'I'm sorry it's so late, I can't make it home, there are no more buses,' he said." She fussed with the baby for a few minutes.

"Were you mad?" I asked.

"Yes! I scolded him in front of his friends. I told him, 'I'm home alone, I'm scared.' He just told me to go to my mother's."

"How did you scold him?" I asked.

"Well, I didn't *scold* him . . ."

"She's scared of him," her mother laughed, appearing in the doorway. "She's scared of Téyipjan, she is . . ."

"I am not scared of him, I just . . . respect him. In front of his friends I called him *sen* ["you" familiar form]," she says, by way of answering my question. "And I always call him *siz* ["you" polite form] out of respect. I respect him, I don't fear him." Remember that Senemgül is eight months pregnant.

In this incident, we see that for men, the increased freedom of mobility they enjoy compared to their wives is both a fundamental condition of inequality and a resource they are glad to draw on in their interactions with their wives, especially during periods of conflict.

This second anecdote shows more of the animosity that routinely colored interactions between spouses. It also shows the common masculine trait of purposefully pushing another to anger in an attempt to demonstrate one's own superiority.

Ablimit Hajim (age 45, also known as Haj'kam) was resting in the shade this hot June afternoon while his wife Anise was baking *nan* bread, which even in winter is a hot job for the person who must crouch over the oven to add and remove the breads. She walked by, her face beet red from the hot sun and the fire, and Ablimit shook his head with disapproval.

"Why don't you let your mother do it?" he said accusingly, as if the diminution of his wife's strength is a loss he resents. He also knew full well that Abidem, at age seventy-six, had stopped baking her own bread several years earlier.

Anise was now "all better," Haj'kam had told me that morning, referring to her recent health problems (possibly related to the tuberculosis she had suffered years earlier) and to the "expensive medicine" he had bought for her with much blustering about the cost. But there she was, baking *nan*, then chopping firewood for a second round of baking. She picked up one of the scraps of lumber that littered their yard while their new house was being built, and immediately he yelled at her, "Hey, we can use that!" Even for him, his attitude today seems excessive, designed to provoke. "He must be angry about something," I thought.

He left the *chayxana* and went into the *dalan*, where thick adobe walls kept the air cool on hot, windless days. He sprawled out on the high *supa*, dangled his feet over the edge, and called Anise in to serve him some tea. Anise walked in when he called, empty-handed, and asked him to move over so she could sit too, even though most of the *supa*'s edge was empty. He stared blankly in her direction, as if she wasn't there, then slowly he extended his raised foot.

"Take my shoe off."

"My hands hurt," she said, then walked away. Haj'kam shook his head, a look of utter disgust on his face.

"Where do you get off putting on airs like a rich person," he grumbled softly after she was out of earshot.

This incident dramatized for me somewhat more openly than I was used to seeing in spousal relations the masculine behavioral trait of purposefully pushing others to anger, a trait I explore in detail in the next chapter.

Once couples were married, patterns of social interaction among men were strikingly different from those among women. Instances of spouses socializing together were not common in the *mehelle*. As a single man, I was only rarely invited to social events that young married couples did attend together. My perception, however, was that such events were rare but growing in popularity among couples in their twenties. At one gathering of married couples I did attend, eight couples shared an evening at one of the couple's homes. As guests arrived, the men sat together on pads on the floor in the *saray* guest room, and the women remained elsewhere out of sight. Only after the last of the couples arrived did the women enter the room and sit together on the floor across from the men. After thirty minutes, the women left, and the men spent the next several hours in each other's company.

Some Zawut residents described a kind of social event attended by men and women, called *wichir*, held in private homes rather than at restaurants or outdoor settings. These were sometimes held before and after weddings and were attended mostly by young people in their teens or twenties. Participants drank tea, enjoyed ballroom-style *tansa* dancing, and shared a meal. As one twenty-something woman, concerned to impress on me the propriety of these events, explained, "Right-minded people play *wichir*, not backward people."

Marriage, Mistresses, and Sexuality

Once I went into a dumpling restaurant at Erduchu. I go in and order ten dumplings. I take a dumpling (*manta*), bite into it, and inside it, there is nothing but onion! So I'm chewing it, saying "*xep xep*" [an expression of dissatisfaction] and the cook gets up and comes over, and says, "What's the matter, why are you saying '*xep*'?"

"Oh, I'm not angry at you. I'm angry at my wife. Whenever I take home a kilo of meat, and I give it to her, she says 'How can I make dumplings with just one kilo of meat?' But look at this, dumplings can be made even with just onion!"

—Hésam Qurban, Yining jokester

Men in the *mehelle* rarely expressed affection for their wives in front of others. Levels of affection between spouses undoubtedly varied, of course, but some recurring features of spousal interactions as I observed them demonstrated to me that, for many couples, relations could often be rocky. One of those features was men's concern that they appear to dominate their wives in all matters.

The joke quoted above was received with special enthusiasm by *mehelle* men, stimulating my interest in it and leading to an analysis that will, I hope, provide a useful entry to understanding men's expressions of masculinity regarding sexual relations with women. First, Hésam's wife's comment that one kilo of meat was insufficient is a barely disguised insult to him, since it implies he is, in her eyes at least, a bad provider. No matter what he brings home for his wife to cook, she is not satisfied. By sharing this with the audience, he is revealing himself to be henpecked by his wife. At this point, the joke usually gets a loud laugh. Then he reveals to the audience, by sharing his astonishment at a meatless dumpling (*manta*), that all along he had taken her statement as culinary fact, not even realizing that she was insulting him. This is the final joke, when he shows that he hadn't even had the acuity to know he was being insulted.

Another layer of meaning in the joke derives from the fact that eating manta is a common folk metaphor for sexual intercourse. His wife's comment that he fails to supply enough meat to make *manta* implies that she withholds sexual activity to spite him for his economic inferiority. His comment that *manta* "can be made even with just onion" is, in my reading, a coded way of saying "Even if I bring home only vegetables, and do not have enough money to always buy what she wants me to buy, she should still give me sex." I am not suggesting this layer of meaning is obvious to an audience of *mehelle* men, only that these tensions are relevant and are associated with the anxiety men often manifested about appearing henpecked to their male friends.

The following verse, described independently by several *mehelle* residents as a sexual allegory, similarly relies on the metaphorical equivalence of eating meat and sexual relations.

At Mullah Axun's house	*molla axunning öyde*
They slaughtered a calf	*topaq soyuptu*
But still his five daughters	*molla axunning besh qizi*
Couldn't get their fill of meat	*göshke toymaptu*
Set out the dough on the kneading plank	*ashni sélinglar taxtida*
Slaughter the lamb in good time	*qoyni soyunglar waqtida*
Play away, young children	*oynanglar yash balilar*

It is worth noting here that the verb *oynash* (to play), which has a wide range of meanings in Uyghur, is used frequently to refer to young adolescents interacting in ways that suggest sexual contact.

Although sexual relations between spouses were virtually never discussed at any of the various kinds of informal all-male gatherings in which men regularly took part, sexual exploits outside marriage were frequently both a topic of conversation and an activity for many men. Below I discuss some of the attitudes men expressed about these activities as revealed in their narratives and folklore.

In the summer of 1995, soon after I arrived to begin fieldwork, two men stepped in to Abidem's courtyard. Both men were in their thirties, acquaintances from a short visit I made in 1992. "Come on," they said, "let's go shoot some pool." We walked toward the *consul,* a plaza in Yining's center that had a cluster of twenty or so outdoor pool tables covered by canvas awnings. As we crossed the street approaching the plaza, one of the men darted into a small shop and emerged a minute later carrying a purple bottle with a label in Chinese that read "God of One Hundred Loves." Just as I pondered his need for cologne prior to shooting pool, he walked off again, "to make a phone call," he explained. When he returned ten minutes later, it was with three young Uyghur women with powdered faces. The men, it seemed, had made other arrangements for the day; namely, they had invited the three women for an afternoon of amusement by the riverside, where we spent the next few hours drinking beer, telling jokes, and chatting, before going to a restaurant on the far side of town for a dish of Big Plate Chicken, a local specialty. Although I was initially surprised at how the day turned out, over the next year I had ample opportunity to accustom myself to participation in gatherings where men and their mistresses were present together and to hear men discuss their trysting activities.

Within the *mehelle,* sexual relations between men and women took place within the bonds of marriage, confined by the spatial configuration of home and hearth and the presence of kin and nosy neighbors. Trysting and extramarital sexual relations, not surprisingly, occurred outside the *mehelle.* A man sometimes met his mistress alone, although more frequently two or three couples met together. Many of these meetings involved socializing without sex, and took place in the more remote corners of the same parks and riverside areas that all local residents visited for picnics. Such meetings also took place in the city, usually in restaurants in the outskirts of the city situated as far as possible from the men's own *mehelle,* where their neighbors would be least likely to see them.

For sexual encounters, the city center, with its several large hotels, offered relative anonymity. The visiting of expensive hotels highlights one key feature of trysting practices—the expenditure. Only men who had the financial means to pay for restaurant meals, hotel rooms, and gifts of cash could afford to maintain mistresses. For these men, trysting was a marker of financial success and of the elevated social status financial success provided. This may help explain why group trysting was common; performing one's ability to tryst to an audience of friends raised one's status in the local community of men. Men also boasted about taking women into the surrounding countryside for sexual liaisons, particularly to the single-room buildings erected by farmers adjacent to fields far from their homes. Several farmers confirmed to me that this actually occurred and was not empty boasting, as I had first suspected.

Another monetary dimension of trysting is made clear in this field note passage, in which a man comments about his mistress, who had gone to Beijing with a friend whose husband was a heroin dealer there.

"She went to sell her cunt," he said gruffly. He took a drag on his cigarette and rubbed his crotch. All of a sudden he laughed, and waved his hand as if to be rid of her. "She'll come back, and I'll tell her it's over. What do I want with her anymore? I even used to give her money, every week, to spend, afterwards. Every time I'd give her something, forty *yuan* or fifty *yuan* [$5.00–6.25]."

"So, you give money then, do you?" I asked. I hadn't yet heard men discuss such things, but had wondered about the financial side of these relationships.

"It's safer if you give money."

"What are you talking about, 'safer'?" I asked.

"If the police ever get involved, they ask 'Did you pay her?' If you did, they let you go right away, since it's not a problem" [i.e., it is not the more serious issue of adultery].

For men who trysted, pagers were essential instruments for arranging meetings with their mistresses. Such men attended to their pagers constantly, conspicuously checking the readouts often in front of their male friends to look at the numbers of women who called them. One interesting inversion of the actual meaning pagers had in men's lives was expressed in several jokes that circulated in the *mehelle*.

A man and a woman were going to get a divorce. They went out in the fields to talk about their problems and sat down on adjacent rows of raised earth.

The man's mother-in-law, she's there trying to patch things up, saying, "Why don't you two try to make things better?"

The man says, "I want to, but she won't." Just then the wife farts, and the man calls over, "My dear, why are you farting?"

And she says, "That's just my boyfriend, he hasn't heard from me, so he's paging my cunt."

A guy and his wife are out in the melon fields, and he's fucking her, and when he's doing it, she farts. So he says, "I must be pretty good, huh, fucking you so hard you farted."

And she says, "No, that was just my boyfriend beeping me."

In these jokes, instead of the pager allowing men sexual access to women outside their marriage, the wife's genitals become the object of other men's "paging" activities. In the second joke, the wife is also unsatisfied with her husband's sexuality, a fact she shares with him just at the moment he reveals his complete confidence in his own ability.

The first of these jokes was related one day in the marketplace among a group of merchants, prompted by an incident in which they overheard a married couple shopping together. A woman examining the wares hung on a clothing rack, behind which the men were hidden, criticized her husband in public, saying, "You don't know how to buy anything, and every time I try to buy something, you say you don't like it." To this her husband replied, "Don't squeeze your cunt!" (*totaqing qisma*). The metaphor of "squeezing one's cunt" expresses the male attitude that a woman is being too aggressive, since, in my reading of this phrase, it is his genitals that should be doing the pushing on her, not hers squeezing on him. Prompted by this overheard comment, in which men's expectations about sexual roles are reversed, one of the merchants immediately recounted the first joke, in which male expectations about sexual roles are also reversed.

Men's attitudes about relations with their mistresses were also expressed in a number of proverbs. One day the mistresses of two merchants paged their men, and when the men telephoned them, one of the women demanded an immediate daytime rendezvous at a spot not far from the men's market stalls. If the men refused, the women threatened to visit them at their stalls, an arrangement men usually avoided. The men spent the next five hours sitting and partying with the women, one of whom was departing for several months and claimed to be quite upset about leaving her man behind. The man presented himself as decidedly cavalier about the separation. At one point in the conversation, he complained to his mistress about the trouble she had caused him that day, saying, "The Mullah who has no donkey has peaceful ears" (*ishigi yoq mollaning qulaqi tinch*).* The meaning this proverb had for him, as a form of self-reflection, seemed clear. If you want to have a donkey, you have to expect it to sometimes bray and be a nuisance; if you have a mistress, you must expect she'll cause you problems every now and then.

Later at that same gathering, during an exchange of angry words with his mistress, the same man exclaimed at one point, "A wooden pot burns once, it doesn't burn twice" (*yaghach qazan bir qaynaydu, ikki qaynimaydu*). This proverb suggests several possible interpretations. The man was attempting to convince the woman that the affair was ended permanently, that there was no going back. Like a wooden pot consumed by fire, of which nothing was left to reuse, the affair had happened and was over, he was suggesting; to think it could continue to go on would be as foolish as to think one could use a wooden pot over and over. It is tempting to also connect this remark to a particular joke I heard this same man tell four or five times in the month prior to that gathering, in which a stirred pot is used as a metaphor for a woman's vagina: "I'd like to have what's in your pot," a man says. "You can't," the woman answers. "Why not?" "Because I'm cooking tomatoes," she says, implying she is menstruating. If this metaphor is relevant here, his comment that the pot is gone may express his feeling that the sexual link that had connected them was gone.

Guests, Gifts, and Gendered Sociality in the *Mehelle*

When you go to a wedding, first eat then go
Leave your children at home, then go

—Uyghur proverb[4]

As a young child, Hésam went along with his mother to be a guest at a wedding. As soon as he saw the tablecloth covered with treats, he starting demanding, "Mom, give me one of those! Oh, and one of those!"

---

*"Mullah" is a title for a Muslim cleric and an honorific for a learned man.

Embarrassed in front of the others, his mother said, "Funny, he never eats candy when we give it to him at home."

"What are you saying?" Hésam piped up. "You yourself always say wait until we go guesting."

—Maxmut Muhemmet[5]

The lives of Zawut residents were woven together with the lives of their friends, kin, and neighbors through many forms of reciprocal exchange. Perhaps the dominant form of exchange in Zawut was reciprocal household visitation. In the local idiom, *mehelle* residents alternated between "being guests" (*méhman bolmaq*) and "making guests [of others]" (*méhman qilmaq*). Guesting, in its two reciprocally linked modes of being and making, formed a single pattern of social exchange central in the lives of Zawut residents, although in many ways guesting and gifting were far more central in the lives of women than men. Consider the following two incidents, paraphrased from my field notes, in which men articulate their views on guesting exchanges.

Aliye and Anwarjan, a married couple in their forties, sit cross-legged in their *chayxana* eating dinner. Both are tired from a hot day tending their busy market stall. The woman suggests that they pay a short visit later that evening to her mother, who lives nearby. The man twists up his face.

"Why? Did she grow horns? Are we supposed to go see if she grew two horns or six horns, or what?" He glares at her, his eyes wide, until she turns away.

On a hot June afternoon, Aliye and Anise walk into the courtyard that their younger sister Maynur (age 34) and her husband and two daughters share with her husband's brother's family. They find Maynur washing clothes at an outdoor spigot.

"We've been waiting for you for an hour," they complain, the "we" referring not only to themselves but also to two other adult women and seven of their children. The group had planned to go by minibus to a village fifteen km away, where they would take tea and exchange gifts at six or eight different households over a two-day period.

Maynur's husband steps out of his house, furious at the conversation he has overheard, and yells at his wife,

"You fucking beggar, you! All of you, you're all beggars. Go on then, get out if you're going." Maynur had anticipated his anger; her overnight bag had been packed the day before, and she had been doing chores for the past hour while she waited for her sisters to arrive and escort her out of the house safely.

These passages, to me, demonstrate something more than the general tensions that existed between married couples in Zawut. Although the two intended visits were quite different (the second was a typical example of what residents called "guesting," the first was a more informal visit), they share one feature: men viewed them with derision and contempt. Indeed, men's attitudes toward informal visiting and more formal "guesting" generally consisted of viewing both practices as more appropriate for women than men. The husband's response in the second incident is best understood in the context of the overall systems of exchange found in Zawut. His anger in itself is not surprising if we see it as a response to the temporary loss of his wife's labor, to her having made an independent decision, to her having successfully hidden the visit from him until her sisters arrived. It is his use of the word "beggar," however, a word not typically used as an insult, that is unexpected, and that hints at the underlying differences that exist between the social ties women create through reciprocal gift exchange and those men create in the agonistic masculine domains of the marketplace and the all-male drinking party.

Guesting and Gifting in Women's Lives

In each of several distinct types of household visitation practices, women participated far more prominently than did men. In kin visitations of the type described in the second incident above, groups of female kin traveled together to visit multiple households in other *mehelle* or in nearby villages. Women gone guesting typically stayed overnight for two or three days, sometimes longer. Exactly when such visits would end guests themselves could not say; to demonstrate their desire to have guests stay as long as possible, hosts often good-naturedly invoked the phrase "When you arrive is up to you, when you leave is up to me!"

On such visits, women usually took daughters of all ages and sons up to the age of six or seven. Once past this age, boys would be left at home on their own to play with friends, perhaps to be supervised by older brothers. In the summertime, guesting between women became more frequent. When all the women and daughters were away guesting for extended periods of time, men at home faced difficulties having food to eat, and perhaps having clean clothes to wear, since men were utterly dependent on women for domestic labor.

Most guesting visits were themselves elements in a broader system of prestations and social relations. Many visits, in other words, were prompted by the occurrence of life-cycle events; births, circumcisions, marriages, and funerals were among the most common reasons for groups of women to undertake visits, although often the visits were delayed for weeks or even months after the events they honored. Abidem, for example, went with several of her daughters and a group of children eight months after her eldest brother had passed away to make a customary visit to one of her nieces "to inform her of the death."

Another occasion on which women gather is the "mothers' tea" (*anilarning chéyi*). Such a tea was held for one young woman in Zawut who was about to give birth to a second child, and whose first child had died shortly after birth. Abidem explained that seven female religious specialists (*büwi*) would visit the woman and prepare seven pieces of *yit*, a fried dough cake. Whereas *yit* prepared for festive holidays were made using wheat flour, eggs, and milk, for this event they would be made from a mixture of rice, oil, and milk. Abidem explained that the tea was held "for our mothers," meaning not only the participants' actual mothers but also their female ancestors. "Büpatime, Büzörem, they are our mothers," Abidem said, explaining that these were the two saintly women whose once-separate graves at Sultan Mazar, a shrine she often visited, had been combined into the single grave described in Chapter 3.

Other occasions for gathering include the "weariness tea" (*harduq chay*), held roughly on the one-year anniversary of a wedding, and the "salutation tea" (*salam chay*). In early May Aliye gave a salutation tea for around twenty married women, with thirty-five persons total in attendance, including numerous children and five adult men who sat outside the house in the courtyard most of the day. All the women brought small cash gifts as well as *edimechilik* gifting objects, which they handed to Aliye as a means of reciprocating for her hosting the tea. She in turn gave gifts to four special guests, all recently married women, gifts that included sets of dishes and other household items. Several weeks later, Aliye's sister Anise had a salutation tea for fifteen different

Fig. 9   In the days after Ramadan and Qurban, men visit the homes of neighbors, friends, and relatives. These visits often last a few minutes, long enough for guests to eat a morsel of food and pay their respects to their hosts. Here friends of Abidem's deceased husband, Tursun, rest for a moment in her *saray* after a long morning of post-Ramadan visiting (photograph by the author, 1996).

women, for which Abidem helped Anise prepare a meal to serve to her guests. Later than night, Abidem chatted with Aliye about the day's events.

"As soon as the guests left, [Anise's husband] Haj'kam asked us what the take in cash was."

"All those people at my *salam chay,*" Aliye interjected, "and 'their father' [i.e., her husband] never asked me how much I took in."

"So I asked him," Abidem went on. "That money, that two hundred and fifty *som,* why don't you give it to me?" She giggled. "He couldn't stand it! He started saying, 'We spent so much money on the food, Mother, we just can't afford it.' And I was only teasing him!"

Holiday visiting is also an important, indeed obligatory, form of guesting in the *mehelle.* Both the Qurban and Ramadan festivals are followed by periods of intensive guesting. After Ramadan, for example, men are expected to make guesting visits to the homes of all their neighbors, kin, and friends within three days. Zawut men traveled alone or in small groups, first visiting every home in their own *mehelle,* then the homes of each of their relatives and friends in other *mehelle.* Initially men traveled together in groups of two or three, but as these smaller groups made their rounds and crossed paths, they often informally merged to form larger groups. Most visits lasted only a few minutes, some a bit longer. At each home, each visitor made an effort to eat at least one mouthful of the food that was offered, although many tried explicitly to take two bites, since just one was considered too cursory. Guests were sometimes poured a bowl of tea, although often none was even offered, or was only offered halfheartedly, and visitors refused as expected. On the first day after Ramadan, more than forty men came to Abidem's home to pay their respects (*hürmet bildürüsh*). On those visits, adults gave money to any children present, usually brand new bills they obtained in advance from banks for that purpose, crisp two-*mao* or five-*mao* notes, which they handed out one at a time. Holiday visiting for women was entirely different; women's visiting began on the fourth day after Ramadan, once men's visits had ended, and lasted an entire month. Like men, women made their rounds to the homes of kin, friends, and neighbors, but women's visits were fewer, and were far more leisurely, often lasting several hours.

For the Qurban Festival, the Festival of Sacrifice, most households in the *mehelle* slaughtered a sheep. A household unable to afford a sheep usually received offerings of raw meat (*qurbanliq*) from those that did. Qurban household visitation patterns were similar to those for Ramadan. Men made obligatory but perfunctory visits to neighbors, friends, and kin, and at each home men were expected to take a bite or two of mutton from the animal sacrificed. And as with Ramadan, women had a month to complete their more leisurely visits after men's visits were over.

Women's household visits of all kinds were in most cases accompanied by a special form of gift giving. The gifting objects exchanged by guesting women were called *edimechilik,* derived from *ademiyetchilik/ ademgerchilik,* meaning "humanity." *Adem,* cognate with the Biblical Adam, is the Uyghur word for "person." These gifts are thus called, in a sense, person-ness, and those who exchange them thereby constitute themselves as persons. As a corollary, we shall see below, women who did not participate in these exchanges stigmatized themselves as being less than fully social beings. The gift objects themselves varied little, and almost all the gifts I saw change hands were one of three things: a piece of manufactured cloth between one and two meters in length, a wrapped package of sugar cubes, or a brick of pressed tea. Less frequently exchanged items included lumps of rock sugar, small blankets or towels, and items of clothing, especially clothing for small children. For most adult women in Zawut, *edimechilik* were exchanged many times each month, whenever women gathered to celebrate or remember some event in their lives or the lives of their kin.

This form of giving can be seen as an instantaneous reciprocation for being treated as a guest, although local women did not necessarily see it in that way. At larger gatherings, where ten or more women arrive with *edimechilik* gift objects to present to their host, the host reciprocates before her guests leave by giving each one a parting gift of a bag containing small breads, fried dough twists, candies, cookies, peanuts, seeds, or nuts. This form of gift giving was called "making *petmus*" (*petmus qilish*).

Only once did I witness a man participating in what I thought was the exchange of *edimechilik* items. When Abidem and her adult daughter visited a local saint shrine, each woman gave gifts to the elderly Uyghur man who had unlocked the gate for them; one gave a piece of cloth, the other a packaged dress shirt. The women told me that such gifts were customarily made to shrine attendants. Later, however, the women made clear that these were not *edimechilik* but simply "offerings" (*nezir*).

Women's complex feelings about this form of gift exchange are demonstrated by several comments Abidem made to me over the course of the year. One day toward the end of my stay, I went into the *saray* to return some of my Uyghur-language dictionaries and reference books to the wooden chest where I stored them. I found Abidem sitting alone on the floor, rearranging pieces of gifting cloth, and contemplating which one to use to make a curtain. She looked up at me, she with her cloth in her hands, me with my books in mine, and said

Crows say "caw"	*qaghalar qagh eytidu*
And make their hearts happy	*könglini xosh étidu*

Before that day I had asked her several times how *edimechilik* gift exchange worked, and she had done her best to explain it to me. But when I chanced upon her refolding and reflecting on these cloths, she appeared self-conscious. Her spontaneous comment suggested to me that she knew the pieces of cloth in themselves might be as meaningless to other people (men, for example) as a crow's cawing was to humans, and that her desire to refold the cloths and to bring back the memories of the friends and relatives who gave them to her might seem foolish; but spending time with the cloths made her happy, contributed to her sense of social being, of belonging, and that was enough for her. But her remark was also offered as a comment on my behavior, I suggest. She knew that books were important to me; I was always bringing home tattered books from the bazaar's lone used-book seller, and she knew I enjoyed working with printed materials in an effort to improve my knowledge of Uyghur language and culture. In this light, perhaps a better translation of the proverb would be "The best thing of all, for the crow, is his caw."

Another of Abidem's comments also influenced my understanding of women's gifting practices. Abidem had gone one day to offer *edi-mechilik* to a woman whose sons (ages six and eight) had been circumcised together a month before. The next day I found her in the *saray* sorting through cloth pieces and packages of tea and sugar cubes. The daughter-in-law of a friend had recently had a baby, and Abidem would have to go visiting again to see her, she explained. She sighed, exhausted, and said, "Farmwork never ends" (*tériqchiliq tügmes*). At the time I heard two layers of meaning in her comment. It expressed her feelings of fatigue, and the seasonal cycle served as a metaphor for the human life cycle, its births, marriages, and funerals, all of which required that gifts be exchanged. As the farmer sows and reaps, so, too, did gifts plant the seeds of the networks and friendships that provided women with social sustenance. Later I began to doubt my field notes, realizing she more likely said "Living never ends" (*tirikchilik tügmes*), but the farming metaphor, even if it had been my own, still seemed to be an apt one.

Women unable to participate in reciprocal gift exchange were singled out for pity, as this field note excerpt reveals.

This morning Abidem walked a few houses down the lane to visit a close neighbor, a woman in her sixties. The woman had injured herself in a fall, and most of the women on our lane had gone as a group to visit her and take her a special present. As I sat writing in my notebook, the calm was broken by a child's scream.

"You child-of-a-whorewife, fuck your mother, you son-of-a-bitch!" yelled naked Ilyar, age seven, at his parents, as they washed him in a basin by the coal shed. I stepped out of the house to take in the scene, just as Abidem's neighbor Méhriban walked into the courtyard.

"What's going on in here?" she asked, and we chatted a bit. Then, as if in an afterthought, she called over to Gülzire (who stayed home, since she always avoided guesting with her mother-in-law), "So, how much was the chip for the gift?"

"Three *yuan* [$0.38]," Gülzire replied. Méhriban nodded and disappeared through the gate.

The scene made sense to me only in light of a confidence Abidem had shared with me earlier: that Méhriban was pitied by all the neighborhood women because her poverty kept her from participating in gift exchange, and therefore in much of women's socializing. When Méhriban's son was married that year, Abidem suggested no one would attend the wedding. "No one will go. They never go to anyone else's things. They don't mix much, they just don't have it in their hands," she said, referring to the family's poverty.

The "money tea" (*pul chay*) was another common form of women's gathering. One morning at breakfast the usually cheerful Senemgül grumbled several times about how broke she was.

"Why should I have to lend her 300 *som* [$37.50]," she muttered about her sister-in-law, "just because Yakupjan has no money." Yakupjan's wife, Gülzire, she explained, had borrowed that amount from her the day before in order to host a tea party for twenty women. Given that Yakupjan indeed had no money—his profits from a year-long sojourn trading in Kazakhstan were still in the hands of his former partner—I was surprised Gülzire would host a party at all.

"If they are so broke," I asked Senemgül, "then what is she doing giving a tea in the first place?"

"Well," Abidem answered, "it's that kind of tea, now, isn't it!"

"That kind of tea," Abidem explained, was a "money tea." The next day, she said, twenty women would come, each bringing 100 *yuan* ($12.50) for their host Gülzire, and Senemgül's loan, used to pay the cost of purchasing sweets and preparing a meal for the visitors, would be paid back to her that same day. The next day twenty-seven of twenty-nine expected women in Gülzire's money-tea group arrived to present their payments, but only sixteen stayed for tea, sitting and chatting for several hours before eating a meal of rice and mutton.

The group that day had been larger than most, judging by the descriptions of money teas past and present that I elicited subsequently; according to women I spoke with, most groups ranged from ten to twenty participants. Women who participated in money teas often joined more than one group at a time, and each group was organized around a fixed payment ranging from 10 *yuan* ($1.25) per person per meeting up to 100 *yuan*, with 50 and 100 *yuan* teas being most common. Numbered lots were drawn, and participants took turns hosting according to the order of the drawn numbers. The day for meeting was set as the same day every month, although both the hosting order and the day of the meeting could easily be switched without consequence if participants required. Many teas were started by women from a single *mehelle*, but women from different *mehelle* were not excluded. Each group met for the same number of months as it had participants and then dissolved. For many women, the dozen or more of these teas they participate in during the course of their lives provide a valuable opportunity to expand their networks for friendship and exchange, which are important assets for all women, especially those with few nearby kin.

Women also recognized the effectiveness of such teas as a means of accumulating money, but the fact that this was rarely highlighted in their narratives is not entirely surprising, given prevailing secular and religious attitudes against displaying emotional attachment to wealth. A few weeks later, I asked Senemgül again why women played money teas.

"To have fun, to get to spend time with your friends."

"But can't you do that without the money?" I asked.

"But people wouldn't necessarily come if they didn't have to bring money," she said.

Her older brother Yakupjan, who had heard our voices and stepped into the room from outside, chimed in, "Yeah, they have cooking and cleaning and stuff. They couldn't come, maybe, but if they don't come when there's money involved, it is ugly (*set*)."

Introducing the exchange of money makes this strictly women's event a social arena in which value and honor are now at stake. Thus, the exchange of money helps enable women to extract themselves temporarily from daily chores and other commitments at home. The men in Abidem's extended family, her eldest son and three of her sons-in-law, frequently dismissed the importance of social visits planned by their wives and often forbade or otherwise successfully blocked their departures by citing a woman's need to remain home to complete chores. When women exchange only *edimechilik*, fabric, tea, and sugar cubes, social events have little or no importance in men's eyes. But when the object exchanged is money, which men view as something earned in the marketplace by men,* men more readily acquiesce to women's participation.

Guesting and Gifting in Men's Lives

Some forms of reciprocal exchange do figure in men's daily lives in Zawut. One example not to be overlooked as trivial is that men who know one another typically exchange handshakes and greetings in the market or on the street. Such greetings often begin with the phrase "Peace be upon you," to which the other man responds, "And upon you peace." After this the men might inquire briefly about each other's business affairs, the health of family members, and so forth. Similarly, a man who takes leave of another man or a group of men generally places his right hand on or below his heart and bows slightly, a gesture described as "expressing respect." Men recognize that mutual greetings are required by Islamic tradition.

That greetings are an important form of masculine reciprocity for *mehelle* men is demonstrated by men's focusing on incorrect greeting practices as a marker of social stigma or inferior status. In the *mehelle*, for example, men at times made fun of residents of nearby villages by parodying the interminable greetings they exchanged, continuing on

---

*Men's trading ventures were often funded using wives' and daughters' factory wages, but this seemed not to influence men's general view that money was an inherently masculine object.

with "And how are your sheep? And the chickens? And how is your cow?" On the other hand, during a visit to Turpan, I witnessed a local man tease an acquaintance who had passed him in the street without a greeting by saying, "Hey, what are you, from Yining? Passing by and not so much as a health-to-you?"

Perhaps the most striking male counterpart to female reciprocal household visitation is a practice known as *qara basti*. The ostensible goal of this strictly male guesting practice is far different from that of women's visiting. *Qara basti*, literally "pressed-by-blackness," is a standard idiom for describing the state of a person who has become delirious or has gone crazy. In this visiting practice, a group of men make an impromptu decision to call unannounced at a friend's house; when he greets them at the door, they explain that they have come to be guests. The host must maintain his emotional composure, acting delighted at and honored by their visit, spread a tablecloth for the men, and serve them whatever snacks he has available. Only after he provides them with a cooked meal, which may take hours to prepare, will they leave.[6] This behavior, and the name that states clearly the group's intended goal of driving the host "crazy," fit into the overall pattern of men's interpersonal agonism discussed more fully in the next chapter.

Another male activity, a traditional children's game enjoyed by young boys, shares the name *qara basti*, and a comparison of the two activities shows that they have more than their name in common. This game proceeds as follows. One boy in a group is selected to be the "mother" (*ana*); he will remain seated on a chair throughout the game. Another boy now gets down on all fours and places his head in the lap of the mother, who covers his eyes tightly with "her" hands. One of the other children, who stand around in a circle, steps forward, slaps the kneeling child on the buttocks, and returns to his place. The kneeling child's eyes are then uncovered, and he is asked to guess who hit him. If he answers correctly, he trades places with the hitter, and the game begins again with the new victim. If he guesses incorrectly, he must kneel and subject himself to another attack. A number of similarities between the two practices are evident. In each, a person is provoked by an aggressive action framed as a form of play. Only when the victim satisfies all others present with his ability to complete a task imposed on him, providing a meal in one case, guessing an identity in the other, does the group relent in their aggression against him, at which point they move on to another victim, in the first case on some other day, in the second immediately.[7]

Adult Male Relationships

The importance of friendship in men's lives is explicitly demonstrated by the great frequency and vehemence with which men debate the meanings and consequences of friendship. A number of words all of which can be glossed in English as "friend" take on distinct shades of meaning in the *mehelle*. The term *adash* can be used as a term of address and reference for a man's actual friends and can also be a term of address used for strangers. A *mehelle* man who regularly uses this term marks himself as slightly tough, cool, and street-smart; he knows everyone, and everyone is his buddy. The term *aghine* refers exclusively to a man's regular companions; usually these are members of the age cohort formed in his *mehelle* during his adolescence, or other close and constant companions. The term *dost* (or *dos*) goes further in implying ideals of friendship, uprightness, and decency. It is a common Uyghur given name, for example, a testament to its propriety, whereas the use of *adash* or *aghine* as a man's name is, to me, unthinkable. Song lyrics invoking friendship invariably do so using variations of the word *dost*, which gives a sense of decorum and serious importance to the relationship. The term *aghine* connotes more frivolity and possibly deviant behavior; these are the friends with whom one regularly drinks, smokes hashish, and perhaps parties with mistresses. *Aghine* suggests a level of mutual intimate knowledge of the private self; *dost* implies the image of friendship between the public selves men present to the community at large. Things *dost* do together are respectable; things *aghine* do are potentially more illicit.

Not all men's interpersonal relationships fall within these categories of friendship, however. In the *mehelle*, each man is either a fictive "younger brother" (*uka*), a "friend" (*aghine, adash,* or *dost*), or a fictive "older brother" (*aka*) to every other man, depending on the relative seniority of the age cohorts to which they belong. When speaking to or about a fictive elder brother, men often added the suffix *aka* to the man's name, sometimes with the possessive suffix -*m* (my) also added to make explicit their mutual relationship. Tursun thus becomes Tursun-*akam*, which is often shortened to Tursun-*kam* or Tursun-*ka*. Although men may have relationships of close camaraderie with men junior or senior to them, I witnessed many scenes in which the *uka/aka* component of those relationships came to the fore and imposed on the men a set of asymmetric expectations and obligations that were never relevant among friends of similar ages.

———

A fuller understanding of men's personal relationships and masculine ideals, however, requires a much more detailed look into men's lives. The next two chapters take that subject as their focus.

7

The Pretty *Olturash*

Masculinity and Moral Order

in Adult Play

A guy (*bala*) arrives late to a drinking party with all of his friends, and because he is late they say, "Hey man, you're late, that's a fine!" and they pour him three shots of liquor. He drinks the first two, one right after the other, but the third, he spills a little bit on the ground. One of his friends says, "Hey, you poured liquor on me, another fine!" and pours another three shots. Again he downs the first two, but spills a little bit of the third on his hand.

"You spilled more! Another fine for that," the other guy says, pouring three more shots. Well, the guy can barely get them down, that was three fines, each one three shots, and pretty soon he is totally wasted. He stumbles outside onto the street and bumps into a cop.

"Hey you!" the cop says. "You're disturbing the peace. I'm going to have to fine you."

"Aww, shut up and pour!"

— Muxtar Hésam, Yining jokester

For many adult men living in Zawut and adjacent *mehelle*, informal all-male drinking parties like the one described in the joke above were a central social activity around which the rest of their days and weeks were organized. Whether measured by the incredible amounts of time men spent in planning, attending, and discussing these gatherings, called *olturash*, or by the emotional intensity of the events that transpired there, these parties were among the most important events in their day-to-day lives. It was not merely that men attended *olturash* perhaps several times each week, and in the summertime more frequently than that; it was not merely that *olturash* often lasted six, eight, even ten or more hours. Rather, the importance of the *olturash* lay in the richness of the expressive culture on display there, the profound and sometimes volatile emotional exchanges among the participants, and the flourishes of verbal skill and wit, not to mention drinking prowess, through which men sought to establish and maintain social position in their own and others' eyes. It was for these reasons that I took the *olturash* to be a key site for understanding the performance and practice of masculine identities among the men of the *mehelle.*

In the joke at the beginning of this chapter, two different worlds of moral order collapse upon the protagonist at the same time. He cannot satisfy both orders, indeed their goals are exactly opposed. The first punishes him, insists that he drink because of his failure to conform to group norms. The other punishes him because he drinks. These elements suggest that an analysis of *olturash* can provide a window into the ideas and behaviors that contribute to the moral ordering of the local community, at least in the eyes of men. In the pages that follow, I discuss a range of men's recreational activities, beginning with the *olturash*, literally "a sitting-together," which was the primary site of men's informal socializing. After this, I look at other common recreational activities, such as hashish-smoking parties, billiards, and card playing. One of my goals in examining these secular forms of associational life and the importance of the interpersonal networks they create for the men who participate in them is to be better equipped to evaluate their significance relative to a very different set of male associational activities, those affiliated with the practice of Islam, which are explored in this book's final chapters.

Olturash

Most men in Zawut participated regularly in *olturash*, and it was not uncommon for men to attend several gatherings each week for much of the year. Summer was an especially active season for these informal gatherings, a time when *olturash* meeting sites shifted from homes and

Fig. 10 Men aged sixteen to sixty regularly gather in small groups to share songs, jokes, and stories about life in the *mehelle*. In the summer these drinking parties are held in parks or, as shown here, along the banks of the Ili River (photograph by the author, 1996).

restaurants to outdoor settings, either to the broad forested banks of the nearby Ili River or to one of Yining's many wooded parks. Near-universal participation in *olturash* created widespread networks of men who came to know something of one another through *olturash*. Although the same close friends often sat together, the exact roster of participants changed with each event, so that by the time a man had reached his forties or fifties he would have sat together with hundreds of other *mehelle* men and heard stories about many more. For men, gaining a reputation on the basis of the performance of proper masculine identity at *olturash* was a main path to establishing and maintaining social status in the local community.

To begin to understand the dynamics of *olturash*, we must first take note of the deep and constant concern participants routinely expressed for evaluating one another's behavior during the event. In evaluating others' conduct, participants routinely invoked the idea that behavior at *olturash* should conform to "rules" (*qaʾide*). Behavior deemed proper was characterized as "pretty" (*chirayliq*); improper behavior was "ugly" (*set*).

Olturash participants regularly discussed the "rules," and actions seen as counter to them frequently gave rise to heated arguments. Other patterns of behavior were also readily apparent, patterns the participants did not make explicit in their narratives of praise and recrimination. In the description of a typical *olturash* offered below, I review all these behavioral patterns in order to demonstrate some of the fundamental features of *mehelle* masculinity.

Before an *olturash* takes place, several friends first discuss a few days in advance their intent to sit together, perhaps to honor some individual or event, such as the return of a friend from a trading excursion, or simply to enjoy themselves. The oft-used phrase "for opening the heart," meaning "for recreation or enjoyment," was a sufficient and commonly stated reason for gathering. Most *olturash* were arranged by and for men who had grown up in the same informal age cohort, usually in the same or adjacent *mehelle*. As such, *olturash* continually reinforced bonds of friendship within these cohorts over many decades. A great deal of "sitting together" also took place across cohorts, since men make and maintain other acquaintances widely, for example, through dealings in the marketplace or by attending Friday prayers. In other words, *olturash* were a primary site for the maintenance of social bonds among men across such groups as are defined by age cohort, *mehelle* loyalties, occupation and status group, and the fellowship of religious congregation.

Although a group of friends and acquaintances lies at the core of every *olturash*, the truly successful event requires one or perhaps two special participants. Exchanges of jokes and musical performances are indispensable elements of *olturash*, and it is not surprising that many of the men who participate in them regularly can and do join in such exchanges often, picking a tune, singing a song, telling a joke or two. Nonetheless, men I saw planning an *olturash* invariably made a concerted effort to invite someone known as a skilled raconteur of jokes, in the local idiom a "jokester" (*chaqchaqchi*), or as a skilled performer of Uyghur folk and popular music. One special guest of either kind was sufficient to raise the standard of *olturash* entertainment above that of the everyday, and a gathering with a top jokester and a top musician was an event long remembered.

The costs of an *olturash* are typically paid by a single individual. By hosting *olturash*, both in financing the events and in attracting high-status performers and participants to make them successful, men compete for social status. Through displays of masculine prowess once the *olturash* is under way, they compete to build wide networks of friends, networks that both elevate a man's status and provide access to the economic resources and social connections that support men's market trading. Through *olturash*, then, men accumulate social status and establish informal and asymmetrical ties of mutual reliance.

The planning of most *olturash* is hardly a rigorous affair, however, and many planned *olturash* fail to materialize, or else come off poorly. Invitations are routinely offered and accepted insincerely, and cancelled plans are common. One day, for example, I watched as three men, visiting from Urumqi, invited two old friends to join them for an *olturash* at a local restaurant that evening, an invitation the men accepted warmly. Hours later, I pointed out to one of the men that the time to meet had passed. "Why would we sit with them?" he scoffed, "Just to get drunk?" His comment expressed his confidence that these visitors from afar would not be able to arrange to have local musicians or joke-tellers attend, and although that is never an absolute requirement for attending, his comment "just to get drunk" highlights the critical importance of those elements.

Olturash take place at private residences or in the small private dining rooms common in restaurants throughout Xinjiang. Men sit together in a circle, either on the floor or the *supa* if at a home, on chairs around a table or on carpeted floors if at a restaurant. In the summer men sit outdoors around the edges of a large sheet or blanket spread on the ground. Participants routinely stress to one another the importance of seating arrangements, a topic I return to below.

Once the men have gathered, but before the event is ready to get under way, the last step is the selection of one man to perform the role of the *saqiy*. The *saqiy* assumes responsibility for pouring all the alcohol consumed and thus for maintaining the rhythm of the event. He also has a certain unspoken informal status as leader of the event, which he may exercise, for example, in resolving disputes. The role of *saqiy* is assigned casually, without any outward display of competition or careful consideration. The role is occasionally passed to another man, but only if the original *saqiy* cannot remain until the gathering has ended. To avoid such a situation, men decline to be *saqiy* if they know they may have to leave early.

The *saqiy* often begins by giving a little speech, stating how nice it is that the friends can gather, and that he will agree to pour in whatever manner the men decide: "I'll do what you want. If you say stop, I'll stop," he promises. At a typical gathering of five to eight men, he always pours into a single shot glass, which is passed in slow rotation among the men. For larger gatherings, and *olturash* with ten to fifteen men present are not uncommon, two glasses are used, but never more. These glasses are always poured as a pair, then passed to and consumed by adjacent men, often but not always simultaneously. Breaks in strict rotation are allowed, such as for special toasts by one man to another, or when men drink three shots in a row for some reason, such as a fine, or to demonstrate their "heart" to their friends before they are permitted to leave the gathering early.

The consumption of alcohol is an indispensable element of any *olturash*. Beer is rarely consumed, the preferred drink being a hard liquor called *aq haraq* ("white alcohol," perhaps a translation from the Chinese *baijiu*). This clear liquor, distilled from sorghum or other grains, varies in strength from 42 to 58 percent alcohol. Most *mehelle* men preferred local brands—understandably so, since Yining-made liquors are distributed throughout China as premium brands. Better brands cost 20 to 30 *yuan* per 500 mg bottle. Lesser brands sold for a half or a quarter of that price, but these were more often drunk unceremoniously by men eating meals at restaurants or food stalls, rather than at *olturash* or other festive gatherings.

The first round of drinks is poured soon after the men have taken their seats. During the first round of drinking, it is common for a number of the men to gently decline or refuse the glass as it is offered to them. Once or twice they will repeat their intention to not drink. When the others predictably insist, most men yield immediately and without resistance. This pretense of refusing is common even for men who arrive expecting and hoping to drink long into the night, and everyone knows that it will be quickly abandoned, once the purpose has been served of dramatizing their willingness to place the group's needs over their own desires. Such men might comment "Well, okay, maybe I'll just give it a little taste" or "But just a small one, okay?"

Disputes occasionally arise if a participant is unwilling to share equally in the drinking. Men are rarely permitted to abstain entirely, and more often such disputes focus on whether a man should be allowed to stop after drinking three glasses, the minimum gesture of respect to the group. Once the drinking is under way, disputes can arise over just about anything. Men will generally consume between 150 g and 400 g of liquor during an *olturash*, although drinking 500 g or even 700 g is not uncommon. As a rough estimate, only one man present at every second or third *olturash* I attended succeeded in convincing the group to allow him to not drink at all. Another two or three were permitted to stop at three shots. Constant mutual encouragement and taunting, the imposition of fines, and other forms of harassment keep men drinking past any point they might privately wish to stop. After such heavy drinking, it is fairly common for one or more of the participants to vomit, either during the event, usually but not always after first exiting the room, or as the men return to their homes amid loud proclamations of eternal friendship, angry threats of violence for perceived slights, or both.

After participants have been drinking and chatting for a while, someone among them will call out for a joke, or for a song, and then after a bit of discussion—perhaps the demand for silence *hapshük!* will be needed to bring the group to order—the men will decide to begin a phase of music or joking. If the group decides to tell jokes, most of the men present will likely take a turn telling a joke or two. The jokes are seldom new, but even a joke that the men have heard at *olturash* many times will still draw a great laugh if they are in good spirits and if it is told well. If an especially skilled jokester is present, he will listen to the others until being invited to take over, and then he will regale the group for ten to twenty minutes by himself. When he is finished, that signals the end of the joking phase, and the men will quickly decide as a group to switch to another activity, either informal chatting, as before, perhaps swapping stories of recent happenings in the marketplace, or playing instruments and singing songs. After a rotation through phases of these other activities, the joking will begin all over again, and the whole cycle recommences.

Most of the jokes that appear in this book were recorded at *olturash* I attended or taken from mass-produced *olturash* cassette tapes. When I first visited Yining in 1992, enterprising local men sat in the marketplace with racks of cassettes, most of them recordings of private *olturash* in Yining attended by renowned local musicians and jokesters. A would-be buyer paid a small fee, and the seller dubbed for him a copy of the desired tape on the spot. By 1995, small-scale cassette production and merchandising were thriving in Yining, and local entrepreneurs released attractively packaged recordings of Yining musicians and comedians in batches of several thousand, which were sold throughout Xinjiang. These tapes, which alternated between jokes and songs, with an occasional poem or two, attempted to capture the feeling of a great *olturash*. Important distinctions between live and prerecorded *olturash* jokes, however, did exist. Manufactured cassettes bore a state-issued publication number indicating that the contents had been vetted by the government and included neither obscene nor explicitly anti-Han jokes; both kinds of jokes, although mostly obscene ones, were routinely told at *olturash*.* Otherwise the jokes told were quite similar, and for good reason; many jokes on manufactured cassettes had been circulating in the *mehelle* for some time, and new jokes that appeared first on such cassettes, created or borrowed from elsewhere by famous jokesters, quickly become widely performed by *olturash* participants.

A distinctive and highly stylized form of laughter was common at (and entirely unique to) *olturash* joke-telling sessions. Such laughter was distinguished by its explosive initialization, which gave it the sound of an abrupt, ejaculatory squawk. This sound differed completely from the informal laughter heard when men responded to a witty remark or a funny incident in their everyday lives. I also never observed this laugh

---

*Although published cassettes had been reviewed by state censors, such reviews were sometimes cursory, with the result that local state agents announced bans on and physically removed from market stalls several popular releases during my research after it was discovered they contained politically sensitive (pro-Uyghur or antigovernment) content. Publishers also circumvented censors by illegally reusing single-use registration numbers.

used when women were present. The extraordinary quality of this laughter is confirmed by an anecdote told by one *mehelle* jokester about a group of neighbors becoming deeply annoyed by the distinctive sound of *olturash* laughter emanating from a house where gatherings were often held. One of the neighbors teases the men that they sound like a bunch of goats. Stylized forms of crying are known in many cultures, as part of mourning rituals, for example, but stylized laughter has received less attention from scholars. Vladimir Propp has argued that the significance of ritual laughter is to mark the boundary between the living and the dead, as well as the creative and sexual life-force.[1] If Propp is right that laughter marks the sexual life-force, then perhaps the sharp ejaculatory laughter of men at *olturash* does relate to the group's sexual energy.

In addition to the recounting of jokes and humorous anecdotes (*letipe*), two other kinds of joking interactions are common at *olturash*. The first involves men making oblique references to other participants' nicknames; the following chapter is devoted to nicknaming, and I describe this kind of joking there. The second is a form of verbal dueling known in Uyghur as "attacking (*hujum qilish*) joking." These lightning-fast exchanges of punning, rhyming insults were the domain of only very skilled jokesters. Since *olturash* rarely had two jokesters in attendance, these exchanges were relatively uncommon. I did witness verbal duels on several occasions, but comprehension of the dialogue in real time remained beyond my ability.

Once someone in the group suggests with sufficient force that it is time to "have a little music," the interactions that follow are much like those of the joking phase. Several of the men might take turns strumming a rhythm on the *dutar*, a long-necked wooden instrument with two nylon strings, perhaps singing to their own accompaniment while the rest of the men watch quietly. More proficient musicians might pick on an even longer-necked *tembur*, whose five steel strings and high action require more technical skill. After other participants have taken turns performing for the rest of the group, the most skilled musician or musicians present will be invited to play, perhaps for a half hour or more. The ideal *olturash* ensemble was two musicians, one on *dutar* for rhythm and another on *tembur* playing lead, with one of the men singing. When such a pair performed, the others listened reverently, punctuating pauses in the beat with words of praise—"Thank you" (*rexmet*), "Marvelous" (*karamet*), or "Oh yeah!" (*way-way*). Often all the men would join in singing the choruses or well-known verses.

After several hours of heavy drinking and cigarette smoking in a small room crowded with friends, with the men's voices booming out in unison the words to a musical refrain, the altered, even exalted, state of consciousness *olturash* participants regularly experienced was perhaps not dissimilar from the state attained by Sufi adherents of old, sitting in circles of their own, performing their *dhikr* chanting long into the evening. When skilled musicians play, one man often rises to dance, inviting another to join him as he circles the room in tiny little steps, spinning himself in circles while his hands swing and wave in smaller circles over his head or at his sides. This dancing style, too, like the unique *communitas* of the singing and of the song, suggests the possibility that the associational forms of *olturash* and Sufi *dhikr* group are but modalities in a single secular-sacred ritual complex.

A distinctive pattern underlies the way in which men exchange the symbolic good that is their participation in the dance. As each man is invited to dance, he rises and dances for a minute or two, during which time the man who invited him sits. The dancer must then invite another man to join him, at which point he, too, can take his seat. In this way, the performance of the dance is "passed" from one man to the next. This exchange is structurally similar to a practice described to me by a Turpan resident; at mixed-gender social gatherings, the man explained, an object, often a belt, was passed at random throughout the group from one individual to the next, often at the beginning of the event. Participants then had to pass back the object in the exact opposite order at the end of the event before they might depart. The same pattern sometimes appears, as we will see below, at the beginning and close of a different form of men's gathering known as the *meshrep*.

Music performed at *olturash* included songs about local history. One song often heard was Canal Song (*Östeng naxshisi*), the lyrics of which I presented in Chapter 2. Other songs dealt with themes of love and romance. This song seemed to be a favorite, since it was often played.

The beauty of my love's heart	*seherde sayrighan bulbul*
Awakes at the lark's dawn song	*köngülning zéhnini achti*
And the red rose that blooms	*échilghan qizil gülni*

Fig. 11 Bootleg recordings of private *olturash* parties circulated in Yining's markets in 1992. By 1996 local impresarios were recording Yining's jokesters and musicians and publishing audiocassettes that captured the feeling of an *olturash* by alternating between jokes and songs. This J-card insert is from *Non-Stop Laughter* (*Üzülmes külkiler*) featuring jokesters Hésam Qurban and his son Muxtar.

Adorns my love's dark tresses long	*yar qulaqqa qisti*
I'll share my moon with the sky	*asmanda méning ayim*
And the flowers can share my home	*gülzarda méning janim*
But listen well, that girl with the rose	*anglanglar xalayiqlar*
I'll keep for mine alone	*gül qisqan méning yarim*

This slightly free translation is offered in the hope of communicating some of the beautiful imagery common to Uyghur romantic songs, although in this instance the figurative language suggests a more interpretive reading as well. This song is known as *Gül qisqan méning yarim* (Flower-clenching love-of-mine), with the literal image being one of a girl with a flower "pinched" or "clenched" behind her ear. Certain metaphorical implications seem apparent in the male singer praising his girlfriend by saying she keeps her flower clenched tightly. Immediately following this song (the two are traditionally sung as a suite without an intermediate pause) comes *Gülshedixan*.

I planted a flower, which sprouted	*gül téridim maysa boldi*
And put out shoots of every hue	*shax chiqardi rengmu reng*
My love lay down in the sunlight	*yarim aptapta yétiptu*
With me, in this golden place	*men bu yerde sewze reng*
Tell me, did you miss me?	*sen séghindingmu méni*

I missed you quite a lot	*xoyma séghindim men séni*
From where inside you did you miss me?	*sen qeyeringde séghinding*
For me it was from the heart	*men yürekimdin séni*
If you go to the countryside on horseback	*at ménip sehragha chiqsang*
I'll be the horsewhip you raise	*qamche desting men bolay*
And when everyone's eyes are upon you	*barche xeqning közi sende*
I'll be the amulet that guards you	*til tumaring men*
from their gaze	*bolay*

Finally, in addition to sharing jokes and songs, men occasionally re-cited poems, most of them works they attributed to Uyghur poets writing early in the twentieth century, whose writings were widely published in the 1980s and 1990s. Poetry was a valorized literary genre among boys and men, and it was not uncommon for adults to confide that when they were young boys they wanted to grow up to be poets. In the 1990s, however, when poetry was presented at *olturash* it was more likely to come in the form of a mass-produced audiocassette of poetry recitation, which the men would listen to in silence for a period of time before shifting back to conversation, joking, or music.

Ugly and Pretty

The word "pretty" (*chirayliq*) was regularly used at *olturash* to describe the performance of a proper male habitus. The central place of "pretty" in men's comments was striking to me, in that it inverted the language women used when speaking about threats to the proper ordering of social interactions. In everyday life, women regularly used the word "ugly" (*set*) to describe behaviors or situations that were, or threatened to become, productive of shame for parties involved. Not once did I ever hear a woman use the word "pretty" as men used it, to describe behaviors or situations in which things were done properly. For men at *olturash*, the exact opposite speaking pattern held. Men used "pretty" to describe and encourage positive behavior, usually many times per event, but they never used the word "ugly" to express their anxiety or disapproval regarding improper behaviors, as women often did in other contexts. But exactly which behaviors cause men to criticize, beseech, and berate others in the quest to be "pretty"?

First, participants are expected to sit roughly in a circle, with each man sitting down squarely and facing inward toward the group. During periods of informal chatting, it was common for men to divide into several smaller separate conversational groups, but with a single comment on the part of one man that the men should be but no longer were sitting "pretty," men usually re-established a single collective conversation. The root of *chirayliq* is *chiray*, "face," and a loose translation of the term might be "facely." In this sense, the use of this word for the core meaning of "men facing one another" is sensible.

Men must sit squarely on the ground. If a man sits with his buttocks tilted up off the ground he is criticized for "displaying his butt." This is not altogether surprising, since gesture and bodily comportment are widely and explicitly read by men as a symbolic language of power and interpersonal aggression, as the following incident demonstrates. On two separate occasions I heard groups of men discussing footage that had recently aired on an official television newscast in which Chinese Communist Party general secretary Jiang Zemin and U.S. president Bill Clinton were shown together, I believe on the occasion of the fiftieth anniversary of the United Nations. Both groups of men discussed the images they had seen at length, mixing playfulness with serious political analysis. Their conversations focused on how Clinton was *intentionally* turning his back and extending his protruding buttocks toward Jiang's face. As the men re-enacted the scene over and over, their portrayal of the interaction became increasingly exaggerated, and more aggression was expressed in and attributed to Clinton's posture. As a corollary to these standards, no one joining or temporarily leaving the group, for instance, "for politeness" (*edep*), as men remarked euphemistically before exiting to relieve themselves, was allowed to pass in front of any other person. A man who did so would be sharply upbraided for "displaying his butt."

A number of other rules apply to *olturash* drinking arrangements. Once a liquor bottle is emptied, for example, it is immediately removed from sight. Even more strictly followed is the practice of never displaying unopened bottles, a number of which are usually kept close at hand. A man hosting an *olturash* at his home might purchase six or eight bottles of liquor, but these will be carefully hidden the entire evening and taken out one at a time after the previous bottle is finished. At riverside parties in 1992, most groups brought their own supplies from home, and perhaps replenished them occasionally at one of the few small stores in the area. By 1995, that popular picnicking area had been greatly commercialized. Several dozen stalls provided every kind of cooked food or beverage, and many stalls had one or two large tables where groups of men would sit for hours, while the stall owner sent out to other stalls for any specialty foods the men requested, and handled all payments for them.

After the drinking has gone on for a while, it often happens that one man wishes to cease drinking, stating that he is physically unable to drink any more; perhaps he will ask to be excused from drinking just for a round or two. Such a man is often criticized for refusing to contribute to making the group "pretty," and the others will respond with a *gradatio* of strategies; first polite words, then sharp teasing, then barely bridled expressions of aggression and hostility. Only if the men are quite drunk can this lead to physical violence, and although extreme drunkenness is routine, physical violence is rare.

The man who wishes to stop drinking will first be told by the *saqiy* or another participant "But it is my heart, here, for my heart" or "Respect, you have to respect us." If appeals to friendship and respect fail, and one of the men present is considered an "older brother" (*akam*) to the others, that older man will inevitably invoke the "rules" (*qa'ide*), holding a glass out to the man while repeating "Rules, rules." These rules are understood to govern behaviors related to when and how much one must drink, including the imposition of fines for arriving late, as was mentioned in the joke given as the epigraph to this chapter. Note that in that joke the man who spills liquor on the ground is accused of pouring liquor on another participant. This phrasing suggests that the spill is taken as an act of disrespect against a person. At one outdoor drinking party I attended, one man tried for several minutes to refuse a glass of liquor placed before him, with no success. Several minutes later a fight broke out among a different group of drinkers, and the men jumped up to take a look. As they looked away, the man dumped his full glass out onto the ground, then claimed to have drunk it. The *saqiy* became suspicious, found the ground under the man to be wet, and the two almost came to blows. "That's my face you poured it on," the *saqiy* yelled. "If you didn't want to drink, why didn't you just say so?" In the end, the man was forced to drink three large shots of liquor as a fine.

Proper *olturash* behavior also requires that no man can be permitted to leave the party until every participant is ready to leave. Consider the tenacity in this exchange, paraphrased from my field notes.

9:00 P.M. Six men are sitting on pads on a carpeted floor in the small backroom of a local restaurant. Four empty bottles of *baijiu* sit hidden in one corner. One man, the host that evening, gets another bottle from the restaurant owner.

"Just one last bottle," he tells the others. Another man tries to convince him not to open it.

"We've drunk enough," he says. They argue for fifteen minutes, each trying in vain to convince the other to yield. Eventually the host relents.

"Okay, okay," he says, seeming to have given in. "So we won't drink it. We'll just . . . taste it." He quickly unscrews the cap, knowing full well that a bottle once opened must be finished before anyone can depart.

For any individual to leave before an opened bottle is finished is extremely difficult, since it is considered a threat to the group's "prettiness."

Drinking is seen as a gift to the group, one that must be made to maintain group "prettiness." It is not simply that one is forced to drink; rather, the drinking event is a series of reciprocal gift exchanges, in which opting out cannot but symbolically remove the individual from the collective.

Several hours into an *olturash* of seven men, Abet was passed the single glass. Holding the glass, he addressed the others, "Some newspaper in America came out with an article, each cigarette takes five minutes off your life," he said, launching into a long-winded rambling commentary about cigarettes and health. Every man there smoked, of course, including Abet himself. Abet went on speaking until the others became bored and turned their attention elsewhere, then he looked to the *saqiy*, who was watching him, waiting patiently to get the glass back.

"Well, I gave a speech," Abet said in a near whisper, "so I don't have to drink this. Pass it on over." He motioned toward his neighbor. The *saqiy* nodded in agreement and took the glass and passed it over to Ömerjan, on Abet's right. Ten seconds later, Abet called out loudly, for all to hear, "Hey Ömerjan, are you gonna drink that or what? Is it going to sit there all night?"

Ömerjan smiled sheepishly. "Sorry, I didn't see it," he said, assuming that it had been poured for him, and gulped it down.

Abet looked at the *saqiy* and squeezed both eyes shut, a triumphant grin on his face.

Those who saw Abet's gesture of the slow blink knew to read it as a sign that the dupe had failed to recognize the interaction had been a prank. Abet's invocation of the rules (implicitly, the rule that men must drink in a timely fashion) was not genuine; it was done just to best the other man in a game of wits. This incident also supports the interpretation that drinking is an offering to the group, one that on rare occasions may be replaced by a commensurate offering. Men are keenly aware that their drinking creates serious short- and long-term health problems, and it seemed to me that men shared an explicit understanding that the sacrifice of their health was a deeply meaningful offering each was making to the others.

Other forms of transgression against *olturash* ideals are deemed more significant than those mentioned so far. It frequently happens, for example, that a man attending one *olturash* temporarily joins or attempts to join another, effectively abandoning his mates. Restaurants may have five or six private back-rooms, each occupied by a separate *olturash*, and outdoors a dozen or more groups of men might sit within sight and hearing of one another. Indoors or out, men sometimes overhear the jokes, laughter, and music of other *olturash* or see individuals they know participating in them, and are lured or physically pulled away. Such transgressions are one of the more regular sources of deep anger and threats of violence at *olturash*, as the following field note excerpt suggests.

In the back room of a restaurant, eight men in their thirties sat partying on a carpeted floor when a man passed in the hallway and peeped in.

"Hey, Ablikim'ka!" yelled Ibrahim, one of the partiers, who recognized the well-known *dutar* player. The newcomer declined an invitation to sit, so Ibrahim stood, walked to the door, pulled him inside and sat him down.

The men began to discuss where they might get their hands on a *dutar* for Ablikim to play. Not long after, an older man, age sixty or so, stepped in, visibly angry. These men had stolen Ablikim, his group's special musician, and although the man spoke directly to Ablikim, his overbearing tone of voice was directed at the entire group.

"Okay, up! Come back to our room! These people are all unknown to us. Strangers," he snorted.

"What do you mean 'unknown'?" Ibrahim said slowly. "Every one of us here knows Ablikim'ka, and he knows all of us."

The older man spoke with an icy voice. "Well, I don't know you." Then even more harshly, "Ablikim, up!" Ablikim stayed seated, but Ibrahim got to his feet.

"Look, you are an 'older brother' (*aka*), we should respect you. But it's not Muslim of you to say what you're saying. If we don't know each other, then we greet, and meet each other." He leaned forward, and the two clasped hands.

"Okay," the man said. "Now we've met. Time to go." The contest continued for ten very emotional and tense minutes. Ibrahim was extremely drunk. Ablet leaned over to me and said chuckling, "He eats dick." His flat tone communicated that these words were not meant as they usually were, as an insult and a provocation, but to indicate that the newcomer genuinely had a reputation for having sex with other men. Finally the two older men left, but the original group of partiers argued vehemently among themselves for a full ninety minutes about how the problem should have been resolved.

During this interaction, I was particularly struck by the rude tone the older man took toward his own party's *dutar* player. *Mehelle* men had a strong sense of the relative skill of dozens of local musicians and jokesters. Men planning a party sought to invite skilled performers by promising to serve them expensive liquor and food at the gathering itself, or by offering them other favors, including cash payments if need be. Once an *olturash* began, most participants treated these invitees with special respect, even reverence. Even those rare participants who admitted to having no appreciation for music or humor still recognized such performers were status symbols for an *olturash*.

On a different occasion, a man stepped into a room where an *olturash* was in full swing and requested that the talented musician sitting there leave temporarily to serenade the man's own *olturash* group in an adjacent room. This request, unreasonable and naïve by any reckoning, was flatly rebuffed. The group's *saqiy* nonetheless offered the man a shot of liquor, a goodwill gesture clearly not appreciated by the rest of the group. The visitor attempted to salvage his status among the men.

"Look, we're not strangers, we are all friends. I know you, Niyaz, we know each other, right?" the newcomer said, looking at one of the seated men. "And I know you, Memtimin. And you are all friends with Xeyret, right, he is my closest, closest friend."

Xeyret, a young merchant of substantial wealth, was indeed an acquaintance of all of the men, but they yielded nothing on this basis. Several of the men spoke up, saying that they had known Xeyret more than a decade earlier, when they were hustling on the streets of Guangzhou together.

"Xeyret? He's like our little brother, he's younger than we are. When he started he was nothing, snot running down his nose, now he thinks he's such a big shot."

The newcomer played his trump card, a reference to a man with claims to an elite social status based on market success, but the men framed the relationship in terms of age cohorts, rejecting the newcomer's claim to equal status by suggesting that they were his older brothers.

Not only must participants' drinking behavior during an *olturash* reflect their concern for the group's reciprocity and symmetry, but decisions to leave the *olturash* must also be collective. It is "pretty" for men to leave together, and anyone wishing to depart before the others is sharply rebuked and spoken ill of. The injury of a person leaving early is perhaps most sharply felt by the host or honored guest of the event, although it is spoken of as disrespectful to all. It is the job of older brothers to keep everyone drinking. One thirty-six-year-old man, Dilshat, had been drinking with close friends for several hours but wanted to leave the group at 9:30 P.M. to return home. Recently his older brother had been hassling him for being a wastrel, a character flaw the brother felt explained some major marketplace losses Dilshat had recently suffered. One of the younger men present took up the cause of giving Dilshat a hard time.

Dilshat, you shouldn't say you want to go. You should be saying "Let's sit a while, enjoy ourselves, drink a little more." But here I am saying it. You're my older brother (*aka*), you should be taking charge. You should be making sure we have a good time.

The concept of rules (*qa'ide*) is often invoked to describe behaviors expected between older men and their fictive younger brothers; this is the case despite the fact that biological brothers, in my experience, strictly avoid drinking in each other's presence.

Men who do wish to leave early typically present a lie to the group. A man will explain he is stepping out "for politeness," to make a phone call, or to check on his assistants who are closing up his market stall at the end of the day. At an *olturash* held in a restaurant, a man might arrange for a third party, perhaps the proprietor, to enter the room at a predetermined time and announce that there is someone asking for him outside, or that he is wanted on the phone. If a man is honest and simply admits to a desire to leave, endless speeches and bodily violence will be used to coax, cajole, and coerce him into remaining until the group as a whole decides to go.

A successful ending to an *olturash* is generally as follows. At some point, with all opened bottles of liquor finished, a brief discussion about leaving will take place, and several men will agree that perhaps it is time to leave. Occasionally the *saqiy* will make a brief speech to close the event. Then, the men will hold their hands up in front of them, palms facing up, close their eyes, and then pass both hands downward over their faces in a wiping motion, saying "God is great" (*Allahu akbar*). Immediately they rise to depart and make their way home alone or in small groups. The abruptness with which a lazily conducted *olturash* of six or eight hours is concluded is extremely striking.

When men leave an *olturash* held at a private residence, the host routinely invites his guests to spend the night. These invitations are offered with utmost sincerity, but are made in the secure knowledge that they will not be accepted. Such a host, for example, displays equal sincerity when insisting that his own next-door neighbor, who lives twenty feet away, also stay the night: "Aren't you going to stay over? It's no trouble, really. We'll stay up and play cards." These offers of hospitality are a general feature of *mehelle* life; several times I saw Abidem pay her fare to a middle-aged male driver of a horse-cart taxi that delivered her home in the evening, only to send him off with the words "Aren't you going to spend the night?"

As a counterpart to the *olturash*, where alcohol, tobacco, and tea are consumed, mention should be made of the kind of men's gathering that focuses on the smoking of hashish (*neshe*). Many *mehelle* men smoke

hashish, starting in their teenage years and continuing through their forties and fifties. Hashish has been widely produced and consumed in
Xinjiang for centuries. In the local vernacular, men referred to hashish
as "goods" (*mal*), in the sense of "market goods," and the metaphor
used to describe the intoxication that resulted from the large amounts
of hashish men consume was that of being "grabbed" (*tutmaq*). Although it was not uncommon for men to casually smoke hand-rolled
cigarettes of tobacco mixed with hashish, distinctively shaped with a
right-angle bend in the middle, men gathering in the daytime or the
evening expressly to smoke hashish together invariably used a water
pipe made from a small gourd. A striking feature of such pipes, which
had a roughly 3-inch diameter orb at the base curving upwards into a
bent shaft 7 inches long and 1.0–1.5 inches in diameter, was that they
approximated the size and shape of a man's genitals.

Men who met to smoke hashish usually did so in the evenings. They
rarely sat together for more than an hour. As with *olturash* drinking, the
men sat in a circle and one man, much like a *saqiy*, prepared the pipe and
passed it to each man in turn. A fresh serving of hashish would be put in
the bowl for each of the men. The man smoking would hold a burning
splint of wood or thick twist of paper to the bowl as he inhaled deeply,
fully inflating his lungs once, exhaling the dense smoke into the room,
then fully inflating them a second time. Men often choked back a cough
as they inhaled, and every now and then one of the men would fail at
this, and an intense spasm of coughing followed. As the pipe was passed
around the group, the men were extremely attentive to each smoker's
performance, and good-natured teasing about men's ability to suck hard
at the phallus-shaped pipe and to endure the effects of the hashish was
common. In their attentiveness to one another's performances and in
their mutual teasing, men seemed well aware that the style of a man's
smoking put his masculine prowess on display.

Games and Frames

As a means of passing time away from their productive activities or passing the slow hours of the day in the marketplace, men participated in a
number of game activities. In the remainder of this chapter, I consider
the two most common game activities, card playing and billiards, as they

relate to the linked themes of symbolic aggression and masculine identity discussed in this and the next chapter. A casual observer watching a group of local men engaged in a game of cards or billiards would soon realize that the men were spending far more time and energy arguing about the game, cheating, and arguing about the cheating, than they were trying to win by obeying the rules. For *mehelle* men it is playing with rules, and not playing according to them, that is the deeper game of play.

Billiards

Billiard tables were visible everywhere in Yining, outdoors in the open-air plazas and street corners of the city center, indoors in most *mehelle* in privately owned, one-room recreation centers. Day or night, active tables were likely to have crowds of men standing around them watching players take their turns. Women never played and, except for the occasional female Han table owner, were virtually never seen. When a ball was pocketed in the course of play, it fell into one of the mesh bags that hung down several inches below the table at each pocket. Men kept score by removing each ball they sank and placing it in one of the table's pockets designated as their own. The more balls they sank, the more that bag bulged. One sign the game took on deeper symbolic meanings for men was found in the routine teasing a man might engage in if his opponent had not sunk any balls, laughing at him, "You are a girl, you have no balls."

Several features of men's billiard playing stand out as distinctive. First, it seemed to be more important to players to fire the cue ball and other balls explosively around the table, snapping them into the pockets, than it was to simply sink their shots. Men regularly missed easy shots of several inches by striking the cue ball with all their strength instead of tapping it gently. Making one's shots was to be desired, of course, but a man who fired his shot in smartly and perfectly was admired, praised, held in respect. This desired trait of snapping the balls hard so that they made a cracking sound evokes the metaphor of "crackingness" (*chaqqan*) used to describe the cracking of jokes and the performance of rapid-fire, witty language.

Further symbolic associations can be made between the game of billiards and the performance of masculine identities. Each man slides his stick back and forth in his hands, trying to demonstrate that his stick is more potent that that of his opponent. The white cue ball explodes away from the tip of the cue, and balls subsequently are slammed into pockets with almost enough force to threaten to break the pocket. As I read these gestures, the player wields his symbolic penis, trying to penetrate a passive receptacle that awaits him, and to do it with a force sufficient to break that receptacle, in order to gain victory over his opponent and demonstrate his masculinity. This interpretation should be seen only as an attempt to foreshadow a far more explicitly made metaphor (described in the next chapter), one in which success at interpersonal symbolic combat is cast expressly as the delivery of a thrust that overwhelms an opponent's anus. Another aspect of men's interest in billiards also leads to this theme of anal symbolism. When men spoke about billiards, I often noticed that a distinctly playful enthusiasm entered their voices as they uttered the game's name. Only many months and many dozens of games later did I fall upon the likely explanation. The word men used for billiards in Yining was *bort*, which most men I asked believed to be the Russian word for billiards.* In vernacular Uyghur, however, *bort* is the standard onomatopoeia for the sound of a loud fart. The question "Should we play billiards?" is thus a homophone with "Should we play fart?"

Perhaps the most distinctive feature of local billiards playing was the drawn-out, good-natured arguing that took place between players, such as when each claimed to have sunk a particular ball (long enough after it was pocketed for the one who sank it to have perhaps forgotten), or when men disputed how many victories each had tallied at a certain point. Men's objectives in these interactions were twofold: first, to provoke the other person to anger, a common and (to men themselves) endlessly entertaining element in all men's interactions; and second, to bring one's opponent around to accepting one's invented account of what transpired; success in either regard meant a treasured symbolic victory over an opponent.

---

*The Russian *bort* means "billiard cushion," according to Wheeler et al., *Oxford Russian Dictionary*, 749.

Playing Cards

A common way for men to pass quiet time in market shops and stalls was playing cards. Just as in billiards playing, certain features of men's card playing highlight the critical importance men placed on transcending the game frame during card playing. True gaming mastery was not limited to play done according to the rules but was manifest in men's constant and endlessly evolving attempts to cheat, and in the bluffing and denials and arguments that followed about whether and how cheating had occurred. The following is a hypothetical example of a typical cheating drama.

The game is a variation of the Chinese game *zheng shangyou* (struggling upstream). North partners with South, East with West. In the counterclockwise play of the game, a player must either put down a card or cards higher than the last cards played or pass to the player to their right; thus, it is both permitted and common for a player to decline to put down cards and pass instead, while retaining the right to enter play later in the same hand.

In the middle of play, South follows the hand by laying down cards but goes out of turn, laying down his cards immediately after his own partner North has gone, without waiting for West to either play or to declare a pass. When West complains that it is his turn to go, South complains even more loudly, "But I've just gone! You don't go after me, you have to wait your turn! What are you trying to do?" South frames the situation such that if the rules *had* been obeyed, his having gone *would* indicate that the person to his left had played. Everyone sees South has broken the rules and is playing with the logic of the rules to get others to accept the frame he has put forward. After more arguing, play will resume.

Attempts at cheating are made often, and many are detected, but given the never-ending nature of the cheating, and given cheaters' aggressive attempts to deny, bluff, or joke their way through without yielding to an opponent's version of what happened, a significant percentage of attempts at cheating are ultimately tolerated, and therefore successful. Cheating does not ruin the game— the dramas it creates *are* the game.

As in billiards, men playing card games regularly competed to see who could display greater prowess, first in conjuring up convincing (though patently false) accounts of what had happened and, second, in forcing opponents into the no-win situation of either acquiescing or allowing themselves to be provoked to anger.[2] Vernacular terms for card playing support this interpretation. Playing cards for money was called "playing for real" (*ras oynash*), whereas playing for amusement only was called "false playing" (*yalghan oynash*). These terms reflect the fact that cheating was far more common when the game was for fun only, whereas people playing for money were more serious.

Although a nimble tongue was a primary requirement for success at "false" card playing, players also placed value on the physical style of play. As with the gestures of shooting billiards, the delivery of cards from hand to playing surface was made with an explosive force that produced a loud smack when the cards hit. If a man let his cards simply drop from his hands without throwing them, others might tease him by saying "Don't plop them down like a cow shitting!"

Other Games

Mahjong was a popular pastime among younger men in the *mehelle*, men in their teens and early twenties. As with billiards playing, an active mahjong table would often have ten to fifteen men crowded around watching. Many billiards halls in the *mehelle* set up a mahjong table or two when they realized that crowds of younger men were drawn in by the telltale rattle of tiles. Gambling with sheep's knuckles was spoken of as fairly common, but it was the domain of more serious competitive gambling, and I never saw it, much to my regret. Local men spoke also of cockfighting as a popular pastime that went on during the summer months. Attempts by friends in 1992 and again in the fall of 1995 to lead me to an active gaming locale, however, turned up nothing. During the winter of 1995, one man I knew was raising a fighting cock, feeding it egg whites and giving it doves to kill to stimulate its bloodlust. I was looking forward to the springtime and the opportunity to see the sport from the perspective of a bird trainer. Unfortunately, the bird died from drinking the wastewater from a hashish water pipe that had been left carelessly in a basin during a party the man hosted while his wife was in the countryside guesting for several days, and my chance at an insider's perspective on cockfighting died along with the bird. Games of chance were played widely in the streets and on inter-village buses in

Xinjiang (as they were throughout China at that time). That gaming participation was seen as a marker of masculinity is suggested in the spiel of one card sharp I heard on a minibus shuttling between Yining and surrounding villages: "Okay okay everybody, let's play! But no Party members, and no one who is afraid of his wife!"

8

"Women have hair, men have nicknames"
Uyghur Nicknaming Practices

The old ones have a saying   *konalarda bardur bir maqal*
"Giving nicknames is a thing for immortals"   *leqem qoyush xizirning ishi*
Goodness, are immortals just like Uyghurs   *towa xizirmu xuddiy uyghurdek*
Among whom no one lacks a nickname   *uyghurda yoqtur leqemsiz kishi*

—Merhum Téyipjan, Uyghur poet

In the *mehelle* surrounding Yining, as the verse quoted above suggests,
all men indeed did have nicknames (*leqem*), and each day I heard countless nicknames invoked by men and women alike. Even before beginning fieldwork in Zawut, I had suspected that Uyghur nicknames could
provide a valuable taxonomic framework for examining the gendered
construction of personality and emotion in men's lives. When I started
my research in Xinjiang, I originally hoped to gain through nicknames
an entrance into the rich lexicon of folk speech, viewing nicknames as a
form of local commentary on folk psychological categories. Later I began to ask: If nickname use is an instrument of social action, a means to
some end regarding identity formation and maintenance, what might
that end be? What, in other words, do nicknames do for the individuals
and groups who use them? By the end of my field research, I realized
that much of what a study of Uyghur nicknaming could offer was lo-

cated not in the names themselves but in the dynamic practices of nicknaming. The need to address nicknames as symbols used in practice became more clear to me when I considered the limited usefulness of extant lists of Uyghur nicknames published with no accompanying discussion of meanings, use, or context.[1] In this chapter I attempt to remedy such shortcomings by considering nicknaming as an institution that comprises both a set of signifying symbols, the nicknames themselves, and a set of signifying behavioral practices.

Why Nicknames?

Four incidents, which took place over a ten-year period, represent some of the stepping-stones on the path of my own interest in nicknames and my discovery of their value for exploring the semiotics of vernacular Uyghur culture. If the cumulative effect of these stories on the reader parallels my own experience, she or he will, I hope, find the analysis that follows a useful attempt to unravel some of the mysteries they contain.

Lesson 1. Osman the "Bulge": Every Nickname Is a Story

August, 1985. I am standing outside a train station in Guangzhou, a city in southern China, on my first day ever in the People's Republic. The train I will take to Beijing departs at midnight, so I check my bags and wander out into the sweltering afternoon heat to explore the surrounding markets. Amid the din of traffic, standing out from the Cantonese spoken around me, a man's voice calls "chain jamani." A group of young men flash some bills, and the meaning becomes clear—"change your money." I knew what they wanted, since I had heard from other travelers that the Foreign Exchange Certificates I had received at the railway station's Bank of China office could be swapped on the black market for *renminbi*, China's regular currency, at a rate of 1 to 1.4. The men who had addressed me stood out physically from the Chinese who passed around us, "like Greeks or Turks," I thought, having never heard of Uyghurs. We quickly negotiated a transaction using hand gestures and a mix of Chinese and English, but when they miscounted the *renminbi* three times, I reached out to intervene. That was the cue they were waiting for. "PO-LICE!" they cried, shoving some *renminbi* in my hands before they rushed away. They had, I found, given me a one-to-one swap, making themselves a profit even if they hadn't exactly robbed me. I had to laugh at the simplicity of their ruse; they had certainly made my first day in China, and my first encounter with Uyghurs, moments to remember.

Years later, in part due to the above incident, I listened eagerly when Uyghur friends in Beijing told stories about the legendary Osman Doqa, a Uyghur from Yining who, for most of the 1980s, reputedly controlled the networks of Uyghur merchants and moneychangers sojourning in Guangzhou, themselves all from Yining. But I was perplexed. I had met dozens of Uyghurs at that point, and all went by a single name. Yet Osman had two. "Why is it Osman Doqa?" I asked. This is the story they told.

Alone, Osman had once walked into the restaurant that served as headquarters for a rival Uyghur gang in another large Chinese city, Zhengzhou, and asked them to hand over a girl from Yining they had lured into their group. Although the men were openly impressed by his boldness, a deeply admired trait, they laughed at his request. Rather than surrender the girl, they beat him severely, broke both his arms, stabbed him with shards from ceramic plates, and dumped him in a corner. Minutes later, when the men had turned their attention elsewhere, he rose silently to his feet and hurled himself at their leader. He knocked the man to the ground and began pounding his forehead into his opponent's face. With both of his arms broken he was quickly subdued, but the gang was so amazed by his boldness, they bestowed on him two items he retains to this day. The young lady (at last count they had three children and lived quietly in a splendid house in the *mehelle*), and eternal renown for his childhood nickname *doqa* (bulging forehead). The friends who told me this story did not mention that "to make a *doq*" also means "to threaten," an interesting semantic association for the nickname of a man reputed to head a major protection racket. But this, the first nickname I ever learned, had sparked my interest in the stories behind men's nicknames.

Lesson 2. The "Anvil": Every Nickname Is a Secret

Between 1985 and 1991 I spent several years in Beijing, and my interest in Uyghur culture and history began then. While pursuing an interest in Uyghur music, I made friends with a number of Uyghur men my own age who also lived in Beijing. For years they continued to speak to me in Mandarin—only after 1991 did I make any progress learning Uyghur—while often speaking Uyghur to one another in my presence. At the time of the following incident, I had not realized that *all* Uyghur men had nicknames; I thought Osman *doqa* was unique in this regard. One day I asked a friend why, when he spoke Uyghur, I often heard him refer to a friend not simply as Peret, the man's given name, but as Peret *sendel*. He reluctantly admitted that *sendel* was a nickname. He warned me gravely, "Uyghurs never mention a person's nickname to his face" (I hadn't known this, and as we will see below the statement is accurate), and insisted I never mention the word to Peret. *Sendel* meant "anvil," he told me, explaining that Peret had once slept with a female prostitute nicknamed *sendel*, a metaphor for her having been "hammered on" by many men. As I began to pay greater attention to nickname use, I realized that men frequently *referred* to people who were absent using name-nickname pairs but never uttered nicknames when those people were present. Years later friends admitted to me the real story behind this nickname. Had I known originally that women were never given nicknames,* I might have guessed something I was told only much later, that Peret himself was metaphorically labeled an "anvil" because he reputedly sought out other men for consensual sex.

This new information made nicknaming practices even more intriguing. If a man's nickname was never uttered in his presence, why was it used so frequently and with such relish by his friends when he was not there? It was, I thought, a strange kind of teasing or insulting behavior that strictly required the butt of the insult to be absent, to remain unaware the insult had been made. If assigning and then using derogatory nicknames were forms of symbolic aggression, what benefit did men seek out or gain by engaging in psychological combat only with absent rivals? The point of this strictly non-addressing nicknaming, I suspected, had as much to do with the speaker's relationship with his audience as it did his relationship with the person assigned the nickname.

---

*In my final list of 550 unique nicknames assigned to specific *mehelle* residents, only two were assigned to women.

Lesson 3. Nixon in China: Nicknames "Sink In"

Early in my field research in Zawut I met several times with the co-author of a published list of local nicknames.[2] This man, a Yining native in his mid-fifties, generously spent many hours discussing with me the meanings of these and other nicknames. On one of those occasions, as we worked through his records of local name-nickname pairs, I came to a strangely familiar-sounding nickname, *néksun.*

"Is that Nixon, like President Nixon?" I asked.

"That's right, it's Nixon," he said. "During Nixon's visit to China in 1972 someone realized that Ablet's nose looked just like his, so they called him Nixon."

"And it 'stuck,' huh?" I asked in Uyghur, just to maintain the patter of an interested listener.

"*Stuck?* Why no, it got digested . . . ."

The Uyghur verb for expressing how nicknames take hold, *singmek,* has two meanings: the first is "to seep or ooze," the second is for food "being digested" (the causative form *singdürmek* refers to what the person does to the food, "causing [it] to be digested"). This metaphor suggests that just as the nourishment of food seeps into and becomes flesh, nicknames are permanently absorbed into the identities of those who bear them. It may also suggest the potential prescriptive capacity of nicknames: they get inside you and affect your behavior, just as much as they may describe it. The Uyghur metaphorical relation between name and named is stronger than its American counterpart, where what merely "sticks" can more easily become "unstuck," and where through verbal formulas (e.g., "I'm rubber, you're glue") one can "stick" bad names back onto the would-be namer. Just as the "sticking" metaphor indicates the relative impermanence typical of American nicknaming practices, the Uyghur digestion metaphor accurately portrays the life-long permanence of Uyghur nicknames. Even more suggestively, it also situates nicknames conceptually in the digestive process, between eating and bodily evacuation. As we will see below, both of these activities are important elaborating symbols for describing all manner of men's shortcomings in the cultivation of a masculine habitus through bodily and psychological self-control.[3] Taken together, these facts suggest that psychological concerns figure as centrally in Uyghur nicknaming as nicknaming use itself figures in the more psychologically nuanced exchanges of Uyghur social life.

Lesson 4. "Can't-Take-It": Provocation and Prank

Despite the best efforts of many *mehelle* residents to unlock the mysteries of certain nicknames for me, explanations for a number of seemingly unrelated nicknames consisted often of the same single word. Over and over informants would say of a particular nickname, "That's for someone who is *chidimas*," and then explain no further. In a literal sense I knew the word meant roughly "cannot take it" or "doesn't tolerate," but it remained a mystery to me why the word occurred so frequently in discussions of interpersonal relations. Insight came unexpectedly with the incident described in this field note excerpt.

Today I was sitting on the *supa* typing field notes. Abdüshükür (16 months old) was happily waving a purple fifty-*tiyin* note. I plucked it from his hand, just to provoke him, and put it in my pocket.* Before he reacted, Senemgül addressed me sharply. "Hey, don't take that money! That money gives birth. If you take fifty *tiyin*, it becomes one *som*—we take interest on that money!"

I gave it back to the baby, apprehensive about her use of the rhetorical figure of money and payments (I was sensitive about this, given my status as a paying houseguest). More important, she hit me this morning as we were teasing each other, grabbing me by the arms, acting angry in a flirtatious way, so I am sketchy about her teasing me today. I didn't want to escalate a kind of playfulness I haven't ever seen among siblings our age, so I just gave in. Then she and her sister Maynur, seeing that I had submitted to her, sang at me in unison

Couldn't take it, couldn't take it	*chidimidi chidimidi*
Pancake asshole	*chelpen qong*
If he leaves, if it's been enough	*ketse yetse*
False asshole	*yalghan qong*

---

*In describing child-rearing practices, I noted that young children, even infants, were often provoked by adults. Such behavior was routine and I often found myself following along.

I had shown that I could be easily rebuked into submission, and they jumped on the opportunity to mock me for not being able to "take it." After I was unable to find *chelpen* in my dictionaries, Maynur stretched her arms wide and explained that *chelpen qong* meant a big, wide, round asshole the size of a washbasin. Later I determined that *chelpen* was a dialectical variant of *chelpek*, a large pancake made by taking a lump of dough and pressing it repeatedly with a wooden rolling pin widening it out until it spreads to full size, an apt metaphor for enlarging someone's anus to the breaking point. By singing "couldn't take it," the women implied they had pushed me to a point where I could no longer tolerate the force of their symbolic aggression. That I yielded in itself proved the superiority of their attack and the inferiority of my verbal and volitional defenses, and the enlarging of the anus was a metaphor of masculine domination used to describe their victory. Only the line "false (*yalghan*) asshole" seemed to me not to fit with the symbolic and social context of the women's performance of this verse.

Since I had long been frustrated in my efforts to better understand *chidimas* in relation to nicknaming, I was glad to have encountered this enlightening rhyme. A short time later Yakupjan came into the room, while I was busy typing field notes, and the women explained to him what had happened. He immediately offered a variant of the above item, one that clarified the reference to the "false" asshole.

Couldn't take it, couldn't take it	*chidimidi chidimidi*
Pancake asshole	*chelpen qong*
In four drops of grease	*töt ser yaghda*
A greased-up asshole	*yaghlighan qong*

The image of the "greased-up asshole" seems more in line with the overall symbolism of the jibe, that the victorious and dominant party in this psychological combat has metaphorically penetrated and overwhelmed the anus of the loser.[4] In the Yining dialect *gh* phonemes that fall between certain other phonemes are often dropped in speech; in this case dropping the first *gh* from *yaghlighan* (greased) gives *yalighan*, a word I suspect has been changed during oral circulation into *yalghan*, "false."

Yakupjan explained to me what kind of person was *chidimas*.

You say to them, "Why can't you keep your word?" Look, it's like, if they lose gambling at sheep's knuckles, and they can't take it [i.e., are provoked to anger], or if they say they will do something, but later they come up with some excuse, and don't do what they said they would . . . or if I say, "I am going to borrow your bike," and you say, "Sure," then you refuse to lend the bike later, turning your back, that's *chidimas.*

"Turning your back" on a friend, as Yakupjan put it, means turning your backside to them. Friends are people who keep their faces turned toward each other, who create social space by forming circles and facing one another when they gather. This was amply demonstrated in the discussion in Chapter 7 of the rules (*qa'ide*) of sociality that men enforce during *olturash.* A man is criticized and often derided for sitting with his face pointed away from the center of the group, or for passing in front of someone with his back to them when entering or exiting a gathering. This helps explain why a man who regularly sat leaning sideways, with his buttocks tilted upward, was assigned the permanent nickname "buttocks"(*yanpash*). In Yakupjan's explanation, the behavior of a man who cannot bear up under the pressures of friendship and who turns away from his promises exemplifies *chidimas.*

In Yining usage, then, *chidimas* means strictly "one whose capacity to tolerate has been pushed, or is easily pushed, to its breaking point." To call someone *chidimas* does not mean that they refuse to accept some form of symbolic domination or aggression and that they respond with some clever or superior counterstrategy of dominance. Such a *refusal* to tolerate is the opposite of the *incapacity* to tolerate expressed by the term *chidimas.* Collections of anecdotes about renowned Yining jokester Hésam's behavior at *olturash*, for example, include many stories in which he purposefully and successfully uses verbal taunts to push victims to the point where they resort to physically threatening him, a response that signals his complete victory over his opponent.[5]

Unfortunately for individuals who have low thresholds for tolerating symbolic aggression, *mehelle* men constantly provoke their friends through such ruses as heaping on them spurious requests for gratuitous favors, requests made only in the hope of causing the targeted person to respond with anger. The attempt to prove others to be *chidimas*, in other words, was neither an occasional nor an incidental feature of *mehelle* social life. On the contrary, the performance of masculine identity seemed to require that men make constant efforts to annoy and aggravate any men around them whom they think they might succeed at "breaking." This field note excerpt describes an interaction typical of a kind I witnessed on a daily basis.

Two men, Abet and Kérim, stand by the side of the road at a public phone. Abet wishes to page someone, so he says casually to Kérim, "Dial *hongshan*," referring to a paging service with live operators. Abet is actually standing closer to the phone than Kérim, but he goes out of his way to place a demand on the other man.

If Kérim complies, Abet wins a small victory; he has been the dominant one. If in refusing Kérim reveals any anger and resentment he might feel, he shows himself to be *chidimas*, and Abet wins an even greater victory. The burden is now on Kérim, who must obey or instantly counter with an artful way of getting out of the obligation.

These kinds of demands were a constant feature of male interaction in the *mehelle*. Stanley Brandes, describing pranks played among men in an Andalusian town, has written

There exists a conscious attempt . . . to arouse a victim to the point of anger. The [prank] becomes the test of a person's ability to maintain control over his emotions. It pits the determination of a group of men to provoke and anger another until he breaks, against the equally strong determination of the victim to maintain his composure or even, ideally, casually to dismiss his aggressors' actions through laughter and humor.

. . . No matter how much they publicly dismiss the incident as insignificant, the aggressors will secretly regard their victim with contempt for his inability to maintain his mastery over the situation and by extension, over his life in general. . . . Men who disintegrate under the threat of aggression are scorned, while those who withstand it courageously are admired.[6]

This captures precisely a key characteristic of a good deal of men's interactions in the *mehelle*, not merely behaviors that fit the category of prank-playing.[7] Men do play pranks, of course. To give just one tragic example, Abidem's first-born son was killed, leaving behind a widow and nine children, when he was hit by a truck driven by a close friend who was attempting to scare him by "pretending" to run him over. A critical distinction exists, however, between the prank as a genre of social interaction and the forms of symbolic aggression that character-ize men's interactions. In the former, a prank is framed as such by par-ticipants through meta-communicative words or gestures, such as the gesture of a double eye blink, as described in the previous chapter. Ge-neric symbolic aggression, on the other hand, was a social constant and was not framed as being distinct in any way from sincere or genuine in-teraction.

Having demonstrated just a few of the more interesting discoveries that led me into the deeper study of nicknaming practices, I turn now to analyses of nicknaming practices and of the names themselves.

Structural Features of Uyghur Nicknaming

In onomastics, or the study of naming, the set of all names in a given language is designated its "onomasticon." Following the derivation of the word "nickname" from "eke" + "name,"* I propose that the term "ekonomastics" be applied to the study of nicknaming and that the set of words used as nicknames in a given language be termed its "ekono-masticon." Before I examine the semantic space of the Uyghur ekono-masticon, I first describe some structural features of nicknames, using a framework that allows me to outline the systemic conditions that make nicknaming coherent as a social institution. The concepts I employ emerged from my consideration of Uyghur materials, but the flexibility of the model should allow it to be easily expanded or modified for cross-cultural nickname analysis.

Uyghur nicknames are combinative. Uyghur nicknames are always com-bined with and are never substituted for given names. Kérim may be referred to as Kérim *shatraq* ("diarrhea," a common nickname) but never simply as *shatraq*.

Uyghur nicknames are non-addressing. Although in many cultures nick-names are used as terms of address, Uyghur nicknames, as we saw above, are strictly non-addressing.[8] Whereas addressing nickname use instantiates a dyadic relationship between addresser and addressee,

---

*Jönsjö, *Studies on Middle English Nicknames*, 11. Originally this was OE *ecan* + OE *nama*, meaning "additional name."

non-addressing nicknaming reflects more how individuals manage others' perceptions of dyadic speaker-referent relationships.

Uyghur nicknames are conditionally referential. The use of a Uyghur nickname as a term of reference is strictly conditional upon the referent's absence. Note that this and the previous condition taken together mean that Uyghur men are unlikely to ever hear their name-nickname pair uttered.[9]

Uyghur nicknames are maximally durable. In minimally durable nicknaming traditions, nicknames assigned to an individual are temporary and plural, and consensus over them is neither sought nor achieved. In maximally durable nicknaming, on the other hand, nicknames are permanent, and group consensus over an individual's nickname is achieved.[10] Uyghur men are assigned a single nickname with a high degree of group consensus, and this typically remains their nickname for life. For some men, however, a second nickname assigned later in life permanently replaces their first nickname.

Uyghur nicknaming is strictly male gendered. A review of nicknaming practices worldwide suggests that nicknaming is a diverse activity—sometimes women and men participate equally, and sometimes men predominate. Existing studies suggest that when nicknames are minimally durable, they are more likely to be gender neutral; when nicknames are maximally durable, they are much more likely to be associated with interactions between males.[11] This pattern is present in Yining nicknaming, where nicknames are highly durable, and only men have nicknames. In the *mehelle*, durable nicknaming systems first take hold during male adolescence, when the majority of names are assigned. This, I suggest, is best understood as reflecting male adolescents' concerns to break away from the female gender identity of their caregivers and to assert their male gender identity and masculine habitus in the local community. Some individuals may be assigned another nickname later in their lives, but this is not the norm. Since men maintain the use of adolescent nicknames throughout their lives to express attachment to aspects of personal identity and gender identity, it is not surprising that adolescent identities and adult masculine identities are critically linked together in the lives of *mehelle* men.

Uyghur nicknames are not inherited. A nicknaming system is heritable insofar as it encourages or permits the passing of nicknames along recognized lines of social reproduction. For example, if a man receives a particular nickname, that name may be bestowed automatically (or upon the fulfillment of some condition, such as at the man's death) on a child or to some other kin group member. In the case of Yining, strict heritability is not found, although it is not unknown for a son to be given a nickname that has a semantic relationship to his father's nickname. A common Uyghur nickname for a tall man, for example, is "camel" (*töge*). The son of such a man may be given the nickname "baby camel" (*botilaq*). One Yining man had the nickname "fly" (*chiwin*); his son received the nickname "mosquito" (*pasha*); that man's son in turn was given the nickname "midge" (*kumuta*). Although I found no indication of its use in 1990s Yining, a separate system of strictly heritable nicknames does exist in other areas of Xinjiang.[12]

Nicknaming in Context and Practice

Perhaps the first point to be made about nicknames in the *mehelle* is that they are used at all. Frequent nickname use, it has been suggested, correlates with dense internal networks of communication typical of village life, networks that tend to disappear under modernization and urbanization.[13] The frequent use of nicknames in the *mehelle* thus attests to the continued existence in the *mehelle* of dense social networks, which I argued in Chapter 7 were maintained in large part through *olturash* participation.

A number of social functions have been associated with nickname use.[14] The utility of nicknames for identification is one widely noted function. In Yining, I often witnessed men and women alike using nicknames in conversation to differentiate men with the same name. Although this confirms that nicknames are regularly *used* to identify individuals, it explains neither the complex features of nickname creation and maintenance nor the rich expressive uses of nicknames.

The role of nicknames in reinforcing social control is also widely acknowledged in Western studies.[15] The importance of stigma management in relation to the development of social competence has been considered central to understanding the social psychology of nicknaming among children, who, it has been argued, use such names to display and maintain both positive and negative affective dyadic bonds.[16] Such findings have little relevance in non-addressing nicknaming systems, which deny any opportunity for impression management by creating a domain in which the person is systematically deprived of any chance to contest or influence (or even to know) the name he is given.

If naming in general is a powerful means for establishing or acknowledging an identity-claim, then in the *mehelle* nicknaming in particular is one means men use to establish their collective identity as a local community of men. As one proverb suggests, "A man without a nickname is not a man" (*leqemsiz er, er emes*). Nickname usage can also reinforce relative degrees of situatedness within this local collective identity. If knowing the name of someone implies at the very least that he is not a stranger, demonstrating knowledge of a man's nickname shows that one has an additional degree of familiarity with him. A man who displays wide knowledge of other men's nicknames shows his participation in a wide network of social relations; in short, nickname use functions as an index of social status.

Nicknames also shape the collective memory of individuals. Most *mehelle* men strolled daily through Yining's markets, stopping to chat or play cards at the stalls of their friends, often leaving others to watch their own stalls or businesses to do so. During my field research, I followed this routine as well, visiting the stalls of merchants in my gradually expanding networks. On such occasions, men I had not yet met often stopped in to join our group, and I would inevitably be introduced in a manner something like this.

This kid (*bala*), he's a good kid, he's living in Zawut *mehelle*, at the house of Memetjan, Memetjan the *rawap* player who left for Beijing, living with Abidem, the wife of Tursun Stovesmith (*meshchi*).

All the men in nearby *mehelle* seemed to know Memetjan's father as Tursun Stovesmith (stovesmithing had been his trade). When family members and close friends spoke his nickname, however, they referred to him without exception as Tursun *tembur*, since he was also a renowned player of that musical instrument. By calling him Tursun *tembur*, family members were remembering him as the valued musician he was within the community, despite the more mundane occupational label that was his consensually assigned nickname.

The final and, in my view, most important function of *mehelle* nicknaming is as a means of displacing aggression. Consider the word *shatraq* (diarrhea, diarrheic), a common derogatory adjective in Yining vernacular meaning "frivolous, skittish." Used in everyday speech *shatraq* is just a word; only when paired with a name does it function as a nickname. A man who says "Kérim is a very *shatraq* person" alone bears responsibility for his decision to employ this particular modifier for Kérim, and the utterance can be viewed as a small but discernible act of personal aggression. If instead the man casually refers to Kérim using the name-nickname pair Kérim *shatraq*, he intensifies the attack—Kérim is so "diarrhea" that he and "diarrhea" are an identity, without the contingencies implied by predication—and at the same time he shifts responsibility for the aggression toward the group, through whose consensus the name was selected. Nicknaming permits men to initiate aggressive acts while disclaiming personal responsibility for that aggression.

Uyghur scholars who have commented on the matter have taken an opposite view, saying that Uyghur nickname use should not be viewed as a form of interpersonal psychological aggression: "Among Uyghurs, the putting of nicknames, or the use of nicknames . . . is absolutely not taken as offensive. On the contrary, it is seen as a pleasing and amiable thing."[17] Even when describing verbal duels that involve teasing through the use of nicknames, Uyghur scholars emphasize the spirit of friendship behind such duels.

Of course, this type of joking is only for opening the heart, for livening up a gathering, for enjoying the richness of language, for raising skill in speaking. These jokes, which center on nicknames, are a kind of Uyghur artistic form, using rhythmic, rhyming, semantic wordplay to create friendly relations— no matter how piercing they may be, this does not in the least affect the friendly affection [between participants]. Invariably, the most scathing jokers at gatherings are found to be the most harmonious of companions in everyday life.[18]

I suggest that, on the contrary, an examination of nickname use in men's joking relationships reveals that nicknames are widely used for psychological aggression; specifically, they are used by men attempting to push others past their breaking points.

In his study of narrative genres of Uyghur folklore, Osman Ismayil considers nicknames as they appear in what he calls "nickname joking."

The objective of nickname joking is to start by making a comment that directs attention to the competitor's nickname, and in so doing to make completely manifest his nickname. . . . In executing his idea, the jokester must display mastery at picking out some characteristic of the thing which is the person's nickname, and incorporating [an oblique reference to] it into the situation at hand, so that those who hear are instantly aware that such a reference has been made.[19]

This kind of joking was common in the *mehelle*, and a man's nickname might be hinted at in his presence as a form of teasing. One man described for me an encounter he had once witnessed at an *olturash* involving three persons, A, B, and C. All were good friends who knew one another's nicknames. One of the men, B, had the nickname "beggar" (*diwane*), assigned not because of his economic circumstances or because he was prone to requesting handouts but because he was in the habit of walking a lot. Early in the *olturash*, A picked up a soft *nan* flatbread from the center of the table, broke it into pieces, and distributed the pieces around the table so that each man present had bread within reach. This gesture, one I witnessed at many *olturash*, momentarily places the actor in the role of host and may be done by anyone present whether or not they purchased the bread or are an actual host of the event. In this case, though, A paused a second, then surreptitiously squeezed both eyes shut for a second or two in the direction of C, a common gestural cue for a joke or prank, in which the closed eyes suggest how the dupe will be blind to the joke. A then reached out and slid the piece of bread nearest B several inches closer to him. Beggars circulating through the *mehelle* were often given small pieces of bread as alms. Thus, A's gesture, his emphasis on giving bread to B, silently invokes B's nickname for the amusement of the other men. In a separate incident, one *olturash* participant collected a few bread crumbs from the table in his hand and casually dropped them in front of another man whose nickname was "chicken" (*toxu*), as if feeding a chicken.

In his discussion of Uyghur nickname joking, Sabitov presents another example of such joking in an exchange that took place at an *oltur-*

ash between three men whose nicknames were "blind" (*qarghu*), "lantern" (*dinhuli*) (from Chinese *deng huo lu*), and "dog" (*it*).

"I hear that at the circus, they light a lantern, and dogs jump over it from one side to the other," said Blind jokingly to the one nicknamed "lantern," causing a third person sitting at his side, whose own nickname was "dog," to start laughing.

Lantern responded . . . instantly, "Oh, so you've seen it yourself, have you? You know, I even heard that all the dogs they trained were blind!"

Thus, even though the two jokesters initiated this exchange through direct reference to each other's nicknames, it is the third party, the one nicknamed "dog," who is the underlying object of their joking, and who remains without a comeback.[20]

Teasing through oblique nickname references can also take place outside *olturash* and this kind of joking duel. The following is an example of a verse used to taunt a man by invoking his nickname "yellow" (*sériq*), assigned due to his light complexion. The following verse was uttered repeatedly by Abidem in the presence of her son-in-law Ablimit to annoy him; the couplet invoked his nickname *sériq* by rhyming with it.

Water that flows is a stream	*sular aqidighan ériq*
What is eaten by chickens is millet	*toxular yeydighan tériq*

Interpretive Content Analysis of Nicknames

An examination of nicknames themselves can provide a unique window into local categories of personal and social identity, insofar as nicknames isolate those psychological and physical traits that Uyghurs themselves find significant. In the sections that follow, a content analysis of nicknames is organized around certain common thematic categories. All terms presented below are nicknames of actual *mehelle* residents collected in Yining in the 1990s.[21]

The Male Habitus and Its Transgressions

Men who exhibit behavior deemed typical of women are often assigned nicknames on this basis. Examples of such names include "pretty" (*hörliqa*), "woman's" (*damsika*, from Russian *damskiy*), "miss" (*xénim*), and "grandma" (*momay*). "Frivolous" (*naynaq*) is for a man whose walk is characteristic of a woman's, who swings his hips while he walks (the verb for this is *naynaqlash*). The nickname *tetey* is also used for "a man who walks like a woman," and by extension a man who is effeminate generally. It derives from the Chinese *taitai* (woman, wife), a euphemism in Yining vernacular for Han bar hostesses.

"Cosmetics" (*pedez*) is for a man overly concerned with his stylish appearance. "Unmarried woman" (*chokan*) is for an effeminate man. Other nicknames used in Yining for men "who act like women" include *shawaxun, zeypane, seteng,* and *hejexan*. Of these, the latter two terms refer specifically (according to Jarring) to a man who plays the receptive role in a homosexual relationship.[22] Other recorded nicknames include "girl" (*qiz*) and "bashful" (*ghiljing*). *Ghiljing* literally means "bashful," but is specifically used to describe a wily woman who merely feigns bashfulness to seduce men.

Walking and gait are associated with issues of bodily control and masculine identity in ways that go beyond associations with being effeminate. *Ship-ship,* the sound of creeping on tiptoe—vernacular Uyghur is rich in onomatopoeias—was assigned to a man who walked with small mincing steps. *Dong-dong,* a clanging, ringing sound, was for a man who walked with big movements. *Ghach-ghach,* another onomatopoeia, was given to a man because of the sound of his new shoes. *Palaximan,* for a man "who went around knocking things over and making a racket," comes from *palaq,* meaning "racket, noisy confusion."

Dildash is for a man who walks like a drunk, whose movements are a bit sloppy. *Pir-pir,* an onomatopoeia for a spinning or humming sound, was for "a man who would walk all around town in the evenings like a crazy person." Such a man, we might well say in English, is one who "enjoys going for a spin." This nickname is likely cognate with *pir,* a title for the leader of a dervish sect, given the association of spinning with the circular dancing of dervishes. "Beggar" (*diwane*) is used for "someone who likes to walk." In the last two nicknames it is not the quality of the man's walking that he cannot control but the quantity. Such a man cannot organize his lifestyle to avoid excessive ambulation. Men seemed to derive great pleasure from commenting on how other men walked too much, one implication being that they themselves had the means to regularly take taxis.

Men who move too quickly are also criticized. "Nerves" (*nérwin*) was assigned to one man: "You'd say one word and the guy got upset, he got upset at everything. His nerves weren't normal, he was a grape salesman, but he'd hit the hands of people touching grapes." "Bolt" (*chichang*), in the sense of a horse "bolting," is for "one who leaps about, one who responds to hearing news he doesn't like by leaping about. He has no self-control." Jarring, I note, elicited the nickname "jumper" (*sékigek*) in 1935 from a southern Xinjiang informant who explained its meaning as follows: "If a man starts to hurry about when doing something, we say something like 'don't jump around like a frog.'"[23] This explanation of *sékigek* (prone to jumping) confirms that being unable to conduct one's affairs according to a properly measured tempo makes a man subject to ridicule.

The nickname *beg*, a local official in Xinjiang prior to Communist rule, is assigned to persons with exemplary self-control. One *mehelle* man explained this nickname by saying

He's a Beg, he's a Khan	*özi beg özi qan*
His own affairs, he himself takes care of	*öz ishi özi bashqurdighan*

Yawbey, from Chinese *yaobai*, "to swing back and forth," was for men who either were known as good dancers or swayed from side to side as they walked. The nickname "chaotic" (*qalaymiqan*) was for one who always made a mess of things. As noted earlier, "buttocks" (*yanpash*) was for a man who couldn't sit down well: "He always stuck his butt out when sitting, as if half on his side." The nickname *binno* was reportedly taken from the name of a Cambodian leader who was shown on television during a visit to China with his head swaying from side to side and was assigned to a man with the habit of swinging his head in the same way.

Bodily Emissions

Body-control issues salient in the life of the young child are extended metaphorically by adolescents to concerns about controlling the physical and emotional self. The word *chichqaq* (prone to shitting) was used to describe infants who shat a lot; at Abidem's I heard it often uttered in anger by a caregiver who had to wash Abdüshükür's swaddling cloths or clean a soiled rug. As a nickname, one informant tried to explain its metaphorical meaning saying: "Someone who likes to shit, he doesn't act like a man, doesn't treat his friends well." To say a man who treats his friends well "doesn't shit" means, in other words, that he has his anus squeezed tight, keeps himself under control. "Keep your asshole squeezed together" is a common expression meaning "don't get upset, keep yourself under control." "Holds his shit" (*chéchimas*) is a nickname for one "who keeps his anger inside." The use of a loose or a tight anus as a metaphor for emotional control over the self and over others is also found outside nicknaming, such as in the following Uyghur proverb.[24]

Know yourself!	*özengni bil*
Squeeze your anus!	*qongangni qis*
Watch your road!	*yolunggha baq*

"Diarrhea" (*shatraq*) is also extended metaphorically to mean "frivolous, unreliable, skittish." One man explained: "Someone who has diarrhea, it's someone who isn't heavy (*éghir*), but watery (*suluq*). . . . To say they shit a lot, shit diarrhea a lot, these two things mean the same." This comment suggests the analogy: this man's shit is to other men's shit (i.e., as liquid is to solid) as his character is to other men's character. Men often expressed the view that a man should be "solid" or "heavy" (*éghir*), a quality associated with traits of reliability, sturdiness, dependability, and competence; being "watery" (*suluq*), on the other hand, indicated the exact opposite of those traits. A man who is solid is one who can control his fluids. The inability to maintain the wholeness of the body suffered by the man with loose bowels becomes a metaphor applied to one who can't keep his social being stable and self-contained. "Prone to urinating" (*süygek*), on the other hand, carries no metaphorical meaning and, as a nickname, is assigned to a man who literally wet his pants or bed as a child.

Sepra, a word meaning both "vomit" and "anger," is another nickname that uses bodily emissions and bodily control as a metaphor for emotional control. "To be *sepra*" means "to get angry, be irritable," and "to do/make *sepra*" means "to vomit." The nickname *sepra* is for one who likes to get angry. "Snot" (*mangqa*) is assigned to a boy or man who literally has a nose that runs a lot, who sniffs frequently. "Saliva" (*shölgey*) was for someone with lots of saliva dripping all the time. "Eye pus" (*cha-paq*) is for a person who has a weeping eye. One *mehelle* resident employed in a government administrative office, who was widely seen as a sycophant, sought favor with a superior whose mother had died by visiting the man's house crying like a relative. For this he received the nickname "entered crying" (*yighlap kirdi*). Note that in this case the emission of a bodily fluid (tears) is recognized as a kind of gift-giving, that is mocked for being made with the explicit expectation of reciprocation.

Full and Empty, Liquid and Solid

Metaphorical meanings of liquidity and solidity go beyond the opposition between reliability and unreliability described above. The nickname "pacifier" (*soska*), for example, was explained this way.

It is like, if there is someone you ask to do something, and they say "Sure, I'll do it," and the next day you ask and they say "Tomorrow, tomorrow," and they always put you off, and never actually do it. That's like a *soska*, where you never really get any milk. Someone who speaks "dry words" (*quruq gep*), someone you can't get a real performance out of, no matter how hard you try, a liar, a false promiser.

Here the adjective "dry" also means "empty, hollow; without foundation." I once observed a *mehelle* man upbraid a female relative who claimed a particular folk belief was Muslim by saying "That's *quruq gep*, it's not in the Qur'an." In the metaphor of the pacifier, a dry breast represents disappointment and unreliability. Good friends are to a full breast, in other words, as bad friends are to an empty breast. Above I noted that the metaphor of penetrating and overwhelming the anus found in the *chidimas* rhyme was also linked with the man who is deficient in friendship. The expectations of reciprocity within friendship, in other words, stand as a bridge between, on one hand, symbols of empty versus full breasts and, on the other, the man who shows his butt when friends make demands of him. The common denominator in these images is that the object, a man, is feminized.

Other nicknames draw on core symbols of emptiness and fullness. A man is nicknamed *koldur*, "a clanging ringing sound," if "he is full of shit about what he will do, what he can do, but it's all empty." The adjective *por* describes rotten wood, or a tree whose core has rotted and become hollow. A fat person is nicknamed *por* to emphasize that he is "empty inside," although by some accounts *por* can also mean simply "fat." *Pok-pok*, the noise made when one thumps on a melon, was assigned to a man who was "hollow, weak, who has no backbone." *Löm-löm*, meaning "elastic, spongy; loose" is used for a slack or negligent person, as is the nickname "wax" (*mom*). *Paxpaq*, "empty, hollow," is used for one who speaks "with empty words," that is, someone who is untrustworthy. To say a man should be heavy (*éghir*) means also that his words should carry weight, that they should not be empty. One folk verse comments on empty people, saying

Outside looks good,	*téshi pal pal*
Inside is empty	*ichi tal tal*

The nickname "noodles" (*leghmen*) was assigned to a man who had an "empty waist" (*béli bosh*), that is, a weak backbone, no strength or ambition.

Another instance in which a watery substance serves as a metaphor for social relations is found in a Hodja trickster tale widely known in Yining, which I heard unelicited several times during my field research, saw in print, and the final line of which I heard used alone as an item of folk speech. In Xinjiang, the protagonist of these tales is called Nasréd-din Eppendi, or simply Eppendi. I paraphrase the story here.

A large group of friends arrived unannounced at Eppendi's house and presented him with a rabbit they had hunted. He served them a meal of the rabbit, and they left.

A week later, another large group of men arrived. They explained that they were friends of the first group of friends, clearly expecting to be treated as guests. Eppendi had little in the house, but hastily prepared a soup out of the remaining rabbit, which they ate with relish. After this they departed.

A week later, a different group of men arrived unexpectedly.

"We're friends of the friends," they explained, taking their seats. After some preparation, Eppendi brought the hungry men steaming bowls of water.

"What's this?" they blustered indignantly.

"Why, that's the soup-of-the-soup (*shorpaning shorpési*)!"

A meal of liquid, without substance, is used as metaphor for friends who are not real friends, those who have no intention of reciprocating. A related nickname is *suyuqash*, the name of a thick soup with square noodles. The word is a compound of *suyuq* (watery) and *ash* (meal) and is used as a nickname for men who are "watery," whose actions are unreliable and unstable, such as those who "act crazy when they drink."

Although the word was not known to be an actual nickname, several times I saw *olturash* jokesters bestow on peasant characters in their anecdotes the nickname "noodle-cooking water" (*menteng*), and their doing so always produced an immediate and intense comic effect. In this case I suspect the reason has little to do with metaphors of liquidity and comes instead from a unique ambiguity regarding the cultural meaning of *menteng*. Alone in Uyghur cuisine, it both is and is not food. *Mehelle* residents widely believed that ending one's meal by drinking a ladle of the water leftover from cooking noodles was good for one's health. In the home, however, any left-over noodle-cooking water was treated as non-food and was poured into a basin and used to wash the dishes. To call a person "noodle-water," something that is and is not a food, is simultaneously to value *and* devalue them. And indeed, *mehelle* residents viewed peasants as the "truest" Uyghurs—this is perhaps a form of romanticization reflecting a nostalgia for their own remembered or imagined more rural backgrounds—but also mocked and denigrated them for their relative poverty.

Reciprocity: The Hard and the Soft

Hardness, in the vernacular of nicknaming, is associated with an unwillingness to give, a reluctance to surrender things to others. "Hard bread" (*qattiq nan*) is for one who is stingy, miserly. Home-baked *nan* does become too hard to chew by the third day after baking and is typically eaten only after being soaked in black tea to which salt and fresh cow's milk or clotted cream have been added. Just as hard *nan* requires tea to soften, a man nicknamed "hard bread" will soften up and yield benefit to others only if there is some "tea" (*chay*) in it for him. "Tea" not only can mean the literal tea one serves guests to honor them but also is an abbreviation for "tea money" (*chay puli*), a euphemism for a bribe or the share given to the middleman in a market transaction. The nickname "tea" for a flatterer makes sense, since such a man heaps words on others to soften them up, to make them yield benefit. The proverbial simile "like trying to pull a hair out of an unleavened *nan*" (*pétir nandin qil sugharghandek*) helps us understand the nickname "hard bread"; any attempt to pull a hair from a hard *nan* would break the hair before the baked dough would yield.

Nicknames for stingy persons that invoke a hardness metaphor include "hard boots" (*qattiq ötük*) and "stone bean" (*tash purchaq*), used for people who "won't let go of anything." Stingy persons were among those described as *chidimas*, since they would become upset when others asked them to give up something. "Dregs" (*dashqal*), a term that specifically refers to dregs of coal left behind in the ashes, was a nickname used for a former Nationalist Party follower who remained behind after Communist rule and was considered "no longer good for anything." This term surely derives from the Chinese *canzha yunie*, "the dregs of the old society," a phrase popularized during China's Cultural Revolution.

Not all nicknames dealing with issues of reciprocity draw on the hard/soft distinction. "Red-eyes" (*qizil köz*) and "jealous one" (*hesetxur*) are used for jealous, envious persons. "Spoon" (*qoshuq*) is for "one who puts just a little food or tea in the bowl when serving others, who puts only a few spoonfuls." "Belly" (*qorsaq*) was used only literally for men of large girth, despite the fact that in other contexts, metaphorical meanings of the belly do relate to reciprocity; to have a "wide belly" is to be generous, and to have a "painful belly" is to be sorry about another's misfortune. A stingy man might also be nicknamed simply "stingy" (*xesis*). "Empty pocket" (*quruq xalta*) was assigned to a man who repeatedly asked others for tobacco to smoke, a reference to the practice of *mehelle* men of keeping loose *moxorka* tobacco in a pants or jacket pocket. "Overripe" (*ching pishshiq*) is for one who does things too carefully: "If you borrow something, he goes over all the conditions of borrowing."

When *mehelle* residents return home after visiting at each other's houses, those who have been guests enjoy commenting in great detail on the treatment they received, and hosts inevitably have much to say about guests' behavior. How much food guests eat is carefully observed by hosts, and gluttony is criticized. One who is *ishteylik*, "with a good appetite," may be nicknamed "whirlpool" (*girdap*), because he sucks everything down. The nicknames "doesn't eat meat" (*gösh yimes*), and "doesn't eat bread" (*nan yimes*), men suggested, also implied criticism of those whose participation in the reciprocal food exchanges of everyday life was deemed inappropriate. The "doesn't eat meat" nickname perhaps arose because the man declined to take even the obligatory single bite of another's Qurban Festival meat offering.

Speaking

Given Uyghurs' great admiration for rhetorical skill, it is not surprising that many nicknames refer to features of an individual's speech. "Stutterer" (*kékech*), for example, is for a person who stammers or stutters. "Sluggish" (*ezme*) is for one who speaks slowly. "Candy" (*tangga*) is also for someone who speaks slowly and unclearly; the word is a shortened version of the local term *tanggaza* (from Chinese *tangguozi*, "candy pieces"), referring to a nougat-like candy made from barley malt sugar. This candy is sold in the streets only in the winter, when the cold temperature allows it to hold its shape. Once put in the mouth, it quickly warms and melts into sticky taffy. One man whose trade was to make and sell this candy was also nicknamed *tanggaza*.

Paxal, meaning "chaff, stalks left after threshing; rice straw," was for "men who speak ambiguously, untrustworthily" (*tutruqsiz gep qildighanlar*); in other words, for men who say things that can be taken two ways, who unscrupulously exploit ambiguity in their interpersonal dealings. "Cotton" (*paxta*) is for one whose words can't be trusted. *Pöshkel* was assigned to a man who was described as an *ösekchi*, someone who speaks in a rambling manner and who says "crazy things" (*ösek*). "Doesn't low" (*mörimes*), in the sense of the lowing of cattle, is for one who never speaks, a quiet person. This nickname implicitly references the derogatory nicknames "cow" (*kala*) and "calf" (*mozay*), which themselves imply a man is unintelligent, by casting him as a cow that is so stupid it is not even able to low.

"Garrulous" (*kaska*), an adjective also used for dogs that bark endlessly, is assigned to men who speak too much. Both "submachine gun" (*aptomat*) and *pilmot* (which men stated was a rapid-fire large-bore gun deriving from Russian *pilimyot*) are for men who speak rapidly. "Mosquito" (*pasha*) is for one who is *ghingshuq*, who whines or speaks too much, prattles on. "Thunder" (*güldür*) is for a man who talks loudly and rapidly. "Talkative" (*kot-kot*) is for a man who talks all the time, especially one who often complains. To clarify, in *mehelle* vernacular a man may be praised as being "exceptional at complaining" if he is skilled at complaining about things in a way that provokes others to anger, which is a desirable masculine ability. In that sense being a complainer is a positive attribute; in this nickname, the sense is negative, suggesting the man is a whiner, not a skilled provocateur. *Qaqash*, possibly from *qaqach* (dried snot), is also assigned to a person who talks a lot. "Calumny" (*pasat*) is for one whose speech is *inawetsiz*, "invalid; lowly regarded, not taken seriously by others." *Pöpek*, presumably an alternative spelling of *pöpük* (tassel), was explained as a nickname assigned to men who are *shipa* (clean), which is slang for "one whose words and actions are elegant, refined, delicate, a person whose life and affairs are in order, a person who is solid, sturdy."[25] This definition nicely captures *mehelle* residents' tendency to conflate verbal control with behavioral control in general.

Gür-gür is an onomatopoeia used for the sounds of speaking, stomach rumbling, and wind blowing. As a nickname it is used for a person who often brags or boasts, a man we might say is a "windbag." *Xing-xing* is onomatopoeic for the sound of nasal speaking and is assigned to a man who speaks that way. "Windpipe" (*kanay*) was for a man who had a loud voice, as was "big-big" (*chong-chong*), a name whose meaning may relate to the term *chongchi*, for a conceited person.

The Body

It should not be surprising that body types draw attention in nickname assignment—a thin person, for example, might be called "skinny" (*oruq*) or "scrawny" (*awaq*)—but perhaps unexpected is the extent to which body characteristics serve as metaphors for masculine conduct. The nickname *erwah* (soul of a deceased person) is also used for a skinny person, but in a manner that relates to the extended meanings of "heaviness" considered above. As one informant put it, "someone who is really skinny, you know, *someone who is unable to accomplish anything.*" Again, the suggestion is that a man must be metaphorically heavy; a skinny man simply doesn't have the weight to accomplish things. The nickname "with mange, scabies" (*qotur*) is also assigned, at least in some cases, strictly due to a person's skinny stature. Tall skinny persons are often nicknamed "camel" (*töge*) or, more rarely, "stringbean" (*jangdu*). *Kisltek* is used for "a person as slender as a child" (*ushshaq balilik adem*), although it may derive from *kiseldek*, "like a sick person." A person with a strong, solid build may be assigned the name "dirt clod" (*pangpa*, or *pampa*).

A short man might be called "short" (*pakar*), or "Japan" (*yapon*). The nicknames "half-height" (*banggaza*; from Chinese *ban gezi*) and "gourd" (*kawa*) were given specifically to men of short stature who were also a bit plump. Another nickname for a short, stout person was "urine-pot" (*kültük*), referring to an accessory for cradling infants. A man with a large belly might be called "blanket chest" (*sanduq*). Individuals with either dwarfism or hunched backs are assigned as nicknames one of the many words describing such physical traits, which include *dok*, *petek*, and *parpa*.

Hair often figures into cultural symbols of gender identity and sexuality and is a theme in nicknaming.[26] The link between nicknames and hair is made explicit in the folklore itself, such as in the proverb from which this chapter takes its name. Perhaps it is not a coincidence that nicknaming begins in earnest roughly during boys' puberty years, exactly when secondary sexual characteristics begin to emerge. Another proverb linking nicknames with gender difference is the following.[27]

Without a nickname one isn't a man   *leqemsiz er bolmas*
Without a thimble, one isn't a woman   *oymaqsiz xotun*

This proverb reinforces the notion that nicknames are potent gendering devices. The analogy between hair and nicknames is perhaps due in part to the idea that women are expected to keep their hair covered—although veiling has never been the norm in Xinjiang, women do regularly wear head-scarves—just as men do not display their nicknames. Furthermore, uncovering another man's nickname, exposing it to the public by uttering it, is an act of aggression itself, much like pulling down a boy's pants to expose his genitals, a common adult male way of teasing little boys discussed in Chapter 5.

One other interpretation of the proverbial equation "hair is for women what nicknames are for men" is that just as hair can mark a woman's advancement through the life-cycle phases of female gender identity and her place in her community of peers, so, too, do men adorn each other with nicknames as markers of advancement through phases of male identity and of their place in the peer group. Consider the following narrative, recorded in 1891.

A maiden (*qiz*) wears her hair in seven braids. This is called *köküle chach*. When she touches a man, she wears it in five braids, which is called *sumbul chach*, and she is called a *chöken*. When she bears one child, she wears two braids, and she is called a *jughan*, and her hair is called *yangaq chach* or *sékilek chach*.[28]

From this account we see that in nineteenth-century Uyghur society a woman's hair marked her social position, much as a man's nickname helps to situate him in the local community of men.

The nickname "beard" (*saqal*) is for a man with a big beard, "moustache" (*burut*) is for one with a moustache, and "goat" (*öchke*) was assigned to one man who wore a goatee. "Beardless" (*kosa*) was for a man without a beard. *Pushkin* was assigned to a man whose curly mutton-chop sideburns resembled the poet Pushkin's. Many examples are found of similar associations based on the distinctive facial hair of famous individuals, including nicknames such as "Hitler" (*gitlér*); *chapayev*, a Soviet hero with a distinctive handlebar mustache; and *zato*, a film hero who hid his identity from his pursuers by growing a huge beard. A number of nicknames are assigned to bald men, including "bald spot" (*paynek*), "bald" (*taz*), and *qashqa*, a term that refers to a white spot on the forehead of an animal.

Not all body part–related nicknames deal with hair, however. "One-handed" (*cholaq*) is for a man missing a hand or the use thereof. "Six fingers" (*alte qol*) is for someone with an extra finger. "Finger" (*barmaq*) was for a man with a disfigured finger, and "crooked" (*dunay*) was assigned to a man with a crooked arm.

A man with a pockmarked face might be assigned as a nickname "veil" (*chümbet*), "pockmarked" (*choqur*), "colorful" (*chipar*), "speckled" (*char*), or "freckled" (*sepkün*). "Tomato" (*pemidur*) is a nickname for a man with a reddish face. "Big eyes" (*chong köz*) and "protruding eyes" (*palköz*) are self-explanatory. *Chekmen*, a type of rough cloth used for sifting soil, is for those who have "speckled" (*chiqir*) eyes. "Melon-seed" (*gazir*; from Chinese *guazi*) is for one whose eyes are shaped like melon seeds. *Jirtaq* is for someone whose eye opens only partially due to illness, whereas "crooked eye" (*alighay*), a word that normally describes the sagging of an eye during old age, was assigned to a young man whose healthy eye merely gave the impression of having this condition. "Blue eyes" (*kök köz*) and "beans" (*purchaq*) are for those with blue or green eyes.

"Galoshes" (*kalach*; also found as *galach*, *qalash*) is for a man with a wide mouth, suggesting a resemblance to the wide opening of the rubber galoshes commonly worn in Xinjiang. "Big mouth" (*dazuy*; from Chinese *dazui*) is self-explanatory. "Lip" (*kalpuk*) was for a man who had a strangely shaped lower lip, and "chin" (*éngek*) was for a man with a long chin.

"Ear" (*qulaq*) was for a man with physically large ears, not one with "long ears," a common folk metaphor for someone who always seems to know the latest news or gossip. "Fly ears" (*chiwin qulaqi*) was for a man with small ears. "Droopy" (*salipang*) was for a man whose ears were large, and "double ear" (*qosh qulaq*) was for a man with a large lump at the base of one ear. "Nose" (*burun*) had a big nose, and "flat-nose" (*pana*) was for a man with a pug nose. "Drum" (*dumbaq*) is for a person with a goiter (*poqaq*) on their neck, a condition common in parts of Xinjiang due to inhabitants' consumption of noniodized salt dug locally from the earth.

Miscellaneous

A number of nicknames refer explicitly to childhood statuses and personality traits and, as such, exemplify the ability of nicknames to serve as emblems of childhood emotions and behaviors. For example, young boys are commonly praised as being *shox* (mischievous) when they behave assertively toward adults and display lots of energy for getting into trouble. Although *shox* is not used in everyday speech to describe adult behavior, it may be assigned as a nickname to a man remembered for his mischievous habits as a child. "Shoeshiner" (*waska*) was the term used for the dozens of young boys aged roughly seven to twelve who roamed Yining's streets or sat in large clusters near market entrances with wooden boxes of polish, brushes, and rags. These children, who were organized by older boys who "protect" them in the streets in exchange for cash payments, typically present themselves as quintessential street urchins—bold, fearless, and aggressively mischievous. As a nickname, *waska* is for persons who are similarly mischievous. "Trouble-maker" (*doden*; from Chinese *daodan*, "mischievous") is a term widely borrowed into vernacular Uyghur, and is used as a nickname with the same meaning. *Gawrush*, which according to one informant was the

name of a young hero in a Victor Hugo novel, was assigned as a nickname to a mischievous orphan.* "Troublemaker" (*chataqchi*), "trouble"
(*joda*), "disturbance" (*kashal*), and "riot" (*topilang*) were assigned to men
prone to get into fights. "Started a fire" (*ot aldurdi*) was assigned to a
man who liked to incite others to fight.

Various other personality types are also bases for nickname assignment. "Knot" (*chigish*) is used for someone who does things by "not being straightforward, who lies and cheats, uses all sorts of messed up
ways, but still fails to get what he wants." A person who cheats might
also be called "mirage" (*ézitqu*), "swindler" (*kazzap*), or "cut ears" (*qulaq
kesti*), the last possibly a reference to the practice of marking a deck by
altering the corners of playing cards. One man was nicknamed "gypsy"
(*sigan*) also for his reputation as a cheater. "Devil" (*sheytan*) is for
"someone who likes to joke, who is a cheater." Although *sheytanliq*
means "teasing, joking," several men agreed that as a nickname *sheytan*
was for persons who cheat, not just jokesters. "Sapling" (*köchet*) was assigned to persons "whose words were without snares or traps." "Unreliable" (*kawbujo*; from Chinese *kaobuzhu*) was assigned to one man
who was untrustworthy. "Knife cut" (*pichaq kesti*) is for a man "who
can take care of things quickly, efficiently, who gets things done." A
brusque, gruff person may be nicknamed "ice" (*tong*). A stubborn man
might be called "mule" (*héchir*). "Holy person" (*ewliya*) is for one with
airs of self-importance. "Mild-mannered" (*yawash*) is for a quiet man,
one "who doesn't like to fool around."

One of the most intriguing nicknames I elicited was "snow fell" (*qar
yaghdi*). This nickname was widely known throughout the *mehelle*, and
more than a dozen people offered identical explanations of its use, stating that it was "for people who aren't quite normal, a little weird," or
"not really crazy, but just a little bit strange." Not one, however, could
offer so much as a guess about the connection between snow falling
and personality deviance. Perhaps the answer to the mystery is that this
nickname was first bestowed on an individual for some reason unrelated to their strange personality and then became associated through
this one individual with the personality trait of behaving strangely.

---

*This is Gavroche, the archetypal street urchin in *Les Misérables*.

Uyghur nicknaming, which encompasses both a world of social relationships and a semiotically rich world of names, brings into play Uyghur cultural ideals about masculinity, identity, and community. Nickname use, like participation in *olturash*, joins men in the *mehelle* through
face-to-face small-group interactions into a single local community of
men, a community that is simultaneously real, since the webs of social
connection truly do link all men, and at the same time imagined, since
the social meanings of the community for the men who belong to it are
conceived in the minds of those members. Up to this point, my focus
has been on the more private side of men's lives, on personal and
sometimes intimate relations between individuals. In what remains of
this book, that focus shifts to examine the lives of men as they participate in the two primary domains of public life for *mehelle* residents, the
world of the marketplace and the world of Islam.

PART III

Markets and Merchants
on the Silk Road

In the name of Allah the merciful

In order to promote the development of market trading, passages from various books have been printed in this pamphlet. He who reads these prayers many times, day in and day out, his position in society will increase.

Should he write them out and keep them in his store, customers will be so plentiful that they will fight with one another in their haste to buy.

— Introduction to a Uyghur-language pamphlet circulating in 1990s Yining

| Control it, it dies | *yi kong jiu si* |
| Release it, it's chaos | *yi fang jiu luan* |

— People's Bank of China researchers on Yining's market environment

After decades of central economic planning and Maoist ideology, Beijing's embrace of the banner of Market Socialism in the 1980s placed unprecedented burdens on local governments to create and regulate new markets and to cope with rising tensions between the mentalities and mechanisms of the market and the slowly eroding infrastructure of the planned economy. By the 1990s, despite the many challenges they confronted, officials at all levels and citizens alike throughout China increasingly recognized in private enterprise their best opportunity for success; Yining's Uyghur residents were no exception. In Part III I consider how men in the *mehelle* responded to the opportunities created by market reforms. The story told is one of enterprising traders who rely on the capital of their social networks to make up for their limited access to financial capital; it is a story of merchants deeply engaged in the pursuit of material success and the social status that wealth could provide. Local marketing practices did more than bring wealth and status to successful traders, however; they also produced a matrix of social differences and a range of occupation-based identities within the *mehelle* community. To demonstrate these social dimensions of economic life, I examine the range of market practices that provided a basis for social mobility and status competition among *mehelle* residents. Uyghurs' personal and collective identities are, I suggest, produced as much through participation in commerce and productive labor as they are through any explicit sense of "ethnic" difference. Economic success has also provided some *mehelle* residents with the means for pursuing an increasingly activist role in their local communities; examining market activities gives us insight into the bases for these changes as well.

In 1990s Yining, private enterprise, specifically market trading, was an engine driving a broad reorganization of social life. In some ways, changing marketing practices conformed to patterns of transformation widespread in China; in other ways, however, local forms of entrepreneurship were deeply particular. Yining's unique geographic position— it is perched on China's border with Kazakhstan along a historical corridor into Central Asia—profoundly influences the forms of marketing available to Uyghurs in their pursuit of wealth. And for a time, wealth there was in Yining, perhaps not enough for everyone, but enough to have deeply captured the imagination and attention of many of the men (and women and children) of the *mehelle*.

Uyghurs' outlook on their economic situation, I realized early in my research, was informed by an unshakable confidence in an imagined historical legacy of entrepreneurship. Uyghurs with whom I spoke, from *mehelle* merchants chatting over a hand of cards to scholars writing historical treatises at universities in Urumqi and in Beijing, seemed certain that their ancestors had long participated in local and long-distance trade in the region in a tradition they dated back to the Silk Road trade of centuries past. Surely there is some truth to their vision. In his 1898 book on Uyghur society based on two years spent in the region, Fernand Grenard reported that every Uyghur peasant dreamed of becoming a merchant.[1] C. G. Mannerheim, who passed through Yining around 1906, observed that Uyghur men seemed to wish to become merchants even when it was economically irrational to do so, simply in order to gain the social prestige associated with that status.[2] Despite the century between their observations and my own, many men I met in Yining seemed as enthralled with the social identity they associated with being a merchant as with the promise of wealth it offered.

Although many Uyghurs were confident their people had enjoyed a glorious past as Silk Road traders, most were decidedly less certain of their future. Although not even Uyghurs knew where their marketing practices would take them, one thing was clear. Nineteen-nineties levels of market success provided *mehelle* residents with a material and affective basis for an increasingly activist engagement with issues affecting their communities. Party leaders in the post-reform era continue to gamble that economic prosperity, a condition they believe will be delivered by correct policies and a willing, industrious citizenry, will bring stability to Xinjiang. Unrest in the streets of Yining during my research, which exploded into violence in 1997 shortly after my departure, portended a different relationship between prosperity and stability than that envisioned by the state. To understand the links between market prosperity and the role of Islam as a basis for social mobilization in Xinjiang, we must first understand local trading practices.

Marketing practices shaped the lives of *mehelle* residents in many ways beyond the merely economic. Ideals of masculinity were inseparable from the public spaces of the market and the street; men and women alike expected that a man should leave home in the morning and return before the evening meal, having spent the entire day in the market. Yining's markets also have a significance that extends beyond the local, since they play a role in economic, political, and social relationships linking Chinese, Central Asian, and global economic spheres of influence. The complex set of marketing relations that link China's coastal regions, passing through Xinjiang, with the former Soviet Union, join these respective economies together through flows of goods, persons, and practices. As such, local marketing practices are an eminently transnational example of contemporary globalization. At the same time, even a casual stroll through Yining's bustling wholesale markets cannot fail to impress upon the visitor the rich local specificity of the marketplace as a concrete sphere of social interaction. It is this social world of the market that I emphasize in the two chapters that follow.

9

Merchants and Markets
in the *Mehelle*

The infant Abdüshükür sneezed unexpectedly from inside his cradle. His grandmother Abidem chuckled, "Hmmm, your daddy must be making a lot of money."
—Field notes, December 1995

Abdüshükür's mother clipped his fingernails and gathered them carefully. Out on the patio she leaned over the courtyard wall and tossed the clippings into the neighbors' garden, saying "Dirtiness go over there, wealth come over here!" She explained the verbal formula as follows: "It's so that blessing (*beriket*) will come into your hands. It's a way of saying of one's hands, may they make lots of money."
—Field notes, May 1996

In this chapter I offer an overview of the social relations and practices associated with retail marketing in Yining, emphasizing marketing arrangements in which Uyghurs participated either as buyers or sellers. Both Han and Uyghurs in Yining demonstrated considerable ethnic solidarity in their personal marketing and shopping practices. Just as Uyghur merchants sold mainly to Uyghur customers, and Uyghur shoppers purchased mainly from Uyghur-owned enterprises, so, too, did Han buy and sell largely within their own networks. This is not to suggest, however, that marketplace interactions were strictly segregated. Given the near absence of other forms of social interaction between Uyghurs and Han in Yining, marketplace interactions, scarce as they were, constituted perhaps the most significant form of face-to-face Uyghur-Han interactions. Below, I first describe some of the social actors of the marketplace and the different kinds of merchandising found in Yining. Next, I describe more fully the spatial arrangement of retail marketing activities in the *mehelle*, the city, and its environs. Finally, I provide additional context for understanding the meanings of marketing practices by addressing complementary and alternative occupational strategies available to suburban residents, including traditional craft production and wage labor.

Merchant Status Categories

Although it is convenient to describe the many kinds of local market actors under the single term "merchants," *mehelle* men and women distinguished a range of diverse marketing activities. Some men (and far fewer women) operated fixed retail stalls, which they rented in predominately Uyghur retail markets. Adjacent to these larger Uyghur retail markets, a few of the newer stalls that sprouted up along sidewalks or inside state-run stores were rented by Uyghurs, but most were taken by Han or ethnic Hui. Owners of retail stalls often left young helpers in charge while they roamed the markets throughout the day, exchanging personal gossip or the latest news about market trends. Other men earned their living in the market without having fixed stalls. Many sold goods from handcarts or donkey carts, from portable cases, from blankets spread out on the ground, or from small carrying racks on the backs of their bicycles. Others sold at flexible times, such as only on Sundays, or for some children, after school. Some men exclusively bought and sold high-priced items like automobiles and motorcycles at weekly specialty markets. Among the highest status merchants were those who traded abroad. Such a merchant might sojourn in Almaty for a year selling goods retail at a market stall, then take one or two years off from full-time productive activity. Other men sought their livelihood working strictly as middlemen in local market transactions. *Yangpungchi*, middlemen who brokered deals between Han wholesalers and trader-tourist buyers from various Central Asian republics, achieved a good degree of success in this role, which I discuss in the next chapter. Men in lower-status trades included those who transported bales of goods on three-wheeled pedicabs and those who sewed up the bales in which market goods were shipped. Day laborers (*yétimchi*, literally "orphan-ists"), who stood in large groups on street corners, were perhaps the lowest in status.

None of these merchant categories were associated by locals with that particular conception of the small-scale entrepreneur most frequently used by state agents and Han entrepreneurs alike, the individual household (Chinese *getihu*).[1] The term *yekke*, the standard Uyghur translation of *getihu*, was used in Urumqi, but only within a select group of more elite Uyghur merchants who were deeply embedded in Han-dominated state administrative networks, the kind of merchants who acquired capital through official bank loans or who participated in state committees on private enterprise. On the streets and in the markets, the term *yekke* had no relevance for the vast majority of Uyghur merchants and how they understood their identities or activities in local markets.

A review of local terms for various kinds of merchants demonstrates the richness of Yining's marketing activities. Many of the terms presented below include the agentive suffixes *-chi*, *-dar*, or *-kesh*, all of which here mean primarily "one whose occupation is" or "one who makes or sells"; in some cases I translate this as "-smith" or "-maker." Frequently used general terms for persons who sell goods at market include *tijaretchi*, one with *tijaret* (business activities), and *oqetchi*, one with *oqet* (market dealings). The roots of these words were employed in common marketplace greetings such as *oqetingiz qandaq* or *tijaretingiz qandaraq*, in each case meaning "How is your business?" Not only merchants had *oqet*; a cobbler, to take one example, who retailed his own products, or an *ashpez* (cook, restaurateur) also would be said to have *tijaret/oqet*. The term *sodiger*, on the other hand, was reserved specifically for people engaged in the buying and selling of goods. This term had distinct connotations of self-importance and of an ambition to build a larger enterprise. *Élipsatar*, literally "buy-and-seller," was a less common term denoting a smaller-scale merchant. Persons who owned and operated *mehelle* shops (*dukan*) were called *dukandar* or *dukanchi*. The term *xojayin* (owner, manager) was a standard term of address for the principal of such an enterprise. Men and women who sold goods by arranging them on the ground, usually on a sheet or blanket, were called *yaymikesh* or *yaymichi*, from the verb *yaymaq*, "to spread," and the noun *yayma*, "a spread."

Some types of merchants had more narrowly drawn labels. A man who buys and sells clothing (*ushshaq mal*, "small goods") is called by the generic term *sodiger*, whereas a seller of grains, cereals, and oils is specifically a *rewende*. Sellers of dried apricots, raisins, and nuts are *gangxochi*, from Chinese *ganhuo* "dried goods" + *-chi*. Sellers of medicine (*dora*), whose wares include a range of spices and other botanical, mineral, and animal products, are called *seksen xalta* (eighty sacks). Traders in raw sheepskins, who are middlemen between those who slaughter sheep (butchers and households) and local tanneries, are called *jallap*. Men insisted that the homophones *jallap* (trader in raw skins) and *jallap* (prostitute) were distinct and unrelated words, despite the apparent semantic connection; a common term for prostitutes in vernacular Chinese, for example, one familiar to *mehelle* men, was *maipi de* (seller of skin).

Not every key player in the local marketplace was himself a buyer (*alghuchi*) or a seller (*satquchi*). A number of intermediary figures played important roles in local market exchange; these included the middleman (*bédik* or *dellal*), the guarantor (*borun*), and the go-between (*elchi*). A description of middleman practices appears later in this chapter. Financial services are provided by *koymochi*, from Chinese *kuai mao* + *-chi*, roughly equivalent to a "dollar-cents-ist." These men exchange Chinese *renminbi* and U.S. dollars in the "dollar market" (*dolar bazari* or *dolar sichang*, from Chinese *shichang*). The pejorative "usurer" (*jazanixor*) was virtually never used by merchants to describe money traders, even though the yearly interest rates they charged for loans ran to 90 percent. The lines between moneychangers and moneylenders were blurred; many men did both, but some who exchanged money did not lend at all, and some who lent money for interest did not exchange.

The attainment of the highest level of merchant status was marked by the application of the honorific *lawben* (from Chinese *laoban*, "boss") following a man's name. Marketplace gossip often revolved around the successes and difficulties of these well-known figures. These "bosses" had more than wealth in common, and many wealthy individuals were not honored with the epithet *lawben*. In addition to their involvement in other entrepreneurial activities, *lawben* were specifically people who pooled funds given to them by large numbers of smaller-scale merchants and who then used those funds to engage in large-scale deals with trading partners in Central Asia. A local perspective on the meaning of the term *lawben* is found in a story that circulated in the *mehelle* for several months, paraphrased in this field note passage.

The well-known Yining figure Osman *doqa* was sitting with friends at a table in the main room of a large and fancy restaurant in Yining, which he in fact owns. A diner at another table, a Han customer, saw he was being treated with great respect by the staff, and approached him, asking him in Chinese, "Are you the boss of this restaurant?"

"No," Osman replied, pointing to the man who managed the restaurant for him. "That guy over there, he's the boss of the restaurant. Me . . . I'm the boss of society."

Men in the *mehelle* could appreciate Osman's comment on two levels. First, as "society's boss," he raises his position above that of boss of a single enterprise, a position in this case held by a man who was his subordinate. The term "society's boss" (*jemiyetning lawben*) has a second meaning as well; in Yining vernacular, "society" at times referred specifically to the world of gangsters and grifters. Osman, as mentioned in Chapter 8, was reputed to be the former head of an illicit organization that ran a protection racket for Uyghur merchants in the city of Guangzhou. Here Osman's comment makes a subtle reference to his status as a leader within the criminal underworld while mocking the Han diner for having underestimated his social position. The currency this story gained, I suggest, had much to do with its resonance with the sentiment in the *mehelle* that Uyghur society had its own forms of authority that were more meaningful for men in Yining than the authority of the state and its agents.

Shopkeeping and Retail Marketing

The physical space of Yining was sharply divided into an urban center and a periphery of residential Uyghur *mehelle*. A limited range of everyday retailing practices took place in the *mehelle* themselves. In Zawut, for example, several residents ran small shops in one-room buildings adjacent to their homes, or in rooms in their homes to which a door or window opening out onto the street had been added. In most *mehelle* the number of such shops had grown quickly throughout the 1990s as enterprising residents sought to profit from an increase in consumer spending. *Mehelle* shops stocked an identical assortment of daily-use items such as candy, razor blades, toothpaste, light bulbs, and candles, plus a small selection of toys, clothing, medicinal products, and special foods that might be needed when guests arrived unannounced, as they so often did. For shopkeepers, customers were also friends and neighbors, which meant that many could be counted on to linger and to chat. Many shops had recently installed phones, registered as residential phones, but which were available to all for a fee. When a call came in for someone living nearby, shop owners would send a child or passerby headed in the right direction to tell the neighbor she or he was wanted on the phone.

Ablimit, the husband of Abidem's daughter Anise, whose efforts to build a new house were described in Chapter 3, was by trade a shop-keeper, a *dukandar*, as was his father before him. With the help of Anise and their three older sons, he ran a small store out of a converted room in their home, which opened onto the dirt lane of his neighborhood through a small door. Although he claimed he could neither read nor write, he kept a small notebook on the counter into which one of his children would record customers' purchases made on credit. Directly across the street a neighbor had almost finished building a small shed by the roadside: "I'm only selling vegetables," the neighbor had re-assured him, but Ablimit was sure the man would soon be selling other items too. Three doors down yet another neighbor was converting a small room in his house into a store, and Ablimit had been extremely displeased about that as well.

In addition to these shops, busier intersections in many *mehelle* were filled in summer with outdoor stalls selling melons and stone fruits, and with refrigerators stocked with popsicles and ice-cream treats. In most *mehelle* a small number of other commercial enterprises also operated, such as pool halls, barber shops, tailors, and health clinics, and these, too, were increasing in number in the 1990s, a sign of residents' rising disposable income and of the new proprietors' entrepreneurial confi-dence. When Zawut residents needed more than a few routine items for the home or kitchen, however, they had little choice but to venture outside the residential *mehelle* and into the southern part of the city cen-ter, where a number of large retail markets opened daily.

One of the main features of Yining's overall marketing organization in the 1990s was a tendency toward spatial clustering, a trait whose exis-tence is well established throughout both China and Central Asia.[2]

Everyday retailing as a whole was clustered into a number of larger retail bazaars. These permanent markets, some located in large buildings or underground rooms, others in the open air, covered with fixed roofs or makeshift canopies, were a main destination for Uyghur shoppers. Yining's larger retailing clusters were typical of *bazar* I saw elsewhere in Xinjiang in that they contained roughly 400 to 600 stalls; these included the Teshlepki, Pediwal, and Galantir bazaars. But the city's largest marketplace was a sprawling collection of more than one thousand stalls, a number that swelled even larger on Sundays. Official municipal publications referred to this market as Longbridge (Chong Köwrük), but *mehelle* residents referred to it only as the "Chinese Market," either Xitay Bazar or Xenzu Bazar.

Another form of clustering was exhibited in the marketing of particular products, both inside and outside these bazaar spaces. Inside large markets most stalls sold only a single kind of item, such as men's or women's clothing, shoes, leather jackets, hats, fabric, or gold jewelry. Sellers of each type of item were often clustered together, with only an occasional outlier. Outside these main markets, similar products could be purchased at privately run stalls throughout the city, and these stalls, too, were often found in small clusters. A typical example of such clustering outside the larger retail markets would be fruit-sellers (*baqqal*), who gathered usually in groups of five to ten vendors selling from permanent stalls or large carts at several dozen sites around the city.

Social Life in the Retail Markets

For men in the *mehelle*, the standard morning meal of hard bread pieces soaked in salted milk tea was often a hurried affair. Women had many household chores to do in the morning and consumed their meal later as time allowed. Men, on the other hand, ate early and rarely lingered around the house. Whether they had already been out for morning prayer at a small neighborhood mosque, or whether it was their first time out the door, men left home immediately after breakfast, and regardless of where they were truly heading, "I'm off to the market" was always an appropriate comment to make as they stepped out the courtyard gate.

Fig. 12   Merchants tending market stalls were sure to be visited many times each day by friends whose daily schedules were more flexible. Here a *mehelle* man just back from a successful sojourn in Almaty has stopped in to play cards with a group of clothing merchants in the back area of a market stall run by two brothers from Zawut (photograph by the author, 1996).

Since only a small percentage of *mehelle* men had permanent stalls at any given time, most could be found wandering about the markets for much of each day, and each day a stall-keeper could count on dozens of friends to stop by and chat long enough to smoke a cigarette, to warm their hands over one of the small coal stoves used in the winter, or to play a hand of cards and trade a few jokes in the summer. Most days passed slowly, with the monotony broken only by a few long haggling sessions with customers, some of them perhaps ending in sales, or by a moment of excitement when a fight erupted or a shopper yelled she had been the victim of a pickpocket.

Magical practices to promote sales were an element of everyday marketing practices I first noticed in a scene much like this one.

Walking around Teshlepki at mid-morning, I saw a young man, perhaps twenty years old, tending a stall whose racks were draped with several dozen pairs of men's dress pants.

He held a green two-*yuan* note in his hand, and for twenty seconds or so he brushed it over all of his merchandise as if the bill were a feather duster. When he was finished, he laid the bill flat on one outstretched hand and slapped the bill several times sharply between his two hands, as if to make sure that profit would not elude him, fixing it in place.

In Part II, I described a range of practices called *irim* performed upon the birth of a child to ensure the health and longevity of the child and to fix the child in "this world" (*bu dunya*). The only other set of practices in Yining described using the same term *irim* were those performed by merchants at the first sale of each day to ensure that other goods would sell. Touching the first income of the day to one's wares on display is easily explained as a form of contact magic, but its meaning may also be influenced by the Islamic concept of baraka, "blessing," well known to Uyghurs as *beriket*. Related practices involve the notion that physical contact with certain blessed objects, especially those that have been touched by holy persons, can transmit that blessing. Stepping on bills or slapping them in one's hands, I suggest, expresses the merchant's desire that the money, representing income generally, remain in his hands.

Men who passed their days in the markets, whether they were among the wandering majority or were more steadily occupied as stall owners, craftsmen, or laborers-for-hire, usually ate a mid-day meal between 11:00 A.M. and 2:00 P.M. Men often went to eat lunch alone or in pairs, rather than in the large groups typical when meals were organized for recreation. Scores of food-stalls and restaurants in the market area's main food court rarely counted *mehelle* men among their customers, however; most of their customers were shoppers and out-of-town travelers, Han and Uyghur alike, whose knowledge of the marketplace was limited. Instead, *mehelle* men frequented a smaller number of less visible but well-established restaurants tucked away in hidden corners of the marketplace, most of which opened only for lunch and sold only a single house specialty, such as rice pilaf with lamb, or hand-pulled noodles.

I discovered one of these restaurants for the first time only after a friend led me through an unmarked door hidden in a far corner of the market. The quietness that pervaded the inside was strikingly different from the scene found in other restaurants, which are often hosting one or more rowdy *olturash* gatherings. All fifty or so seats were taken, and we waited several minutes until two seats opened up. The restaurant served only a single dish, *chaynek shorpa*, a rich meaty broth with chunks of freshly boiled lamb and turnip, to which a raw egg was added, served with a warm bagel-like *girde nan* fresh from a wood-fired oven. On my first visit three women were present, two sat together and one with her husband, all villagers shopping in town for the day who had stumbled in. All the other customers were men from the marketplace. On the walls colorful plastic signs written in Chinese, placed there by Yining's Health Bureau, challenged diners to *Promote Food Cleanliness, Reduce Intestinal Infection, and Thoroughly Implement the Control of Defecation* and also to *Promote Regulations for Defecating in Latrines.* Both slogans struck me as ironic—the municipal government campaigned endlessly to discourage people from defecating and urinating on public streets, yet the only public toilets located near the bustling markets were padlocked shut in the evenings and on weekends, when the food court was routinely filled with upwards of 250 customers and 120 stall workers. Overshadowing those official messages, on a much larger poster hung by the restaurant's owners, was a slogan in Uyghur that read *Such is the law of Allah: Any ethnic group that finds its condition to be backward or lowly must first change on its own before Allah will change it.* Men eating in these workingman's lunch restaurants rarely spoke to each other and usually ate their meals in silence. When men did speak, perhaps commenting briefly about some recent news, greetings were almost never exchanged first. This alone gave these spaces a special quality, as if they were places of refuge from the world of ordinary social intercourse. Here men's interactions were serious and reserved, and there were no signs of the constant teasing, insulting, symbolic aggression, and jockeying for social position that dominated men's interactions during meals at most other Uyghur restaurants in town.

Street-side Selling, Sunday Markets, and Spatial Control

For the many individuals who lacked the capital needed to rent and stock a permanent market stall, the greater flexibility of mobile peddling arrangements allowed them to participate in private trade. Most mobile and street-side selling took place outside the *mehelle* in the central parts of town. Itinerant retailers did occasionally circulate through *mehelle* lanes, but the number of products they offered was limited. Fresh cow's milk, for example, was purchased this way by households in Zawut, either for the children of the household or to use in making savory tea when the more preferred clotted cream (*qaymaq*) was unavailable.

Sunday was an especially busy market day in Yining, and the sidewalks around the bazaars on the city's southern edge would be filled with men and women selling items spread out on blankets or stacked in boxes. Although more shoppers and more sellers were present on Sundays, the same kinds of merchandise were sold then as were sold on other days. On a typical Sunday, 800–1,000 separate displays of goods by mobile sellers were present on the busiest marketing streets around Teshlepki and Xenzu Bazar. Sunday densities of sellers elsewhere in the city were far lower, but still considerable.

By far the items most commonly sold by peddlers were clothing and fabric, and men, women, and children lined up along the streets by the hundreds to sell shirts, trousers, socks, and underwear that they displayed on their blankets. Starting at one end of a typical street on which more specialized street-side selling occurred, a group of ten to fifteen women sold sweet clotted cream, spooning it from their bowls into buyers' own jars. Farther down stood several tinsmiths selling assorted ladles and pails, then tinkers selling miscellaneous items like mousetraps, wooden rolling pins, and *shümek* tubes for cradling children. Next to them came several booksellers offering mimeographed booklets and prayer guides to *mehelle* residents who were considering participating more fully in prayer practices. After them came a cluster of broom sellers, then the sellers of large *kigiz* felt mats. Beyond them a few dozen men stood together, each one holding a single pair of leather shoes or displaying a single cashmere-blend scarf draped on the rear rack of a bicycle. Hawkers wandered through the crowds selling fresh or dried

Fig. 13　Many men earn their livelihood as retail or wholesale merchants without any fixed place of business. Peddlers sell from mobile carts, blankets, or the backs of bicycles. At this intersection, which stands near the boundary between Zawut and the city center, men gathered each day to buy and sell raw and processed sheepskins (photograph by the author, 1996).

fruits. In summer, seasonal stands would appear in prominent positions around the marketplace selling homemade ice cream, candied haw fruit kebabs, or sour yogurt mixed with chipped ice and sugar. In autumn these stalls would disappear, to be replaced in winter by stalls selling locally made horsemeat sausages and barley malt sugar candy.

Although street-side selling flourished during my research, changes under way in Yining affected many *mehelle* residents' ability to earn their livelihood. Parts of the city that had for decades been public space were increasingly being "privatized," and many residents, merchants and non-merchants alike, resented the loss of what they felt should be public space. One scene I witnessed, described in this field note passage, captured vividly for me the concerns *mehelle* residents often expressed about the pressure of in-migrant Han on local resources, not least among which, all recognized, was space.

10:00 A.M. on a December morning. On the wide sidewalk across the street from the post office, a Uyghur man, 5' 2", who looked to be about sixty, dropped a large bag of knitted woolen underwear down on the ground and bent over to spread out a dirty cotton sheet. His ragged and unstylish clothes marked him as visiting from a nearby village. His wares, most likely, had been knitted by his female kin in the hope of supplementing their farming income.

A second man, a Han, 5' 10", in his late thirties, came over immediately. He spoke with authority, although he wore no sign of any office except perhaps his expensive leather jacket, a favored symbol of financial success for Uyghur and Han men alike.

"No, no, you go across the street," he insisted several times, pointing to a much narrower sidewalk one hundred feet away, which had only a trickle of foot traffic, and most likely had its own "guardian" as well. "Look, you can set up across the street, but we have to clear snow here."

The older man didn't seem to understand, perhaps because he spoke little Chinese, perhaps because the previous night's snowfall had obviously already been shoveled, and more than three dozen women and men—all of them Han, not one Uyghur—stood minding similar blankets piled with goods on either side of the opening where he wanted to set up.

The old man was furious, stood his ground, and repeated a single phrase four or five times in thickly accented Chinese,

"Go back to Jiang Jieshi, go back to the *gomindang.* Go on, get out . . ." The younger man placed his hands on the old man's shoulders, as if to escort him off, but the peasant kept repeating his line about the Guomindang, the political party whose army controlled Xinjiang more than fifty years earlier, before the Communist Party took over.

The peasant kept up his ranting, his anger pushing him beyond reason, never once speaking in Uyghur. Finally he moved his blanket ten feet or so, to the far edge of the Han vendors.

I had been standing off to one side waiting to see how the Han man would respond, when a group of seven young Han women recently arrived from Jiangsu walked by chatting loudly as they peddled the t-shirts that they carried draped in thick stacks over their arms. Squads of such women, always carrying shirts or socks, were a common sight in Yining, soldiers in the floating population of Han that are slowly pushing the demographic balance in the region toward Han majority. One of the women waved a shirt in my face as she passed, hoping for a sale. On the shirt was a drawing, with palm trees in the background and a wooden pier piled with coils of thick rope and bales of goods. The caption read COLONIAL—RAW MATERIALS.

Increasingly, street-side sellers were expected to obtain licenses and permits from local authorities or from these quasi-legal private retail space brokers. Zawut residents often discussed cases of neighbors or kin being fined for selling on the streets without a license, but no one seemed interested in or informed about obtaining one, and no peddlers I knew had one.

Retail Shopping Practices

Shopping responsibilities in Uyghur households were shared between men and women. Clothing, personal items for women and children, and household cleaning or cooking supplies were likely to be purchased by women; men purchased larger items such as appliances, as well as their own clothing and personal items. Both men and women shopped for food.

Retailers selling domestic manufactured goods bought at set prices did not engage in bargaining. A customer might comment that a certain item was cheaper elsewhere or had been cheaper in the past, but these comments did not lead to price flexibility on the part of sellers. Retailers who purchased goods imported by private Uyghur merchants, such as fabrics and clothing from Turkey, or miscellaneous items from various Central Asian republics, themselves bargained over the prices they paid, and they passed on this price flexibility by allowing customers to haggle; stall-keepers and customers bargained directly, and once negotiations were *pishshiq* (ripe, cooked), the deal was made. *Mehelle* shopkeepers rarely seemed interested in bargaining, perhaps because the assistants who minded shops when proprietors were absent were often young children and could not be trusted to negotiate with customers. Nor were prices for commodities such as sugar, oils, or eggs negotiable, since these had government-regulated or otherwise generally stable prices. Some *mehelle* shops, however, had on their shelves specialty items brought back by people returning from the *haj*, pilgrims for whom this sideline trading helped offset the cost of the trip. For items of this kind, identifiable by their Arabic labels, shopkeepers were willing to dicker.

Mehelle residents also occasionally bought items from merchants who had no places of business, not even temporary ones. Merchants of this type bought goods in bulk and peddled them directly through networks of friends and acquaintances. One man from Zawut, for example, purchased fifty refrigerators in Urumqi and shipped them to Yining, where he sold them through personal networks at a 32 percent discount off the retail price (2,200 *yuan* marked down to 1,500). Direct-selling and multilevel marketing organizations, which recruited millions of new members throughout China in the 1990s, had no presence in the *mehelle.*

For many *mehelle* residents, of course, shopping had meanings that transcended the practical aspect of exchanging money for needed goods. For women, especially younger women, shopping provided an opportunity to temporarily absent themselves from household chores. For men, familiar habits of pushing others to anger often entered into otherwise routine market transactions.

9:00 P.M. on a November evening. Eight men sit in the dark on wooden bed frames in the small guard booth outside the factory gate at Zawut. The office, with its door and windows open, is bitter cold, but the men have smoked several joints of hashish mixed with cheap *moxorka* tobacco, and they sit chatting happily. The sound of approaching footsteps is heard, and a man steps through the doorway. He is a stranger, but he greets them all warmly and asks if anyone is interested in buying a pair of boots.

"Boots? Sure, I was just talking about wanting to buy a pair of boots," Rexmetjan says, spotting his opportunity. "You have boots? Bring 'em in!" The man goes out to where his two associates, young teenagers, have dropped the piles of boxes they were carrying. The men in the guard booth quickly exchange winks before the stranger returns holding a pair of leather dress boots. At 180 *yuan* a pair, they are being sold as top-of-the-line footwear, but it is hard to check their quality in a dark room whose only light comes from a small bulb outside the room, shining through the open window. Each man in turn looks carefully at the boots and gives Rexmetjan his opinion. Abruptly Rexhmetjan says, "Oh, I guess I don't want boots after all." The seller realizes he has been manipulated and stomps out angrily, yelling out with his back turned to the men, "We wasted half an hour coming here." The men sitting in the dark burst out laughing. They have pushed him until he became *chidimas*, and they have won.

Shopping and the State

The masculine disposition that transforms a marketing interaction into a contest of manhood found a slightly different expression in the context of marketing relations between Uyghur shoppers and the Han sales clerks who worked in state-run retailing enterprises. As mentioned, Zawut residents purchased goods mainly from other Uyghurs, whether at *mehelle* shops, hawkers' handcarts and street-side spreads, or bazaar stalls. They also, although less frequently, visited Yining's several state-run department stores, mainly when shopping for more expensive consumer goods not sold elsewhere such as electronic appliances, cameras, or propane cooking stoves. Uyghur and Han sales clerks, most of them women, worked side by side behind the counters in these enterprises, although they informally self-segregated by ethnicity, standing in clusters throughout the day speaking their separate languages.

In these stores I regularly observed small groups of Uyghur men approach Han sales clerks and play the role of customers needing help locating or selecting items to purchase, doing so essentially for entertainment. Sometimes men would use these opportunities to purposefully abuse or harass the Han sales clerks, such as by making requests designed to force a clerk to make repeated trips to a back room. When the sales clerk was female, these interactions contained an unmistakable element of sexual predation, albeit one the male shoppers encouraged the female sales personnel to suspect was a form of flirting, hoping the same would be reciprocated. At first I was quick to interpret this behavior as a kind of "weapon of the weak" used by members of an ethnic minority who resented (as men often explained in just so many words) what they viewed as Han exploitation of their homeland.[3] Similar incidents between Uyghurs, however, such as the one presented above, in which a group of men pretend to be interested in buying boots from a peddler, suggested to me that the agonistic aspect of Uyghur-Han shopping interactions, although undoubtedly also an expression of ethnic hostility, was but a particular variation within a more general pattern in Uyghur men's sociality, a pattern in which strategies of symbolic aggression and contests to establish interpersonal dominance are routinely enacted and performed for audiences of other men.

Cannibalization of Public and Private Space for Retail Use

No discussion of retailing in 1990s Yining would be complete without mentioning the widespread rush to convert open spaces, public and private, indoor and outdoor, into new retail marketing sites. One striking characteristic of the physical layout of Yining, a remnant of state-planned urban construction, was the broad sidewalks that separated city streets from the prominent facades of large buildings. Throughout the 1990s these once-spacious walkways gradually became clogged with newly erected rows of small roofed sheds of painted steel, glass, and aluminum, retail stalls that were immediately rented to Han vendors. The prominent facades of older buildings, designed to impress the citizenry with the grandeur of state power, were increasingly obscured by booths selling costume jewelry and women's underwear, an ironic commentary on the victory of the market over Maoism. The force behind these changes was plain from the conversations of the city's business elite. It was the lure of income from renting these sites to vendors that caused individuals and organizations with control over space of any kind to scramble to convert it into rentable retail stalls.

The cannibalization of interior spaces for retail use was, if anything, even more widespread. In buildings of all kinds, from established state-run retail stores to bus stations, even in banks and post offices, managers filled any available floor space with empty booths, cabinets, and counters that they rented out (for around $20 per month, payable six to twelve months in advance) to people selling wares like socks and shoelaces, cheap paperbacks, and cigarette lighters. The goods sold in these new commercial spaces varied widely, but what such stalls had in common, whether indoors or out, was that virtually all were rented and operated by Han individuals hoping to turn their single glass counter into a source of household income. Uyghurs were almost entirely absent from this new form of retailing. At outdoor sidewalk stalls in the area around Yining's main wholesale markets, the only significant exceptions to this pattern of Han predominance were the dozen or more small stalls, out of many hundreds, rented by Uyghur vendors of manufactured audio and video cassettes, the contents of which included a mix of Uyghur popular and folk cultural performances, mainly of music but also of jokes, poetry, comedy sketches, and dramatic readings.

Specialty and Secondhand Markets

A number of smaller specialty markets added to the diversity of goods available for sale in Yining. These included a large, covered food court with more than seventy small restaurants, a flea market (*pit bazari*), and markets for the private resale of secondhand items such as televisions, bicycles, motorcycles, automobiles, and livestock. Transacting through middlemen was common in secondhand markets, and I describe that practice here using examples taken from my visits to Yining's used-motorcycle market, known to residents as the *motobazar*. This market had for years been located on the grounds of the dormant factory in Zawut, where it drew a strictly Uyghur clientele. During the winter of my research that market was shut down, and buyers and sellers relocated to a much larger Han-owned combined automobile and motorcycle market in a *mehelle* beyond the east edge of the city. With this shift, the fee to enter the market grounds with a motorcycle increased from one *yuan* ($0.13) to five *yuan* ($0.63), although when I entered, each time on the back of a motorcycle driven by a Uyghur acquaintance, the driver routinely avoided paying this fee, either by slipping through the gate unnoticed or else simply refusing to stop.

When private parties bought and sold items at these specialty resale markets, their transactions were almost always brokered by men who specialized in that activity. Although the description that follows uses examples from the *motobazar*, in its general outline it applies equally to the practices of men buying and selling televisions, livestock, or other specialty items.

Men who had motorcycles to sell would often spend hours scrubbing and polishing every visible part of the machines before taking them to market. Sellers arrived between 9:00 A.M. and noon, parked their motorcycles on the dirt field, and then squatted or stood several meters away. On most days I visited there were between forty and eighty motorcycles for sale. The crowd of men would grow throughout the morning, usually peaking at around 300 persons, all Uyghur. And men it was—one typical head count was 281 men and 3 women—since interest in motorcycles was a distinctly masculine preoccupation.

Potential buyers and their friends would circulate among the machines, one person occasionally stepping forward to ask a price. Sellers responded by stating prices they knew were unrealistically high, even sellers I knew were anxious or desperate to sell, and buyers rarely replied. Any buyer who expressed an interest more serious than that initial inquiry was quickly descended upon by one of the many roving middlemen (*dellal*), who competed to earn the "tea" or "tea-money" (*chay* or *chay puli*) buyers paid them for arranging such transactions. The *dellal,* in order to broker the deal, would first have to talk the buyer out of a token amount of money, usually a single 50- or 100-*yuan* note. He would then approach the seller, and while stating a price the buyer had agreed to pay, he would attempt to slap the folded banknote loudly into the hand of the seller; if he succeeded at this, he would then try to shake the seller's hand with the money squeezed between their palms, often by grabbing their clasped hands with his other free hand to prevent the man's escape. A seller who refused to be manhandled into completing this handshake thereby signaled his unwillingness to settle for the stated amount. A good *dellal* reared his hand back behind his head and waved it in the air several times before slapping it down dramatically with a sharp crack. This gesture, like the *irim* money-slapping gesture described earlier in this chapter, can be viewed as an attempt to fix the money in place, as if with a forceful enough slap one could fix the money in the hand of the seller, sealing the deal.

At the first sign that one *dellal* was losing momentum in brokering a deal, another would step in to take his place, wrenching the buyer off to one side for a private chat, where he would try to convince the buyer that he could get the seller to accept a suitable price where the last *dellal* had failed. Since only one person at a time could hold a buyer's token money, competition between *dellal* involved a good deal of physical jockeying for access to that money and to buyers' and sellers' bodies. Sellers had to pull their hands and bodies away from *dellal,* who grabbed them violently with their arms around their shoulders. In descriptions of Uyghur-Han business transactions presented in the next chapter, we will see these same gestural motifs and the dramatization of physical coercion by middlemen take on new meanings in the very different frame of Uyghur-Han relations.

To succeed as a *dellal,* a man had to possess a combination of highly valorized and highly maligned masculine traits. A good *dellal,* men said, needed to be "a master speaker" (*gepte usta*), but also "a man who knew no shame," who was "thick-faced" or "brazen." "*Dellals,*" one man explained succinctly, "they're like beggars." The *dellal* must possess verbal skill, perhaps the most valorized of masculine traits, yet like a beggar he is seen as standing outside the local moral community, someone who wanders, taking without giving. This suggests that the *dellal* is in some way a scapegoat in the transaction; his function is to serve as a symbolic locus of greedy profit-seeking behavior, and the sympathetic positioning of the money within the men's handshake, the symbolic center of trust and friendship, can be read as an attempt to situate the cash transaction into a moral order.

In addition to the maneuverings of middlemen, two other market institutions were available to parties to transactions at the *motobazar*, the down payment (*zakalat*) and the services of the guarantor (*borun*). Down payments were usually understood to be nonrefundable, though whether this varied in practice was unclear. Guarantors were recruited when parties were not able to establish sufficient trust between them for a transaction that involved the extension of credit of some kind. Guarantors were used not only in private market transactions but also in loans of money between individuals.

Regional Markets

The Ili River Valley that extends eastward from Yining is characterized by a wide, flat, and fertile valley floor dotted with villages inhabited by Uyghurs, some ethnic Hui, and increasingly by Han in-migrants. Agriculture is the dominant form of productive activity in these villages, and crops include wheat and other cereals, corn, sugar beet, legumes, and vegetables. To serve the marketing needs of village residents, Sunday markets and a system of rotating daily markets operate throughout the valley. Many of the merchants at these markets are *mehelle* residents who travel back and forth from Yining by public bus; these merchants are called "countrysiders" (*sehrachi*), and their occupation is known as "countrysiding" (*sehrachiliq*). I visited several of these rotating markets, including those at the villages of Dong Mazar, Chighliq Mazar, and On Yer, all between ten and forty kilometers from Yining. One other market I learned of, a Monday market at Hangda, I was not able to visit. At a typical Sunday bazaar at Chighliq Mazar, there were between five hundred and one thousand people in attendance. Most of the forty or more stalls inside the market sold clothing. Five or six stalls sold seeds and pesticides, wares rarely displayed at markets in Yining itself. A ring-toss game did an active business, with players attempting to throw a motorcycle inner tube over clocks and basins in order to claim them as prizes. Restaurants set up around the market's periphery were run by local families who farmed during the week. Behind the market grounds' perimeter wall of rammed earth, men looked over a small number of donkeys and sheep for sale. Abidem had spent two years "country-siding" in the late 1980s, and knew many of the clothing sellers from that time, suggesting this was a flexible market niche for *mehelle* residents, long-term for some, temporary for others.

Other Occupations

The two main economic alternatives to market trading available to *mehelle* residents were craft production and wage labor. A third alternative—employment as a skilled administrator, manager, or professional in a government work-unit or state-run enterprise—was rarely available to Uyghurs in Yining, and because so few residents had such positions, I do not consider them here.[4]

Yining and the surrounding Ili River Valley have a long history of craft production. Figures for craft production in Yining and its environs for the two years 1875 and 1876 show that craft production has long been a significant part of the local economy.[5] Yining may have become Xinjiang's largest craft production center by the early part of the twentieth century; certainly, at least, it was one of several such centers.[6] In the 1990s, craft production remained a strong sector of the local economy, providing goods that were retailed in local markets, often directly by producers, and wholesaled throughout Xinjiang. This mode of production was on the decline, however, due to the inflow of manufactured goods from the factories of China's coastal areas and from smaller household putting-out systems in the villages and towns of Jiangsu, Zhejiang, and Anhui. China's national shift from small-scale craft production to large-scale manufacturing, in other words, was a process in which Han factory workers laboring in distant manufacturing centers displaced Uyghurs from local craft production. Despite this trend, the production of certain handcrafted consumer goods remained an important source of income for some *mehelle* residents.

The list of craftsmen (*kesipdar* or *hünerwen*) in Yining who still relied on traditional materials and technologies in their handicraft production includes: the *meshchi* (stovesmith), who makes stoves, pails, scoops, ladles, dust pans, water troughs, and flour holders out of sheet metal; the *tonurchi*, who makes clay liners for *tonur* beehive ovens; the *mozduz*, or cobbler; the *seypungchi*, or tailor; the *mölchi*, maker of donkey saddles; the *sazchi*, or luthier, who makes musical instruments like the *dutar*, *tembur*, and *rawap*; and the *zerger*, or goldsmith. Goldsmiths were numerous in Yining, with more than a hundred operating in the main market area alone. Of all local handicrafts, goldsmithing was the only one I observed with regularity. Between my visits to Yining in 1992 and 1995, the work of the goldsmith changed significantly. This trade, which until recently required that men spend hours, even days, laboring to fabricate a single chain or filigreed ring or pair of earrings, had been transformed by the popularity of small plaster molds brought in from Fujian province by traveling Fujianese salesmen. In the space of a few years, most goldsmiths had entirely abandoned their earlier methods; now, female Uyghur customers flipped through glossy catalogs provided by the mold manufacturers and selected a design, then the goldsmith would pull the corresponding mold from his stock of molds and produce a ring or a chain necklace in under an hour. Apprenticeships of several years were a common practice in most local trades, and many craftsmen had from one to three apprentices, who helped with both the production and the retailing of produced goods.

Other market stalls produced and sold certain prepared or specialty foods, which I consider here, despite the fact that these were not seen as *hüner* (crafts). Examples found in virtually every Xinjiang market include the *naway*, who bakes and sells *nan* bread, and the *qazzap*, or butcher, who buys live sheep to slaughter and then sells the meat. In Yining a kind of horsemeat sausage (*qéza*) was widely enjoyed during the long winter, as it was considered a "hot" food. Individual *mehelle* households produced *qéza* in small batches for resale through informal networks of vendors. Another local specialty product is *moxorka*, a cheap tobacco smoked by many *mehelle* men, who roll it into cigarettes by itself or mixed with hashish. The plant is grown locally, prepared by roasting over a fire, and sold from handcarts by vendors throughout the city. One sunny day in December a temporary booth appeared on the sidewalk in front of Yining's largest department store. Han sales personnel were promoting a new brand of filter-tip cigarettes, Celestial Horse, made from 100 percent *moxorka* tobacco, by giving away free samples, and several dozen Uyghur men crowded to get in line. It

seemed unlikely to me that manufactured *moxorka* cigarettes would succeed, but if they did, another set of local occupations would disappear:
those of the men who prepared the tobacco, those who sold it in the
markets, and those whose sole trade was selling for a few fractions of a
penny slim packets of old newspaper cut to size for use as cigarette rolling papers.

Labor

Perhaps the strongest theme that emerged in conversations with men
about local marketing activities was the deep value placed on the enterprising individual who relied on cleverness, financial acumen, and social
connections to succeed in the marketplace. The inferior position of the
person who labors for another in exchange for a payment of money, by
contrast, was thoroughly disdained by most *mehelle* men. Nonetheless,
opportunities for individuals to sell their labor for money did exist.
Forms of labor that did not enter directly into the cash economy, for
example, household labor, the overwhelming bulk of which was performed by women and female children, are not considered here.[7]

One source of income for men in the *mehelle* was working as skilled
laborers. As noted earlier, most residential construction labor and virtually all commercial construction labor was provided by Han workers. In
residential construction, teams of ten to twenty Han men and women
worked together under the supervision of a Han entrepreneur who
handled all negotiations with Uyghur clients. Nonetheless, some Uyghurs pursued building trades; primary among these were the *yaghachchi*,
or carpenter, and the *tamchi*, or mason (literally "wall-ist"), also known
as *laychi* (mud-ist), whose building techniques included fired brick and
mortar masonry as well as rammed earth and unfired clay brick construction. Since even new homes had no indoor plumbing, and electri-
cal needs were met by tacking a wire from the street to an exposed roof
joist, most homes could be completed by masons and carpenters alone.

Uyghur merchants and craftsmen viewed unskilled manual labor, in
their words "black work" (*qara ish*), to be highly stigmatizing. Among the
most visible forms of manual labor in Yining were those that supported
the functioning of the city's large wholesale markets; these included
loading and unloading trucks, transporting bales of goods to and from

market stalls, and preparing bales of goods for shipping. Men who labored at such jobs in and around the marketplace, receiving compensation on a per piece basis, were treated with a mixture of pity and disdain by the other *mehelle* men active there as merchants or middlemen.

Adult and adolescent females made up another category of *mehelle* residents who routinely sold their labor for cash payments. Many wives and daughters in Zawut families labored in factories. Most of these women worked at one of the several large spinning and knitting plants on the outskirts of town. Two of Abidem's daughters, for example, had worked in these factories. Senemgül did so from the age of sixteen to twenty-six, before she had her first child; her older sister Aliye had already completed twenty-five years, for which she received a monthly retirement payment of 200 *yuan* ($25.00). Women also labored in other ways to provide household income. By the late spring of 1996, for example, eight months after his return from a year-long sojourn trading in the former Soviet Union, Yakupjan still had not resolved the dispute with his partner that was tying up his income from that period. As a result, his wife began to hem scarves, for which she earned 0.15 *yuan* ($0.01) for the half hour it took to complete each scarf. She also occasionally went out with her eldest daughter to pick crops in nearby villages for a small daily wage.

Women supported their households with income from other sources as well. Another of Abidem's daughters, for example, had for years received 60 *yuan* each month for conforming (on paper, though not in practice) to a state birth control plan. Shortly before my field research the monthly payment had been reduced to 30 *yuan*, and payment in cash was replaced by a system in which monies were paid into a state-managed fund. The contributions of wives and daughters to a household's economy, whether these involved earning money at factory labor, temporary forays into marketing or handicraft work, or laboring at household chores, were rarely if ever discussed among men or between married couples or families in my presence. Although discussions of men's market activities were common, women's work rarely emerged as a topic of discussion, disagreement, or resentment. Whether this represented a symbolic erasure of women's economic contributions, or whether the topic was avoided in my presence, I cannot know, although I suspect both factors were relevant.

A final group of sellers of labor, all of them men, were referred to as *yétimchi*. This word compounds *yétim* (orphan) with the agentive suffix *-chi* (-ist) to make "orphan-ists." On most days twenty or more *yétim-chi* stood in loose groups at an intersection near Yining's largest retail bazaar. In their grimy coats and shabby trousers, they stood out plainly from the passing crowds. Living at Abidem's with the orphan Aysajan, I saw firsthand why those without kin to support them symbolized the most helpless, most exploited, and most suffering of all. Day laborers were "orphans" in *mehelle* residents' eyes, first, because they occupied the lowest status position in the local economy, and second, because (in theory, at least) only a man with no kin to rely on could be driven to sell his labor to strangers for a cash payment. *Mehelle* men, I noted earlier, participate in a fictive kinship system in which each man recognizes men more than a few years junior or senior to him as younger or older brothers. Day laborers, I suggest, were so low in socioeconomic status that they could not readily participate in this fictive kin community, an additional sense in which they were "orphaned."

Not all *mehelle* residents' marketing activities took place in Yining itself, however. Yining's position near China's border with Kazakhstan meant that flows of people and goods across that border also figured prominently in merchants' activities. To understand the source of the rising levels of prosperity enjoyed by many *mehelle* residents throughout the 1990s, I turn now to examine those border-crossing trade activities.

10

―――――

Yining's Border Trade

Trader-Tourism and

Uyghur Sojourning

All of you know, we have an in-law, Bolus, that guy is really a jokester, he is. And as you know, he's a cook, he's got his own restaurant.

One day, back when he opened a restaurant on the border [with Kazakhstan], he's sitting in the place, and a group of beggars walks in, right inside. They're inside, and Bolus, he grabs one of them and asks him, "What have you guys come here to the border for?"

And one of them goes, "We're beggar-tourists."

— Muxtar Hésam, Yining jokester

During the early 1990s, Yining grew to become a key entrepôt along the overland trade routes linking the economies of China and the former Soviet Union. Entrepreneurial Han men and women by the thousands arrived in Yining from China's coastal regions and established businesses selling consumer goods shipped in from their home provinces, often from their hometowns. And throughout the 1990s, weather and road conditions permitting, trader-tourists (*sayahetchi-sodiger*) from Kazakhstan and Uzbekistan, some from as far away as Azerbaijan and Chechnya, crossed daily over the Chinese border at Horgos just 88 km from Yining. Most hurried on to Yining, with its large wholesale bazaars, where they hustled to fill their trucks and buses with clothing and other consumer goods before their three-day visas expired. When they departed, they took with them bales of socks, track suits, and t-shirts decorated with familiar pop-culture icons like Mickey Mouse, Michael Jordan, and the Marlboro logo. Virtually all *mehelle* residents recognized in this stream of cash-carrying visitors the lifeblood of their city, but the visitors were no less resented for that fact. In the joke above, this resentment is expressed by substituting for "trader-tourists" the jarring compound "beggar-tourists." This neat trick downgrades these visitors from a position of superior wealth, merchants who travel *because* they have extra money to spend, to the stigmatized position of vagrants, those who travel because they have no money at all.

Mehelle men referred to trader-tourists most often using the term *sowetlik* (Soviet). Given Yining's proximity to the former U.S.S.R., the fact that many *mehelle* residents had kin ties with ethnic Uyghurs living in Kazakhstan, and the significance Uyghurs placed on the establishment of independent republics by other Turkic ethnic groups in Central Asia, it surprised me that in Yining vernacular the former U.S.S.R. was called simply *sowet*, and its residents *sowetlik*, with no reference to their changed status. Although trader-tourists were lumped together as *sowetlik*, men were nonetheless keenly aware of differences in trader-tourists' national origins and associated patterns of difference in their buying and shopping preferences.

As trader-tourists hurried around Yining to find the goods they needed at the right prices, they were assisted by groups of young Uyghur men who rarely left their sides from morning until night. These men, called *yangpungchi*, interpreted between Russian and Chinese to help trader-tourists in their negotiations with Han sellers, and they also helped locate desired goods through information-sharing networks they maintained with one another for just this purpose. This arrangement is effectively the reverse of the situation of Xinjiang in the 1920s and 1930s, when Han Chinese traders were "little more than middlemen between the [Uyghur] natives and the Russians."[1] The term *yangpungchi* derives from Chinese *yangpin* (sample), pronounced *yangpung*, to which has been added the suffix *-chi* (-ist). This term is a reference to the common practice of sellers and buyers of circulating samples among middlemen. Han vendors did so to advertise their wares and to bribe middlemen with free samples, and trader-tourist shoppers did so to provide *yangpungchi* with examples of the kinds of goods they wished to purchase.

In 1990s Yining, these flows of people, cash, and goods catalyzed dramatic changes in life for *mehelle* residents, some of whom achieved unprecedented wealth through trading. In the economic transition away from state socialism throughout Central Asia, trader-tourism has emerged as a social phenomenon of considerable economic conse-quence. In this chapter, I review some quantitative indices of the im-portance of this form of exchange for Yining's economy, describe how these marketing activities worked, and examine their relation to the categories of social identity—place, gender, status group, religion, and so forth—explored in other chapters. My goal, in other words, is to consider how Uyghur identities find expression in and are shaped by the everyday practices of translocal marketing.

Background to Trader-Tourism in Yining

The Horgos border station near Yining was first opened under the People's Republic in 1950. By 1959 annual exports leaving China through Horgos amounted to $13,250,000.[2] When Sino-Soviet relations became strained in 1962, trade through Horgos declined continuously until 1967, when it ceased completely.[3] Not until five years after China initiated broad economic reforms in 1978 was the Horgos station re-opened, in 1983. The flow of goods through the town increased dra-matically, and three years later exports leaving China through Horgos had surpassed their highest levels from the 1950s, totaling $13,500,000 in 1986.[4] By 1993 annual trade had skyrocketed to $119,470,000.[5] Given that the total border trade in Xinjiang was estimated to be around $700 million in 1996, Horgos clearly had a large share.[6]

Horgos was officially opened to bus traffic on March 1, 1989, with traffic going from China to Kazakhstan on even-numbered days and re-turning on odd-numbered days. Trader-tourists were quick to take ad-vantage of this new opportunity, and in 1990 there were 53,300 entries into China through Horgos. In August 1991 Yining was officially opened to receive cash-carrying trader-tourists arriving on three-day visas.[7] That year the number of border entrants rose to 75,000, of which 23,000 were now officially recorded as trader-tourists.[8] Within twelve months, trader-tourists had purchased a total of $5,870,000 worth of goods and services and paid $1,430,000 in taxes and fees to local governments.[9] A separate report estimates that trader-tourist exports worth $10 million passed through Horgos in 1992 and 1993 combined, although it is more likely that these numbers contain inaccuracies than that the amount of trade declined.[10] By 1994, the number of annual trader-tourist visits to Yining surpassed 100,000, an indication that Yining's economy had found its fastest growing marketing system.[11] One final marker of the importance the state placed on border trade is the fact that although Horgos had a fixed population of only 1,500 in the early 1990s, state planners projected in 1993 that by 2050 it would be home to 50,000 permanent residents.[12]

The expansion of market trade in Yining in the 1990s was not without historical precedent, however. Russia has played a critical role in marketing relations in Yining at least since it began to extend its influence into Central Asia in the mid-nineteenth century. During the 1840s, Russian merchants, despite restrictions on their activities (which they largely ignored), annually made the two-month journey from Semipalatinsk or other cities to trade in markets in and around Yining. In 1851 the Qing government and Russia signed the Yili-Tarbaghatai Regulations on Commercial Relations, which led to Yining's emergence as a major commercial center.[13] Through the 1870s, when Russia annexed Yining and the surrounding area during a period of unrest in south Xinjiang, the amount of trade not surprisingly continued to grow in both directions between Yining and the Russian-dominated cities of Central Asia.[14] Even after China reclaimed the area in 1881, the trend toward trade continued, and in 1906–7 nearly 3,000,000 Chinese *liang* worth of border trade took place between the Ili-Tarbaghatai area and Russian Central Asia.[15] In May 1920 the Soviet Union and Xinjiang's regional government signed the Yining Temporary Agreement on Commercial Relations, creating new guidelines to replace the earlier treaty. At that point Soviet merchants established markets on both sides of the border. For the next ten years, an estimated 80 percent of Xinjiang's border trade passed through this region.[16]

Han traders and sojourners also have a long history in Xinjiang. By the mid-eighteenth century, increasing numbers of Han merchants traveled to Xinjiang to conduct trade.[17] In several Uyghur-language private business documents from 1815, a time before the introduction of modern ethnic labels, when official documents in Xinjiang referred to

Han simply as *min* (people), Han are categorically referred to using the vernacular term *maimaichi*, derived from Chinese *maimai* (buying and selling) plus the Uyghur *-chi*.[18] Perhaps the greatest impetus for the incursion of Han merchants into Xinjiang came when General Zuo Zongtang led an army of Hunanese soldiers into the region to put down the rebellion of Yakub Beg in the 1860s. Many of these soldiers had long been active in financing mercantilist activities and using their affiliation with secret societies such as the Gelaohui to protect long-distance shipments of goods.[19] Large numbers of those soldiers and their dependants remained in Xinjiang to establish commercial enterprises. The Han who sold consumer goods from rented stalls in Yining's large wholesale markets in the 1990s, however, were far more recent arrivals. Most of those I spoke with had come from major urban areas such as Shanghai and Ningbo or from smaller cities and towns in Zhejiang, Anhui, and Jiangsu, and most intended to remain no longer than a year or two.

The Wholesale Markets

Three wholesale markets in Yining competed for trader-tourists' attention in the mid-1990s. The largest of these, with around 240 stalls, had the Chinese name Zhongya shichang (Central Asia Market) and was referred to by *mehelle* men as Jungya, or simply Sichang (market). Second largest, with more than 200 stalls, was Qingnian shichang (Youth Market), known among Uyghurs as either Chingnen, Yashlar (Youths), or Bide Bazar (Clover Market), for the site on which it had been built. The third market was Ghulja Saray, named for the Ghulja Hotel across from its entrance. The first two of these were indoor warehouses, the last was an outdoor market of booths with corrugated steel roofs. Each of these wholesale markets grew in importance after trader-tourism began in 1991; before that time, Teshlepki had been Yining's main wholesale market.[20]

Inside the markets, stalls rented by groups of two or three Han sojourners typically displayed only a few sample items, mostly seasonal clothing of various kinds, although goods always in demand, track suits, children's clothes, and socks, were displayed throughout the year. A

Fig. 14 Many men earn their living by acting as middlemen (*yangpungchi*) between sojourning Han wholesalers and visiting trader-tourist buyers. Here *yangpungchi* follow their clients through a local wholesale market waiting for an opportunity to help close a transaction, or to be dispatched in search of a better deal (photograph by the author, 1996).

range of other items could also be found, such as doorknobs, pens, adhesive tape, foam shoulder pads, and toys. Almost always, the goods on display were manufactured in the vicinity of the Han sojourners' natal homes and were acquired by wholesalers through personal networks. When these markets were at their busiest, they might be filled with hundreds of Uyghur *yangpungchi* shuffling about looking for new and interesting wares or sniffing for a bargain. As many as 20 or 30 separate groups of trader-tourists would meander from stall to stall, each one accompanied by a small cluster of *yangpungchi*; every now and then one of the groups would rush off, perhaps having heard reports of a shipment of new merchandise being unloaded from a Chinese truck outside. Other men wandered through the markets waving bundles of cloth strips, which they used to sew plastic burlap bales around merchandise being readied for transport.

Outside the markets, massive bales of goods were unloaded from Chinese trucks arriving from the railhead in Urumqi; trucks carried 50 to 60 bales, with bales ranging in size from 0.5 to 1.5 m³. After Uyghur laborers unloaded and stacked the bales in piles, individual bales were either taken inside to the stall owners who had arranged for their delivery or transferred directly to a waiting buyer; when trade was brisk, bales were often sold before they were unloaded. To move these large bales of goods from place to place inside the market, transport-laborers (*kirakesh*) with sturdy handcarts stood at the ready. They could move two bales at a time and earned 1 *yuan* ($0.13) for each bale they moved.

The loading of goods into the vehicles that trader-tourists drove across the border, passenger buses stripped of all but a few seats or massive Russian Kamaz trucks, took place away from the markets at special loading sites scattered around the *mehelle*. The largest was a twenty-truck capacity warehouse not far from Ghulja Saray, an operation overseen by Téyipjan "Sparrow" (*qushqach*), a *lawben* who lived in a prosperous *mehelle* next to Zawut; smaller loading sites were found throughout Yining's suburban periphery. To move bales of goods from site to site around town, trader-tourists hired Uyghur pedal-tricycle operators known as *salurchi* (from Chinese *sanlun*, meaning "three wheel"), whose vehicles' oversized rear racks were capable of holding three or four massive bales of goods. Motorcycles with sidecars also taxied trader-tourists and their *yangpungchi* from market to market for a few *yuan* per trip.

Many trader-tourists cultivated relationships with particular *yangpungchi* middlemen to assist them every time they came (most visited Yining from two to eight times each year, depending on the distance they traveled). *Yangpungchi* also hoped to establish long-term relationships with visiting traders. Early in my research, I noticed large crowds of Uyghur youths loitering outside the hotels where trader-tourists stayed, and assumed that they were hustling for clients. Eventually *yangpungchi* explained to me that the main purpose of these loiterers was to watch for the arrival of their own or friends' regular clients. Every *yangpungchi* was in business for himself, but cooperation and loose temporary partnerships were often of mutual benefit, and so were common. If a group of trader-tourists emerging from a hotel did not have established *yangpungchi*, however, a cluster of young men would follow them around for the remainder of the day. Within that group, inevitably one or two men would take charge, moving forward to assist with translation when the traders entered the markets. The others waited alongside hoping to be dispatched by their "leaders" to search for some desired goods.

One subtle indication of the equivocal feelings toward visiting traders (beyond that suggested in the analysis of the joke quoted as the epigraph to this chapter), and toward ethnic Russian trader-tourists in particular, can be discerned in the habit of young *mehelle* men of shouting (usually from a safe distance) the word *barat* at any Russian-looking traders they saw walking around town unaccompanied by *yangpungchi*. This, they explained to me, was the Russian word for "brother" or "friend." In fact *brat* is "brother," but the near homophone *brat'* is Russian for "to screw or hump," a word young *mehelle* men were sure to know. Since *yangpungchi* typically expressed contempt and revulsion for Russians in private, it seemed to me that men used this ambiguous vocative to express their equivocal feelings, feelings that combined aggression toward Russians with a desire for the wealth that relations with Russians could bring.

To be a successful *yangpungchi*, a man had to possess some ability to negotiate in both Russian and Chinese. Although I had initially assumed that middlemen mainly served as interpreters, I learned that most saw their role as far more entrepreneurial. The *yangpungchi* who followed trader-tourists in packs, men explained, were not the only ones who performed middleman services, just the most visible. Others, for example, bought salable goods outright from Han vendors, and then marketed them through those *yangpungchi* who did have steady trader-tourist clients. One trader explained as follows.

Like the other day I made 450 *yuan* in one day. We'll hear one day that such and such goods are coming the next day. So we go there, to where the truck from Urumqi is being unloaded. We'll see the stall number of the receiver on the bag, and see what's in it by recognizing the packing style, like with socks, or else by just prying into the container. And if it's fast [i.e., highly salable] goods, we'll go right in and either buy it there with cash, or pay a down payment, then later that day, the *yangpungchi* will ask who has such goods, and we'll sell them.

Successful middlemen possessed the additional skill of being able to discern subtle differences in quality between seemingly identical goods.

One man, a *yangpungchi* in his twenties, explained that what to me looked like identical goods were actually produced in a number of different factories. "Unless you have no eyes," he explained, "you can tell that clothes from one of those factories are better than clothes from the others, and so the prices are different." No amount of looking at apparently identical children's dresses enabled me to detect the difference in quality between one "obviously worth 11.30 *yuan*" versus one for which "only a fool would pay more than 10.50 *yuan*." Yet this specialized appreciation for fabric and sewing quality was a skill critical for success as a middleman.

Yangpungchi, like other local merchants, spent much of their time seemingly idle. The many indoor and open-air pool halls near Yining's wholesale markets, for example, were always crowded with men, several dozen of them watching a few others play. Most of these men were traders of one kind or another, who used this time to chat about shipments of goods that had recently arrived or were scheduled to arrive in coming days. Even the most successful middlemen spent only a small fraction of their time visibly active in the markets. For an outside observer, it would not be easy to distinguish between men who were truly idle 100 percent of the time and those who used this "idle" time to build social networks and exchange information in order to line up a profitable deal, although the difference between wealth and poverty hinged on just this distinction.

Yangpungchi middlemen took their payments for brokering deals sometimes from Han sellers, sometimes from trader-tourist buyers, and occasionally from both at once.

At Chingnen this morning I saw Dos speaking Russian with two Russian women in their early forties, who were buying 400 shirts at 16 *yuan* apiece. A young Han woman, the seller, said to him quietly in Chinese, "You know, right, that that's the price I really take." She wanted him to acknowledge that he would take his "tea" only from the buyers and not expect a kickback from her as well.

The money earned by *yangpungchi*, like the money earned by *dellal* middlemen, was called "tea money" (*chay puli*) or simply "tea" (*chay*). *Yangpungchi* were generally unwilling to reveal accurate information about their earnings. On one hand, men frequently exaggerated their incomes, I suspected in order to enhance their reputations and thus the value other men placed on networking with them. On the other hand, *yang-pungchi* might wish to downplay their success in order to protect relationships with particular clients; revealing a profitable client to other men might risk ruining a good thing.

A small, but highly visible, minority of visiting trader-tourists were ethnic Uzbek and Uyghur women from Kazakhstan. These women all used *yangpungchi*, and seemed to quite enjoy having a group of men at their beck and call. The following incident, which involves a female trader-tourist, reveals details about the issue of collecting pay.

Today Hakim didn't open the cassette stand he runs across from the entrance to Teshlepki. Friends came to his house last night to say they had spotted a regular client of his arriving at a hotel. He went today to look for her, first without success at Bide Bazar, then he grabbed a sidecar for Sichang, where she was getting into a minibus. She was Uyghur, born in Almaty. A big woman, 170 pounds, forty-ish, hair dyed bright red, pink head-scarf, lots of makeup, red roses on her socks, colorful *etles* fabric dress.

Dozens of men standing around could have helped her to negotiate for goods in Chinese, but she smiled when she saw Hakim, and told him she had waited, had known he would find her.

They went back inside to look around, and after a while bought 120 Mercury brand striped dress shirts labeled "Made in Ningbo" from a Shanghainese seller who yelled loudly that at 10.25 *yuan* apiece he was selling at a loss.

They broke for lunch, a bowl of *chaynek shorpa*, then returned to Jungya to look for Marlboro socks. No luck, but she bought 215 more shirts from a different seller, a Han woman, for 10.50 *yuan* apiece. Hakim convinced her he had gotten her a great price, and she gave him (he reported to a group of friends that evening) 0.50 *yuan* for each shirt they got that day. He also told me he had negotiated earlier with the woman seller to give him a *chay* kickback of 0.30 *yuan* per shirt.

For this one day's work, Hakim calculated he had earned 232 *yuan* ($29.00), far more than he would have earned selling cassettes for 7 to 9 *yuan* apiece, tapes that cost him 4 to 5 *yuan* wholesale. Hakim's flexibility, switching between other market activities and *yangpungchiliq*, was characteristic of Yining marketing practices.

Two days later, an incident occurred that gave me a sense of how difficult it was to obtain reliable information about traders' financial arrangements.

This morning Jungya was fairly dead. The Han woman that Hakim and his buyer had bought shirts from [with me accompanying them] recognized me from across the aisle and ran over to tell me, "We just got more shirts in. This time, *you* tell her, *the price is 9.50.*" The intensity with which she spoke made it clear. Hakim must have taken 1.00 *yuan* from the seller, plus the 0.50 *yuan* from the buyer. That is more than I have heard most *yangpungchi* ever speak of getting.

Han sellers wanted to attract trader-tourist buyers with low prices, but they also needed to avoid angering the *yangpungchi*, many of whom were skilled at steering traders to sellers they preferred, something not hard to do given that sellers' wares were often nearly identical.

Despite their interdependence, relations between *yangpungchi* and Han wholesalers were often marked with considerable animosity. *Yangpungchi* for their part were always ready to exploit what they saw as Han sellers' reliance on their services in order to extract additional profit from the relationship. One common technique was to demand a sample item of clothing from a seller's wares. Nearly every *yangpungchi* who looked over a bale of goods under the pretense, genuine or not, of having a ready buyer at hand, asked if he could take an item without paying. Such a demand puts the seller in a position of either losing part of his inventory or being forced to present himself as ungenerous. *Yangpungchi* usually insisted they were just taking a sample to show a potential buyer, but these claims were often empty, and men laughed heartily about them afterward. Antagonistic and aggressive banter often accompanied negotiations over free samples, and when the outcome involved a *yangpungchi* walking away with an item while the seller screamed "No!" behind him, the line between negotiation and theft was often blurred.

Uyghur-Han Relations in the Marketplace

The deep resentment *mehelle* men felt toward Han in Xinjiang, a feeling they voiced widely in their everyday conversations, was further highlighted by the routine acts of violence between Uyghur and Han that occurred throughout my field research.[21] The following incident is taken from my field notes.

It was rainy and quiet this afternoon at Qingnian, not many "Soviets" in town, it seems. A Han woman, in her early thirties, sat behind a small table displaying samples of the goods she had in stock, two-piece dress outfits for young girls in Daffy Duck and Atlanta 1996 Olympics designs, which wholesaled for $1.30–$2.00.

A Uyghur *yangpungchi*, he looked about eighteen years old, ran up the aisle and stopped, breathing heavily, directly in front of her table. "You mother-fucking—," he snarled, then ran away.

The woman calmly reached down to pull a hammer from beneath her feet and placed it on an empty stool next to her. She reached down again, this time retrieving half a building brick, which she held in her lap. The youth was back in twenty seconds with a half brick of his own. The guy selling half bricks is the only one doing any business today, I thought to myself. They screamed at each other for a while, waving their bricks.

"I'm not scared of security, let's go!" the man yelled, referring to the market's private guards. People were holding them apart. Bared fangs on both sides, no blood.

When Uyghurs interacted with Han wholesalers to buy goods for themselves, for instance, to supply their own cross-border retailing operations, antagonism between parties was even more exaggerated, and conflict over the terms of the deal at times turned on an explicit verbal and gestural rhetoric of violence.

I saw Alimjan and Kérim in front of Jungya this morning. I didn't know either of them did *yangpungchiliq*. I asked Alimjan what they were there for.

"Oh, I've got a little business," he said. Inside, a few minutes later, they stood with three other Uyghur men, talking in Chinese to a Han merchant from Zhejiang. Alimjan wanted to buy several bales of track suits the man has had in stock since last year.

The Han man groaned that at 23 *yuan* he was "selling at a loss of 30 *yuan* per item."

"Not a penny less—and no tea!" he insisted, referring to the payment middlemen take for brokering a deal. The five men accompanied him to the second floor, used only for storage. The man seemed uncomfortable going up alone, but he had little choice. Uyghurs always greatly outnumber Han in the markets, and the Han that are around are usually busy tending their own stalls. When trader-tourists are buying, Han are all busy with their own sales.

Upstairs the men pulled three grimy bundles from a storage cage. Immediately a strong sour smell spilled into the hallway. The first track suit they pulled out was dirty.

"Forget it," Alimjan screamed, wrenching himself away from his friends, who grabbed him and pulled him back. "Even for 20 *yuan* I wouldn't take these," he yelled, meaning that for 20 *yuan* he would actually be very happy to take them.

Alimjan acted the part of the buyer reluctant to part with his money, while Kérim and the others played the role of the *dellal* competing to "convince" him to agree to a price. Whereas actual *dellal* compete to bring buyer and seller closer together, and receive "tea money" for their efforts, this act was orchestrated to convince the seller to lower his price, or to much the same effect, to give one of the "middlemen" a kickback.

As the incident continued, dramatic violence quickly became a critical part of the negotiations.

Kérim loudly demanded "tea money," first 1.00 *yuan* per item, then lowering his demand to 0.50 *yuan*, all for the service of convincing Alimjan to accept a price. The Han man was literally screaming, "No way, forget it! Not a penny less!"

Kérim grabbed the man's collar firmly, lifted his other hand behind his head, and quickly swung his fist toward the man's head, stopping it just before impact with no contact. Kérim glared into the man's eyes, "You mother—," he growled in Uyghur, leaving the "fucker" to be understood. There was no genuine competition between *dellal* here, no one said "I'll cut the deal." The men were planning to split the *chay* no matter what, so there was simply a combined effort to say the goods were inferior.

Finally, Alimjan said, "Okay, I'll take them." The men dragged the bales over to an open area to rebag them, rejecting those too dirty to sell, while the seller screamed that at that price they had to take them all. A number of minor matters were negotiated with much screaming, histrionics, and more threatening gestures.

Hakim bummed a cigarette from one of the other men, and the Han seller waved his hand. "No, don't light that here, they'll fine you 50 *yuan*."

Hakim just laughed. "Hey, don't worry. I'm not worried. I have money. I can pay." I'd witnessed the same exchange numerous times before, Uyghur smokers presenting themselves to Han sellers as empowered by wealth and fearless of authority.

Kérim suddenly aimed another false blow of his fist at the seller's head, who was adamantly refusing to give tea. Some more bickering. Hakim was holding the money for Alimjan, a common ploy; the top man, by refusing to deal with the details of paying, adds a barrier to be exploited in negotiations. Even as Hakim was handing cash in payment to the seller, Alimjan screamed, "Forget it!" and walked away, demanding an additional discount. In the end he paid 22.50 *yuan* apiece. The men went downstairs to arrange shipment of the goods to Alimjan's partner in Almaty.

"Okay," Alimjan said to the others, "you who are getting tea, how about a hand?"

When *yangpungchi* worked to broker deals for trader-tourist buyers, most displayed a cooperative and positive attitude in their marketplace interactions with Han sellers. When buying inventory for their own retail operations, however, they were far more likely to resort to harsh language and violent gestures. This incident not only illustrates the mistrust and antagonism characteristic of marketing relationships between Uyghurs and Han, it also introduces us to the activities of men like Alimjan, men who form sojourning partnerships in which one partner resides outside the country for a period of time selling retail the goods continually resupplied to him by the other partner, who remains in Yining.

Uyghurs Sojourning Abroad

One day, the Americans decide to send a ship to the moon. They send the ship up to the moon, it lands, and they do their experiments, and then they take off to go home. They turn on the engines, but they can't lift off. They try it again, turn on the engines, nothing. Finally the third time the captain says, "You. Go outside and see what's the matter!"

The American guy goes outside and looks under the ship, and there are two guys there, two Uyghurs. The American says, "What are you doing here?"

"We were just up here doing business, and we thought we could hitch a ride home."

—Joke circulating in Yining, 1995

For men in the *mehelle* the most desirable method of participating in border trade was to undertake a cross-border retailing operation. One response to the official opening of the border at Horgos in 1991 was a steady increase in the number of Yining merchants who traveled to cities in the newly independent Central Asian republics to sojourn there and trade in local markets. For most of these men, the principal destination was 262 km beyond the Horgos border station, in the city of Almaty, and specifically the large market there they referred to as Baraxulqa, from the Russian *baraholka* (flea market). Almaty has its own small population of Uyghurs, many of whom fled Yining in 1962 to escape persecution and famine, and given the numerous ties Yining residents had with kin across the border in Almaty, it is not surprising that many *mehelle* merchants were pulled in that direction.

Partners

A good wife doesn't give you good morale	*yaxshi xotun roh bolmaydu*
A good partner gives you good morale	*yaxshi shérik roh bolidu*
	—Yakupjan, citing a Uyghur proverb

Partnerships are necessary for men who wish to participate in the so-journing trade, but much like marriages, as the proverb suggests, men do not enter partnerships lightly, and often find them fraught with disputes and difficulties. Below I combine multiple descriptions given by *mehelle* men of their partnerships, taken from my field notes, to provide an overview of how such relationships worked.

Suppose two men, Yasin and Adil, agree to become partners. They decide that Adil will sojourn in Almaty for a period of time, typically six to twelve months, selling goods in the marketplace there, while Yasin remains in Yining to purchase goods and send them by truck to Adil in Almaty. They share the expenses involved in sending Adil to Almaty—the cost of the documentation required to obtain a visa (referred to as the *paks*, because it often arrives by fax), the visa itself, and travel costs. In practice, costs were not shared according to any one standard or formula. Men paid up to $350 for the *paks*, and visas ranged from $100 to $500 or more, depending on the type and duration. Most traders arranged to travel on single-entry family-visitation visas. One enterprising trader purchased a student visa and paid to study Russian and Kazakh at a school in Almaty. After paying only $500 for the visa and another $200 for language study, he received a coveted one-year multiple-entry visa.

Together the two traders use whatever money they have left, the remainder of their capital, to purchase the initial inventory, which is either taken along with Adil to Almaty or shipped separately by truck. When Adil arrives in Almaty, he rents his own stall in Baraxulqa or pays for a share in a stall with other Yining traders. For his residence, he pays a share in a private home already rented by other Uyghur sojourners. Now Adil can begin to sell his goods, typically selling both retail to customers and wholesale to other traders. For his goods he is paid in tenge, the currency of Kazakhstan. He keeps some of this income for his expenses and sends the rest back to Yasin to purchase more goods to send to him. The Uyghur partner who remains in Yining assumes a role that combines the activities of the trader-tourist and the *yangpungchi*. Like a *yangpungchi*, he roams the wholesale markets, identifying desirable goods at the stalls of Han sellers, and negotiating, alone or with the help of friends, to make his purchases. Now, however, he is also the buyer, a fact that introduces a new element into his relationship with Han sellers. I pause in my account of the hypothetical Adil and Yasin to present in detail an actual incident involving such a transaction.

Went to Jungya at 8:30 A.M. All doors were locked but one, which had a desk positioned in front of it allowing people to squeeze through single-file. Tensions have been running high since a fight broke out inside the market last week between Uyghurs and Han, a fight in which six men were seriously injured.

All this week entrance has been limited, and Uyghurs must be accompanying trader-tourists or else must convince the guards they are buying goods for themselves in order to get in. Here is a huge warehouse, five to six hundred people inside, the stalls all filled with clothing, many people are smoking, and all doors but one are chained shut. An incredible safety hazard.

Inside Memtimin was looking to buy goods for his wife's father in Almaty. Several days earlier he bought ten bales of goods for his own partner [who was also in Almaty], today he was stepping in to help his in-laws. His wife's younger brother was maybe eighteen, Memtimin was trying to show him how to buy, and the younger man was taking notes in a little blue book. Memtimin massaged his own shoulders, revealing a small flower tattoo on the middle joint of his right middle finger.

"Man, yesterday I helped a friend harvest wheat," he said as we walked around, "my back is killing me." Memtimin knew what he wanted and where to get it. At the stall of some Han sellers whom he seemed to know well, he quickly settled on three bales of low-end track suits, 360 suits per bale, at 18.70 *yuan* apiece. Next, he wandered around looking for something with more profit in it.

At another stall he agreed to pay 2,240 *yuan* for 280 pairs of track suit pants, at 8 *yuan* apiece, then spent fifteen minutes negotiating an additional 20 *yuan* discount for *chay*.

"That's for lunch," he said, winking at his brother-in-law. Outside he smiled at his good fortune. "That's four bales, three of *jin* (real), one of *ja* (fake). You can't make money on the quality stuff these days. It's got to be the cheapest there is, and it will sell."

The term *jin*, from Chinese *zhen* (real), was used to describe quality goods, a designation assigned partly on the basis of fabric and stitching quality and partly for the quality of the packaging and labels. Even the most cheaply made items of clothing, as long as they came with individual color-printed cardboard hang-tags attached, were on that basis taken at face value as *jin*. During the 1990s China's national press sustained a discourse of vigilance against shoddy goods, routinely describing them in Chinese as *jia* (fake).

In Yining's wholesale markets, the meanings of *jin* and *ja* took on an additional significance.

Memtimin then walked behind the main building to talk to Ablet, the front man for a transport enterprise.

"500 a bag," Ablet said, giving the fee for shipping.

"But the bags are all small," Memtimin argued.

"500."

"But there are only 280 pieces per bale," he said, even though three of the bales were 360 pieces each.

"500."

"At least let me show them to you."

"It'll still be 500. Oh yeah—" Ablet hesitated, "is any of it *ja?*"

Memtimin knew that he would probably have to pay more to ship *ja* goods. Chinese newspapers reported frequently on the growing resentment of "fake" Chinese goods in Central Asia among consumers and governments alike. Transport companies were wary of taking "fake" goods into Kazakhstan, perhaps because of the associated costs of any necessary bribes, or because of the extra effort required to place bales of *ja* goods at the bottom of loads, a practice traders said was routine.

"Only one bag, the others are all good stuff," Memtimin continued, unhappy about the fee Ablet had quoted. "Look, there are others who ship goods, you know. I didn't go to the *xitay* [i.e., Han-run transport companies], I came to you, out of my heart." He walked away in disgust. He had gone twenty feet when Ablet called to him,

"Okay, look, as low as I can go—400 a bag. But bring it now."

Memtimin went inside and found a *kirakesh* to take the bales around to the back. Once the bags were at Ablet's feet, Memtimin said without the slightest trace of flexibility, "Look. I won't say this and I won't say that, okay? I'll pay fifteen hundred for all four sacks. That's it, what do you say?" He must have been convincing. Ablet nodded, then handed Memtimin's brother-in-law a can of red paint and a brush.

The young man began to paint twelve-inch-high letters over the fertilizer brand logos printed in blue on the plastic burlap sacks. He painted the names of the shipper and receiver in Uyghur, then added an Almaty phone number prominently in the center. He painted the total number of pieces, 1,360, and after a brief calculation he painted the shipping cost per item, 1.10 *yuan*. Finally, he painted the price he had paid per item on each bale, writing 10.20 *yuan* for the 8 *yuan* pants (was this to deceive one of the parties to the transaction, or just to disguise the fact that the goods were of lowest quality, I wondered) and 20.70 *yuan* for the suits.

The younger man filled out some forms and got a receipt. The goods will leave today.

This incident shows how partnering relationships, which men tended to portray in interviews as involving only the two primary individuals, were in fact more flexible and often incorporated the participation of others in various capacities; in this case a father-and-son team relied on the assistance of an in-law. Sojourners, I gradually learned, often took advantage of their position in Almaty by selling on the side merchandise obtained from men other than their primary partners. Serving as a secondary supplier to a sojourner abroad represented one more way *mehelle* men participated in border trading, as this field note passage shows.

Iminjan and his wife's older brother went in together on two bales of socks, 9,000 pairs total, for 0.97 *yuan* per pair, 8,730 *yuan* total. They also spent 550 *yuan* in transport and 142.32 *yuan* on phone calls to a Uyghur sojourner in Almaty, for a total cost of 9,422.32 *yuan*.

They arranged over the phone to sell the socks outright to the man in Almaty for 12,350, giving a profit of 2,927.68. Each man kept half the profit, or about 1,464 *yuan* ($183).

In small-scale side deals such as this, the profit earned on a single bale of goods was enough to satisfy the monetary needs of a *mehelle* household for about three months. Four bales of goods sold during the year would be enough for a man to provide for his household while he schemed about and pursued other more substantial marketplace ventures. This was another reason why so many men were seemingly idle for long periods; even a few deals were enough to keep them going.

In most sojourning partnerships, revenues collected in Kazakhstan tenge had to be converted into U.S. dollars and sent home for the Yining partner to use to purchase and send back new inventory. Repatriating profits presented a significant challenge for small-scale Uyghur traders, who worked under the assumption that Chinese customs agents would confiscate any dollars they attempted to bring into the country openly. Even though Soviet trader-tourists routinely entered China carrying dollars without apparent difficulty, Uyghur traders uniformly avoided doing so. Given the elaborate transactions traders used to circumvent this obstacle, I often wondered why *mehelle* men did not arrange to have trader-tourists transport cash for them; perhaps the potential profits could not offset the deep distrust between the two groups. Instead, Uyghur traders described two main methods for sending money home.

In the first method, a trader in Almaty would exchange tenge for U.S. dollars, then give the dollars to a border-crossing Uyghur truck driver to smuggle in. I was told the cost of this service was very low, some drivers charging as little as 0.04 *yuan* per dollar, so that sending $1,000 would cost only 40 *yuan* ($5.00). Although the cost here was negligible, traders agreed that this method was rarely used, for it was considered extremely risky. Not only would the money be confiscated if found, but other problems could arise. For example, a group of traders at one point approached me to inquire about the U.S. government's policy on replacing damaged currency; a driver had put $30,000 in currency somewhere inside the tire or wheel assembly of his truck, and most of the bills had been either partially or entirely burned by the time they had arrived in Yining.

By far the most common method of currency repatriation was itself part of a larger set of transactions between small-scale and larger-scale Uyghur merchants. To describe this method, I return to my account of the trading arrangements between the hypothetical partners Yasin and Adil. To recap, once Adil arrives in Almaty, secures a place to live, and secures a stall or a portion of a stall in the retail market, he is ready to receive goods to sell. Yasin purchases bales of clothing in Yining, spending Chinese *renminbi*, and has the goods transported to Almaty. Adil sells the goods for tenge, which he converts using local money-changers into U.S. dollars. To repatriate the money Adil gives the cash to another man, whom we'll call Küresh, a prominent wealthy Uyghur trader from Yining or Urumqi. Because of his wealth and the role he plays in these exchanges, Küresh is one of the individuals known widely among Xinjiang traders as a *lawben*. Most likely Küresh is not himself a sojourner, but he travels to Almaty frequently on business and has personal agents there who conduct his business for him in his absence. Küresh or his agents collect dollar payments in Almaty from dozens of small-scale traders like Adil and use the funds to finance the purchase of steel, cotton, or other commodities, which they ship back to Xinjiang. There Küresh or his agents arrange to sell the goods for *renminbi*, ideally as soon as the goods are cleared through customs. Weeks or months after Adil has loaned the use of his cash to the operations of Küresh, Küresh or his agent in Urumqi or Yining pays Yasin a negotiated amount of *renminbi*, which Yasin uses to purchase more inventory, and the cycle begins again.

As I learned more about the circular nature of these flows, I understood why local traders instinctively measured the scale of their trade activities for me in terms of "money-in-circulation" (*pul oborot*); their money always was quite literally in motion. Between the *lawben* who borrowed dollars in Kazakhstan and the Yining merchants whom they repaid in *renminbi*, exchange rates were negotiated for each transaction by weighing the banking services larger traders provided against the effective extension of credit by the small trader, balancing these in the specific context of the short-term cost of capital in the region.

The description of a typical partnership is now almost complete. Every month or so Adil will send money home. He'll write in his book, "I gave $1,600 to Küresh *lawben*, whose partner in Yining is Murat." Weeks or months later Murat will give Yasin the money in *renminbi*. After one year and perhaps dozens of currency repatriation transactions, Adil returns home. As a final step before the partners end their relationship, they sit down together to calculate how much profit has accumulated. Accounting practices are straightforward; the partners combine their cash holdings, subtract the amount of their original contribution to the joint capital, and split the remaining profit evenly. All of Adil's expenses, such as rent for a stall, taxes, licenses or fees paid in Almaty, and rent for living quarters and food, were paid out of Adil's earnings in Almaty, and do not enter into their final calculations.

Yakupjan, Abidem's son, described for me the common practice of not recording and deducting expenses.

Before the one partner leaves for Almaty, the other one says to him "Come on now, friend (*adash*), don't bother writing down that which has been eaten-and-pissed (*yégen-süygen*)." Or he'll say "Aww, friend, don't write down that which has been pissed-and-shat (*süygen-chichqan*)."

These metaphors suggest that concern over the sojourning partner's expenses is treated by both men as something to be denigrated and dispensed with. Note also that Yakupjan's hypothetical speaker reinforces the bond of partnership with the word *adash*, emphasizing his willingness to forgo market accounting based on a social bond of friendship that marks membership in the moral economy of the community. *Mehelle* men believed partnerships formed by Han merchants to be very different from their own. As Yakupjan put it:

The Chinese (*xitaylar*), they calculate every little penny. We just, whatever is left, we just split it, we don't worry about all of the little costs here and there. If you are partners in town here with someone, sure, you'll write down who spends what. But when a partner goes abroad, what good does it do to have him write down what he spends, since you don't know anyway?

Ideals of friendship between Uyghurs could also be set to the side during business deals. Yakupjan and several other *mehelle* traders, when describing their attitudes toward partnerships, used some variant of the proverb

| Friends may be friends | *dostqa dost* |
| But be proper in your calculations | *hésapqa durus* |

This proverb often came up when men spoke of the difficulties partners faced when settling accounts. Yakupjan, for example, was in the middle of a long and unresolved period of animosity with his own recent partner, who told him on his return that there was no profit left to share with him. To avoid problems of trust, men often established partnerships with siblings or other male kin. One successful Zawut trader, for example, was the youngest of six brothers, three of whom had left to sojourn abroad in countries including Romania, Bulgaria, Russia, and Kazakhstan. The other three brothers remained in Yining to ship goods to their brothers abroad, who sold the goods or sent them back and forth among themselves to seek further benefit from regional variations in market demand.

Cross-border sojourning partnerships were generally seen as the most profitable kind of marketing arrangement available to men in the *mehelle*. A few more ambitious merchants, however, were exploring even more entrepreneurial activities. For those with both capital and confidence, even higher profits could be made by ordering custom-made goods from manufacturers in China's coastal regions and having them shipped to Yining for eventual sale in Almaty or elsewhere in Central Asia. Soon after I arrived in Yining, a pair of brothers, Zawut residents with a history of successful sojourning, asked me to print the words *United States of California* in English on a slip of paper. They explained that they were preparing to contract with a Han man from Fujian to supply them with 5,000 track suits with a customized embroidered logo. Track suits were in great demand throughout Central Asia and constituted a large share of all adult clothing that passed through Yining. By ordering a logo of their own design, the men hoped to secure a unique product unavailable to other traders. Three months later the suits had been shipped to Yining and then across the border to a sojourner the men knew in Almaty. One of the brothers told me in secrecy that the suits were emblazoned with a picture of a wolf leaping from a rock. The wolf was widely considered by Uyghurs to have a long history as a symbol of Uyghur cultural identity; as such, wolf imagery was often taken by Uyghurs and state agents alike as symbolic of Uyghur separatism.[22] The idea that these clothes contained a political message intrigued me.

"If I go to Almaty," I asked him, "would I see them for sale at Baraxulqa?"

"No, they're already gone. They went on, one load to Vietnam, one load to Europe." An unmistakable expression of pride on his face suggested that his trading gave him a sense of personal connection with those far-off places.

"Why didn't you save some here, like you said?" I asked. He had promised me one of the suits in exchange for helping with the design.

"No way! It's much too dangerous," he blurted out. I immediately assumed this was due to the dangerous political meanings of the wolf image. But I had misunderstood. "What if someone else saw them," he said, "and had the same kind made!"

Months later at his home I saw the one jacket he had saved for himself. The picture on the back was actually of a tiger, a popular Han icon, and not a wolf at all.

———

Given the flow of trade goods through Yining and the many opportunities Uyghurs found to participate in local and cross-border marketing, it is not surprising that there were numerous signs of increasing wealth in the *mehelle*. Throughout the 1990s, it seemed that more and more residents were able to build fancy new houses, dress themselves and their children in colorful new clothes, and generally enjoy higher levels of consumer expenditure than ever before. Not all this newfound wealth was spent on consumer goods, however. Residents also used their earnings to build neighborhood mosques, undertake the *haj* pilgrimage to Mecca, and initiate and support philanthropic activities to address local social problems. The resurgence of *mehelle* residents' participation in Islam, and the meanings they associated with that participation, are the subject of the next part.

PART IV

——

Islam in the *Mehelle*
The Social Dimensions of Uyghur
Religious Practice

If a whirlwind passes alongside a person, they face in its direction and slowly say the name of God, and then breathe in a way that looks like spitting. We say that a whirlwind is a ghost or a demon. . . . If you don't spit at the whirlwind, you'll fall sick, or else some other disaster will befall you.

—Uyghur man describing a local folk belief in 1892

At present, the religious faith of the ethnic masses and all legitimate religious activities are protected. The broad patriotic masses of religious believers and religious specialists alike uphold the principles of national unification and ethnic unity. They are respectfully obeying laws and diligently laboring; they are struggling to construct a more beautiful and fertile, prosperous and thriving, modernizing socialist Xinjiang.

—Luo Yingfu, *Discussing the Problem of Religion*

Neither the sentiments of piety nor the practices of Islamic life of *mehelle* residents in the 1990s can be understood without reference to ongoing struggles in the region between Uyghur and Han over access to resources, including, ultimately, political power. The significance of Uyghur religious practices, however, should not and cannot be simply reduced to sets of political strategies or aspects of those larger struggles. Regrettably, this is often how Islam in Xinjiang is viewed. Islam has been an easy scapegoat for the Chinese state, which blames religious leaders and adherents for large-scale demonstrations of popular dissatisfaction

251

with party rule.[1] Given state leaders' firm control over the production of scholarly research in Xinjiang and the priority they place on stability, there has been virtually no call in China for a meaningful examination of religious life in Xinjiang in recent decades from any perspective other than that of state security. As a result, much like a man facing a whirlwind, the Chinese state demonizes what it cannot see into and is unwilling to understand. The bullets that spray from the weapons of the People's Armed Police are far more lethal, of course, but the metaphor of spitting into the wind is still apt. Throughout the 1990s, *mehelle* residents increasingly involved themselves in local philanthropy and social activism with the goals of strengthening their communities and playing a role in shaping their own future. The state responded with mass arrests, harsh prison sentences for activists, and a broad intensification of its military presence and administrative control, measures that in my view are no more likely to prove effective in resolving the troubles created by Xinjiang's ethnic and religious plurality than spitting into the wind.

When Kashgar ruler Satuq Bugra Khan converted to Islam in 934 C.E., prompting the inhabitants of southwest Xinjiang to follow suit, a centuries-long rift was introduced between those western oases and the eastern oases that did not fully convert until the fourteenth century. Since the fourteenth century and up to the present day, Uyghurs as a whole have embraced Islam, and the roots of Islam have sunk deeply into all aspects of regional life.[2] In the 1990s, after decades during which devotional practices had diminished under Communist Party rule, interest in Islam was on the rise, and an increasingly sharp divide between secular and religious lifestyle choices was a key element shaping the personal experiences and social identities of *mehelle* residents.

In Chapter 11, I describe the practice of Islam in the *mehelle*, emphasizing an emerging tension between religious and secular orientations within men's efforts to accumulate social status and masculine prestige. To this end I introduce a type of men's social gathering known as *meshrep*. On February 5, 1997, thousands of Uyghurs in Yining's suburbs took part in one of the largest ethnic uprisings in the history of the People's Republic. Over 200,000 state military personnel were mobilized to swiftly strike back; dozens of Uyghur activists were executed immediately, and hundreds were detained indefinitely. Drawing on ethnographic, historical, and official materials as well as popular culture and folklore, I present an account of the social and political forces that led to that unprecedented event. In my analysis, a primary catalyst for this large-scale collective action was the practice of holding *meshrep*, a form of gathering that had become increasingly politicized and Islamicized in the 1990s. In Chapter 12, I present a detailed ethnographic account of the Uyghur passage of Ramadan, the month-long fast incumbent upon Muslims as one of the five pillars of their faith.

In presenting my personal observations of and reflections on the varied meanings and experiences of Islam among *mehelle* residents, it is not my intention to suggest that some Uyghurs are "more Muslim" or are "better Muslims" than others, even if this view was routinely expressed by residents themselves when they encountered differences in their beliefs about Islamic practice. The challenges of exploring those differences as an outsider became clear to me one day when speaking to an intelligent young man in his mid-twenties, who at the time was considering making a major shift in lifestyle from praying once each day to praying five times each day. As we discussed my interest in Uyghur culture, I referred to variations I had observed within the local *örp-adet* (customs and traditions) of Islam. He seemed to lose any sense of understanding my meaning, and our conversation foundered until I gradually realized that the term *örp-adet* for him referred exclusively to *secular* aspects of Uyghur culture. All cultures exhibited variation, he explained in an authoritative tone, hoping to set me in the right, but variation could have no place in religious practice, he continued, since in that domain there was only one way things should be done. We agreed to disagree on the matter, and I can only hope others will be as generous to me as he was by not reading into this account anything other than my deep respect for the beliefs and practices of the men and women of Zawut.

II

The False *Hajim* and the Bad *Meshrep*

Piety and Politics in Uyghur Islam

For several years we have gone down to conduct firsthand research and arrived at these conclusions.

Youths younger than eighteen are participating in religious activities and lack a scientific world view. Middle- and elementary-school students attend illegal scripture schools to study the Qur'an, seriously disrupting the normal progress of state education. Scripture schools imbue youths with unhealthy, even extremely reactionary, thoughts, causing some students to take part in illegal activities that seek to split the nation and damage ethnic unity.

> —"On the Serious Problem of the Existence of
> Religious Faith Among Xinjiang Youth"

The greatest threat to Xinjiang is: (pick two)
   1. Ethnic separatism
   2. Lack of economic development
   3. Illegal religious activities
   4. Don't know

> —"Survey on Conditions of Thought, Morality,
> and Culture Among Youth"

The pervasive influence of Islam on social life in Zawut was manifest in a broad range of associated practices, cultural forms, institutions, and sensibilities. In the 1990s, Yining displayed many signs of *mehelle* residents' increasing attention to religious life. In the marketplace, for example, private booksellers did a brisk business selling both typeset books and mimeographed handwritten pamphlets on Islamic faith and

255

practice, most of which provided instructions on performing daily prayers. The women and men who purchased these materials, usually in their twenties and thirties, were among the growing number of *mehelle* residents who were increasing their efforts to maintain what they viewed as an Islamic lifestyle.

To understand the factors contributing to this increase in attention to Islam, I suggest we must consider the place of religious practice within the broader set of practices that provided the symbolic and organizational bases for status competition among men. In the status-conscious world of Yining's *mehelle*, secular and religious activities were often seen as offering alternative, even competing, sets of resources that individuals could draw on to establish and maintain their social position in the community. A primary manifestation of this division between the religious and the secular was the growing rift between the majority of men who participated in *olturash*, the marathon drinking parties described in Chapter 7, and the smaller but increasing number of men who were gradually rejecting *olturash* in favor of daily prayer and participation in a form of men's gathering known as *meshrep*. At *olturash*, I have argued, men sought status by demonstrating an ability to dominate others, particularly through verbal jousting and other techniques of self-presentation. Men deepening their relationship with Islam also elevated their social status, but did so by demonstrating the strength of their ability to submit their personal will to the will of Allah. In the 1990s, the number of *mehelle* men who gained prestige in the community by demonstrating religiosity through prayer, *meshrep* participation, and good works, was unmistakably on the rise. To shed light on the differences between these opposed lifestyle choices, I address two questions in the pages that follow. First, how did *mehelle* residents incorporate Islamic practice into their lives? Second, how did they incorporate outward expressions of Islamic practice, as signs of their Muslim identity, into their overall presentations of self? In invoking the idea that all social behavior exhibits elements of performativity, an idea richly developed by Kenneth Burke and Erving Goffman, I hope to avoid any implication that performativity is equivalent to insincerity, even though admittedly that interpretation might correspond better with *mehelle* residents' occasional skepticism toward overly pious behavior.

Development of Religious Sensibility

From almost the first moments of life, the sonic and scriptural presence of Islam imprints itself on the world of the infant. Simultaneous with his or her being named as a person (as we saw in Chapter 4), the child hears the *tekbir*, the affirmation "God is great," whispered into her or his ear. When the newborn begins to be cradled on the seventh day after birth, pamphlets of Islamic prayer texts are placed under her or his head. Long before the child is capable of prayer, fasting, professing submission to God, or undertaking the *haj* pilgrimage to Mecca, the requisite amount of alms are given in his or her name at annual festivals, thereby allowing the child to fulfill at least one of these five Muslim duties. The time when children truly assume responsibility for their conduct as Muslims, however, comes much later, usually at or near the advent of puberty. It is then, for example, that children begin to participate in the month-long Ramadan fast that comes once each lunar year. A second marker of the child's maturation as a Muslim comes with their receiving training in the bodily practices of prayer.

During the mid-1990s, the Chinese state repeatedly sought to eradicate private religious education in Yining and the surrounding Ili Valley through measures such as shutting down schools and threatening teachers, parents, and pupils alike with the punitive power of its security organs and political-legal apparatus. For those parents who intended for a son to continue with religious education for a long period of time, this crackdown was particularly worrisome. One Zawut man, whose son was in his second year of such an education, was visibly distraught when rumors circulated in the *mehelle* alleging that 990 such students had been secretly detained by the police in southern Xinjiang. For most parents, however, the goal of sending their child to a religious specialist was to have the child learn to participate in the prayer practices of the adult community. Such parents were concerned less with being targeted for punishment and more with the consequence of the ban, namely, that their children were being deprived of the opportunity to learn to pray as Muslims.

A historical perspective on the impact of the state's recent policies targeting religious education is available in the figures Pantusov recorded for the numbers of "Taranchi schools in the homes of Clerics and at *medresse* [seminaries]" for the area in 1875.[1] In Yining proper, 19 such schools served a total of 398 male and 162 female students. For Uyghurs in the surrounding Ili Valley, an additional 210 schools taught 2,286 male students and 1,095 female students. These figures support *mehelle* residents' claims that all children, not just boys intending to become religious specialists, have long been sent to such schools for short-term religious education. Combining these numbers with population figures for the same year, we see that 5.4 percent of the total city population (560 students per 10,311 residents) and 8.1 percent of the rural population (3,381 students per 51,891 residents) attended religious school.[2]

The practice of providing children with short-term religious schooling remained the norm throughout the decades immediately prior to Communist rule. Abidem, for her part, recalled that in the late 1920s and early 1930s she attended three schools, each one at the private home of a teacher. These three teachers she named as follows: Ishen *qariy* (literally, the "one-handed *qariy*"), who lived near the burned mosque; Sherinxan *imam*, who lived in Térek Mazar *mehelle*; and Cholaq *qariy* (literally, the "one-handed *qariy*"), who lived in Qazanchi *mehelle*. Each week, she recalled, she gave a *peyshembilik* (Thursday offering) of bread and cloth to the teacher's assistant as payment for her education. When I asked why she had attended three schools, she smiled and explained that she had been a willful and mischievous little girl who often got in trouble with her teachers. With this foundation, Abidem began to perform her five daily prayers at the age of ten. For the generation of children I came to know during my research, opportunities for short-term religious training of this kind were nonexistent. Among Abidem's kin, only Ablet, her daughter Anise's eldest son, had received religious training, in his case because he had embarked on the long-term course of study needed to become a Qur'anic reciter, and he swelled with pride when speaking of his plan to study for ten years.

Three Degrees of Supplication:
Patterns of Uyghur Prayer

Men and women in the *mehelle* recognized a range of acceptable prayer activities, and there was no pervasive stigma influencing a man's choice to pray once a week, once a day, or five times each day, depending on his personal inclination. Once men selected levels of prayer that suited them, however, their prayer patterns were stable, and the decision to increase one's commitment to prayer was a matter for serious consideration. At a minimum, men were expected to attend collective Friday prayers at a mosque, and virtually all did. Some men were occasionally unable to attend, usually because they were caught without the time needed to bathe and perform ablutions before prayer. No repercussions befell men who were negligent about attending mosque, and the fact that men were not expected to and at times did not attend the same mosque each week meant that missed days went unnoticed. For those who prayed five times daily, rare instances of missing a prayer session were always made up for later with a supernumerary prayer.

Although many men prayed only on Fridays, growing numbers of *mehelle* residents switched to praying once each day (usually first thing in the morning) or five times daily; this trend was a common subject of conversation throughout my year of research. Many men and women, mainly in their twenties and thirties, contemplated such a decision for months, using the long period of time to slowly inform others of their intentions and to seek guidance and advice. Men who prayed daily did so either at home, alone or in small groups with other men, or at one of the dozens of smaller mosques scattered throughout the *mehelle*. Uyghur mosques are traditionally divided into three categories: *heytgah meschit* are physically the largest and are used for holiday prayer gatherings; *jame meschit* are for Friday prayers; *shuma meschit* are small mosques used by neighbors for daily prayer.[3] *Shuma* mosques were proliferating in Yining in the 1990s, their construction funded by wealthy merchants, especially men returned from the *haj*. Women in the *mehelle* prayed only in private homes, either alone or with co-resident female kin or visiting guests.

Some individuals did follow the canonical practice of five daily prayers (*besh waq namaz*), but they were in the minority. Such persons can readily be divided into several subgroups. First, older women and men were far more likely to pray this way than were younger adults. Seniors generally had fewer productive responsibilities, and they were also, in my experience, more likely to be openly concerned with their passage into the next world. As a result, women and men nearing or passing the age of fifty generally began to make a transition to performing five daily prayers. Both men and women acknowledged a stereotype that women were more likely than men to shift to five daily prayers, but I was not able to determine the accuracy of that view. Except for my own observations in private homes, mostly of Abidem, her daughters, and their frequent guests, I learned little about women's praying activities; men rarely, if ever, discussed such things. According to one Uyghur eyewitness, however, a large demonstration in Yining in February 1997 was precipitated when state security officials tried to stop a group of more than 40 women from praying together in a private home during Ramadan.[4]

Most of the younger adults who prayed five times daily either were *haj* veterans or were planning to go on the *haj* within the next year or two. One of Abidem's neighbors, for example, a 36-year-old man who sold overcoats at a retail market stall, had decided the year before I arrived to increase his prayers from one to five times daily, in preparation for going on the *haj* several years later with his father. Such persons, once they completed the pilgrimage, were then regularly addressed or referred to by their personal name followed by the honorific *hajim* or *haji*. *Haj* veterans generally continued to pray five times a day for the remainder of their lives.

A final group of *mehelle* residents who prayed five times daily were women and men in their twenties and thirties whose decision to embrace daily prayer had been a fairly recent lifestyle choice. The decision to commit to this prayer regimen was not taken lightly, for it could not easily be abandoned. The strength of this trend was impressed on me by the regular visits I made to the four or five vendors who sold religious pamphlets from handcarts each day in the marketplace. They sold a wide range of mimeographed and printed Uyghur-language materials, including texts of prayers, explanations on how to perform prayers, and tracts on the meanings of being Muslim. Sales of such materials were brisk, mainly to men and women in their late twenties to early forties.[5] People that age, I presumed, relied on printed materials in part because they were less likely to have received religious training during the Cultural Revolution (1966–76) and in the early post-1978 reform years. Abidem's son-in-law Téyipjan (age 26) was among those who deliberated for months over his intention to commit to five prayers a day.

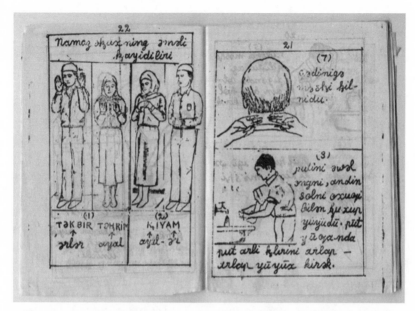

Fig. 15 All adult *mehelle* residents participated in prayer; some once a week, some once each morning, and others five times each day. During the 1990s, many younger adults sought to strengthen their devotional practice, often by consulting inexpensively produced religious booklets sold by booksellers in Yining's market. This image is from one such pamphlet, *Five Pillars and Six Beliefs: An Illustrated Guide to Prayer.*

After numerous conversations with friends and kin alike, in the summer of 1996 he joined the growing numbers of his age peers who chose to follow this more religious path.

One common situation in which the topic of prayer activity was discussed openly was when men asked to be excused from drinking alcohol at *olturash* or other social gatherings. Alcohol consumption, which is proscribed in much of the Islamic world, was common in the *mehelle*, where many men drank alcohol regularly without expressing (or encountering among others) much concern that it endangered their status as good Muslims. A man who prayed every day, and not only on Fridays, however, could excuse himself from the obligation to drink without too much difficulty, as long as he declined the invitation with a firmness sufficient to demonstrate his own sincerity and therefore the sincerity of the invitation itself. A man who prayed five times a day might be cursorily asked to drink but would be expected by all to refrain from drinking, and would certainly be permitted to decline when he requested to do so, as such men always did.

Prayer activities introduced an additional set of gendered differences into local social life. Women regularly prayed apart from men when praying in private homes. When a group of kin or friends gathered in a home to socialize, the men would pray first in a single row of two to four persons, or in two rows for larger groups. After the men had finished, the women would pray together. More typically though, men prayed in larger groups at mosques, from which women were excluded. Praying in the company of others reinforced men's shared identity as members of a Muslim community. Women were more likely to pray alone or within their immediate kin group. This is a familiar division: like *olturash* participation, men's prayer interactions cut across kin ties and linked men into a wider local community; for women collective prayer, like guesting and visitation practices, mainly reinforced social bonds within kin groups.

Attitudes toward other forms of everyday prayer were even more decidedly gendered. Men, for example, cared little about after-meal "tea prayers" (*chay duasi*). When the last person at a meal had finished eating, Abidem called back to the table everyone present who had shared in the meal. She first covered any dish of unfinished tea or food with a plate or her hand—perhaps something had been left for a child to eat later, or a bowl of tea saved for taking pills after the meal—and then recited a brief prayer. Men in her kin group who prayed five times each day consistently acted as if such things were only for women or were not to be taken seriously, the reason given being that they were not Qur'anic in origin. Written charms produced locally by religious specialists were also used primarily by women. One of Abidem's daughters had obtained such a charm to protect her household against burglary, but was embarrassed to have it be known even within her family, because some in the community argued that such charms were contrary to true Islam.

Patterns of prayer in the *mehelle* were also shaped in part by state efforts to curb religious practice. By the end of my year of research, most of the men I knew who regularly prayed once each morning or five times daily claimed to have lessened or ceased altogether their custom of visiting small neighborhood *shuma* mosques to perform those prayers, citing their fear of the state's antireligion campaigns. Attendance at Friday mosque continued as usual, however, and was not considered likely to provoke a response from the state. Investigations by Pantusov documented that in 1875 there were 59 mosques in Yining and an additional 260 mosques in the surrounding Ili Valley.[6] This represented one Uyghur mosque per 188 Uyghur urban residents and 172 rural residents.[7] Although exact figures for active mosques in Yining in the 1990s are unavailable for comparison, official reports on the state's religious crackdown suggest collective forms of worship were on the rise. After the protests of February 1997, which occurred several months after my departure, local authorities in Yining and the surrounding area "[stopped] the construction or renovation of 133 mosques . . . broke up 105 illegal religious classes teaching the Qur'an and dispersed 499 students."[8]

Secular and Spiritual Paths to Status

For many successful merchants, undertaking the *haj* brought wide recognition that they had achieved a position of special status in the social hierarchy of the community. Insight into *mehelle* residents' attitudes toward *haj* participation is available, I suggest, in the following joke, which circulated in Yining during my research.

So there was this *hajim*, just back from the *haj*, who was a really sincerely pious guy. One day he's going to a wedding banquet, right, and so he's at the wedding, and some other guy goes right to the seat of honor and starts off, "I'm that kind of *hajim*, and this kind of *hajim*." You know the kind of guy I mean, shooting off his mouth.

So the first *hajim* goes, "Brother *haji*, how many times have you been on *haj* then?"

The guy goes, "I've gone eighteen times."

"Eighteen times, you don't say. So you must have seen *hijil ekber** then, I guess."

---

*I found it not a little ironic that the identity of the object referred to here was unclear to more than a dozen men, including two *haj* veterans, from whom I sought clarification. I suspect that the object might be the Hajaru al Aswad, the black stone set in one corner of the Ka'bah, the stone building at the center of the mosque in Mecca.

The guy goes, "I saw him, big beard, tall fellow, yeah sure."

And the first guy starts cracking up. "Huh? When I was there, it was a stone."

The other guy sits up for a second, "Well, when he was young, he sinned so much, he ended up turning to stone."

This joke is best understood in the context of a long local tradition of satirizing those who would use religiosity to gain social status, especially those who do so hypocritically or fraudulently. Anecdotes (*letipe*) in which the trickster Nasréddin Eppendi outwits local clerics, together with numerous proverbs expressing the hypocrisy of religious leaders, are examples of this tradition.[9] In this joke, the false *hajim* confuses a sacred object—perhaps the most baraka-filled object in all of Islam—with a person. In Yining's local community of men, interpersonal relationships are the basis for gaining social position in the secular world. A relationship with God, at least ideally, is cultivated in order to attain spirituality and to ensure one's status in the next world. The false *hajim* assumes that any marker that could validate a claim to social status must be a person, since he can understand the *haj* only as an instrumental means for achieving social status, not as a pathway to spirituality. The joke suggests what men are less willing to state directly—that in Yining, there is a widespread low-level resentment of persons, especially men, who publicly flaunt their religious identity in pursuit of social status.

If my analysis of this joke were to end here, however, a critical element would be missed. According to *mehelle* men's standards of wit and verbal dueling, the false *hajim* can also be seen as winning the interaction. Although exposed as a liar and a braggart, he keeps his cool and has the quick-wittedness to put forward a coherent narrative, however fantastical it may sound. If the interaction described here were to occur, many participants at the gathering, I suggest, working within the standard secular frame of social interaction and status competition, would likely view the false *hajim* as the victor, given his quick wit. Those using a religious frame would see him as a fraud and as the loser. That this narrative takes the form of a joke permits the audience to share in both viewpoints simultaneously: men who attempt to pass themselves off as devout are not all of a kind; some are sincere and pious, others are empty braggarts.

In the mid-1990s, several Uyghur-language guidebooks for those planning to undertake the *haj* were printed and sold throughout Xinjiang. Among local merchants, plans to make the long journey, often paying to take a parent along, were widely discussed. Attaining *haji* status was inevitably a marker of economic success, given the expenses pilgrims undertaking the trip incurred. The journey also typically involved visiting a number of other countries, and *haji* I spoke with had visited several Central Asian republics and other Middle Eastern countries on the way.

The image of the returned *haji* was exemplified in Zawut in the person of Ömer *haji*, a man in his mid-thirties who lived in Zawut's first three-story house. He was reputed to have visited nine countries and to have spent one year in Moscow and two years in Almaty as a sojourning trader. Other men referred to him admiringly as a "tough guy" (*lükchek*), although he himself emphasized that he did not smoke cigarettes or hashish and did not drink alcohol at all. The merit of his pilgrimage was heightened, people readily acknowledged, by his having taken his father along with him.

Mehelle women also had opportunities to undertake the *haj*, and residents' attitudes here, too, revealed a tension between secular and spiritual domains as alternative bases for status acquisition. An example of this is shown in the following field note passage. Female religious specialists (*büwi*), generally older women who were widowed or divorced, were active in visiting *mehelle* households in groups of seven women to perform ritual services. Abidem had been active in such a group for several years (as one of four helpers to three *büwi*), but was no longer a regular participant.

This evening I returned home from the bazaar, there was no electricity, but a *büwi* was here, a huge woman with a pug nose and a masculine face, talking with Abidem in the candlelight. She told Abidem that she was preparing to undertake the *haj*. If Abidem came up with 5,000 *yuan*, the *büwi* said several times, she would gladly take Abidem along. Abidem deeply wishes she could go, I know, but she hasn't the means, and I suspect resents the woman's flaunting her intention and ability to go.

"But it is said," Abidem finally interrupted her, "that if you have a son, he has to take you, you shouldn't go alone." She knew the other woman had no living sons, whereas she herself had two.

"That's not in the books." The *büwi* shot back. "I've read the books, I've read all of them, and I know that isn't in the books."

Faced with a woman drawing attention to her future status as a *haji*, Abidem essentially counters by saying, "But I have sons and you don't, which gives me a status in the secular world superior to yours."

Another joke that circulated in the *mehelle* during my research demonstrates this same tension between the secular and the sacred as bases for social status. The version presented here is transcribed from a performance by Muxtar Hésam, a nineteen-year-old up-and-coming Yining jokester, told at an *olturash* organized by a local cassette-tape producer for the purpose of recording material for a new release.

These kids today, some of them don't know anything about rules of behavior (*qa'ide*). In our *mehelle*, there's this kid Rexmetulla, Rexmetulla is his name, and this kid, he doesn't know the first thing about Islamic rules.

So one day, I'm going to Friday prayers, I put on my clothes, get washed up, and I go out to the street corner. Who's there, standing on the corner, but Rexmetulla.

So I say, "Hey Rexmetulla, come on, we'll go over to Friday prayers," and he says, "Friend, but I don't know the rules."

So I say, "But you're a Muslim just like I am. We'll go into the mosque, and you just do whatever I do, right?" and he says, "Okay."

So we got washed up and went into the mosque. After everyone in the mosque was finished performing two *reket*,* it's time to perform the Salaam, so I look to my right and I say, "Peace be upon you (*es-salaam u eleykum*), Rexmetulla." Then he up and says, "And upon you, peace (*we eleykum es-salaam*)."

For most readers, a word of explanation will be in order. As the joke suggests, during Friday prayers in Yining men gathered in groups of a hundred or more to pray together at mosques. In daily life, men greet each other often with the phrase "Peace be upon you," to which the appropriate reply is always "And upon you, peace." The Salaam, on the other hand, is a specific point within the sacred space of prayer when each man wishes peace on his neighbors, saying "Peace be upon you." They in turn wish him peace by repeating the exact same phrase. In other words, the mundane secular reply, which itself is a grammatical inversion of the question, is again inverted, producing the original sen-

---

*Reket (in Arabic *rakat*) are cycles of Islamic prayer that include postures of standing, bending, and prostration.

tence. That everyday speech patterns are inverted in prayer is not surprising, since reversal is among the features that commonly mark the
distinction between sacred and profane, between ritual and mundane.
The audience bursts out in laughter when Rexmetulla treats the sacred
language of prayer, an exchange between man and God, as an everyday
social interaction between man and man. Even on its surface, the joke
reveals tensions in Uyghur communities about the meanings of being a
Muslim, and tensions within male cohorts about knowing the basic
rules of and practicing a Muslim lifestyle.

The opposition between the secular and the spiritual is also expressed in the following anecdote about Yining jokester Hésam, the father of Muxtar, who recounted the joke above.[10]

The Imam of the *mehelle* thought to test Hésam and asked him, "How many
duties (*perz*) are there?"

"Eleven," guessed Hésam confidently.

"Incorrect!" said the Imam, furrowing his brow.

"Psst—say five," whispered a guy standing at Hésam's side.

"What are you talking about?" Hésam whispered back. "If he won't take
eleven, how is five going to be enough?"

Hésam, like the man who completed the *haj* eighteen times, applies the
more-is-better logic of market exchange to his interaction with this religious leader, rather than framing the encounter as expected within the
nonnegotiable logic of canonical Islamic conduct.

In previous chapters I described how men competed to gain status
in local society by performing their masculinity through dominating
other men in verbal jousting and other forms of interpersonal competition. If we accept that submission to God is an alternative, and in some
ways contrary, path for seeking status, we are perhaps better able to
understand the enigmatic proverb recorded in Xinjiang by Grenard.[11]

Two Mullahs equal one man   *ikki molla bir kishi*
One Mullah equals one woman   *bir molla xotun kishi*

Just as women do not participate in the interactions that determine men's
status relative to each other, men whose participation in social networks
of pious men keep them from participating in the full range of secular
activities of the male community, men such as religious leaders, for

example, are viewed as somehow less than full men or, as this proverb states, equal to women.

If the narrative materials analyzed so far bring to light an underlying tension between secular and spiritual modes of status acquisition, only a careful look at the ethnographic context of this tension in the community can reveal its consequences for local social life. In the remainder of the chapter, I consider some of the contradictions men faced in reconciling the spiritual and secular dimensions of *mehelle* social life.

In the *mehelle*, young boys form cohorts with their age peers from the same or adjacent neighborhoods. For most men, these cohorts remain their core group of friends throughout their lives. Most men also involve themselves deeply in the social life of the street and marketplace where they spend their mornings and afternoons, and where additional groupings and networks of friends and colleagues are formed, for example, among those who share a similar trade, who occupy adjacent stalls in a market, or who exchange information about potential and pending deals. As noted, most men also attend Friday prayers, and residents from several *mehelle* usually gather at the same Friday mosque, again allowing men to establish bonds across neighborhood boundaries. Working either through or against these diverse social bonds, individual men's social lives in 1990s Yining tended in one of two directions.

In the first pattern (described in Chapter 7, and reviewed here briefly for comparison), men attended all-male *olturash* gatherings, where they consumed alcohol, usually to excess, and perhaps attended hashish-smoking parties as well. Men who attended *olturash* did so once, twice, even three or more times each week. At these informal gatherings, lasting from four to eight hours, and sometimes longer, men sat in circles, drank strong liquor, told jokes and stories, sang songs, played instruments, listened to poetry, and, despite the nonstop teasing, generally enjoyed one another's company. *Olturash* participants argued frequently, sometimes violently, over whether certain participants had broken the "rules" of decorum, rules that were always understood to apply only to conduct at the *olturash* itself. If a man spilled his liquor, for example, he was punished by a fine, measured in shots of alcohol. When no rules were broken, men congratulated each other on how "prettily" they had sat together. Through participation at such events, I have argued, men established and maintained their reputations as members of the local community of men by performing their masculinity in demonstrations of bodily and emotional control, verbal duels, musical performances, and drinking ability, before an audience of peers. A subset of men in this category also participated in romantic trysting and extramarital socializing with women, a fact that they may have wished to hide from some men (certainly their own kin) but were quite willing to flaunt in front of select peers as a sign of masculine prowess.

In the second pattern, men attended gradually fewer and eventually no *olturash*. One reason they did this was because they chose to avoid consuming alcohol. Men in this category turned toward Islam more strongly. Instead of praying only on Fridays, they began to pray daily, usually in the morning; men whose commitment continued to grow might eventually begin to pray five times a day. For these men, behaviors they associated with Islam, including daily prayer, abstinence from alcohol, and forming the intention to undertake the *haj*, were incorporated more deeply into their presentation of self, and secular symbols of masculinity, like their ability to outdrink or outtease other men, were downplayed.

For men in this second category, participation in *olturash* was replaced by participation in a form of gathering called *meshrep*. *Meshrep* gatherings differed from *olturash* in having a fixed membership, regularly scheduled meetings, and a more formal repertoire of participatory roles and ritual actions. Like *olturash*, *meshrep* were played according to rules, and rule-breakers were sanctioned with punishments. Codes of conduct invoked at *meshrep* drew not on secular ideals of masculinity, however, but on Islamic ideals of propriety. As such, *meshrep* rules were applied to behaviors exhibited not only during but also outside *meshrep*. Men were punished and fined at *meshrep* for infractions against these codes of conduct committed at any time in their daily lives since the last weekly or monthly meeting. It was this consensual, collective policing function that transformed *meshrep* into an important though largely invisible force in local society in the 1990s. In the remainder of this chapter, I consider in detail the features of these gatherings in both their historical and ethnographic contexts.

A Brief History of *Meshrep*

In the 1870s, Russian Turkologist N. N. Pantusov directed a Yining resident to write an account of local *meshrep* gatherings. The account he provided is brief but illuminating.[12]

Older men will sit on one side and younger men will sit on the other side when they play this game. Rich people will play this game spending 20 or 30, 40 or 50, even up to 100 *yuan* apiece, with 20 to 30 people playing. Some people who play *meshrep* spend ten or more *yuan*, some play spending as little as four or five *tengge*.

First, books are read aloud. Books like *Qisasi l'ambiya, Tezkiretü' l'ewliyeh, Nafahat, Rashahat, Shahname, Jimshit, Émir Hémze,* and *Aba Muslim* are read.

Afterward, the *dutar* and *sitar* will be played. When the *dutar* is being played, two men will get up and dance the *sédri* and the *séma*.

Then all kinds of heard [i.e., orally circulating] witty words are exchanged.

Then, after a meal is eaten, they all disperse.

From this passage it is apparent that *meshrep* of the 1870s share a number of features with 1990s *olturash* activities. Musical instruments such as the *dutar* were played; men got to their feet and danced two at a time. Pantusov explains in a footnote that the *sédri is* "a fast dance, with rapid swinging of the arms while keeping the feet and knees fixed on the ground" and that the *séma* is "a gentle dance, with light swinging of the arms." This *séma,* or *sama,* dance, according to another source, evolved from a shamanic dance (the word *sama* is described as cognate with *shaman*) that dates to at least the sixteenth century. This reputed early predecessor of the *sama* dance

possessed a mysterious religious character. It could not be performed with musical accompaniment, only utterances such as *eh* and *ha* were used to add atmosphere. Later on, Uyghurs regularized the motions of this shamanic dance, aestheticized it, added musical accompaniment . . . and this became the *sama* dance.[13]

Nineteenth-century *meshrep* differed from 1990s *olturash,* however, in their emphasis on religious teaching. Many of the works Pantusov's informant says were read aloud to participants are well known to scholars of Central Asian Islam.[14] The first, *Qisasi l'ambiya,* is a work by Nesridin Rabghuzi that has been described as "a voluminous *roman* that combines the forms of Uyghur prose and special historical tales and legends in recounting the personalities of the Islamic world, their activities, and their miraculous adventures." *Tezkiretü' l'ewliyeh* contains "saints' legends, tales, and cautionary sermonizing promoting civility and morality." *Nafahat* is described as a work by Abdurehman Jami, written in 1461–62, that contains biographies of religious personalities. Pantusov identifies the fourth work as *Rashahat ayn alhiwet*, another compilation of biographies of religious personalities. This firsthand account attests that the Yining area can claim a tradition of *meshrep* gatherings involving religious teaching and the collective seeking of moral guidance dating back to at least the 1870s, although almost certainly much further.

If this were the only account of *meshrep* activities available, however, we would not recognize the wide range of gatherings that have been, and to this day continue to be, labeled as *meshrep*. Consider this nineteenth-century account by Grenard, in a passage based on the two years he spent in south Xinjiang in the 1890s.

Private gatherings where music is played take place mainly at night, and in the main covered courtyard of the host's home, although sometimes, in the summer, during the day, in the garden. They are favored equally in the countryside and in the cities; as many people attend as can fit in the courtyard or garden, one day I counted more than 300 persons in the courtyard of a Beg. One gives to these gatherings the name *machrab*, which is, I think, the Arab word signifying "drink." And indeed, tea and yogurt are served, also fruits and snacks, and then, toward the end, dinner, consisting of the traditional pilaf and the no less traditional mutton soup.[15]

The distance between the first type of *meshrep*, a collectively financed inspirational religious teaching session, and the second, a large party hosted by a wealthy individual, may at first glance seem quite great.

One way of making sense of the variation in these accounts is recognizing that the term *meshrep* has a general categorical meaning that encompasses many divergent variant forms. A 1995 Xinjiang encyclopedia names no less than eleven different kinds of *meshrep*, categorized by place, activity, and season, although it otherwise offers no indication of what specific differences, if any, might exist between these forms.[16] A different possibility, however, is that these disparate types of gatherings might be separate modalities within a single tradition, in which each variant manifests secular and religious elements differentially depending on constraining material, political, or historical factors.

One link between the diverse elements of music, dancing, intoxicating drink, and the pursuit of religious knowledge, for example, is found in a type of ecstatic Sufi gathering long widespread in Xinjiang. Nathan Light has noted that the term *meshrep* (which he translates as "drinking, place for drinking, social gathering") suggests the name of the Sufi poet Mashrab, who took his pen name from drinking.[17] This historical personage, Baba Rahim Mashrab (1657?–1711), Light writes, was "an ecstatic Sufi, who publicly violate[d] taboos in order to bring people to mystical understandings that transcend[ed] the superficial obedience to doctrinal rules."[18] Light, writing about the Uyghur classical musical tradition known as Muqam, notes that *meshrep*

is also a Uyghur term for an outdoor gathering with songs and sometimes dances in parks and at mazârs (tombs). Because this term is used for Sufi gatherings as well, the final section of Muqam songs are called *meshrep*. These songs are [also] performed separately from the Muqam tradition by Sufi performers known as *meshrepchi*.[19]

In his review of lyrics in the Muqam tradition, Light notes that the most recent of the poems sung as lyrics to Muqam are compositions by this dervish mystic Mashrab.[20] Whether specific historical ties might connect the Sufi gathering, the Yining *meshrep*, and the contemporary *olturash* is a tantalizing question, one that regrettably must remain unanswered here. Whether further evidence will support a model of modal variation within a single tradition, or whether *olturash* and *meshrep* are best viewed as distinct though historically related forms of gathering, remains a subject for future inquiry.

Meshrep in 1990s Xinjiang

The social impact of *meshrep* gatherings in the 1990s is highlighted by the active role *meshrep* participants played in leading both community activism and resistance to state authority in that period. Several months before I arrived in Yining to commence fieldwork, *meshrep* had already been banned, exactly because participants were credited with organizing various forms of collective action.[21] Despite this ban *meshrep* groups remained active, as is attested by the role they played in a later series of demonstrations that culminated in a large-scale protest and military crackdown in Yining in 1997. Before turning to the politicization of *meshrep* activity, however, I first describe the general features of Yining *meshrep* as they have been played over the past several decades. The following description of the contemporary Yining *meshrep* is based on conversations with men of different ages who were present or past *meshrep* participants.[22]

In men's descriptions of Yining *meshrep*, a number of features appeared with regularity. As a general summary, *meshrep* are gatherings convened at regular periods by fixed groups of men to discuss matters of mutual interest relevant to their communities, to discuss and promote Islamic practice, and to collectively regulate group members' conduct through the application of certain ritual punishments. Participants offer their collective services to their communities in various capacities. They also contribute dues to defray the costs of group functions and to support philanthropic activities, such as making gifts of cash or food to needy persons.

The men who join together to form a group of regular *meshrep* participants are spoken of as "the thirty boys" (*ottuz oghul*). *Mehelle* residents speaking of the recent increase in *meshrep* activity among younger adults most often referred to participants collectively as "*meshrep*-playing kids" (*meshrep oynaydighan bala*). Men who participated in *meshrep* recalled beginning to do so usually in their twenties and continuing to play into their fifties. A group of men who form a *meshrep* unit keep their membership fixed throughout the life of the group, insofar as men are expected to attend each meeting of the group and are not expected to stop participating. I am not aware if membership was strictly closed, however, and suspect that groups could add members if they wished to do so. Men did not participate in more than one group at a time.

Once membership in the group has been determined, participants select a number of individuals to assume certain offices, and once assignments are made, the same men keep these offices permanently for the life of the group. According to some men, only three such offices were necessary. The leader, known as the "head-of-the-lads" (*yigit besh* or *yigit béshi*), presides over the group and its meetings, and always sits at the seat of honor. Second in command is the *pashshap*, who sits to the right of the *yigit besh*. The *pashshap* is charged with executing punishments and penalties on participants. *Mehelle* residents also knew *pashshap* as the name for the person who delivered corporal punishment in the Islamic courts of days past. One Uyghur dictionary, however, defines *pashshap* as "patrolling policeman, beat cop," and according to an annotated list of offices in traditional Uyghur society, the term *pashshap* derives from the Persian *padishahi sheb* (king-of-the-night), and "refers to the official who kept peace in the evenings in the cities and villages by catching and punishing burglars and escaped convicts."[23] Grenard, on the other hand, states the "padchah chab, or padchab for short" was a much higher-ranking official, one he considered a "police commissioner."[24] In any case, it is clear that the office is historically related to the policing function of civil authority.

On the leader's left sits the *kökbéshi* (also given as *kölbéshi*) who performs the duties of the host, such as pouring tea, serving food, and getting water when needed. The phrase *qatar meshrep* (literally "line *meshrep*" or "row *meshrep*") refers to the typical arrangement whereby participants convene one *meshrep* gathering at each member's house in turn. The master of the house (*öy igisi*) where the gathering is held never performs the duties of a host and has no special status in the proceedings. Instead, the group's coffers pay for any food and (nonalcoholic) drink consumed, and the group's *kölbéshi* acts as permanent host. This is in sharp contrast to social events that are part of everyday reciprocal exchange relations, in which a household member is always the host. As with the *pashshap*, the title of *kökbéshi* is taken from the term for an official in traditional society, in this case a local-level official in charge of the distribution of water.

One *mehelle* man in his mid-twenties, who had been playing *meshrep* for several years when the crackdown on *meshrep* was announced, spoke not of three but of five leadership offices in his *meshrep* group. In addition to the aforementioned *yigit besh* and *pashshap*, a *qazi* (Islamic judge) and a *saqchi* (policeman) assisted in deciding and administering punishments within the group. A fifth man served as *kassir* (cashier), an office that may be a more recent addition to the *meshrep* lineup, since by all accounts *meshrep* groups in 1990s Yining were increasingly concerned with collecting funds and using them to organize community activities.

Punishments

If old folks see a youth fighting in the market, they say "that kid's never seen a *meshrep*."
—Anwarjan'kam, Zawut resident (age 49)

At the beginning of a *meshrep* gathering, conversations among the "thirty boys" are brought to a halt with the call to order *Yektiz!*, which is literally the command "Sit on one leg!"—in other words, assume a position with one knee on the ground and one knee in the air. Just as men at *olturash* must be seated properly, the regulation of body position and gesture are also characteristic of *meshrep*. Once the men are assembled, an important aspect of the *meshrep* event is a collective discussion of participants' conduct since the previous meeting. A man whose improper conduct, perhaps involving prayer participation, alcohol or hashish consumption, or extramarital relations, was reported to leaders would likely face a punishment or threat of punishment, as determined by consultations between the *yigit besh* and the *pashshap* (and if there is one, the *qazi*). Men who had played *meshrep* inevitably broke out grinning when they described the punishments they had witnessed.

"Taking a photo" (*resim tartish*) begins with the subject being made to stand outdoors against an earthen wall, with his arms raised at his sides. A bucket of water is then thrown directly at him, leaving his silhouette on the wall behind him.

"Catching a fish" (*béliq tutush*) involves placing an object that does not float, such as a key, in a basin of water several inches deep. The subject must kneel with hands behind his back, then lean over and grab the object in his mouth. Many subjects fall helplessly headfirst into the basin.

"Cooking lungs" (*öpke pishish*) references a dish sold in Yining's markets, one whose preparation involves soaking sheep's lungs for hours in water, causing them to swell up. In this punishment, two pails of water are poured on the subject.

"Giving a baked dumpling" (*samsa bérish*) derives from the baking of *samsa* dumplings in clay *tonur* ovens. In baking *samsa*, uncooked meat dumplings are slapped vigorously by hand against the curved walls of the *tonur* so that they stick in place to bake over the coals below. In this punishment the subject is slapped on one or both sides of the face.

"Airplane" (*ayrupilan*) involves the subject being made to stand upright then bend forward at the waist. A pair of chopsticks is placed in his mouth, one pointing forward and the other sideways, then a full bowl of tea is placed on the nape of his neck.

Men also suggested that it is common for extended conversations to take place in which members debate whether to punish a particular individual, "just to scare him," men explained, to send the message that the group could carry out punishments against him any time it chose.

In addition to punishments, fines are also imposed for lesser offenses against behavioral norms. Men described a coded vocabulary unique to *meshrep* that was used to specify fines, fines that the subject paid by bringing a specified amount of fruit to the group's next meeting. Someone subjected to a fine of one or more "camels" (*töge*) would arrive at the next meeting with the corresponding number of watermelons. A man told to bring so many "sheep" (*qoy*) would arrive with that number of melons. Other men with whom I spoke insisted that "sheep" was a code word for apples, however, not melons, suggesting some degree of variation in the use of these terms. A frequent reason men gave for the imposition of fines was a member arriving late, the same reason given for a fine at an *olturash* in the joke presented at the start of Chapter 7. Clearly, however, *meshrep* fines (demands for offerings of fruit) differ from *olturash* fines (coerced alcohol consumption).

One older man recalled a game that was sometimes played in years past at the beginning of a *meshrep*, in which an object was handed in random order from one participant to another, until each man had handled it exactly once. He described the object, which he called a *putaq* (branch) or *putaqliq yaghach* (branched piece of wood), as a carved wooden object with many "branches and leaves." If one of the leaves fell off while the object was being passed, the man passing it was fined five apples. Later, at the end of the meeting, the same object had to be passed from man to man in exactly the reverse order. Any man causing pieces to fall, or who passed it to the wrong person, was also fined.[25]

It is not possible to describe exactly the various transformations *meshrep* may have undergone in recent decades. One informant in his fifties commented, "These days kids just play *meshrep* for fun; they don't punish for bad behavior outside of the *meshrep*, only inside." This may have been his view, but it was clearly in disagreement with the views of a number of younger men active in *meshrep* at the time. Whether or not the policing of everyday behavior within *meshrep* may have waned in the 1970s or 1980s, by the 1990s it was just this aspect of *meshrep* practice that transformed the groups into such consequential vehicles for personal and social change.

Liquor Boycotts, Soccer Protests, and Martial Law

Meshrep groups came dramatically to the forefront of community activism in Yining during the spring and summer before I began fieldwork. Soon after I arrived in July 1995, friends I had made during a short visit three years earlier told me that younger men, men in their twenties, no longer drank as much as men that age used to do. Instead they participated in *meshrep*, whose purpose, they said, was to provide members with moral guidance. Leaders of dozens of *meshrep* groups in and around Yining had recently initiated a boycott of liquor, which was so successful in the villages around Yining that shops were refusing to stock liquor for fear of community protest. Visiting the nearby village of Turpanyüz that summer, I accompanied a mixed group of visiting *mehelle* residents and village men as they went in search of alcohol for an *olturash*. None of the Uyghur-run roadside stands they passed sold alcoholic beverages, and the men ultimately made their purchase at the lone shop in town run by Han proprietors. According to local gossip, the effectiveness of this grassroots alcohol boycott had been the main reason the government had banned *meshrep* participation in April of that year. My understanding at the time was that local officials were unhappy about the alcohol boycott for two reasons. First, because the boycott meant a loss of revenue to local state-run distilleries; second, because local officials felt threatened by a form of community activism they did not initiate and could neither supervise nor control. It struck me as an indication of the boycott's effectiveness that throughout the period of July 1995 to August 1996, Yining's liquor factories were continually engaged in high-profile advertising, sponsoring lotteries and prize giveaways, and hiring high school students to pass out glossy promotional materials in stores and on sidewalks.

After *meshrep* were banned, the task of policing against *meshrep* within the *mehelle* was assigned to local residential committees (*juweihui*), basic-level organs of the state apparatus, which reportedly fined any man caught participating 50 *yuan* ($6.25). When I inquired about this ban in August, men smiled and said that *meshrep* still went on, but acknowledged that some groups had probably chosen to lay low during this crackdown.

The liquor boycott was not the only sign of *meshrep*-sponsored community activism. One day in early August, while walking on the dirt lane that connected Zawut with the city center, I was surprised to see two skinny eleven- or twelve-year-old boys walk past me wearing iridescent green jerseys, neon yellow socks, and red sneakers. They were wearing immaculate new soccer uniforms, and one of the boys carried a shiny soccer ball under one arm. As the boys passed the shady stoop of Ghopur Hajim's shop, the men who sat there each day playing checkers looked up from their conversations to stare and smile. Everyone in the *mehelle*, I soon learned, knew where the boys were headed. *Meshrep* groups had organized a league of sixteen youth soccer teams, and everyone in the *mehelle* had been talking about it all summer. Each team was named for the *mehelle* from which it drew all or most of its players, and financial support came from *meshrep* participants themselves, supplemented by donations solicited from wealthy local merchants. The teams had been practicing for weeks, and the boys I saw were headed to their final practice, literally a dress rehearsal for the league's grand opening, a round-robin tournament to be held one week later. *Meshrep* participants had gone out to assist in preparing the field, located at a school facility, by leveling the ground with hand tools and building new goals. The marketplace buzzed with conversations about the upcoming tournament, and in their words I could hear residents' pride, pride in their community's ability to create such a league.

Several days before the tournament, municipal officials announced that the field was needed for military exercises, and sent a number of tanks to occupy the site. *Mehelle* residents had many views on why the state chose to crack down so harshly on a soccer league; most convincing to me, as noted earlier, was that the state felt its legitimacy threatened by any form of community activism it did not initiate and control. *Mehelle* teams promoted *mehelle* loyalties and rivalries, and as described in Chapter 2, the state's vision of civic identity in Xinjiang had no place for the neighborhood as a basis for social belonging or grassroots social action.[26] Once tanks had occupied the field, *meshrep* organizers stood little chance of negotiating approval for their tournament (rumor had it that the written permission they had secured in advance had been rescinded), but they did not simply go away.

A day or two after the military exercises were announced and the field occupied, several hundred Uyghur men marched in silent protest down a main city street past Yining's government offices one morning at around 8:00 A.M., then disappeared into the surrounding suburban neighborhoods. By 10:30 A.M. the city was effectively under martial law. At a main plaza in the center of town, a crowd of approximately 700 Uyghur men watched as snipers took positions on rooftops overhead. Paramilitary squads installed themselves at the city's main intersections, which they blocked partially with barbed wire barriers. Many hundreds of soldiers armed with assault weapons patrolled the streets on motorcycles and personnel carriers. Despite the menace, no violence erupted at any time. Within a few days, things returned to their normal state of guarded tension. A number of alleged *meshrep* leaders were detained for a few days after the protest, but of these only four young men were kept in detention, where, according to the brother of one of the detained men, they remained for more than three months.

The Bad Meshrep

In the days following the soccer crackdown, Yining's Uyghur-language radio station repeatedly aired a twenty-minute critique of the "illegal gathering" that had been planned on the soccer field. News editorials such as these were but one of several weapons in the state's propaganda arsenal. Throughout the Maoist period of 1949–78, the Chinese state sought to manage minority ethnic identity within its borders in part through its administrative control over cultural production. By selecting and promoting only those aspects of minority culture considered safe by party officials, the state hoped to co-opt the symbolic bases of ethnic group identity. Ironically, in the case of Uyghurs, a form of social gathering called *meshrep* had been regularly promoted in print and broadcast media, and more recently within the tourism sector as well. *Meshrep* events portrayed in state media were sites of leisure and frivolity replete with boisterous games, singing maidens, and laughing children. These staged events blended elements of folk practice with scripted performances by professional entertainers.

It was not altogether surprising, then, that on the evening of the day after the demonstration, the local television station broadcast a program called *Ili Meshrep*, which had been made by a state-run production unit several years earlier. In the program, a large *meshrep* held at a park in Yining was shown to be a festive party where men and women gathered to watch dancers and singers. As it aired, Abidem sat with Yakupjan and his children on the patio watching the slightly fuzzy images on the family's small black-and-white television set. The program opened with a woman dressed in flowing gowns dancing a "Butterfly Dance" in a meadow. The scene then cut to the park, where more than one hundred people had gathered, the men seated around an immense tablecloth while the women stood together in the background; almost all the women were conspicuously adorned in traditional-style dresses sewn from *etles*-type fabric, garments that most *mehelle* women wore rarely or never. A costumed *pashshap* acted as master of ceremonies, announcing upcoming acts to the audience. A female soloist sang *Harvest Song (Oma naxshisi)*, and then a group of women sang *Gardening Girls (Baghwan qizlar)*. Six male dancers performed a dance alone for several minutes before being joined by six female dancers. The scene then cut to a young couple on a motorcycle visiting some of Yining's best-known picnicking and tourism sites. With the sound track playing a romantic duet, the camera showed the couple walking the floor of one of Yining's spinning factories and gazing at each other longingly. The film as a whole was a confusing hybrid of musical *meshrep*, modernization propaganda, and television variety show, but the intention behind its being broadcast that evening seemed transparent: to project and promote a state-scripted meaning of *meshrep* over the actual folk practice of the event.

The validity of that interpretation is demonstrated even more clearly by a series of events that transpired after I had left Yining. In February 1997 a day of intense protesting and rioting took place in the streets of Yining, leading to a number of arrests and executions of alleged organizers. According to Uyghur groups in Almaty, 103 Uyghurs were killed by Chinese military forces during the incident.[27] Central authorities determined that fault for this "instability" lay with a lax local government, and in June *Xinjiang Daily* reported that 260 grassroots officials had been fired, including "35 party bosses of villages and towns in Yili district . . . and 19 village mayors or factory managers."[28] Then, in July, six months after the unrest and subsequent crackdown, Amudun Niyaz, the Uyghur chairman of the Xinjiang Regional People's Congress, made a visit to peasant townships several kilometers from Yining, where he spoke briefly to his media escort condemning terrorist activity and separatism. Later that evening, as reported in Xinjiang's main daily newspaper, Amudun

took part in a *meshrep*, a traditional Uighur recreation, at a vineyard in Turpan Yuzi township. Young men and women, dressed in colorful ethnic costumes, sang, danced, and told jokes and stories; a merry and tranquil atmosphere prevailed throughout the evening. Amudun Niyaz said, "*Meshrep* is a popular activity among the Uighurs. However, a handful of national separatists, in order to realize their ulterior motive, have manipulated this recreation to establish illicit ties, using *meshrep* as a ground for disseminating speeches, undermining national unity and motherland unification, and for carrying out illegal religious activities.

"This is absolutely not permissible. We must expose such tricks and conspiracies by refusing to participate in their kind of '*meshrep*' and must crack down on such unlawful activity. Meanwhile, we must actively promote and organize the healthy, traditional *meshrep* to enrich the masses' cultural and recreational life and to praise our new life, thereby promoting the advancement of Uighur culture."[29]

Note in particular the subtle misdirection embedded in his claim that *meshrep* promoted illegal religious activities; in fact, the state had determined that they themselves constituted an illegal religious activity. The author of the epigraph at the start of this chapter relies on the same type of misdirection when he writes that scripture schools had been "causing some students to take part in illegal activities," when in fact it had been made illegal to attend those schools at all.

For at least a century before the 1990s, *meshrep* organizations in Yining had been formed by groups of men to provide service to communities and to promote moral behavior among participants. In the 1990s these groups linked together to form a loose activist network intent on social and political mobilization. *Meshrep* groups were the key mobilizers of the collective action that led to the social unrest that occurred in 1990s Yining, and *meshrep* leaders and participants became the primary victims of subsequent state reprisals.

———

If Islamic practice in certain aspects engendered divisions in *mehelle* communities, as with the opposed orientations of *olturash* and *meshrep* participants, or bestowed distinctions of privilege, such as on residents who could afford to undertake the *haj*, in other aspects Islamic practice created a deeply felt common bond between *mehelle* residents, a bond based on their shared experiences as coreligionists. In the next chapter I explore this other side of Islam by examining in detail the devotional practices of Ramadan fasting and their almost supernatural capacity to incorporate participants' most profoundly personal experiences into a powerful dramatization of the community's collective identity.

12

The Hungry Guest

Rhetoric, Reverence, and Reversal

in a Uyghur Ramadan

This fast is for thirty days, it is a guest	*bu roza ottuz iken méhman iken*
Those who do not hold fast are beasts	*rozini tutmighanlar haywan iken*
Another fast will come, after this fast goes	*bu roza ketse yene roza kiler*
Who will die before it comes only God knows	*kim ölüp kim qalidu allah biler*

—Abidem, reciting a Uyghur folk verse

For the residents of Yining's *mehelle*, Ramadan is a special month, a month when time itself becomes special. During Ramadan, the routines and rhythms of everyday life are set aside, and the community as a whole embraces new routines and new rhythms. Marking the passage of this holy month, best known among non-Muslims for its daytime fasting, are altered patterns of virtually every aspect of social exchange, including taking meals, household-to-household visitation, the buying and selling of goods in the marketplace, and the giving and seeking of alms. In and through all these transactions, *mehelle* residents experience the difference of this month from the rest of the year.

In this chapter, I describe the passage of Ramadan in Zawut during the winter months of early 1996. The ethnographic observations I made in Yining do not enable me to determine how similar Ramadan in

Yining's *mehelle* may be to Ramadan as passed elsewhere in Xinjiang, nor can I speak to the question of whether certain features of Ramadan as passed in Xinjiang might not be unique to that region.[1] The materials I offer, however, do raise two distinct topics of interest, and the analyses of these two topics, which I summarize briefly here, form the greater part of the chapter.

In the previous chapter, the joke of the false *hajim* hung on a misrecognition in which a sacred blessing was taken to be a social being. In my analysis of that and related narratives, I argued that they revealed a tension between, on one hand, individual piety and inner spiritual life, and especially the presentation of self associated therewith, and on the other hand, the demands and rewards of secular masculine sociality. In the practices of Ramadan, a different pattern emerges, one in which periods of sacral and sacred time become expressed through, or embodied in, imaginary and supernatural beings. In the first example I give, the entire month of fasting is personified in a human figure known as Roz Ghojam (Master Ramadan). This figure projects Ramadan's metaphorical connections with the human life cycle into the realm of local forms of social exchange, in which the guest is a central paradigm. Roz Ghojam is a guest who ages an entire lifespan during a single Ramadan, a reminder to pious fasters that they, too, are temporary guests in this world. In the second example, a different segment of sacred time is refigured in *mehelle* folk belief as a supernatural luminosity known as the *shiwéqedir*. Narratives of encounters with this spirit entity reveal a range of folk beliefs about piety and reward.

Finally, to end the chapter, I describe a form of ritual begging associated with Ramadan, one that remains widespread in Yining and, by all accounts, throughout Xinjiang as well. I present English translations and original texts of the begging verses I recorded during my field research along with the texts of verses published by other scholars. An analysis of these texts and the context of their performance reveals their importance in marking the reversal that characterizes the ritual process.[2]

From the Beginning: Body as Metaphor

The most perfect account of a concept that words can convey will consist in a description . . . of the kind of action to which it gives rise.

—Charles S. Peirce[3]

In Yining vernacular, the lunar month of Ramadan was most often referred to as *roz* or *roza* (the latter is the more standard Uyghur spelling) and less often as *ramizan*. At Abidem's house the first day of *roz* began, according to my field notes, at 3:45 A.M.

First day of *roz*. Abidem was just getting up as I awoke, she hadn't yet started cooking. By 4:00 A.M. or so almost everyone was out of bed, Maynur, and the girls Mahire and Tohtagül.

Senemgül didn't stir; she was breastfeeding the newborn and would not fast this year. Aysajan also slept on, as he was neither encouraged nor expected to participate.

While Abidem cooked, the others began to playfully tease each other about where they would "grab" or "hold" themselves. The girls giggled and grabbed themselves in various places, on the legs, on the arms.

"If you grab yourself in the head," Abidem explained, "you can fast thirty days. If you grab yourself at the arm, you can fast twenty days, if you grab yourself at the leg, maybe five or ten days." Already the girls were teasing each other about whether they were *roza* or *koza*, meaning whether they were fasters or non-fasters.

The action of fasting is expressed using the verb *tutmaq* (to hold, to grab), which suggests the participation of one's entire body, unlike the more distancing metaphor that the fast is something to be "observed." The playful practice of grabbing their own bodies helped children gain confidence in expressing their commitment to fast. Rather than attempt to explain to children with words the significance of "holding" fast, adults encouraged them to hold their bodies in this way, guiding them both literally and metaphorically to exercise control over their bodies. Rather than describing in words the actions *roz* entails, this holding stands both as a metonym for and a pragmatic explanation of what is to come. The question the girls teased each other with that first day, "Are you a *roza* or a *koza*?," was one I heard children ask one another many times throughout the month.

Not all *mehelle* residents began the fast on the same day. At most *mehelle* mosques, leaders relied on their own independent judgment to decide when the month's new moon was visible, giving rise to variation regarding when the fast began. Households based their decision to commence fasting on the announcement issued from the Friday mosque attended by the men in the family. Since members of the same congregation were generally close neighbors, decisions to commence fasting roughly followed *mehelle* boundaries. This year, it seemed, the population had become divided between those who started on the first or the second of two adjacent days. Mild teasing took place between residents of different *mehelle*, partly over which *mehelle* were right and which were wrong, but the main focus of conversations on this matter was whether the official first day of Ramadan as determined by the Yining Municipal People's Political Consultative Conference, or *siyasi kéngish*, was correct or not. Although the government wished to promote unified and centralized control of religious institutions, here we see that heterogeneity and heterodoxy characterized both organization and belief in local Islamic practice.

Virtually all adults I knew began the fast with the expectation that they would try their best, and the majority completed the fast successfully. This was strikingly different from my experience two years earlier passing Ramadan in Urumqi, where Uyghurs I knew, most of them urban intellectuals, did not fast. Supererogatory fasting in various forms was also undertaken by especially pious persons. Abidem's daughter Aliye, for example, had fasted for nine days during *barat*, the month before Ramadan, on the first, middle, and final three days of that month.

Throughout the month of *roz*, the predawn quiet was broken each morning by the loud cries of the *allahchi*. In each of Yining's *mehelle*, one man with a sure reputation as an earlier riser was chosen to serve as *allahchi*, the "one who cries Allah." Although older residents recalled the days when *allahchi* recited more complicated verses, on the several occasions when I heard a crier pass by our house, I never heard anything more complicated than various permutations of the words "Get up!" (*qopanglar*) and "Allah," or slightly longer phrases such as "Allah, if you espouse faith in God, get out of bed!" (*allah huda diseng qop orningdin*). As with many aspects of traditional practice, suburban Uyghurs suggested that "these days only in the countryside do they sing all the old verses (*beyt*)." Abidem also explained that in the old days it was customary for people "crying Allah" to rattle a *sapay*, a short wooden staff with iron rings attached, an instrument still carried by beggars as they walk through neighborhoods.

Like most women in the *mehelle*, Abidem rose each day that month around 4:00 A.M. to prepare the predawn meal or to warm up a meal she had prepared the evening before. Those fasting ate a meal between 4:30 A.M. and 5:30 A.M. and brushed their teeth or rinsed out their mouths when they were done. By 5:55 A.M., as the muezzin called out from nearby mosques for the faithful to come to morning prayers, fasters would recite the prayer of *roz niyéti*, literally the "fasting intention." From that moment until the fast was ritually broken at sundown, no food or drink could be consumed.

During Ramadan, *mehelle* eating patterns differed from the everyday routine in a number of ways. First, instead of the usual three meals each day, only two meals were eaten. Another distinguishing feature was that meals had special names. Throughout the year, the three meals taken by *mehelle* residents at morning, mid-day, and early evening were virtually never referred to by name. People spoke of eating, eating "food" (*tamaq*), or eating a "meal" (*ash*) but did not refer to meals by name. During *roz*, however, the evening meal was called *iptar*, from Arabic *iftar*, literally "breaking (of a fast)." In *mehelle* homes, *iptar* typically began with the reciting of a prayer, immediately followed by the eating of a sliver of pear or the drinking of a bit of blessed *dimidi* water. By far the most common meal prepared for *iptar* was a minestrone-like broth of vegetables, meat, and noodles (*suyuqash*). Most nights Abidem prepared such a soup, but like other women she also occasionally made one of the other typical wintertime evening meals, such as rice pilaf with horsemeat sausage, or boiled or steamed dumplings.

The name of the meal consumed just before dawn (at least, the name as I first recorded it in my field notes) was *zor*, or alternately *zorluq*, which I took to be the familiar words for "force, coercion" and "forced, coerced," respectively. This name seemed sensible to me given the special effort required of fasters to rise between 3:30 A.M. and 4:30 A.M., to prepare the meal (even if some of the work had been done

the evening before), and to force down food even when not particularly hungry, in order to fortify oneself for the coming day. For these
reasons it seemed self-evident that *zor* the meal was cognate with *zor*
meaning "force." Later, several *mehelle* residents attributed its derivation
to the Arabic *sahar*, which they explained meant "dawn," and indeed in
Arabic the name of this predawn meal is *sahur*, "of the dawn." Still, in
Yining vernacular, people spoke of this meal as *zor* or *zorluq*, and I wondered if the name had undergone a shift in pronunciation from *sahar/
sahur* or from the Uyghur word *seher* (dawn) to *zor* due to the semantic
associations I initially registered.

A number of special foods were associated with Ramadan. Savory
nan stuffed with mutton, not typically sold in the market, were available
at most bakers' stalls. Another special type of *nan* bread covered with
white sugar was also served. People ate preserved figs from Saudi Arabia brought back by *haj* pilgrims. *Rishale*, a meringue served either raw
or cooked, was made at homes and enjoyed widely.

During Ramadan, the ritual purity of the daytime fast could be
threatened not only by the intentional consumption of food but also
possibly by vomiting or receiving an injection. Abidem, for example,
threw up one day from illness, and expressed sincere and grave concern
that the validity of her fast was imperiled. She continued fasting, however, and took solace in the fact that her nausea was not voluntary. She
also stated her intention to fast an extra day in the month following
Ramadan to make up for the day she vomited. Abidem's daughter
Maynur cut her finger one day with a knife, and several women present
all agreed that bleeding from a cut was considered especially bad during
roz. Receiving a hypodermic injection was more serious, and was seen
as definitely constituting a breaking of the fast; when Maynur went to
the clinic for a flu shot on the fifteenth day of *roz*, she and others took
it for granted that there would be no reason for her to continue fasting
for the rest of the month. Indeed, there were even signs at the time that
she might have claimed the need for an injection in order to cease fasting without facing disapproval from family or community.

Prayers

The arrival of Ramadan also meant the recitation of special prayers. Some prayers were recited in Uyghur, others in Arabic, presumably in a form fairly uniform throughout the Islamic world. Intentionality was of central importance to the ritual state of the faster during the day. Within Islamic devotional narratives, intention is made explicit through a prayer type known as "intention" (*niyet*), the performance of which has been called a universal custom of Islam.[4] During a typical Ramadan morning, those who fasted would complete their predawn *zor* meal, drink their tea, and then possibly recite an everyday "tea prayer" (*chay duasi*). After this they would brush their teeth or rinse their mouths with water and then individually recite the prayer that expressed their "fasting intention" (*rozining niyéti*). To learn this Arabic-language prayer, I was able to purchase from a street-side vendor the prayer handwritten in Uyghur script.

In the evenings the fast was broken with the recitation of the *iptar* prayer (*iptar duasi*), also transliterated from Arabic. This prayer was spoken each evening before consuming a first sip of water or slice of pear. Typically, after this prayer was recited, a shorter prayer in Uyghur was added. A variant of such a prayer uttered by Abidem on one evening was the following.

My fast	*tutqan rozam*
Abstinence from dawn prayer	*subhi-sadiqtin*
to evening prayer	*namashemgiche perhiz*

The following day she altered this final prayer slightly, adding two words.

My fast, if accepted,	*tutqan rozam qobul bolsa*
Abstinence from dawn prayer	*subhi-sadiqtin*
to evening prayer	*namashemgiche perhiz*

Each evening of Ramadan, Abidem recited some variant of this same verse. While sharing *iptar* with a group of men late in the month, on a visit I describe more fully below, the men recited a number of other short Uyghur prayers in place of the variants given above, including the following.

| I have held fast, in my faith | *roz tuttim iman bilen* |
| I have opened my mouth, in obedience | *éghiz achtim perman bilen* |

Another was the following.

I have held fast for my soul	*roz tuttim jan üchün*
For the faith that is in my soul	*janda iman bar üchün*
May the fast that I have held be accepted	*tutqan rozim qobul bolsun*
For the sake of my faith at Judgment Day	*axiret iman üchün*

In addition to these prayers, which are used throughout the month of Ramadan, an additional special "intention" prayer was recited during the three-day festival (*roza heyt*) that followed the last day of fasting.

As a comment, perhaps, on my interest in learning and recording prayers during Ramadan, one woman in her mid-thirties, a relative of Abidem's who was visiting from another *mehelle* and who was herself fasting, parodied the recitation of prayer as she knelt over a pan to wash her mouth out after her morning meal. In the rhythm of the prayer of intention she recited several times the words

| Chive-filled steamed dumpling | *jiusay manta* |
| Chive-filled steamed dumpling | *jiusay manta* |

While most practices related to Islam were treated with great reverence by most people most of the time, this moment of frivolity suggested to me that, just as jokes occasionally poked fun at Muslims who drew attention to their own performed piety, the sincerity of personal prayer could also be cast by some residents in a humorous light.

Exchanges Associated with Ramadan

A range of special exchange practices was associated with the passage of *roz* and with the three-day *roza heyt* holiday that followed. Here I consider three such practices: the giving of alms, special market exchanges, and household visitation.

Although the giving of alms to beggars was a daily practice in the markets and *mehelle* of Yining, alms-giving during *roz* differed in that all persons were expected to give the same proportion of their accumulated liquid wealth. This collective giving of alms was another feature that marked this period as one of communal action and *communitas*. The giving of alms (*öshre-zakat*) is recognized as one of the five duties of Islam, and each household must give a "fasting alms" (*roz zakat*) at some point during the month. Throughout the first and second days of Ramadan, Yining's Uyghur-language radio station repeatedly aired an announcement about *zakat* requirements, telling people to give one-tenth of their accumulated cash wealth to the needy, first giving to any close relatives in need, then to other needy persons. Within Abidem's extended family, most household heads did not look beyond their own kin group. The nuclear families of most of her children gave, as they did each year, to the children of Abidem's first-born son, Iminjan, who had been killed in a prank years earlier, run over by drunken friends driving a large truck, leaving a widow and nine children behind. The only nuclear family that gave elsewhere was that of Abidem's daughter Anise, whose husband gave to his widowed younger sister, who year-round sold boiled lungs and sausages in the market to support her children.

Another main form of almsgiving was the giving of *sadigha pétir*. The term *pétir* is cognate with *iptar*, "breaking," and *sadigha pétir* means "the alms (*sadigha*) of the Festival of the Breaking of the Fast." At the end of Ramadan, each household gives this alms to a needy person before the *roza heyt* festival begins. The amount given each year was always set by religious leaders to be the same for everyone in Yining (several residents told me it was the same throughout Xinjiang) and was always stipulated as the price of 1.5 kg of wheat. That year the amount was set at 3 *yuan* ($0.38) per household member. As household heads, both Abidem and her son Yakupjan calculated their donation based on who was recorded in their official household registration booklets, rather than on any independent notion of who they counted as members of their family, or who physically resided in their home. Abidem gave her *sadigha pétir*, as she had done in past years, to a needy woman in the neighborhood, one who was poor, sickly, and without male children to support her.

The altered rhythms of *roz* were also manifest in patterns of market exchange. Full participation in the fast required that adults spend the other nine-tenths of the money they had saved during the past year. As one man put it, "All year you work and work, and then during *roz*, you're supposed to eat up all you've saved." Above I mentioned that Yakupjan purchased a refrigerator directly from a neighbor who had

brought several truckloads of the appliances from Urumqi. It was no
coincidence that this occurred during *roz*, since the seller knew that
many families would be interested in making large purchases with their
savings. Because of this imperative to spend, prices for many privately
sold everyday goods, especially foodstuffs, rose sharply.

Patterns of household visitation also changed during *roz*. My impression was that invitations to visit the homes of friends and relatives were
exchanged more frequently than normal, but were not necessarily accepted with greater frequency. During *roz*, friends had repeatedly invited me to visit their homes for *iptar*. Abidem was quite against it, however, saying forcefully that it was ugly (*set*) for me to eat elsewhere.
Despite my interest in seeing how other families passed the meal, I was
reluctant to do something Abidem believed would bring dishonor on
the household. The reason for my hesitation was practical; as the
month went on, I realized how dependent I was for my caloric intake
on Abidem's mood and her goodwill, as these influenced what and how
much she served at meals. On more than one occasion when Abidem
was tired or irritable, I spent a day fueled by nothing more than a predawn meal of bread and tea. As a result, I was not inclined to offend
her over a point of propriety I did not understand. I did eventually
spend an evening with a group of men sharing an *iptar* meal and found
a scene far different from what I had encountered at Abidem's and her
relatives' homes.

Twenty-fourth day of *roz*. Abdulsemet had nine men over to his house for *iptar*
today. Most were in their mid-thirties, two were older, in their late forties. His
wife served *suyuqash*.

After our meal, we watched videos. Memet was there, just back from sojourning in Almaty, and he had brought five videos back with him. Customs
agents viewed them all and confiscated two, leaving him with Tom and Jerry
cartoons, *Rambo Part I: First Blood*, and *Kickboxer*. The men first watched *Kickboxer*, with Jean-Claude Van Damme speaking in dubbed Russian, which only
Memet understood.

After that was over, they settled in to watch a three-hour video on the life
of the Prophet, a Saudi film dubbed into Uyghur in Kashgar (according to
screen credits), though I can't imagine it had passed through state regulatory
channels. The men sat watching the video and chatting, all the while taking
turns doing bong hits of hashish, between which they passed around several
joints.

As the men smoked they talked about the film and about the state's regulation of Islam. The men lamented their inability to learn more about Islam, an inability they attributed in part to state control.

"They don't care as long as it's in Arabic," one man said about the Qur'an. "But as soon as it comes out in Uyghur, they limit it and control it."

"Yeah—the people might understand," another replied sarcastically. And it is true that Chinese translations of the Qur'an are widely available, stocked at every bookstore in Xinjiang, but I have never seen a Uyghur translation ever, not at a store, a library, or in private hands. I had never reflected on this prior to his comments.

That evening these men joked, exchanged good-natured insults, and smoked hashish, all typical elements of their routine social gatherings, but none of this diminished in their eyes the importance of maintaining their fast and of using the evening to reflect on the Prophet and his, and their, religion.

The Daytime Guest, Roz Ghojam

The practice of children grabbing their bodies to demonstrate a commitment to fast was not the only metaphor used to express sentiments about the period and practices of fasting. Another metaphor related to Ramadan known to all in the *mehelle* was the personification of the period of the fast itself in the being of Roz Ghojam (Master Roz), who was also called Roz'kam (Elder Brother Roz).[5] One older man explained Roz Ghojam to me by describing this scene from years past.

The last day of *barat* [the lunar month before *roz*] we would go to pray at the mosque, and when we returned home we would walk in the house and say, "Hey, I brought Roz'kam back with me." The others all greeted him just like they were greeting a person, but there'd be no one there! We'd sit him down at the seat of honor, and the next day we'd hold *roz*.

In the person of Roz'kam, the fast is figured as a metaphorical guest. I learned more about Roz'kam in the following incident.

Ninth day of *roz*. Abidem stepped into the *dalan* after a trip to the store and asked Senemgül if she wanted some lunch.

"I'll go get you some bread," she said, stepping into the *saray*. Her daughter wasn't fasting, as she had just given birth.

I said to Senemgül, smiling, "All right, lunchtime! My stomach is growling."

"You can't say that," Senemgül said quietly, looking truly shocked. "If you do, it means you're not holding *roz*." Just then Abidem stepped into the room. "Ismayil says he's hungry," Senemgül blurted out [referring to me using my Uyghur name]. Her mother just laughed.

"So no one says that ever, huh? I didn't know," I said.

Abidem answered, "If people don't fast well, Roz Ghojam 'is ashamed / goes without' (*xijalet bolidu*)."

"I didn't say I was hungry," I quickly recovered. "What I said was, my stomach was making noises. It's saying 'I'm full, oh, I'm so full, and I too am holding *roz*.'"

The presence of Roz Ghojam serves to remind people not to say they are hungry. By displacing criticism of the "you should be ashamed" type onto Roz'kam, he also becomes a scapegoat and a repository of shame for human impropriety. Someone who participates in the fast in bad faith or in bad style transfers that shame onto Roz Ghojam.

Toward the end of the fast Abidem explained the impending departure of Roz Ghojam to her granddaughters in this way.

"Roz Ghojam? Why he comes right in the house. White, white hair. And his beard? My goodness, it is way down to here. He comes in, and we ask him 'Have we angered you? Are you happy as you depart from us? Are you leaving us with a smile, or are you leaving angry?'"

Suddenly she changed to a more serious tone of voice and said to the two young girls, "Once Memetjan [her youngest son] and I really did see him. Of course most folks never see him, but we really did once."

Abidem had previously explained to me that Roz'kam arrives at the beginning of the month as a young man, handsome and healthy, and by his departure at the end of the month he has aged and become old.

Twenty-eighth day of *roz*. Tonight Abidem said suddenly at *iptar*, "Roz Ghojam is an old man now." When I asked what she meant, she explained. "Téyipjan said 'I'm hungry.' Didn't you hear him? Roz Ghojam goes to people's houses, and they don't feed him well. They say 'I'm hungry,' and so he turns all old, he's getting all old now, his hair is turning white."

Her comment again suggests that Master Roz is "fed," not by the food consumed at *iptar* and *zorluq*, but by fasters' proper behavior, by their ability to control their bodies and overcome their desires. Others confirmed that although it is perfectly acceptable to feel hunger and to admit those feelings to oneself, one must not make them known to others. By making such feelings public, one makes Master Roz grow old.

Through the figure of Roz Ghojam, Ramadan's symbolic link with the human life cycle is made manifest. Roz Ghojam passes through his adult life cycle in the course of *roz*, even though he returns every year. Recall the final two lines of the epigraph given at the start of this chapter: "Another fast will come, after this fast goes / Who will die before it comes only God knows." These lines evoke an idea I heard repeated in different forms by many people during *roz*, to the effect that only God can know who will be here next year and who will be gone. In my own experience, this was one of the deepest messages Ramadan delivered, this emphasis on the temporary nature of human life, the sense that all of us are guests, visitors in this world, one day here and the next gone.

One morning several days after the fast had ended, Abidem and I sat over our morning bowl of tea and bread. I admitted to a feeling of sorrow and of lack. It felt, I told her, exactly as if a good friend had just been visiting and had gone away. She reminded me about Roz Ghojam. Perhaps the metaphor is even more apt than I first suspected. Holding *roz* was indeed like entertaining a guest in one's house, in that the everyday actions through which one sustains one's physical self are set aside, replaced with a life that revolves around a duty to something outside oneself. During Ramadan, those actions that satisfy and nourish Roz Ghojam (i.e., proper fasting and other actions demonstrative of piety), are placed above the mundane needs that preoccupy residents in their secular social lives.

The Nighttime Guest, *Shiwéqedir*

Whereas Roz Ghojam personifies the month of Ramadan as a whole, a second folk belief substitutes a different supernatural being for a shorter segment in the passage of Ramadan. During *roz* I began to hear accounts of a supernatural entity, the name of which was not recorded in any of the Uyghur dictionaries I had at hand.

Tenth day of *roz*. Aliye came by this morning to drop off tomatoes and turnips for Abidem. As the three of us chatted, Aliye said, "Today is the tenth, the *shiwéqedir* will be walking." I had never heard of *shiwéqedir*, and asked her to explain.

"On the 10th, 23rd, 25th, and 27th days of *roz*, the *shiwéqedir* comes out. Only people who are very close to Allah ever see it. It is a bright, bright light, like a lantern."

Exactly what kind of light she was talking about was a mystery to me, but I noted that Aliye, a devout and generally serious woman, had gone on to joke lightheartedly that newborn Tewsiye "was a *shiwéqedir*," indicating that the association was neither stigmatizing nor impious. In any case, I was intrigued, and looked forward to asking friends later about this mystery. That very night, however, as I lay in the *saray*, I saw a brilliant light suddenly flicker against the wall in the *dalan*, where Abidem, Aysajan, and Senemgül and her two children lay sleeping. "*Shiwéqedir!*" I thought, as I leaped to my feet. Looking through the glass pane in the door between the rooms, I recognized the beam of the flashlight I had lent to Senemgül for her to use when she nursed Tewsiye during the night. My momentary excitement quickly faded.

The next day, at my prompting, Abidem recounted her own tale of seeing a *shiwéqedir*.

"On the 27th day we saw it, Memetjan and I, a bright light. It came right up near me, then went toward the outhouse. 'Who's waving that light around?' I thought, then it flew up in the sky. That was when Memetjan was leaving for his studies.

"Even if there are ten people together in one house, only one sees it, the one who is closest to God," she emphasized, unconcerned that this contradicted the statement she had just made, that she and her son had seen it together. Unlike Roz'kam, whom all adults recognized was an imaginary visitor believed in only by children, here there seemed no doubt that this was very real to her.

On the thirteenth day of *roz* the previous year, Aliye herself had also seen a *shiwéqedir* while in the presence of both her son Ablikim, then age 12, and her mother-in-law. "It touched Ablikim on his back and his chest," she told me. *Shiwéqedir* were beginning to seem quite common.

A man in his sixties who lived in a nearby *mehelle*, a skilled raconteur, had his own views on *shiwéqedir*.

"Have you seen any *shiwéqedir*?" I asked.

"Well now, I'd be rich if I did, wouldn't I?" he scoffed. "If you see it, you can ask Allah for anything. One woman asked for her husband to be turned into gold. For one year she did no work, had no troubles. She just cut off one of his little fingers of gold and passed her days well. A year later she saw another *shiwéqedir*, and that time she had gathered up some other things, rubbish, and asked for that to be turned into gold, and to have her husband back. . . . Then there was a bald girl [i.e., afflicted with favus], *phew*, she stank! Who'd want her? She went out to the hay barn, saw a moon, and then someone came in and asked for her hand in marriage, the son of a rich man."

Since others had always described this entity as a bright light or "like a lantern," I asked him about his use of the word "moon."

He nodded matter-of-factly.

"It can be seen on the 7th, the 17th, and the 27th. A moon comes right into the house. If ten people are there, only one person sees it," he said, using the exact phase Abidem had used.

Of course, his term for "a moon," *bir ay*, also means "one month," the period of fasting.

The detail of the *shiwéqedir* touching the body of Aliye's young son reminded me of a similar account I had heard several years earlier, which at the time had made little sense to me. In Urumqi in 1994, a wealthy Uyghur merchant had told me of an incident that took place in 1971.[6] At the time of the incident, she was away from her native Aqsu, spending the night in a hotel with her son (age 7) and her younger brother. She recalled that earlier on the night in question she had been crying terribly from her wretched condition and had prayed to God to help her out of her poverty. In the middle of the night, a ball of light entered the room, causing her to awake. She screamed, rousing her brother, who had been drinking heavily the night before. He woke still groggy, and mistaking the light for a burglar, he chased it with a large knife and cursed at it. The light moved toward her son, touched him in the face, then disappeared through the closed door, which they were amazed to discover was still locked from the inside. The boy's face immediately began to swell and became very swollen. The next day she took the boy to a local religious leader, who told her that the encounter was an auspicious omen. "Such a thing is seen by people only once in a hundred years," she recalled him telling her. In her narrative, the cleric interpreted the encounter to mean that she would become not just wealthy but, more important, a great leader of the Uyghur people. By the evening of the second day, her son's face had returned to normal.

It is tempting to read these examples of stories about encounters with the supernatural, a genre of narrative known to folklorists as the "memorate," as a kind of projective device revealing something about individual personality. The wealthy merchant, who was also active in both state-sanctioned and grassroots political activities, understood the incident as a sign she had been chosen as a leader of her people. Abidem took it as a sign of her closeness to God. The older man, who had spent his life as a poor farmer, saw it as a chance for riches and a life of leisure. It is also intriguing that three out of three firsthand *shiwéqedir* stories I encountered involved a mother together with a male child between the ages of circumcision and puberty. Symbolic meanings of Ramadan are clearly linked with the individual's capacity to control the body and its fluids—full participation in fasting begins for boys and girls at puberty—and it is even more curious that in two of these narratives the boys' bodies are touched by the light, and in one the boy's body swells out of control as a result.

The reader familiar with Islam may, at this point, have anticipated that there is more to my story about *shiwéqedir* narratives. Throughout the Muslim world, Ramadan is considered to be a sacred time for one reason above all others: it was during this month that the first portions of the Qur'an were transmitted from Heaven to the Prophet. The exact time when this first transmission was made is not known with certainty, Abidem and others explained, but is generally taken to be the evening of the twenty-seventh day of Ramadan, and on each anniversary of that night "angels and spirits descend to the earth."[7] This time is known in Arabic as the *laylat al-qadr,* or "Night of Power"; in Persian the same phrase becomes *shab-e-qadr,* and it is from this term that the name *shiwéqedir* assuredly derives. In Yining, and in at least some portions of southern Xinjiang, where the third encounter I described took place, that particular night has become personified, transformed into a supernatural entity whose name is eponymous with the time of its visitation.

Ramadan Singing

In the final section of this chapter, I consider an additional form of social exchange uniquely associated with the passage of *roz*. The practice of *ramizan éytish*, literally "singing/saying Ramadan," consisted of the fairly aggressive and even rude requesting of handouts by select *mehelle* residents from their neighbors, beginning on the tenth or fifteenth day of the month (opinions on this point varied, but these visits began in Zawut on the tenth) and lasting until the month's end.

In the 1990s, it was mainly children between the ages of seven and twelve who visited others' homes to demand handouts of food or money by singing Ramadan. Most but not all singers were male. Men and women over the age of fifty-five or so recalled that in their youth this activity was associated not with children, but primarily with adults. In 1996, however, only once during the month did an adult make ritual begging rounds through the lanes of Zawut. This man appeared to be in his sixties, was extremely gaunt, and carried a large cloth sack over his shoulder. More than a dozen neighborhood children, who had been out in the streets for the same purpose as he, tagged along behind him, giggling in amazement as he undertook in somber seriousness what for them was a form of outrageously exciting play.

Beginning on the tenth day of *roz*, these young children went door to door in small groups through the *mehelle* lanes after the *iptar* evening meal. Each group of children would stand at a courtyard gate and sing verses requesting gifts of food from the residents. If they received no response, they would cease singing, and yell loudly "Is anyone home?" Either the homeowner would come out to give them pieces of bread or candy, or else the singers would begin to bang even more loudly on the front gate and would sing verses that teased and insulted the residents, usually accusing them of being either stingy or slow. Several adults suggested that in recent years local authorities tried to discourage people from singing Ramadan (exactly how I did not learn), and that the number of singers had subsequently declined.

Answers to the many questions I had about the history and meanings of these practices remained elusive. One older *mehelle* man from whom I sought answers gave this explanation.

Way back in the past, twenty or thirty people would go around together, carrying lanterns (*panos*) and singing *ramizan*. These people would go around together with others, who walked about playing boats (*kémélerni oynitip mangidu*).[8] These boats were made of paper and were worn over a person's entire body. The person's head was not visible, as it was inside the boat. People who played boats had made them themselves. They went only to the homes of rich persons, people who had government positions.

Adults went singing with lanterns, but only younger people played in the boats, at the oldest, sixteen years old, or younger. The singers went together with the boat dancers, because they received more offerings that way. Those who played boats danced around and pretended that they were on the water.

In addition, other persons played "flower-vases" (*gül deste*). These were bigger than the boats, and were made of paper flowers. The "flower-vases" had lanterns with candles inside them. Singers started coming out after evening prayers and would come any time up until the predawn meal.

Neither historical nor contemporary materials available to me mention activities similar to the boat dancing and flower-vase singing he described, nor was I able to learn more from other *mehelle* residents; it may be significant, however, that the saintly figure Qizir, generally taken to be the Prophet Elijah, popular throughout Xinjiang and Central Asia as the patron saint of water, is elsewhere associated with the use of boats during festivals.[9] Abidem herself could remember when boat players and flower-vase singers visited wealthy homes, recalling that they received money and pieces of cloth. What kinds of verses they sung, however, no one in the *mehelle* could recall.

Although some of the songs and lore associated with past Ramadan traditions may be lost to us, Ramadan singing of the kind now done mainly by children was still very much a part of the month's activities, and the verses they sang provide an interesting and unique glimpse into social relations in the *mehelle*.[10] A few days prior to Ramadan, before I had even heard of this tradition, I coincidentally had reached the phrase "singing *ramizan*" in a Uyghur folk-speech dictionary I was translating into English. I asked Abidem if she knew what it meant, and she replied by singing this verse.

Singing Ramadan I come to your door	*ramazan étip keldim ishigingge*
May a ram-like child be given to your cradle	*qoshqardek bala bersun böshüküngge*

Ramadan, Allah, the month of Ramadan	*ramazan allah shexri ramazan*
Happy blessings have come this Ramadan	*xosh mubarek keldi shu ramazan*

The first couplet was a verse, she explained, and the second couplet was a refrain sung between verses. The term "ram-like" (*qoshqardek*) was commonly used in the *mehelle* as a word of praise for a healthy male child. The next day a verse recalled for me by Abidem's daughter Aliye was my first indication that singers occasionally taunted those listening inside the house.

White hen, do you limp and wobble?	*aq toxu ongghaqmusen dongghaqmusen*
Are you so lame you can't get up?	*ornidin qopalmaydighan tokurmusen*

Dos'kam, a *mehelle* resident in his mid-sixties who previously had recounted numerous tales as part of a local folklore collection project,[11] sang for me a number of verses, this time with one of the lines doubled, and also offered a variant refrain couplet, which I give here only once (after the first verse), though he sung it after each verse.

Rich ones who obey God's commands	*xudaning permanigha patqan baylar*
Peace upon you reposing rich ones	*es-salaam aleykum yatqan baylar*
Peace upon you reposing rich ones	*es-salaam aleykum yatqan baylar*
Ramadan, Allah, the month of Ramadan	*ramazan allah shexri ramazan*
Happy Barat has come, la, this Ramadan	*xoshni barat keldi la shu ramazan*
Behind your house a pony's hoofprints	*öyüng arqisida tayning izi*
Behind your house a pony's hoofprints	*öyüng arqisida tayning izi*
At night the rich one's daughter gives a scarf	*kechte yaghliq béridu bayning qizi*
In Mecca there is a black-topped tree	*mekeda bir yaghach bar béshi qara*
In Mecca there is a black-topped tree	*mekeda bir yaghach bar béshi qara*

May God give you a son with a black brow	*xudayim oghul bersun qashi qara*
White chicken, do you limp and wobble?	*aq toxu ongghaqmusen dongghaqmusen*
White chicken, do you limp and wobble?	*aq toxu ongghaqmusen dongghaqmusen*
Are you so fat you can't rise from your seat?	*oruningdin qopalmighan bordaqmusen*

Although *mehelle* residents did not share with me any of the more ribald verses included in this tradition, published sources show that singers who did not receive the offerings they desired from a particular home had recourse to a more serious, sometimes obscene, verbal attack. Verses published in contemporary works by Uyghur scholars in China and the U.S.S.R., for example, include the following.[12]

This room is long, it is not divided	*bu saray uzun saray bölgenmigen*
My rich master doesn't get up, is he dead?	*bay ghojam qopmayidighu ölgenmigen*
Chickens on a roosting perch go cluck-cluck-cluck	*qondighanda toxuliri qaqaqlaydu*
Your stingy wife gives no bread, just prattles on and on	*pixsiq xotun nan bermey walaqshidu*
His donkey's head is mottled black	*ishékining béshida tim tum ala*
He didn't give even one cent, that black heart	*bir tiyinmu bermidi köngli qara*

Verses collected by Pantusov in Yining in the 1870s and published in Uyghur under the heading "Ramadan calling" (*ramzan charlishi*) make it clear that verbal attacks could intensify even further, with singers completely transgressing normal bounds of propriety. Here are two examples from Pantusov's collection.[13]

Next to your door, there stands a dog	*ishikning béshida it turadur*
On the head of your dick, there stands a louse	*chuchaqning béshida pit turadur*
Behind your house is a broken-down stove	*öyingning arqisida eski ochaq*
May God give you a huge dick	*xudayim bersun sanga yoghan chuchaq*

The materials presented in this chapter demonstrate that Islamic senti-ments in the *mehelle* were about more than the emerging opposition be-tween secular and religious lifestyles and the politicization of Islamic gatherings described in the previous chapter. Through their fasting dur-ing Ramadan, I saw the community of all *mehelle* residents being united in an expression of their faith, united in their intention to fulfill the du-ties they embraced as Muslims, united by a month in which the every-day itself was transformed into something at once deeply communal yet profoundly personal, something so transcendent that it seeks expres-sion in the imagery of Roz Ghojam, the reversal of Ramadan singing, and in the form of supernatural encounters with *shiwéqedir.*

Epilogue

Nine million Uyghurs constitute the largest ethnic group in Xinjiang, China's largest provincial-level administrative unit. For more than a half century since the establishment of the People's Republic in 1949, first-hand investigation into social, economic, religious, and political life in Xinjiang has been restricted by the Chinese state. As a result of these restrictions, scholarly studies of identity in Uyghur society in Xinjiang have focused almost entirely on ethnic identity and on ethnonationalism as a force uniting Uyghurs and mobilizing them to participate in various forms of collective action against or engagement with the Chinese nation-state.

In this book, I have sought to demonstrate that there is more to Uyghur identity than ethnonationalism. My approach has been based on my belief that the dimensions of social identity that motivate individual and collective action in the lives of Yining's Uyghur residents are numerous, that they must be traced from the ground up through ethnographic investigation, that the everyday expression of social identities for Uyghurs is linked with participation in a wide range of social activities and cannot be reduced to a strictly ethnic or ethnonationalist identity. Beyond this, I have also described how various aspects of social life in Uyghur communities express and are in critical ways shaped by the assertion of personal autonomy and a concern over the male individual's capacity to take his place in an agonistic world of interpersonal status competition. Throughout the chapters of the book, we have seen manifestations of this theme; it is apparent in the earliest moments of the child's life and continues to be expressed in adolescence and in adult social life. A review of how this theme has been elaborated may be useful here.

The first part of the argument emerges in Chapters 4–6, which focus on the gendering processes of child rearing, childhood play activities, and adult gender relations, and which emphasize the position of boys and men in those activities. At infancy, as we saw in Chapter 4, all children have walnuts smeared on their mouths at birth in the hope that this will improve their ability to speak "crackingly." This metaphor of "crackingness," I have suggested, is best understood in the context of the verbal dueling so prominent in adult interactions, in particular as a metaphor for the capacity of the dominant individual to "crack" a cognitive frame offered by an opponent through a witty or aggressively assertive remark. Male infants are further made aware of their gendered sociality in infancy through the playful interactions of adult female kin, who symbolically consume boys' genitals, reinforcing for boys their need to continually demonstrate their masculinity through personal display. The language of endearment used for boys one to four years old is explicitly recognized as a potentially feminizing influence that boys must be sure to reject as they grow out of early childhood. When boys mature to the ages of four to seven, older men taunt them by pulling down their pants, asking them if they are boys or girls, continuing this process of gender identity enculturation. In the semi-autonomous play activities that preoccupy boys during the years from seven to puberty (these include kite flying, top spinning, and hoop rolling), older boys continue to express a concern with keeping themselves or their symbolic extensions in erect postures, a trait that continues to be used as a key metaphor of domination throughout adult life. Also in their play activities, boys begin to express a concern with performing dominance in front of audiences of other boys. In adult gender relations, these same concerns are repeatedly expressed in men's attitudes toward sexual relations with women, as revealed in narratives that convey men's anxieties regarding their ability to dominate women and to render women's sexuality subordinate to their own.

In Chapters 7 and 8, my concern shifts to the lives of men and to the significance of men's continual attempts to maintain personal status by symbolically dominating other men. It is, I suggest, through the two social institutions examined in detail in these chapters—the *olturash* drinking party and the assignment and use of men's nicknames—that the individual masculine identities of Yining men are rendered collective, as these institutions meld individuals into a single imagined local community of men. The *olturash* is a critical site for the performance of masculine identity through attempts to dominate other men, as expressed through joking behavior, verbal dueling, and the status competition inherent in hosting and being invited to such parties. Through the imposition of a code of behavior invoked through reference to "rules" (*qa'ide*) or by stating the need to be collectively "pretty" (*chirayliq*), men subordinate their own individuality to the collective experience of the *olturash* group. Through the group's insistence on symmetrical behavior, and aided in no small part by group members' consumption of large amounts of alcohol and tobacco, as well as by bodily expressions of unity such as sustained group singing, laughing, and dancing, the participants of an *olturash* attain a temporary *communitas*. Because men participate in *olturash* on a regular basis throughout their lives, these gatherings become the primary site for the maintenance of social bonds among men across the groupings defined by age cohort, *mehelle* loyalties, occupation and status group, and congregation at formal prayer activities. Men in Yining come to know hundreds of other men personally through *olturash* participation, and know from stories exchanged at *olturash* intimate details about the reputations of many hundreds more. In this way, ongoing *olturash* activities and narrative recollections of past *olturash* create a tightly integrated imagined local community of men. The nicknaming system examined in Chapter 8 provides a semiotic field of verbal play that sustains the collective imagining of this local male community, insofar as men know hundreds of men by nickname, many of whom they may never know in person. Nickname-related practices also demonstrate in a unique way the behaviors labeled *chidimas*, behaviors that emerge in men's interpersonal battles to provoke other men to anger in order to achieve a kind of symbolic domination over them.

In Chapters 9 and 10, I consider the role of private entrepreneurship and merchant culture as domains in which men contest not just for wealth but also for social status. Marketing relations are shown to be a key site of interaction between Uyghurs and Han, as well as between Uyghurs and trader-tourists from the republics of Central Asia. Against the backdrop of our understanding of men's interactions in Uyghur society, the apparent antagonisms and dramatized violence that characterize Uyghur men's attitudes toward Han vendors is revealed to be a variation on an established cultural theme, rather than a *sui generis* expression of hostility. Uyghur transactors in general are accustomed to relying on bluffs, threats, and the insistent assertion of personal will in their own interactions, as we saw for example in Chapter 7, in the context of cheating at games such as cards and billiards. In the context of interactions with ethnic others, Han or Russian, however, this familiar trait of aggressive self-assertion takes on new meanings.

Finally, in Chapters 11 and 12, I consider how concern for social status shapes local religious sentiments and activities. Through an analysis of jokes and other materials, I suggest that secular and religious domains offer separate reservoirs of cultural capital that individuals avail themselves of as they seek to establish their social position in the local community of men. Some men seek social position by demonstrating that they possess a superior capacity to force others to submit to their will, the epitome of Uyghur masculinity. Others seek to establish for themselves a superior social status through the display of piety and proper conduct, in a sense reversing the secular ideal of masculinity by showing their capacity to submit their individual will to the will of God. Parallel codes regarding normative behavior, *olturash* invocations of "rules" (*qa'ide*) and the need to be "pretty" (*chirayliq*), on one hand, and the Islamic-based codes of behavior used by *meshrep* leaders in meting out humiliating ritual punishments to participants, on the other, integrate agonistic male individuals into temporary collectives. By producing in men a shared identity of membership in these groups and a commitment to group ideals, these institutions create social bonds that cut across other associational groupings, divisions, and networks in local society. In the case of *meshrep* in the 1990s, members' commitment to collective goals transcended the boundaries of *meshrep* participation and grew into a concern among participants for their communities at large. The increased role of *meshrep* groups in community activism and social mobilization, in forms such as an anti-alcohol campaign and a youth sports league, led to a realization on the part of local government officials that unregulated grassroots organizations in Uyghur neighborhoods were proving more effective than official campaigns and state institutions at mobilizing Uyghurs to embrace and work toward a vision of Xinjiang's future. Understood within the ethnographic context presented in this book, the large-scale and at times violent social protests that rocked Yining in the mid-1990s emerge as a highly particular form of social contest between local Uyghur communities and state agents, rather than a generic case of nationalist separatism. Although parts of this book can be read as a linear narrative leading from the cultivation of masculinity in childhood to the contentious collective expression of that masculinity in the actions of Uyghur protestors, other parts emphasize that Uyghur piety cannot be reduced to political motivations. Thus, I end by considering the sincere pursuit of piety in the *mehelle* during Ramadan, an event that opens a window into the unique power of local place to shape belief and action.

It has also been my purpose to demonstrate that in the everyday life of a face-to-face community, the stylized narratives of folklore play an important role in creating shared social identities. Based on my interpretations of such narratives, I have suggested that an important theme in Uyghur social life is the cultivation and public display of masculinity by men. Whether the reader has found my interpretations compelling or not, she or he will agree with me, I hope, on the basis of the materials presented in this book, on two final points. First, the world is changing rapidly for the Uyghur residents of Yining's *mehelle*, and they are, and will continue to be, forced to change along with it. And second, if we are to render intelligible the dynamics of local society in Xinjiang, and in particular if we wish to understand how Uyghurs will respond to the personal, political, and economic challenges they will surely face in the coming decades, then only a broad consideration of the patterns of Uyghur social life, based on a deep understanding of Uyghur cultural beliefs and practices, will be adequate to the task.

Reference Matter

Glossary

Chinese Terms

fen	Monetary unit equal to 1/100th of 1 *yuan*
mao	Monetary unit equal to 10 *fen*, or 1/10th of 1 *yuan*
renminbi	Chinese currency
yuan	Unit of *renminbi*, 1 *yuan* equals approximately $0.13

Uyghur Terms

chamadan	Tin flour container
chaqchaqchi	Jokester, a skilled joke raconteur
chay	"Tea," i.e., a bribe, or the payment to a middleman
chayxana	Outdoor eating pavilion in a residential courtyard
dellal	Deal-broker for secondhand goods
etles	A particular style of brightly colored fabric
haj	The pilgrimage to Mecca
haji[-m]	Veteran of the pilgrimage to Mecca
kigiz	Decorative felt pad used under or instead of a carpet
kirakesh	A laborer who moves heavy bales with a handcart
lawben	Honorific used for elite merchant

mazar	A saint shrine, or tomb of a holy person, visited for pious veneration
mehelle	Neighborhood
meschit	Mosque
meshrep	A form of men's social gathering
nan	Flat bread, a staple food
olturash	"Sitting-together," i.e., a men's drinking party
öy	Home, household
som	Vernacular term for Chinese *yuan*
supa	Raised sitting platform inside a Uyghur home
taranchi	Uyghurs who settled in the Ili Valley circa 1755–60, and their descendants
tiyin	1 Chinese *fen* = 1/100th of a *yuan*
ulugh	"Great," a term of reverence
yangpungchi	Deal-broker between trader-tourists and wholesalers
Zawut	A Yining *mehelle*, the site of my field research

Notes

Introduction

EPIGRAPHS: Certeau, *Practice of Everyday Life*, 115; Pantusov, *Obraztsy*, 100.

1. Like most population centers in multiethnic Xinjiang, Yining has several names. I follow most contemporary scholarly and popular works in referring to the city as Yining. In Uyghur, however, and for the *mehelle* residents who are the subjects of this book, the city is known as Ghulja, a name that sometimes appears on maps of the region, often as Gulja or Kuldja. Although it is significant that Uyghurs and ethnic Han use separate vocabularies of place in Xinjiang, a point I discuss in some detail in Chapter 3, my decision to use the name Yining and not Ghulja was made only to conform to the usage most common in English-language written sources.

Part I

1. I selected this home as a field site after visiting in 1992 for one month with Abidem's son, a professional musician who had been a close friend of mine in Beijing since early 1987. Although his departure for Beijing more than twenty years earlier was a special situation for the family, in many other regards the family seemed, and later proved, to be typical of other large extended native Yining families.

Chapter 1

1. Mazzoleni, "City and the Imaginary," 289.
2. Menges, *Volkskundliche Texte*, 2: 74–79.

3. Högberg, *Ett och annat från Kinesiska Turkestan*, 48; cited in Jarring, *Matters of Ethnological Interest*, 17.

4. Jarring (*Matters of Ethnological Interest*, 7) finds three separate instances, recorded by Swedish missionaries in 1907, 1917, and 1920, respectively, in which a difficult labor is addressed by killing an animal, which itself must be stolen and its blood allowed to drip down through the skylight. In these accounts, we find again the two themes of market exchange (here necessarily transgressed) and lowering through the roof.

5. This summary of Malov's findings, which he published in Russian only, is taken from Molnár, *Weather Magic*, 86.

6. Molnár, *Weather Magic*, 118–19; Frazer, *Golden Bough*, 292–95.

7. Dundes, "Wet and Dry."

8. Menges, *Volkskundliche Texte*, 1: 117.

9. Mannerheim, *Across Asia*, vol. 1; Lattimore, "Chinese Turkistan," 193.

Chapter 2

1. Fletcher, "Heyday," 386.

2. Translation, slightly modified, from Jarring, *Materials*, 2: 130.

3. Certeau (*Practice of Everyday Life*, 115–22) calls such walking directions an "alphabet of spatial indication" to suggest their role as constituent units of narrative actions that form "itineraries," a category he opposes to "maps." In Chapter 3, I suggest just such an opposition holds between the indication of spatial relations through narrative and the state's mapping of local place.

4. For song author Yasin Muxpul's thoughts on the meaning the song has for him, see Muhemmet Yunus and Dilshat Hoshur, "Xelq heqiqi bahalighuchi."

Chapter 3

EPIGRAPH: Pantusov, *Obraztsy*, proverb no. 408.

1. For more on population transfer into Xinjiang, see Rose Maria Li, "Migration to China's Northern Frontier"; Yuan, "Population Changes"; Tien, "Demographic Significance"; and Freeberne, "Demographic and Economic Changes." For Han populations in the Ili Valley under the Qing, see Xu Bofu, "Qingdai qianqi Xinjiang diqu de mintun."

2. Li Xichun and Niu Shuhua, "Xinjiang chengshi fazhan."

3. Segregation of residential areas has been the norm in Xinjiang for more than a century. See, e.g., Zeng Wenwu, *Zhongguo jingying xiyu shi*, 328; and Lin En-hsien, *Qingchao zai Xinjiang*.

4. See, e.g., McMillen, *Chinese Communist Power*; idem, *Urumqi Military Region*; and idem, "Xinjiang and the Production and Construction Corps."

5. Requirements for borrowers include, for example, the creation of a "Re-settlement Action Plan." For information regarding World Bank policies on involuntary resettlement and related materials, including *Involuntary Resettlement Sourcebook: Planning and Implementation in Development Projects* (World Bank, August 2004), see World Bank website permanent URL http://go.worldbank.org/0WWXTSXYO1, accessed May 2007.

6. Cf. Pantusov, *Obraztsy*, 141.

7. See, e.g., Gheyretjan Osman, "Uyghur ejdadlirining millet nami."

8. This is how most observers have read the situation. See, e.g., Gladney, "Ethnogenesis" (following Warikoo, "Chinese Turkestan"); and Chvyr, "Notes on the Ethnic Self-Awareness of the Uighur."

9. This interpretation is supported by Gladney's argument that "the categorization and taxonomization of all levels of Chinese society . . . represents a wide-ranging and on-going project of internal colonialism" ("Internal Colonialism," 47).

10. Castagné, "Culte des lieux saints," 48.

11. Le Coq, *Buried Treasures*, 93.

Part II

1. Benveniste (*Indo-European Language and Society*, 191) has noted that in Indo-European languages terms for grandchild often derive from the words for "little grandfather."

2. Jarring, *Moen Collection*, 23.

3. During the final month of my research, Abidem successfully entered Aysajan into a newly opened local orphanage established for Uyghur children by a wealthy Uyghur merchant. The opening of this orphanage was perhaps the most widely admired and discussed act of Uyghur-to-Uyghur philanthropy in Yining during my stay, but it exemplified a wider spirit of community-based civil society that was growing in the region and causing great concern among state officials, not least because of its roots in an ongoing Islamic revitalization.

Chapter 4

1. Abdukérim Raxman, *Uyghur folklori*, 342–44.

2. Ibid., 344–45.

3. This practice has a considerable history. Pavet de Courteille (*Dictionnaire Turk-Orientale*, 374–75) locates the term *syonji* in a passage from the *Baburname* (composed prior to 1530), which he renders as "Bykkynä had come to bring me the good news of the birth of the son of Hamayun." He notes that *syonj* means

"bonne nouvelle, joie," and that *syonji* equals "bonne nouvelle, *présent donné à celui qui apporte une bonne nouvelle*" (italics added).

4. Attractive prayer rugs were owned by a few wealthier individuals, but most *mehelle* residents used something similar to Abidem's plain white cotton sheet, onto one end of which was hand-sewn a chevron of blue cloth to be pointed toward Mecca during prayer. Poorer men often walked to Friday mosque carrying only pieces of corrugated cardboard to lay in the dirt.

5. *Muhammedansk vantro och vidkepelse*, 42, cited in Jarring, *Matters of Ethnological Interest*, 13. Neither this nor Abidem's account, of course, is reliable enough to rule out this being a legend with no basis in fact.

6. Alan Dundes (private communication) suggested that this practice, found throughout Southeast Asia, relates to the evil eye belief complex and may be an attempt to disfigure the child.

7. Jarring, in his 1933 dissertation (*Studien*, 22–23, 50–51), presents Uyghur texts in which the phrase *dem qilish* (literally "to do or make breath") means "to pray," a usage I have not seen elsewhere.

8. According to Abdukérim Raxman (*Uyghur folklori*), the "cradle-mother" strokes the child lightly before putting it in the cradle, in order "to make *irim*" (*yumshaq silap irim qilidu*). I never observed this practice.

9. Brandes, *Metaphors of Masculinity*, 35.

10. Menges, *Volkskundliche Texte*, 1: 70–73; my translation, with minor changes from the original text made for clarity.

11. Abdukérim Raxman, *Uyghur folklori*. Some details regarding cradle preparations given here are taken from this account.

12. For more details on the forty water ceremony, see Abdukérim Raxman, *Uyghur folklori*, 353–55. Several interesting features that author describes as typical elements in this ritual were not present on the occasion I witnessed. Of these I mention (1) the older woman who prepares the water and oversees the event is spoken of as the child's *qirqi-anisi* (forty-mother); (2) a barber is invited to cut the infant's hair, which is made into an amulet for the child's cap; (3) the washing itself is called *yawash-yawash*, which may perhaps be related to the use of the term *yuwash* above as a wish that the child be "docile, mild-mannered."

13. Shinjang Uyghur aptonom rayonluq til-yéziq xizmiti komitéti lughet bölümi, *Uyghur tilining izahliq lughiti,* 1: 31; my translation.

14. A sixty-two-year-old Uyghur man from Kashgar, in explaining to me the term *chachratqu*, said: "When someone is sick, they call a female ritual specialist (*büwi*) to remove the illness and send it somewhere else, for example, into an old wall. In return they give her *chachratqu*, which is a payment for her services." This practice of imprisoning maleficent agents into the crumbling

earthen walls of abandoned homes may partly explain why crumbling walls appear in Uyghur folk narratives as superlative examples of undesirable objects.

15. In an analysis of the role of saliva in the evil-eye belief complex, Dundes ("Wet and Dry," 277) describes a person collecting spit in a jar outside a mosque in Saudi Arabia, specifically noting that people "expectorated into the container (or made a pseudo-spitting gesture)." This pseudo-spitting gesture has been widely described in Xinjiang folk practice and, to my knowledge, is always meant to be an aspirated passing of breath, never an actual spitting of saliva.

Chapter 5

EPIGRAPH: Abrahams, "Introduction," xv.

1. This argument is set forth by Dundes in "Traditional Male Combat," 39–40, who credits Chodorow, *Reproduction of Mothering*; Ong, *Fighting for Life*; and Stoller and Herdt, "Development of Masculinity."

2. Some of these names are from my field notes, others come from Abdurehim Hebibulla, *Uyghur étnografiyisi*, 582.

3. Literally, *jalap anang a güy*. As for the term *güy*, several people suggested it derived from Chinese *gui* (ghost). I judged it to be approximately as harsh as "son-of-a-bitch" or "bastard." Variants include *lata güy* (rag ghost) and *maz güy* (filthy-cotton ghost).

4. Pantusov, *Voyna musulman*, 20–21. Texts taken from Pantusov's publications (here and below) are shown as they appeared in those publications and are not rendered in modern Uyghur unless otherwise noted.

5. Similar items are found in Jarring, *Materials*, 2: 119; and Malov, *Uigurskiy yazik*, 42.

6. For related texts, see Pantusov, *Igra Maylise*, 21–30; and Malov, *Uigurskiy yazik*, 31. *Barbira*, Abidem explained, was "an expensive medicine" (*pulluq bir dora*). Pantusov's variant has for this line *bar boyi altun yigit*, which I render "that lad who has a golden stature."

7. This game, as played in Zawut, does not differ substantially from the description in Opie and Opie, *Children's Games with Things*, 56–72. For more on Uyghur *beshtash*, see Jarring, *Materials*, 4: 138–39.

8. Muhemmetjan Abliz and Yünüs Yoldash (*Uyghur ösmürlirining en'eniwi oyunliri*) give the name as *jildirchaq*, a more likely name given the etymology of *jaldur* (onomatopoeia for clanging sound, e.g., jingle-jangle) + *chaq* (wheel).

9. For a discussion of frames in general and the play frame in particular, see Bateson, "Theory of Play and Fantasy"; Handelman, "Play and Ritual"; Huizinga, *Homo Ludens*; Callois, *Man, Play and Games*; and Goffman, *Frame Analysis*.

10. Sanches and Kirshenblatt-Gimblatt, "Children's Traditional Speech Play."

11. For more on Qitmir in Central Asia, see Lemercier-Quelquejay, "Lions pieux et chiens mystique." For this legend in Islam generally, see, e.g., Kandler, *Die Bedeutung die Siebenschläfer.*

12. The elderly shrine keeper of a *mazar* in the village of Tuyuq near Turpan recounted this tale to a group of Uyghur scholars with whom I visited the *mazar* in 1994. These elements are from that narration.

13. Jarring, *Moen Collection,* 23. I have modified Jarring's translation.

Chapter 6

1. Pantusov, *Igra Maylise.* For participants' accounts of similar courting parties in the Turpan area, from where many Yining-area Uyghurs' ancestors originally came, see Menges, *Volkskundliche Texte,* 1: 42–46.

2. The brief account presented here does not address the full range of Uyghur wedding traditions; Abdurehim Hebibulla (*Uyghur étnografiyisi,* 261–88), for example, presents a lengthy account of the 23 separate events that constitute a traditional wedding ceremony. See also Abdukérim Raxman (*Uyghur folklori,* 371–84) for a comprehensive review of wedding traditions.

3. This account draws on Abdurehim Hebibulla, *Uyghur étnografiyisi,* 261–88, from which these quotations are taken.

4. Jarring, *Moen Collection,* 56.

5. *Hisam chaxchaqliri,* 37–38.

6. This account draws on Abdurehim Hebibulla, *Uyghur étnografiyisi,* 530.

7. For a full account, see Muhemmetjan Abliz and Yünüs Yoldash, *Uyghur ösmürlirining en'eniwi oyunliri,* 212–14.

Chapter 7

1. Propp, "Ritual Laughter in Folklore."

2. Herzfeld (*Poetics of Manhood,* 149–62) interprets numerous elements of the speech and gestural actions that accompany men's card playing in Crete as symbolic demonstrations of masculinity. In his analysis (at p. 162), however, card games provide "a clearly framed setting" for contest; in my reading, it is exactly the ambiguity over frame that provides the main medium of contest.

Chapter 8

EPIGRAPH: As cited in Is'haq Basiti and Ablimit Muhemmidi, "Yene Uyghur isimliridiki leqemler toghrisida."

1. For such lists, see Menges, *Volkskundliche Texte*, 1: 70–73; Is'haq Basiti and Ablimit Muhemmidi, "Yene Uyghur isimliridiki leqemler toghrisida"; and Abdurehim Hebibulla, *Uyghur étnografiyisi*, 582–84.

2. This was Is'haq Basiti. This list of nicknames, published with no accompanying explanation or analysis, was a useful starting point for eliciting nickname explanations, and I owe a great deal of my original understandings about nicknames to his generous and animated explanations.

3. Ortner, "On Key Symbols."

4. For other examples of the anal penetration metaphor in men's interactions, see, e.g., Brandes, *Metaphors of Masculinity*, 95–96; and Dundes, "Traditional Male Combat."

5. See, e.g., Maxmut Muhemmet, *Hisam chaxchaqliri*, 5–6, 22.

6. Brandes, *Metaphors of Masculinity*, 122–23.

7. Radcliffe-Brown, in his efforts to understand relations between kin that involve "joking or teasing . . . horse-play . . . [and] elements of obscenity" ("On Joking Relationships," 90), offers a classic comparative structural analysis of kin relations between such persons. His approach disregards the narrative and gestural features of such teasing and, aside from noting that those who do not tease are considered "boorish," is largely indifferent to local actors' own views on the significance of this behavior. These are exactly the features I wish to emphasize.

8. Most works on nicknaming focus only on addressing nicknaming; of these most valuable is Morgan et al., *Nicknames*. Because addressing and non-addressing nickname systems are analytically distinct and are embedded in such different social configurations, the insights of studies on addressing nicknaming are of limited application here.

9. By this I mean that such utterances play no role in everyday social interaction. It is of course possible, even likely, that a man might at some point be told his nickname by a close friend.

10. This contrastive pair lumps together three independent variables: (1) number of concurrent names for a given individual; (2) number of different namers; and (3) duration of name use. To divide these variables here would introduce a degree of complexity unnecessary for my purposes; future studies may require that these traits be separated.

11. For studies of nicknaming practices that considered differential use of nicknames between males and females and concluded that males used nicknames more than females, see, e.g., de Klerk and Bosch, "Nicknames as Sex-Role Stereotypes"; Phillips, "Nicknames and Sex Role Stereotypes"; and Busse, "Nickname Usage." See also Alford, *Naming and Identity*.

12. See Dautcher, "Folklore and Identity," app. 3.

13. Barrett, "Village Modernization and Changing Nickname Practices"; Brandes, "Structural and Demographic Implications of Nicknames."

14. See, e.g., Brandes, "Structural and Demographic Implications of Nicknames"; Breen, "Naming Practices in Western Ireland"; Gilmore, "Some Notes on Community Nicknaming"; and Orgel and Tuckman, "Nicknames of Institutional Children."

15. See, e.g., Morgan et al., *Nicknaming*, 3.

16. Goffman, *Stigma*, as cited in Morgan et al., *Nicknaming*, 13.

17. Abdurehim Hebibulla, *Uyghur étnografiyisi*, 584.

18. Is'haq Basiti and Ablimit Muhemmidi, "Yene Uyghur isimliridiki leqemler toghrisida."

19. Osman Ismayil, *Uyghur xelq éghiz edebiyatidiki zhanirlar*, 190. In the paragraphs before this one, Osman inexplicably reproduces verbatim several identical passages that appear in an article by Sabitov published ten years earlier in the U.S.S.R.

20. Sabitov, "Hejviyler" (Humor). This passage ends with the word "remains," from the verb *qalmaq*, "to be left, to remain," a term often used to describe the loser of a verbal interaction. I understand the meaning to be that the person is left speechless, incapable of offering a suitable comeback. Brandes (*Metaphors of Masculinity*, 117) has aptly described the momentarily speechless man as "conversationally impotent."

21. The names discussed here are drawn from a list of more than 550 names, of which approximately 450 came originally from the list published by Is'haq Basiti and Ablimit Muhemmidi, which proved an invaluable resource for my study. In conversation with co-author Is'haq Basiti, I was able to confirm the reliability of their collection methods.

22. Jarring, *Materials*, 1: 129*n*2.

23. Translation, slightly modified, from ibid., 4: 180.

24. This proverb is given twice in Jarring, *Moen Collection*, 35, 42.

25. Ghulam Ghopuri, *Uyghur shiwiliri sözlügi*, 176.

26. For more on the sexual significance of hair symbolism in Turkic culture under Islam, see Delaney, "Untangling the Meanings of Hair," whose argument draws on important related works by Charles Berg (*Unconscious Significance of Hair*) and Gananath Obeyesekere (*Medusa's Hair*).

27. Abdurehim Hebibulla, *Uyghur étnografiyisi*, 583.

28. Menges, *Volkskundliche Texte*, 1: 80. My translation. *Sumbul chach* means literally "Valerian hair." Valerian, a plant whose leaves spread out in a pattern similar to the braids on a woman's head, is commonly used in Uyghur medicine. *Yangaq chach*, literally "walnut hair," most likely refers to the hair being

divided into two halves, like a walnut. *Sékilek chach* is literally "temple hair," i.e., the temple on the head.

Part III

SECOND EPIGRAPH: Zhongguo renmin yinhang Yilizhou fenhang diaocha yanjiu shi, "Jiji kaituo zijin shichang," 63.

1. Grenard, *Mission scientifique*, 2: 158.
2. Mannerheim, *Across Asia*, 1: 47.

Chapter 9

1. For more on *getihu*, see, e.g., Gold, "Guerilla Interviewing"; and idem, "Urban Private Business."
2. See, e.g., Skinner, "Marketing and Social Structure."
3. Following Scott, *Weapons of the Weak*.
4. For a detailed quantitative analysis of Uyghur employment in this sector, see Ji Ping, "Frontier Migration."
5. Pantusov, *Sviedieniya*, 89–90.
6. Herold Wiens makes this claim in "Change in the Ethnography and Land Use of the Ili Valley," citing Ying Zi, *Xibei fengguang hao*, which is little more than a Han travelogue.
7. Forms of coerced and unrewarded labor extracted by the state from Uyghurs, a modern-day corvée documented elsewhere in Xinjiang by Bellér-Hann ("Peasant Condition," 89), were not required of *mehelle* residents in the 1990s. The only form of compulsory labor I observed in Yining, one also present in Urumqi, was the routine forced recruitment of urban workers to shovel snow from city streets and sidewalks in front of their places of work.

Chapter 10

1. Lattimore, "Chinese Turkistan," 192.
2. Guanghui de sishi nian bianji weiyuanhui, *Guanghui de sishi nian*, 188. This conversion is based on the same eight *yuan* to the dollar rate I use throughout the book; admittedly it may be a crude estimate, but it is likely more meaningful than the official (and artificial) rate of 2.46 *yuan* to the dollar of the era.
3. Chi Zhenyu, "Xinjiang Weiwuer zizhiqu yu Sulian, Bajisidan bianjing maoyi," 164. The station was not officially closed, however, until 1971.
4. Li Ruobin, "Cangsang bianqian hua 'silou.'"
5. Guanghui de sishi nian bianji weiyuanhui, *Guanghui de sishi nian*, 189.

6. "Xinjiang Border Trade Booming." For a thorough overview of events in border trade in Xinjiang in the 1980s, see Chi Zhenyu, "Xinjiang Weiwuer zizhiqu yu Sulian, Bajisidan bianjing maoyi."

7. Xiao Pengjun et al., *Xinjiang ji zhoubian guojia duiwai jingmao zhishi daquan*, 19.

8. Abulaiti Abudurexiti and Han Xueqi, *Duiwai kaifang de Xinjiang kouan*, 87.

9. Xiao Pengjun et al., *Xinjiang ji zhoubian guojia duiwai jingmao zhishi daquan*, 19.

10. Guanghui de sishi nian bianji weiyuanhui, *Guanghui de sishi nian*, 191.

11. Wang Bolang, "Zaiban xuyan," v.

12. Abulaiti Abudurexiti and Han Xueqi, *Duiwai kaifang de Xinjiang kouan*, 89.

13. Guanghui de sishi nian bianji weiyuanhui, *Guanghui de sishi nian*, 33; Li Ruobin, "Cangsang bianqian hua 'silou,'" 84. The Li article usefully summarizes the place of the Ili Valley in Silk Road trading.

14. Pantusov, *Sviedieniya*, 93–97.

15. Zhong Yong, *Xijing jiaoshe zhiyao*.

16. Yilizhou jingmao ju, "Yilizhou duiwai maoyi fazhan gaikuang," 92, is the source of data for this paragraph.

17. Millward has an excellent study on this topic (*Beyond the Pass*, see esp. pp. 136–37). Fletcher ("Heyday," 385), however, suggests that Han merchants were permitted to trade in Ili only beginning in 1845, a shift in policy prompted by the inability of local authorities to obtain adequate amounts of cloth for their monopoly trade with Kazakh nomads. For more on Qing trade in the area, see also Ma Ruheng and Ma Dazheng, *Qingdai bianjiang kaifa yanjiu*.

18. Hori, "Turfan Under Qing rule," 9.

19. See, e.g., the memorial to the throne of Liu K'un, governor of Hunan in 1867, in Ch'en, "Rebels Between Rebellions," 814.

20. Yili diqu difangzhi bianzuan weiyuanhui, *Yili fengwu*, 207.

21. Several times during my stay in Xinjiang I became aware that security agents were clandestinely monitoring my activities, something I had expected, given the state's efforts to control social research in Xinjiang. In such an environment, I avoided pursuing interests in a number of sensitive topics, including ethnic relations, that were outside the boundaries of research established for me by my host unit. Knowing my field notes might conceivably be examined or confiscated, I also avoided making any notes on such topics, so as not to endanger my host family and friends, my research unit, and my status as a researcher. Eventually, gradually, I did begin to document those Uyghur-Han interactions that arose during my observations of market trading. The biggest distortion in this book's portrayal of *mehelle* life, by my own estimation, is that it erases many of the manifestations of interethnic antagonism between Uyghurs and Han that I observed to be present in nearly all aspects of daily life throughout Xinjiang.

22. The use of the word "totem" to describe the wolf image has become popular among urban intellectuals, in part due to views expressed by author Turghun Almas in a series of books on Uyghur history and culture. See, e.g., his *Qedimki Uyghur edebiyati*, 7–12. Rudelson ("Uighur Historiography," 74–75) suggests that a government decision to ban another of the same author's books was based in part because of its use of a wolf image on the cover.

Part IV

EPIGRAPHS: Menges, *Volkskundliche Texte*, 2: 74; Luo Yingfu, *Zongjiao wenti jianlun*, 39.

1. For a review of state repression of Islam in Xinjiang, see Human Rights Watch / Asia, *China: State Control of Religion*.

2. For an overview of Islam in contemporary China, see, e.g., Dillon, "Muslim Communities." For the history of Islam in China, see Broomhall, *Islam in China*; Khan, "Islam and Muslims in Eastern Turkestan"; Hartmann, *Zur Geschichte des Islam in China*; and Dabry de Thiersant, *Le Muhometisme en Chine*. For English-language works on Islam in China, see Pickens, *Annotated Bibliography*; for works in Russian, see Loewenthal, "Russian Materials"; and in Uyghur, see Haji Nurhaji and Chén Goguang, *Shinjang Islam tarixi*.

Chapter 11

EPIGRAPHS: (1) This unpublished paper by Nuermaimaiti circulated at a closed conference at the Xinjiang Academy of Social Sciences in the spring of 1994. Elisions from the original, made without distorting the meaning, have been left unmarked in this translation. (2) This question is taken from a twelve-page questionnaire circulated in May 1996 among Xinjiang Communist Youth League members. Its stated purpose was to "provide data for the policy-making of relevant departments."

1. Pantusov, *Sviedieniya*, 112.

2. Ibid., 147–48. This difference is presumably due to some combination of two factors: first, that sib-group size differed between rural and urban/suburban areas; and second, that rural children did not attend school with the same frequency as suburban and urban children.

3. Haji Nurhaji and Chén Goguang, *Shinjang Islam tarixi*, 323.

4. Dautcher, "Protests, Popular Culture and the Politics of Religion."

5. Locals referred to all such prayer pamphlets as *risale*, even though scholarly works (e.g., Gavrilov, "Les corps de métiers") suggest that this term refers exclusively to occupation-specific collections of prayers, charms, guild rules, and technical expertise, such as for blacksmiths or carpenters. Pamphlets of

the latter kind were available at some Uyghur-run book stalls in Xinjiang but were less common than general prayer guides.

Many other Islamic religious commodities were sold in Xinjiang, including printed materials, audiocassettes, posters, Qur'an texts (in Arabic or Chinese translation only, never in Uyghur), and various other markers of religious devotion. Stores that sold Chinese-language versions of such goods were maintained throughout Xinjiang by Mandarin-speaking ethnic Hui. Uyghur sellers and Uyghur-language materials were more often found at smaller street-side stalls and carts. The two groups maintained a strict segregation between themselves regarding the distribution of such items.

6. Pantusov, *Sviedeniya*, 128–29.

7. Ibid., 147–48. This calculation is based on population figures for that same year and includes a correction that accounts for the presence of Hui residents and Hui mosques.

8. Lim, "China Fires Officials."

9. These tales are known to folklorists as belonging to the tradition of Hodja tales.

10. Maxmut Muhemmet, *Hisam chaxchaqliri*, 24. This translation is slightly abbreviated. Hésam, who is active throughout Xinjiang as a comedian and performer, typically narrates in the first person humorous anecdotes about his life. In published collections of Hésam's witticisms, which are edited for popular consumption, these narratives are placed in the third person.

11. Grenard, *Mission scientifique*, 2: 237.

12. Pantusov, *Igry taranchinskih détey i muzhchin*, 5, 10–12. In my translation here from the original Uyghur, I have repositioned one line for clarity.

13. Xinjiang Weiwuer zizhiqu minzu shiwu weiyuanhui, *Xinjiang minzu cidian*, 235.

14. Quotations and information on works described in this paragraph come from Shinjang Uyghur aptonom rayonluq az sanliq millet qadimki eserlirini toplash, retlesh, neshir qilishni pilanlash rehberlik guruppa ishxanisi, *Uyghur, Özbék, Tatar qadimki eserler tizimliki*. For *Qisasi l'ambiya*, see p. 11; for *Tezkiretü' l'ewliyeh*, p. 14; for *Nafahat*, pp. 235–40; for *Rashahat ayn alhiwet*, pp. 212–13. For a critical review of scholarly research on *Qisasi l'ambiya*, see Dankoff, "Rabghuzi's Stories."

15. My translation from the French (Grenard, *Mission scientifique*, 2: 141).

16. Xinjiang Weiwuer zizhiqu minzu shiwu weiyuanhui, *Xinjiang minzu cidian*, 235.

17. Light, "Slippery Paths," 30, 179–81. In this passage I have for the sake of clarity changed Light's romanization of the terms *meshrep* and *meshrepchi* to conform to my own.

18. Ibid., 179. On pp. 179–93, Light presents a fascinating analysis of the life of Mashrab based in part on a Russian translation of the *Divana-i Mashrab* (Lykoshin, *Divana-i Mashrab*).

19. Light, "Slippery Paths," 181, footnotes omitted.

20. Ibid., 121.

21. Artoush Kumul ("'Separatisme' Ouïgour") cites a *Le Monde* article by Jean Baptiste Naudet ("Quand la Chine écrasa la révolte des Ouïgours du Xinjiang") dated May 23, 1997, in support of his claim that the groups were banned in August. I first arrived in Zawut in late July, and by August I had heard from residents that fines of 50 *yuan* per person were being levied for anyone who continued to participate; this had been going on, I was told, since early April.

22. A valuable account of *meshrep* playing can be found in Abdukérim Raxman et al., *Uyghur örp-adetliri*, 141–47. At the time of my research and writing, that source was unavailable to me, and I have chosen to leave this record of my own research unchanged.

23. Mutellip Sidiq, *Uyghur kishi isimliri*, 167.

24. Grenard, *Mission scientifique*, 2: 275.

25. An obvious structural similarity exists between this practice and the dancing invitations and belt-passing game noted in Chapter 7.

26. The following summer a state-organized tournament brought together for competition teams from different oases. These matches aroused modest interest in the *mehelle*, far less than had been the case the previous year.

27. "Uighur Emigres Warn Central Asia of Conflict." For a detailed description of the events surrounding those protests, see Dautcher, "Protests, Popular Culture and the Politics of Religion."

28. Lim, "China Fires Officials."

29. Lou Wanghou, "Determined Efforts."

Chapter 12

1. The paucity of comparative studies of Ramadan is noted by Marjo Buitelaar in her fine monograph, *Fasting and Feasting*. Readers interested in a review of the few monographs on Ramadan that are available are directed to this work.

2. Various works on mumming and festivals of reversal have proven useful to me in understanding these materials, including Abrahams and Bauman, "Ranges of Festival Behavior"; Sider, *Class and Culture*; and Glassie, *All Silver and No Brass*.

3. Peirce, *Collected Papers*, 5: 491, as cited in Singer, *Semiotics*, 304.

4. Padwick, *Muslim Devotions*, 49; see esp. chap. 3 on prayers of intention.

5. Despite the fact that Roz Ghojam's visit was widely discussed in the *mehelle* as a part of the experience of Ramadan, I have found no mention of this practice in published sources. Buitelaar, writing about 1980s Morocco (*Feasting and Fasting*, 53), notes the existence of verses sung by children on the first day of Ramadan about "papa Ramadan." She adds: "While in daily life children are expected to show respect for adults, the first night of Ramadan they are allowed to tease and taunt grown-ups with [such] verses." She notes that similar verses were recorded by Legey circa 1926 (*Essai de folklore marocain*, 117–18), who indicated that adults often reciprocated with gifts of coins. This practice thus appears to combine a figure of personification akin to Roz Ghojam with elements reminiscent of the Uyghur practice of singing Ramadan.

6. The account of that incident given here is based on field notes I recorded in 1994 immediately after discussing the incident (in Mandarin) with each of the three persons in the room.

7. Grunebaum, *Muhammadan Festivals*, 52.

8. In addition to referring to such boats as *kéme*, people described the boats as *lotka*, *qolwaq*, and *kéyiq*, all of which are types of small boats.

9. See, e.g., Garcin de Tassey, *Muslim Festivals in India*, 86, 133, 179.

10. For a complete presentation of sixty-two additional verses available in printed sources, only a small number of which are given here, see Dautcher, "Folklore and Identity," 356–65, drawing on Abdurehim Hebibulla, *Uyghur étnografiyisi*; Elaxunov, *Uyghur xeliq qoshaqliri*; idem, "Balilar qoshaqliri"; Muhemmetjan Abliz, *Uyghur ösmürlirining en'eniwi oyunliri II*; Osman Ismayil, *Uyghur xelq éghiz edebiyatidiki zhanirlar*; and Pantusov, *Taranchinskiya piesni*.

11. These tales were published circa 1989 in Tursun Yasin, *Ghulja xelq chöchekliri*.

12. These three verses are taken from Osman Ismayil, *Uyghur xelq éghiz edebiyatidiki zhanirlar*; Abdurehim Hebibulla, *Uyghur étnografiyisi*; and Elaxunov, "Balilar qoshaqliri," respectively.

13. Pantusov, *Taranchinskiya piesni*, 65–67. I have rendered these verses in Uyghur according to modern orthography, adding vowel markers omitted in Pantusov's modified Arabic script.

Works Cited

Abdukérim Raxman. *Uyghur folklori heqqide bayan.* Urumqi: Shinjang dashö ne-shriyati, 1989.

Abdukérim Raxman, Reweydulla Hemdulla, and Shérip Xushtar. *Uyghur örp-adetliri.* Urumqi: Shinjang yashlar-ösmürler neshriyati, 1996.

Abdurehim Hebibulla. *Uyghur étnografiyisi.* Urumqi: Xinjiang renmin chubanshe, 1993.

Abrahams, Roger D. "Introduction: Getting to *It,* or A Special Way of Begin-ning." In *Counting-Out Rhymes: A Dictionary,* ed. idem and Lois Rankin, xi–xix. Austin: University of Texas Press, 1980.

Abrahams, Roger D., and Richard Bauman. "Ranges of Festival Behavior." In *The Reversible World: Symbolic Inversion in Art and Society,* ed. Barbara A. Bab-cock, 195–208. Ithaca: Cornell University Press, 1978.

Abulaiti Abudurexiti and Han Xueqi, eds. *Duiwai kaifang de Xinjiang kouan.* Urumqi: Xinjiang renmin chubanshe, 1993.

Ahlbert, G. "Muhammedansk vantro och vidskepelse: Kulturbilder från Ost-Turkestan." *Missionsförbundet* 1920: 42.

Alford, Richard D. *Naming and Identity: A Cross-Cultural Study of Personal Naming Practices.* New Haven: HRAF Press, 1988.

Barrett, Richard A. "Village Modernization and Changing Nickname Practices in Northern Spain." *Journal of Anthropological Research* 34 (1978): 92–108.

Bateson, Gregory. "A Theory of Play and Fantasy." In idem, *Steps to an Ecology of Mind,* 177–93. New York: Ballantine, 1972.

329

Bellér-Hann, Ildikó. "The Peasant Condition in Xinjiang." *Journal of Peasant Studies* 24, no. 4 (1997): 87–112.

Benveniste, Émile. *Indo-European Language and Society*. Trans. Elizabeth Palmer. Coral Gables: University of Miami Press, 1973.

Berg, Charles. *The Unconscious Significance of Hair*. London: George Allen and Unwin, 1951.

Brandes, Stanley. *Metaphors of Masculinity: Sex and Status in Andalusian Folklore*. Philadelphia: University of Pennsylvania Press, 1980.

———. "The Structural and Demographic Implications of Nicknames in Navanogal, Spain." *American Ethnologist* 2 (1975): 139–48.

Breen, Richard. "Naming Practices in Western Ireland." *Man* 17 (1982): 701–13.

Broomhall, Marshall. *Islam in China: A Neglected Problem*. New York: Paragon, 1966 [1910].

Buitelaar, Marjo. *Fasting and Feasting in Morocco: Women's Participation in Ramadan*. Oxford, UK: Berg, 1993.

Busse, Thomas V. "Nickname Usage in an American High School." *Names* 31, no. 4 (1983): 300–306.

Caillois, Roger. *Man, Play and Games*. Trans. Meyer Barash. New York: Free Press, 1961.

Castagné, Joseph. "Le culte des lieux saints de l'Islam au Turkestan." *L'Ethnographie*, new series 46 (1951): 46–124.

Certeau, Michel de. *The Practice of Everyday Life*. Berkeley: University of California Press, 1984.

Ch'en, Jerome. "Rebels Between Rebellions: Secret Societies in the Novel, *P'eng Kung Au*." *Journal of Asian Studies* 29 (1970): 807–22.

Chi Zhenyu. "Xinjiang Weiwuer zizhiqu yu Sulian, Bajisidan bianjing maoyi." In *Zhongguo bianjing maoyi gailun*, ed. Yang Deying, 161–205. Beijing: Zhongguo shangye chubanshe, 1992.

Chodorow, Nancy. *The Reproduction of Mothering: Psychoanalysis and the Sociology of Gender*. Berkeley: University of California Press, 1978.

Chvyr, Liudmilla Anatol'evna. "Notes on the Ethnic Self-Awareness of the Uighur." *Anthropology and Archeology of Eurasia* 34, no. 3 (1995–96): 48–67.

Dabry de Thiersant, Claude Philibert. *Le Mahometisme en Chine et dans le Turkestan oriental*. Paris: E. Leroux, 1878.

Dankoff, Robert. "Rabghuzi's Stories of the Prophets." *Journal of the American Oriental Society* 117 (1997): 115–26.

Dautcher, Jay. "Folklore and Identity in a Uyghur Community in Xinjiang China." Ph.D. diss. in Anthropology, University of California, Berkeley, 1999.

————. "Protests, Popular Culture and the Politics of Religion on China's Northwest Frontier." In *China Beyond the Headlines: A Global Dialogue on the Search for China's Future*, ed. Lionel Jensen and Timothy Weston, 273–94. Boulder, CO: Rowman and Littlefield, 2000.

de Klerk, Vivian, and Barbara Bosch. "Nicknames as Sex-Role Stereotypes." *Sex Roles* 35 (1996): 525–41.

Delaney, Carol. "Untangling the Meanings of Hair in Turkish Society." *Anthropology Quarterly* 67, no. 4 (1994): 159–72.

Dillon, Michael. "Muslim Communities in Contemporary China: The Resurgence of Islam After the Cultural Revolution." *Journal of Islamic Studies* 5 (1994): 70–101.

Dundes, Alan. "Traditional Male Combat: From Game to War." In *From Game to War and Other Psychoanalytic Essays on Folklore*, ed. idem, 25–45. Lexington: University of Kentucky Press, 1997.

————. "Wet and Dry, the Evil Eye: An Essay in Indo-European and Semitic Worldview." In *The Evil Eye: A Casebook*, ed. idem, 257–312. Madison: University of Wisconsin Press, 1992 [1981].

Elaxunov, A. "Balilar qoshaqliri." In *Uyghur edibiyati ve folkloridiki zhanrlar*, ed. Q. Tokhtamov, 178–95. Almaty: Nauka, 1980.

————. *Uyghur xeliq qoshaqliri*. Almaty: Nauka, 1977.

Fletcher, Joseph F. "The Heyday of the Ch'ing Order in Mongolia, Sinkiang and Tibet." In *The Cambridge History of China*, vol. 10, pt. 1, ed. John K. Fairbank, 352–408. Cambridge: Cambridge University Press, 1978.

Frazer, James George. *The Golden Bough: A Study in Magic and Religion*, vol. 1, *The Magic Art and the Evolution of Kings*. 3d ed. London: Macmillan, 1911.

Freeberne, Michael. "Demographic and Economic Changes in the Sinkiang Uighur Autonomous Region." *Population Studies* 20 (1966): 103–24.

Garcin de Tassy, J. H. *Muslim Festivals in India and Other Essays*. Trans. M. Wasseem. Delhi: Oxford University Press, 1995 [1831].

Gavrilov, Michel. "Les corps de métiers en Asie centrale et leurs statuts (*rissala*)." Trans. Joseph Castagné. *Revue des études islamiques* 2 (1928): 207–30.

Gheyretjan Osman. "Uyghur ejdadlirining millet nami bilen atalmay, tewelik jay nami boyiche atalghanliqi heqqide." *Shinjang tezkirisi* 2 (1993): 31–33.

Ghulam Ghopuri, comp. *Uyghur shiwiliri sözlügi*. Beijing: Minzu chubanshe, 1986.

Gilmore, David D. "Some Notes on Community Nicknaming in Spain." *Man* 17 (1982): 686–700.

Gladney, Dru C. "The Ethnogenesis of the Uighur." *Central Asian Survey* 9 (1990): 1–28.

————. "Internal Colonialism and the Uyghur Nationality: Chinese Nationalism and Its Subaltern Subjects." *Cahiers d'études sur la Méditerranée orientale et le monde turco-iranien* 25 (1998): 47–63.

Glassie, Henry. *All Silver and No Brass: An Irish Christmas Mumming.* Bloomington: Indiana University Press, 1975.

Goffman, Erving. *Frame Analysis: An Essay on the Organization of Experience.* Cambridge: Harvard University Press, 1974.

————. *Stigma.* Harmondsworth, UK: Penguin, 1963.

Gold, Thomas B. "Guerilla Interviewing Among the *Getihu.*" In *Unofficial China: Popular Culture and Thought in the People's Republic,* ed. Perry Link, Richard Madsen, and Paul G. Pickowicz, 175–92. Boulder, CO: Westview Press, 1989.

————. "Urban Private Business and Social Change." In *Chinese Society on the Eve of Tiananmen: The Impact of Reform,* ed. Deborah Davis and Ezra Vogel, 157–78. Cambridge: Council on East Asian Studies, Harvard University, 1990.

Grenard, Fernand. *Mission scientifique dans la haute Asie, 1890–1895,* vol. 2, *Le Turkestan et le Tibet.* Ed. J.-L. Dutreuil de Rhins. Paris: Ernest Leroux, 1898.

Grunebaum, Gustav Edmund von. *Muhammadan Festivals.* London: Curzon Press, 1981.

Guanghui de sishi nian bianji weiyuanhui, ed. *Guanghui de sishi nian (1954–1994).* Urumqi: Xinjiang renmin chubanshe, 1994.

Hahn, Reinhard F. *Spoken Uyghur.* Seattle: University of Washington Press, 1991.

Haji Nurhaji and Chén Goguang. *Shinjang islam tarixi.* Beijing: Milletler neshriyati, 1995.

Handelman, Don. "Play and Ritual: Complementary Frames of Metacommunication." In *It's a Funny Thing, Humour,* ed. Anthony J. Chapman and Hugh C. Foot, 185–92. Oxford, UK: Pergamon, 1977.

Hartmann, Martin. *Zur Geschichte des Islam in China.* Leipzig: Heims, 1921.

Herklots, G. A. *Islam in India.* London: Oxford University Press, 1921.

Herzfeld, Michael. *The Poetics of Manhood: Contest and Identity in a Cretan Mountain Village.* Princeton: Princeton University Press, 1985.

Högberg, L. E. *Ett och annat fran Kinesiska Turkestan (Vastra Kina) af L. E. Högberg.* Stockholm: Svenska missionsforbundet, 1907.

Hori, Sunao. "Shindai no Torufan: Kakei nenkan no 3-tsu no genchi bunsho no shōkai tsujite" (English title: "Turfan Under Qing Rule: Three Turki Manuscripts in the Jiaqing Period"). Paper presented at the International Symposium on Non-Chinese Sources for Late Imperial History, University of California, Santa Barbara, 1998.

Huizinga, Johan. *Homo Ludens: A Study of the Play Element in Culture.* Boston: Beacon, 1955 [1950].

Human Rights Watch / Asia. *China: State Control of Religion.* New York: Human Rights Watch, 1997.

Is'haq Basiti and Ablimit Muhemmidi. "Yene Uyghur isimliridiki leqemler toghrisida." *Shinjang tezkirisi* 3 (1995): 60–64, 59.

Jarring, Gunnar. *Materials to the Knowledge of Eastern Turki: Tales, Proverbs, Riddles, Ethnological and Historical Texts from the Southern Parts of Eastern Turkestan.* Vols. 1–4. Lund, Sweden: C. W. K. Gleerup, 1946–51.

————. *Matters of Ethnological Interest in Swedish Missionary Reports from Southern Sinkiang.* Lund, Sweden: C.W.K. Gleerup, 1979.

————. *The Moen Collection of Eastern Turki (New Uighur) Proverbs and Popular Sayings.* Malmö, Sweden: C. W. K. Gleerup, 1985.

————. *Studien zu einer osttürkischen Lautlehre.* Lund, Sweden: Borelius; and Leipzig, Germany: Harrassowitz, 1933.

Ji Ping. "Frontier Migration and Ethnic Assimilation: A Case of Xinjiang Uighur Autonomous Region of China." Ph.D. diss. in Sociology, Brown University, 1990.

Jönsö, Jan. *Studies on Middle English Nicknames.* Lund: CWK Gleerup, 1979.

Kandler, Hermann. *Die Bedeutung die Siebenschläfer (Aṣḥāb al-kahf) im Islam: Untersuchungen zu Legende und Kult in Schrifttum, Religion und Volksglauben unter besonderer Berücksichtigung der Siebenschläfer-Wallfahrt.* Bochum: Brockmeyer, 1994.

Khan, Azmat Hayat. "Islam and Muslims in Eastern Turkestan." *Central Asia* 30 (1992): 55–73.

Kumul, Artoush. "Le 'separatisme' Ouïgour au XXe siècle: histoire et actualité." *Cahiers d'études sur la Méditerranée orientale et le monde turco-iranien* 25 (1998): 83–91.

Lattimore, Owen. "Chinese Turkistan." In *Studies in Frontier History: Collected Papers, 1928–1958,* ed. idem, 183–217. Paris: Mouton, 1962. Reprinted from *Open Court* 47, no. 2 (1933).

Le Coq, Albert von. *Buried Treasures of Chinese Turkestan: An Account of the Activities and Adventures of the Second and Third German Turfan Expeditions.* Hong Kong: Oxford University Press, 1985 [1928].

Legey, D. *Essai de folklore marocain.* Paris: Librarie Orientaliste Paul Geuthner, 1926.

Lemercier-Quelquejay, Chantal. "Lions pieux et chiens mystiques dans la tradition chrétienne et musulmane." In *Turco-Tatar Past, Soviet Present: Studies Presented to Alexandre Bennigson,* ed. idem, G. Veinstein, and S. E. Wimbush, 31–41. Louvain, Belgium: Editions Peeters, 1986.

Li, Rose Maria. "Migration to China's Northern Frontier." *Population and Development Review* 15 (1989): 503–38.

Li Ruobin. "Cangsang bianqian hua 'silou.'" In *Yili Hasake zizhizhou jingji shehui fazhan yantao wenji*, ed. Yilizhou jingji yanjiu zhongxin, 81–86. Yining: Yilizhou jingji yanjiu zhongxin, 1987.

Li Xichun and Niu Shuhua. "Xinjiang chengshi fazhan yu buju yanjiu." *Xinjiang shehui jingji* 2 (1991): 8–16.

Light, Nathan. "Slippery Paths: The Performance and Canonization of Turkic Literature and Uyghur Muqam Song in Islam and Modernity." Ph.D. diss. in Folklore, Indiana University, 1998.

Lim, Benjamin Kang. "China Fires Officials in Muslim Region Crackdown." Reuters Wire Service, June 26, 1997.

Lin En-hsien. *Qingchao zai Xinjiang de Han Hui geli zhengce*. Taipei: Taiwan shangwu yinshuguan, 1988.

Loewenthal, R. "Russian Materials on Islam in China: A Preliminary Bibliography." *Monumenta Serica* (Nagoya) 16 (1957): 449–79.

Lou Wanghou. "'Determined Efforts Must Be Made to Eliminate 'Vermin' and Eradicate Poisonous Weeds,' says Amudun Niyaz During Inspection of Ili Prefecture." *Xinjiang ribao*, July 28, 1997, 1. Appears as "Xinjiang Official Says 'Poisonous Weed' Separatists Must Be Eliminated," in *BBC–Summary of World Broadcasts*, Aug. 13, 1997.

Luo Yingfu. *Zongjiao wenti jianlun*. Urumqi: Xinjiang renmin chubanshe, 1992.

Lykoshin, Nil Sergeevich. *Divana-i-Mashrab: Zhizneopisanie populiarnieishago predstavitelia mistitsizma v Turkestanskom kraie*. Samarkand: Samarkandskii oblastnoi statisticheskii komitet, 1910.

Ma Ruheng and Ma Dazheng, eds. *Qingdai bianjiang kaifa yanjiu*. Beijing: Zhongguo shehui kexue chubanshe, 1990.

Malov, Sergei Efimovich. *Uygurskiy yazik*. Moscow: Akademiya Nauk, 1954.

Mannerheim, C. G. *Across Asia from West to East in 1906–1908*. Vols. 1–2. Helsinki: Suomalais-Ugrilainen Seura, 1940.

Maxmut Muhemmet, ed. *Hisam chaxchaqliri*. Urumqi: Xinjiang renmin chubanshe, 1982.

Mazzoleni, Donatella. "The City and the Imaginary." In *Space and Place: Theories of Identity and Location*, ed. Erica Carter, James Donald, and Judith Squires, 285–301. London: Lawrence and Wishart, 1993.

McMillen, Donald H. *Chinese Communist Power and Policy in Xinjiang, 1949–1977*. Boulder, CO: Westview Press, 1979.

———. *The Urumqi Military Region: Defence and Security in China's West*. Canberra: Research School of Pacific Studies, Australian National University, 1982.

————. "Xinjiang and the Production and Construction Corps: A Han Organisation in a Non-Han Region." *Australian Journal of Chinese Affairs* 6 (1981): 65–96.

Menges, Karl Heinrich. *Volkskundliche Texte aus Ost-Türkestan.* Vols. 1–2. Leipzig: Zentralantiquariat der Deutschen Demokratischen Republik, 1976 [Berlin: Verlag der Akademie der Wissenschaften, 1933, 1943].

Millward, James A. *Beyond the Pass: Economy, Ethnicity, and Empire in Qing Central Asia, 1759–1864.* Stanford: Stanford University Press, 1998.

Molnár, Ádám. *Weather Magic in Inner Asia.* Bloomington: Indiana University Research Institute for Inner Asian Studies, 1994.

Morgan, Jane, Christopher O'Neill, and Rom Harré. *Nicknames: Their Origins and Social Consequences.* London: Routledge & Kegan Paul, 1979.

Muhemmet Yunus and Dilshat Hoshur. "Xelq heqiqi bahalighuchi— kompozitor Yasin Muxpul bilen söhbet." *Shinjang iqtisad gazéti,* Apr. 29, 1995, 4.

Muhemmetjan Abliz. *Uyghur ösmürlirining en'eniwi oyunliri II.* Kashgar: Qeshqer Uyghur neshriyati, 1994.

Muhemmetjan Abliz and Yünüs Yoldax. *Uyghur ösmürlirining en'eniwi oyunliri.* Kashgar: Qeshqer Uyghur neshriyati, 1990.

Mutellip Sidiq. *Uyghur kishi isimliri we uning menisi.* Kashgar: Qeshqer pedagogika instituti pen tetqiqat bashqarmisi, 1992.

Nader, Laura. "Controlling Processes: Tracing the Dynamic Components of Power [with comments and reply]." *Current Anthropology* 38 (1997): 711–37.

Obeyesekere, Gananath. *Medusa's Hair: An Essay on Personal Symbols and Religious Experience.* Chicago: University of Chicago Press, 1981.

Ong, Walter J. *Fighting for Life: Contest, Sexuality and Consciousness.* Amherst: University of Massachusetts Press, 1989.

Opie, Iona, and Peter Opie. *Children's Games with Things.* Oxford: Oxford University Press, 1997.

Orgel, S. Z., and J. Tuckman. "Nicknames of Institutional Children." *American Journal of Orthopsychiatry* 5 (1935): 276–85.

Ortner, Sherry B. "On Key Symbols." *American Anthropologist* 75 (1973): 1338–46.

Osman Ismayil. *Uyghur xelq éghiz edebiyatidiki zhanirlar.* Urumqi: Shinjang yashlar-ösmürler neshriyati, 1994.

Padwick, Constance Evelyn. *Muslim Devotions: A Study of Prayer-Manuals in Common Use.* London: SPCK, 1961.

Pantusov, N. N. *Igra Maylise i proiznosimye vo vremya eya ctihi.* Materialy k izucheniiu nariechiia Taranchei iliiskago okruga, vol. 13. Kazan: Tipo-litografiia Imperatorskago Universiteta, 1907.

————. *Igry taranchinskih détey i muzhchin.* Materialy k izucheniiu nariechiia Taranchei iliiskago okruga, vol. 9. Kazan: Tipo-litografiia Imperatorskago Universiteta, 1907.

————. *Obraztsy taranchinskoi narodnoi literatury: teksty i perevody.* Kazan: Tipo-litografiia Imperatorskago Universiteta, 1909.

————. *Sviedieniya o Kuldzhinskom raionie za 1871–1877 gody.* Kazan: V Univer-sitetskoi tipografii, 1881.

————. *Taranchinskiya piesni.* St. Petersburg: Tip. I. Akademii nauk, 1890.

————. *Voyna musulman protiv kitaytsev,* vol. 2, *Appendix Piesni Taranchei.* Kazan: V Universitetskoi tipografiya, 1881.

Pavet de Courteille, Abel. *Dictionnaire Turk-Orientale: destiné principalement à facili-ter la lecture des ouvrages de Bâber, d'Aboul-Gâzi et de Mir-Ali-Chir-Nevâï.* Paris: Imprimerie Impériale, 1870.

Peirce, Charles. *Collected Papers of Charles Sanders Peirce.* Ed. Charles Hartshorne, Paul Weiss, and Arthur W. Burks. 8 vols. Cambridge: Harvard University Press, 1931–58.

Phillips, Betty S. "Nicknames and Sex Role Stereotypes." *Sex Roles* 23 (1990): 281–89.

Pickens, Claude L. *Annotated Bibliography of Literature on Islam in China.* Hankow: Society of Friends of the Moslems in China, 1950.

Propp, Vladimir. "Ritual Laughter in Folklore." In idem, *Theory and History of Folklore,* ed. Anatoly Lieberman. Minneapolis: University of Minnesota Press, 1984.

Radcliffe-Brown, A. R. "On Joking Relationships." In *Structure and Function in Primitive Society,* ed. idem, 90–116. New York: Free Press, 1965 [1940].

Radloff, W. *Proben der Volkslitteratur der nördlichen türkischen Stämme,* vol. 6.1, *Dia-lect der Tarantschi.* St. Petersburg: Tip. Imperatorskoi Akademii Nauk, 1886.

Rudelson, Justin Jon. "Uighur Historiography and Uighur Ethnic National-ism." In *Ethnicity, Minorities and Cultural Encounters,* ed. Ingvar Svenberg, 63–82. Uppsala: Center for Multiethnic Research, 1991.

Sabitov, R. "Hejviyler." In *Uyghur xeliq éghiz izhadiyiti,* ed. Gh. Sadvaqasov, 227–57. Almaty: Nauka, 1983.

Sanches, Mary, and Barbara Kirshenblatt-Gimblett. "Children's Traditional Speech Play and Child Languages." In *Speech Play,* ed. Barbara Kirshenblatt-Gimblett, 65–110. Philadelphia: University of Pennsylvania Press, 1976.

Scott, James C. *Weapons of the Weak: Everyday Forms of Peasant Resistance.* New Haven: Yale University Press, 1987.

Shinjang Uyghur aptonom rayonluq az sanliq millet qadimki eserlirini toplash, retlesh, neshir qilishni pilanlash rehberlik guruppa ishxanisi, ed. *Uyghur, Öz-bék, Tatar qadimki eserler tizimliki.* Kashgar: Qeshqer Uyghur neshriyati, 1989.

Shinjang Uyghur aptonom rayonluq til-yéziq xizmiti komitéti lughet bölümi, comp. *Uyghur tilining izahliq lughiti*, vol. 1. Beijing: Milletler neshriyati, 1990.

Sider, Gerald M. *Culture and Class in Anthropology and History: A Newfoundland Illustration.* Cambridge: Cambridge University Press, 1986.

Singer, Milton. *Semiotics of Cities, Selves, and Cultures: Explorations in Semiotic Anthropology.* New York: Mouton de Gruyter, 1991.

Skinner, G. William. "Marketing and Social Structure in Rural China." 3 pts. *Journal of Asian Studies* 24 (1964–65): 3–43, 195–228, 363–99.

Stoller, Robert J., and Gilbert H. Herdt. "The Development of Masculinity: A Cross-Cultural Contribution." *Journal of the American Psychoanalytic Association* 30 (1982): 29–59.

Tien, H. Yuan. "The Demographic Significance of Organized Population Transfers in Communist China." *Demography* 1 (1964): 220–26.

Turghun Almas. *Qedimki Uyghur edebiyati.* Kashgar: Qeshqer Uyghur neshriyati, 1989.

Tursun Yasin, ed. *Ghulja xelq chöchekliri.* Yining: Ghulja sheherlik xelq éghiz edebiyati ishxanisi, 1989.

"Uighur Emigres Warn Central Asia of Conflict." *BBC–Summary of World Broadcasts,* Nov. 6, 1997.

Wang Bolang. "Zaiban xuyan." In *Yili fengwu,* ed. Yili diqu difangzhi bianzuan weiyuanhui, v–vi. Urumqi: Xinjiang renmin chubanshe, 1994.

Warikoo, K. B. "Chinese Turkestan During the Nineteenth Century: A Socio-Economic Study." *Central Asian Survey* 4 (1985): 75–114.

Wheeler, Marcus, et al., eds. *The Oxford Russian Dictionary.* Oxford: Oxford University Press, 2000.

Wiens, Herold J. "Change in the Ethnography and Land Use of the Ili Valley and Region, Chinese Turkestan." *Annals of the Association of American Geographers* 59 (1969): 753–75.

————. "The Ili Valley as a Geographic Region of Hsin-Chiang." *Current Scene* 7, no. 15 (Aug. 1, 1969): 1–19.

Xiao Pengjun, Fu Gao, and Zhong Lifen, eds. *Xinjiang ji zhoubian guojia duiwai jingmao zhishi daquan.* Urumqi: Xinjiang keji weisheng chubanshe, 1993.

"Xinjiang Border Trade Booming." Xinhua Wire Service, Sept. 16, 1997; in *BBC–Summary of World Broadcasts,* Sept. 17, 1997.

Xinjiang Weiwuer zizhiqu minzu shiwu weiyuanhui, ed. *Xinjiang minzu cidian.* Urumqi: Xinjiang renmin chubanshe, 1995.

Xu Bofu. "Qingdai qianqi Xinjiang diqu de mintun." *Zhongguo shi yanjiu* 2 (1985): 85–95.

Yili diqu difangzhi bianzuan weiyuanhui, ed. *Yili fengwu.* Urumqi: Xinjiang renmin chubanshe, 1994.

Yilizhou jingmao ju. "Yilizhou duiwai maoyi fazhan gaikuang." In *Yili Hasake zizhizhou jingji shehui fazhan yantao wenji*, ed. Yilizhou jingji yanjiu zhongxin, 92–93. Yining: Yilizhou jingji yanjiu zhongxin, 1987.

Ying Zi. *Xibei fengguang hao.* Hong Kong: Wanqian chubanshe, 1955.

Yuan Qing-li. "Population Changes in the Xinjiang Uighur Autonomous Region (1949–1989)." *Central Asian Survey* 9 (1990): 49–73.

Zeng Wenwu. *Zhongguo jingying xiyu shi.* Urumqi: Xinjiang Weiwuer zizhiqu difangzhi zongbianshi, 1986 [1936].

Zhongguo renmin yinhang Yilizhou fenhang diaocha yanjiu shi. "Jiji kaituo zijin shichang cujin Yilizhou jingji fazhan." In *Yili Hasake zizhizhou jingji shehui fazhan yantao wenji*, ed. Yilizhou jingji yanjiu zhongxin, 60–67. Yining: Yilizhou jingji yanjiu zhongxin, 1987.

Zhong Yong. *Xijiang jiaoshe zhiyao.* Taipei: Shangwu yinshuguan, 1963 [1911].

Index

Harvard East Asian Monographs
(*out-of-print)

Harvard East Asian Monographs

Harvard East Asian Monographs

Harvard East Asian Monographs